KU-732-447

STOP!

This is the back of the book.
ou wouldn't want to spoil a great ending!

This book is printed "manga-style," in the authentic Japanese right-to-left format. Since none of the artwork has been flipped or altered, readers get to experience the story just as the creator intended. You've been asking for it, so TOKYOPOP® delivered: authentic, hot-off-the-press, and far more fun!

DIRECTIONS

If this is your first time reading manga-style, here's a quick guide to help you understand how it works.

It's easy... just start in the top right panel and follow the numbers. Have fun, and look for more 100% authentic manga from TOKYOPOP®!

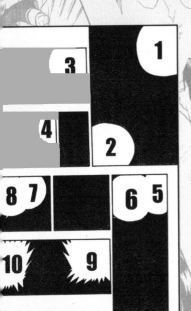

1

LUPIN III

VOLUME 2 PREVIEW

Cloaked in a trench coat, a Fedora set jauntily on his head and horn-tipped sunglasses hiding his shifty eyes, Lupin stumbles in on a femme fatale... train explosions, shady villains, creepy mansions poised atop picturesque hills...

... volume two continues the extraordinary exploits of international master thief Lupin III.

LUPIN III

By Monkey Punch

Volume 1

Los Angeles • Tokyo

Translator - Toshi Yokoyama
English Adaptation - Matt Yamashita
Retouch & Lettering - Monlisa De Asis
Cover Layout - Patrick Hook

Senior Editor - Luis Reyes
Production Manager - Jennifer Miller
Art Director - Matthew Alford
VP of Production & Manufacturing - Ron Klamert
President & C.O.O. - John Parker
Publisher - Stuart Levy

Email: editor@TOKYOPOP.com
Come visit us online at www.TOKYOPOP.com

A **TOKYOPOP**® Manga

TOKYOPOP® is an imprint of Mixx Entertainment, Inc.
5900 Wilshire Blvd., Suite 2000, Los Angeles, CA 90036

ISBN: 1-59182-252-1

First TOKYOPOP® printing: December 2002

10 9 8 7 6 5 4 3 2 1
Printed in Canada

LUPIN III

INTRODUCTION

The inspiration for *Lupin III* is turn-of-the-century French novelist Maurice LeBlanc's Arsène Lupin. Monkey Punch borrowed the debonair French rogue, rendered him with the art style of *Mad Magazine*'s Sergio Aragones and placed him in the action-packed milieu of cold war espionage and high society megalomaniacs. Lupin wears so many hats, it's hard to pin him to any one profession - a master thief, a spy, a mercenary, a bodyguard, a lover, a fighter, a burr in the drawers of the underworld, and a colossal pain in the ass for Interpol's Inspector Zenigata, a man whose life mission has become the pursuit of this incorrigible miscreant. Monkey Punch's original international man of mystery is James Bond, Philip Marlowe, The Shadow, The Phantom, The Saint and Spy vs. Spy all rolled into one dynamic package, tinged with a uniquely wry wit, a penchant for trouble, and an insatiable prurience. Making his debut in 1967, *Lupin* has become a national icon for Japan, and today it continues to entertain audiences around the world.

LUPIN III VOLUME I

TABLE of CONTENTS

CHAPTER 1
"ART OF THE ENTRANCE"

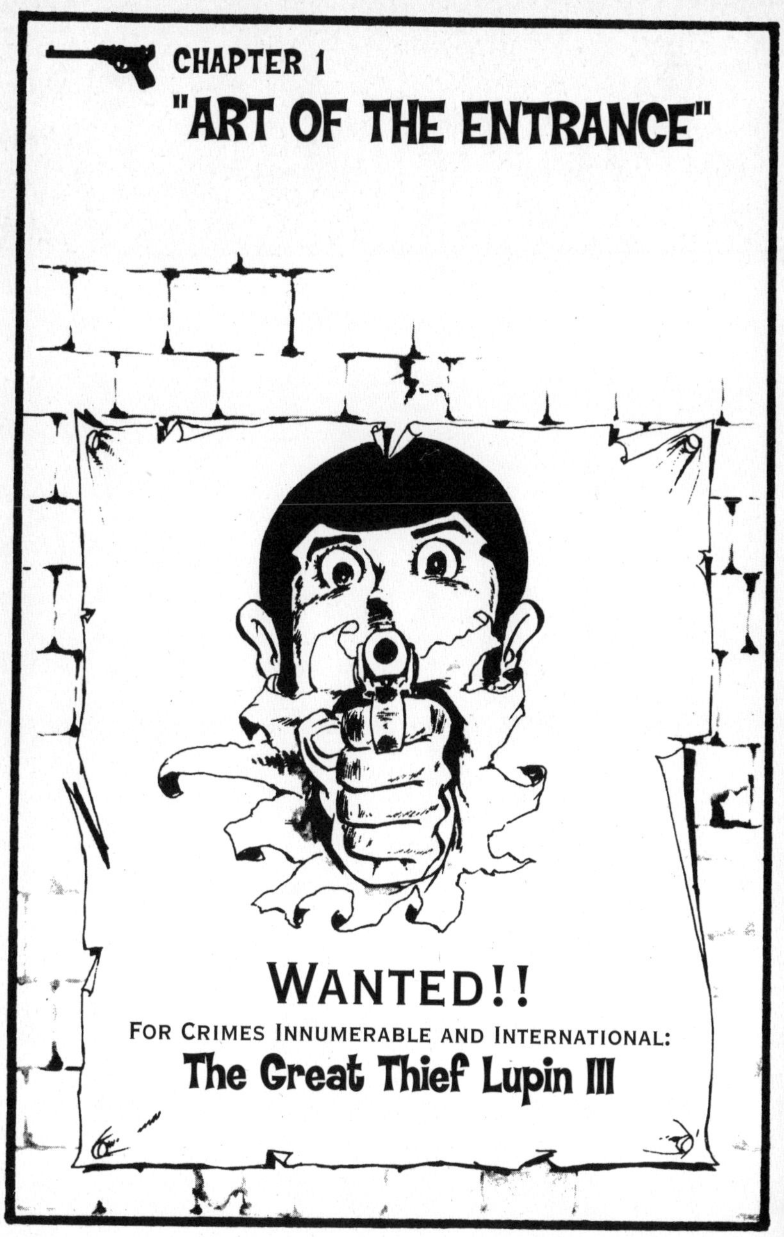
WANTED!!
FOR CRIMES INNUMERABLE AND INTERNATIONAL:
The Great Thief Lupin III

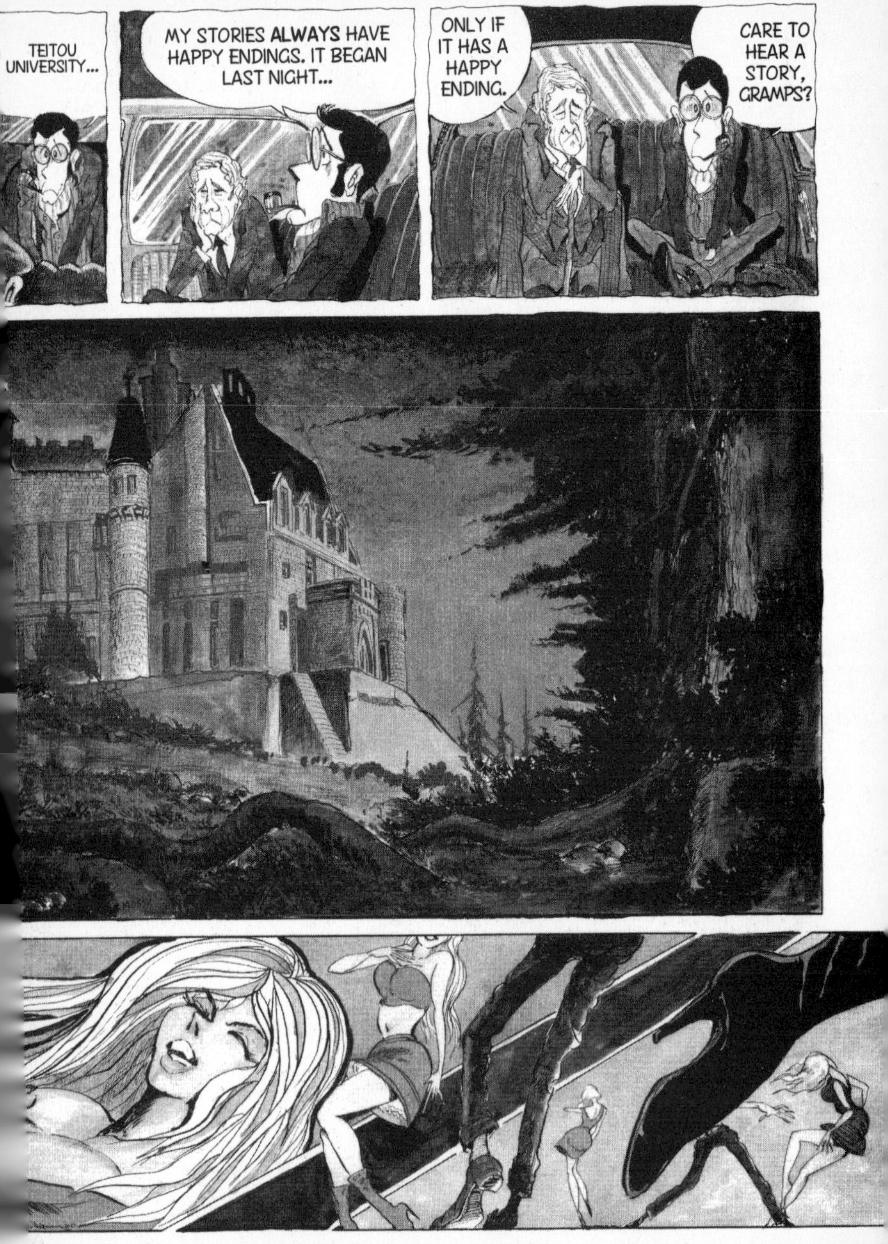
CARE TO HEAR A STORY, GRAMPS?
ONLY IF IT HAS A HAPPY ENDING.
MY STORIES ALWAYS HAVE HAPPY ENDINGS. IT BEGAN LAST NIGHT...
TEITOU UNIVERSITY...

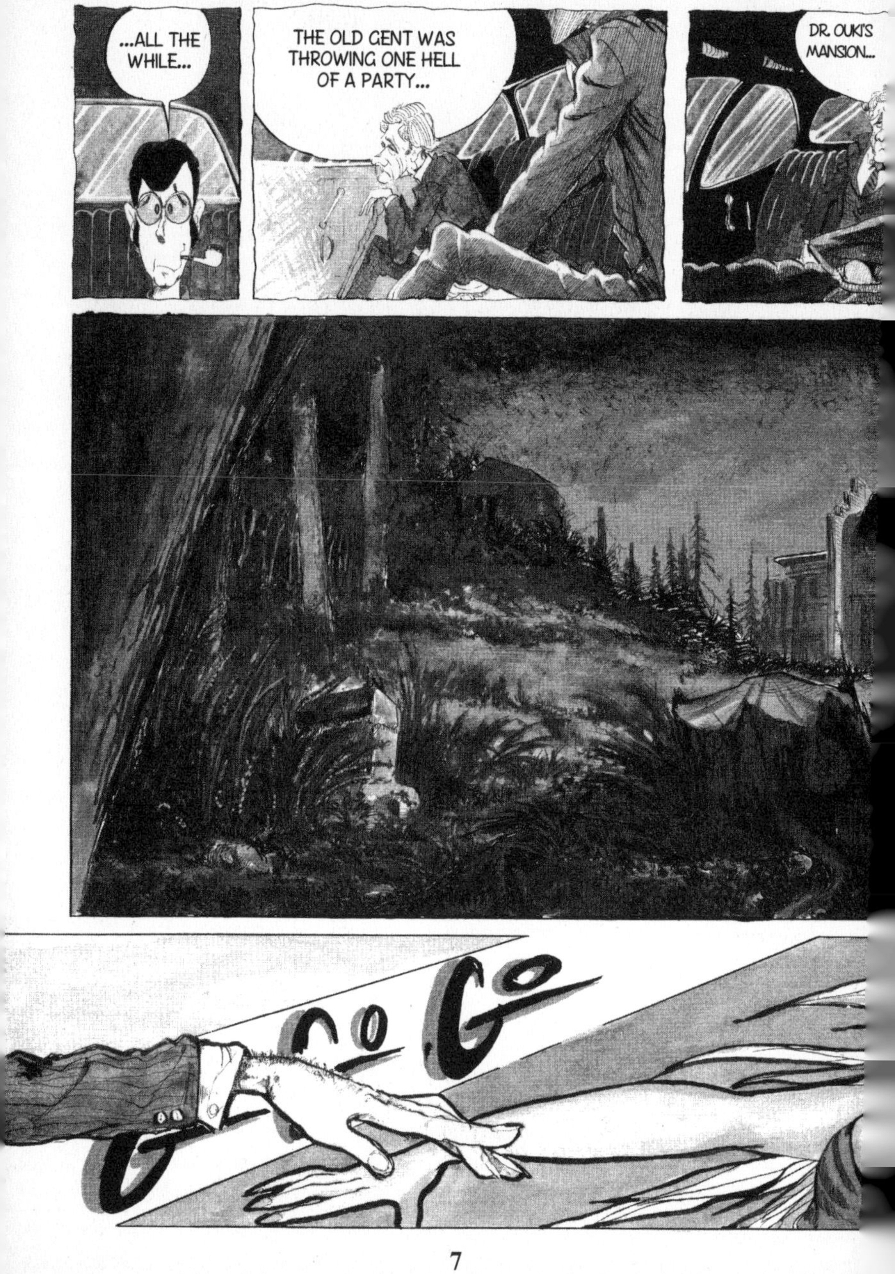
DR. OUKI'S MANSION...
THE OLD GENT WAS THROWING ONE HELL OF A PARTY...
...ALL THE WHILE...
Go Go

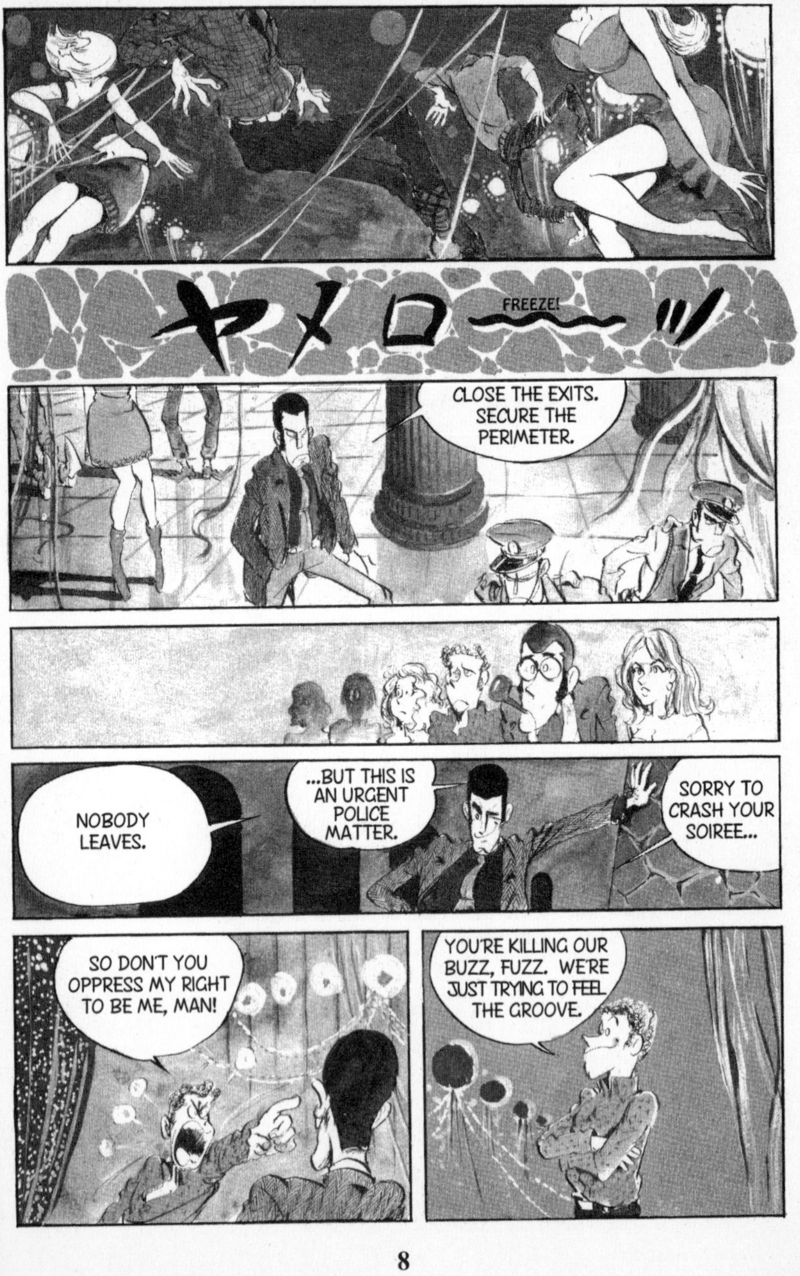
ヤメローーッ
FREEZE!
CLOSE THE EXITS. SECURE THE PERIMETER.
SORRY TO CRASH YOUR SOIREE...
...BUT THIS IS AN URGENT POLICE MATTER.
NOBODY LEAVES.
YOU'RE KILLING OUR BUZZ, FUZZ. WE'RE JUST TRYING TO FEEL THE GROOVE.
SO DON'T YOU OPPRESS MY RIGHT TO BE ME, MAN!

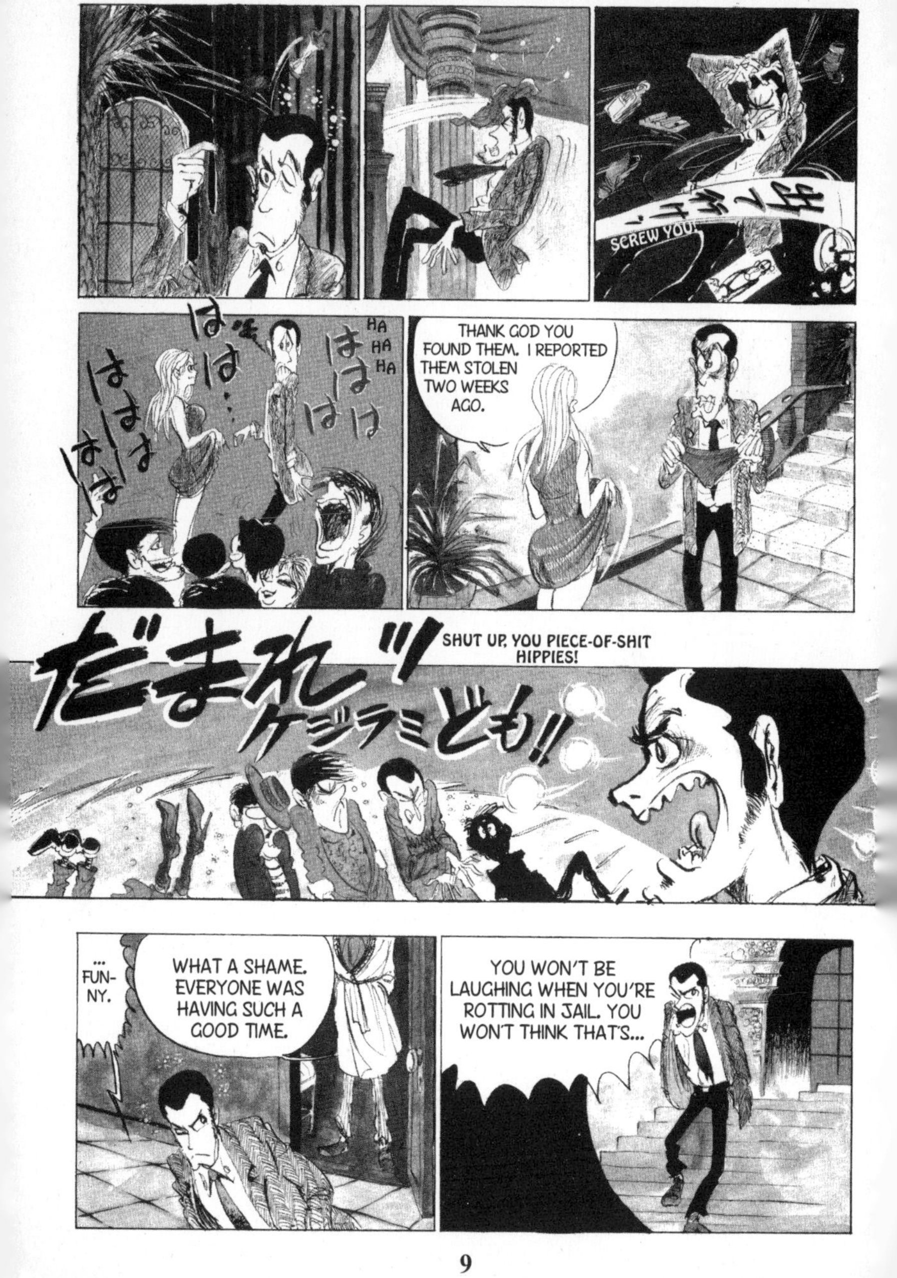
SCREW YOU!
THANK GOD YOU FOUND THEM. I REPORTED THEM STOLEN TWO WEEKS AGO.
HA HA HA
だまれッ ケジラミども!!
SHUT UP, YOU PIECE-OF-SHIT HIPPIES!
YOU WON'T BE LAUGHING WHEN YOU'RE ROTTING IN JAIL. YOU WON'T THINK THAT'S...
WHAT A SHAME. EVERYONE WAS HAVING SUCH A GOOD TIME.
... FUN-NY.

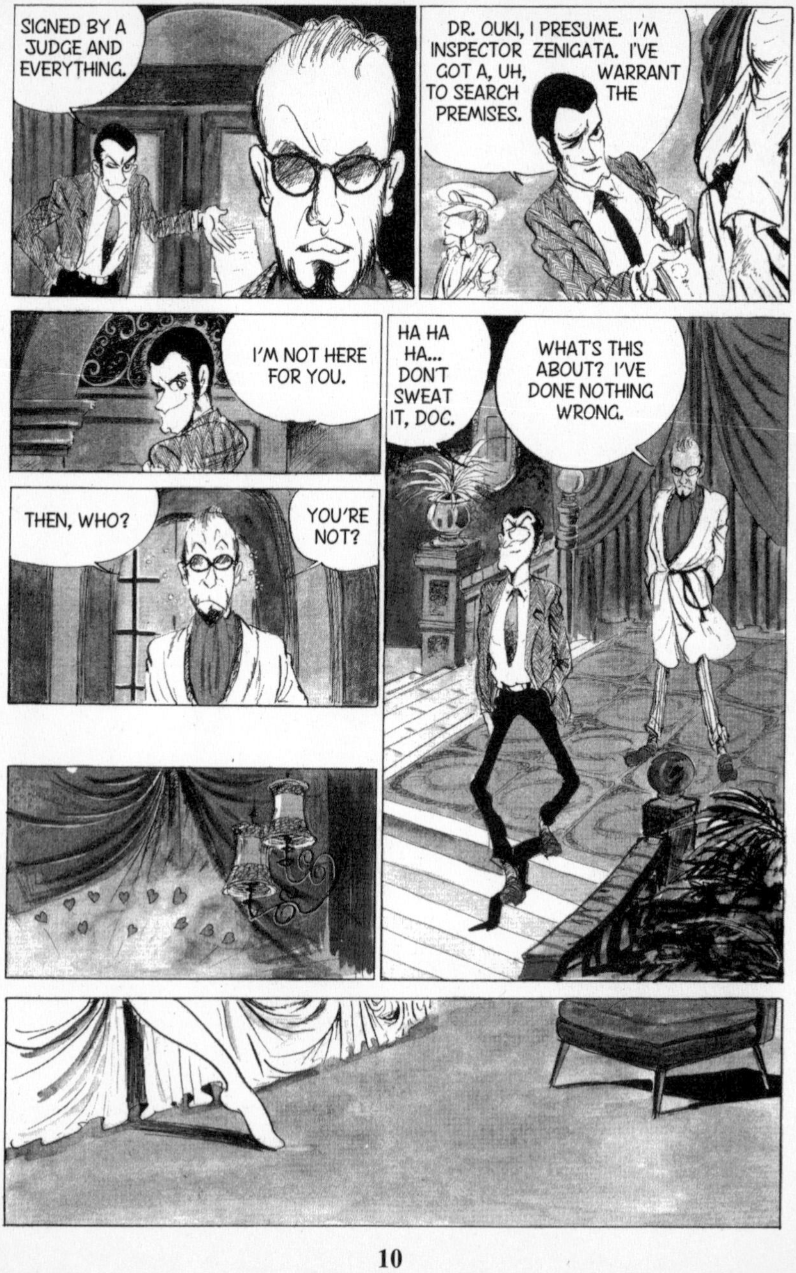
DR. OUKI, I PRESUME. I'M INSPECTOR ZENIGATA. I'VE GOT A, UH, WARRANT TO SEARCH THE PREMISES.
SIGNED BY A JUDGE AND EVERYTHING.
WHAT'S THIS ABOUT? I'VE DONE NOTHING WRONG.
HA HA HA... DON'T SWEAT IT, DOC.
I'M NOT HERE FOR YOU.
YOU'RE NOT?
THEN, WHO?

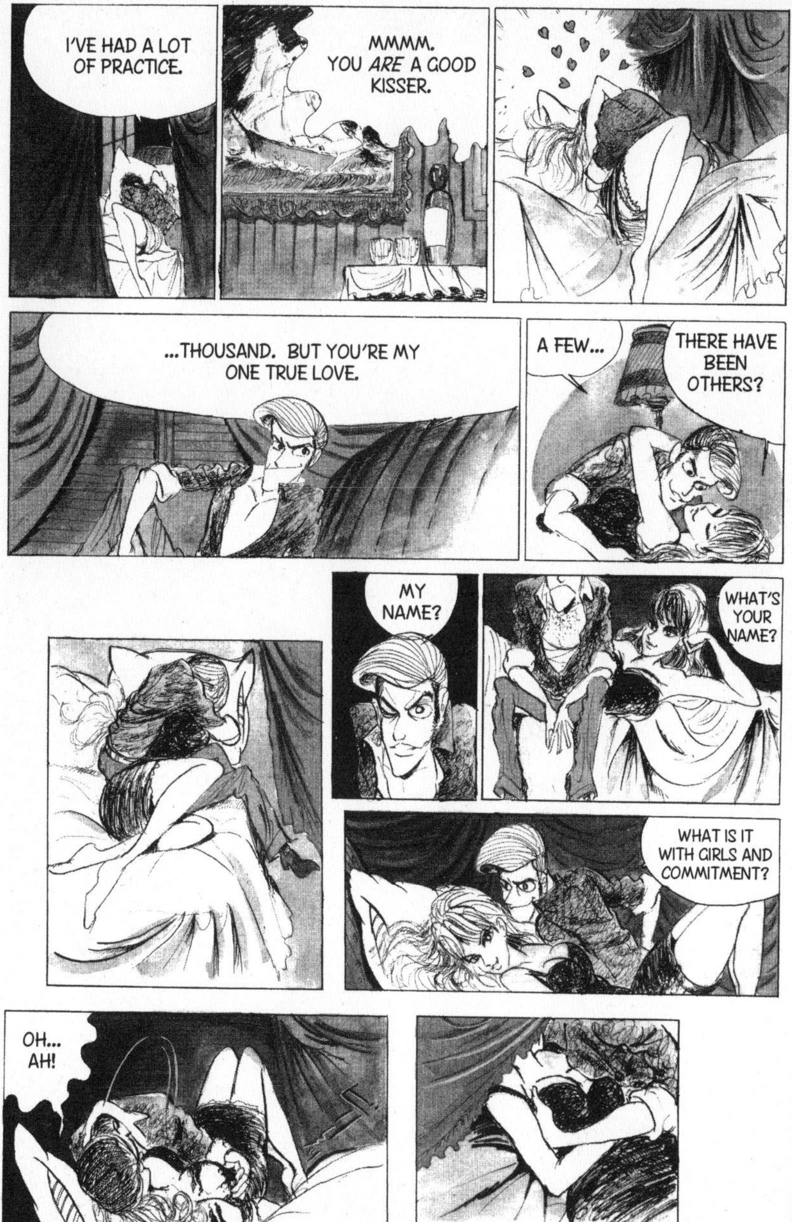
MMMM. YOU *ARE* A GOOD KISSER.
I'VE HAD A LOT OF PRACTICE.
THERE HAVE BEEN OTHERS?
A FEW...
...THOUSAND. BUT YOU'RE MY ONE TRUE LOVE.
WHAT'S YOUR NAME?
MY NAME?
WHAT IS IT WITH GIRLS AND COMMITMENT?
OH... AH!

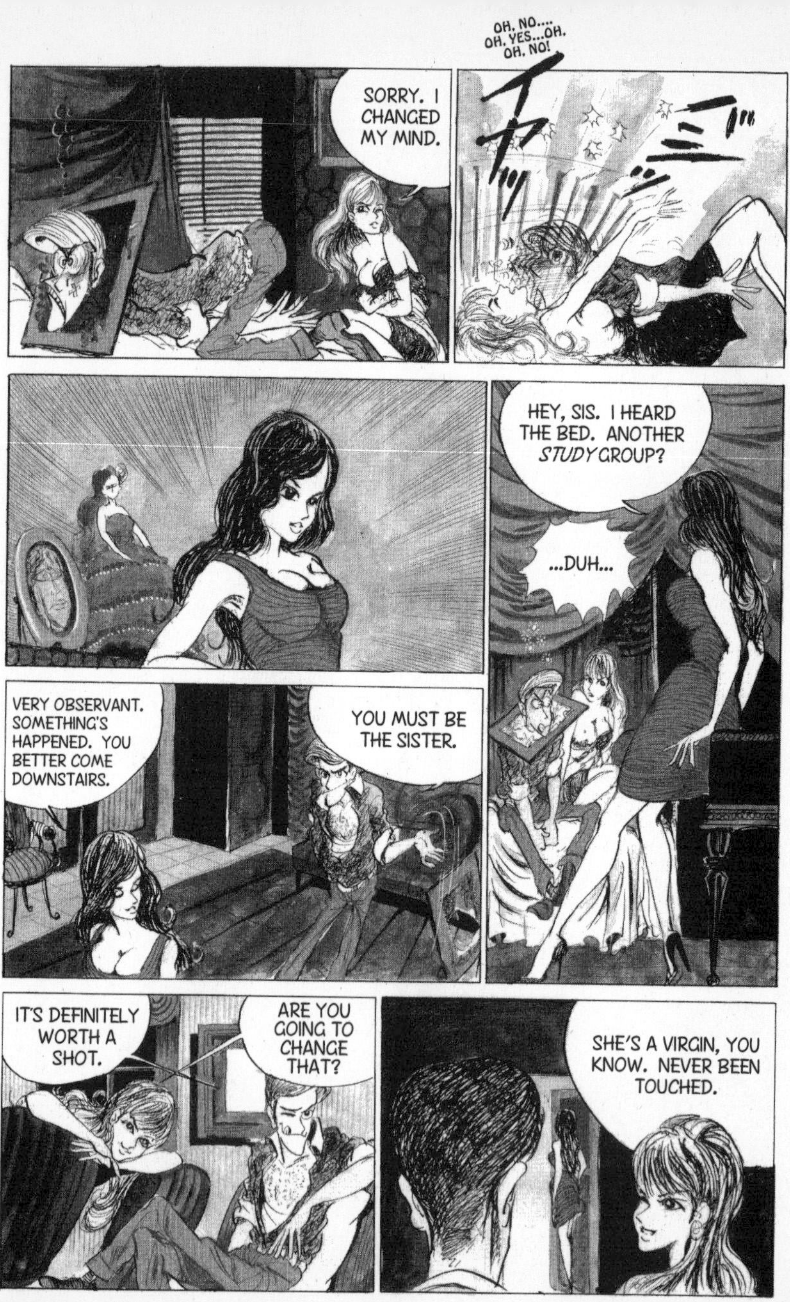
OH, NO.... OH, YES...OH, OH, NO!
SORRY. I CHANGED MY MIND.
HEY, SIS. I HEARD THE BED. ANOTHER *STUDY* GROUP?
...DUH...
YOU MUST BE THE SISTER.
VERY OBSERVANT. SOMETHING'S HAPPENED. YOU BETTER COME DOWNSTAIRS.
SHE'S A VIRGIN, YOU KNOW. NEVER BEEN TOUCHED.
ARE YOU GOING TO CHANGE THAT?
IT'S DEFINITELY WORTH A SHOT.

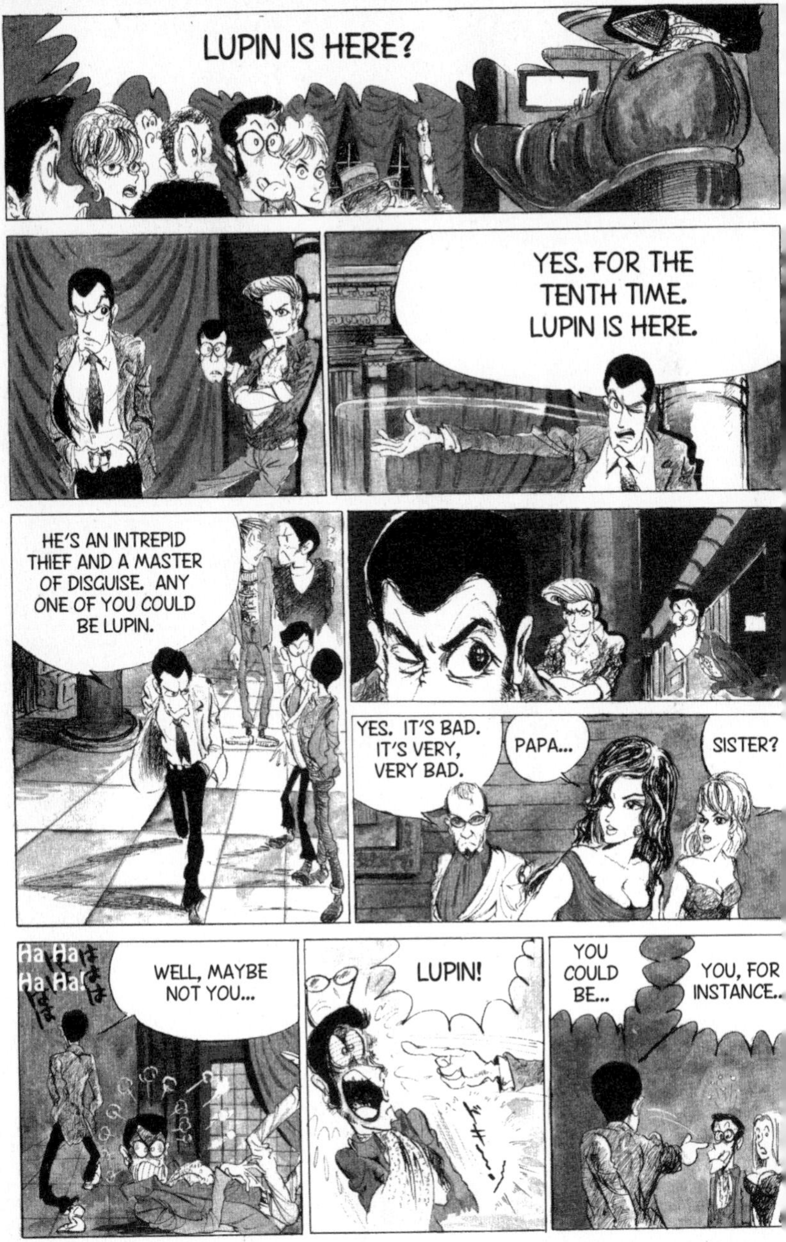
LUPIN IS HERE?
YES. FOR THE TENTH TIME. LUPIN IS HERE.
SISTER?
PAPA...
YES. IT'S BAD. IT'S VERY, VERY BAD.
HE'S AN INTREPID THIEF AND A MASTER OF DISGUISE. ANY ONE OF YOU COULD BE LUPIN.
YOU COULD BE...
YOU, FOR INSTANCE...
LUPIN!
WELL, MAYBE NOT YOU...
Ha Ha Ha Ha!
ははははは

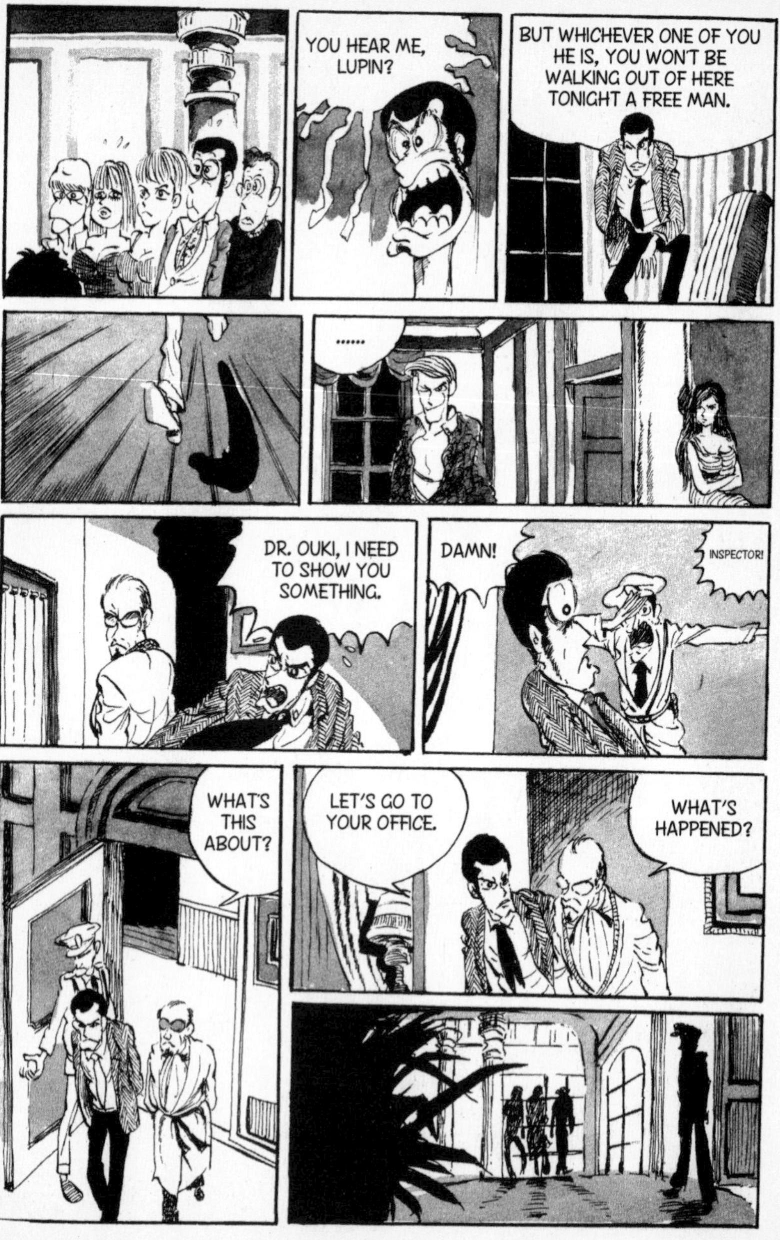
BUT WHICHEVER ONE OF YOU HE IS, YOU WON'T BE WALKING OUT OF HERE TONIGHT A FREE MAN.
YOU HEAR ME, LUPIN?
......
INSPECTOR!
DAMN!
DR. OUKI, I NEED TO SHOW YOU SOMETHING.
WHAT'S HAPPENED?
LET'S GO TO YOUR OFFICE.
WHAT'S THIS ABOUT?

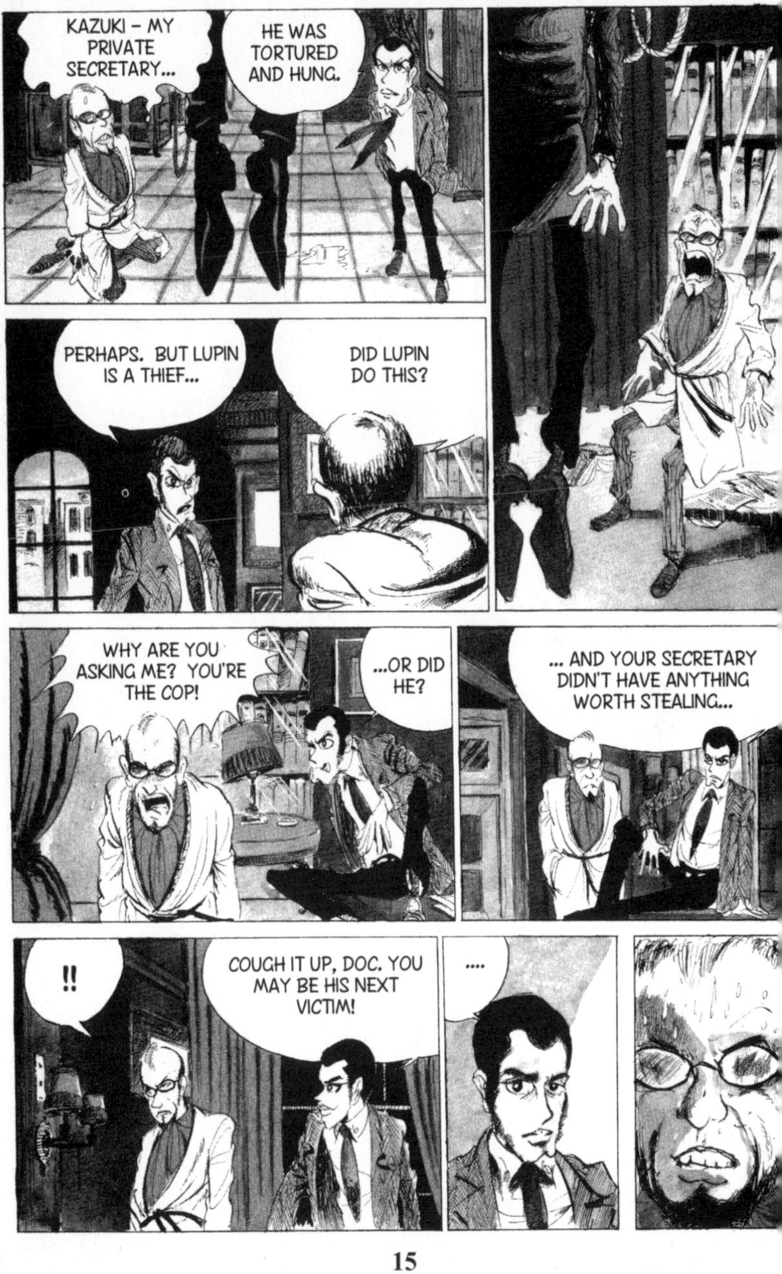
HE WAS TORTURED AND HUNG.
KAZUKI - MY PRIVATE SECRETARY...
DID LUPIN DO THIS?
PERHAPS. BUT LUPIN IS A THIEF...
... AND YOUR SECRETARY DIDN'T HAVE ANYTHING WORTH STEALING...
...OR DID HE?
WHY ARE YOU ASKING ME? YOU'RE THE COP!
....
COUGH IT UP, DOC. YOU MAY BE HIS NEXT VICTIM!
!!

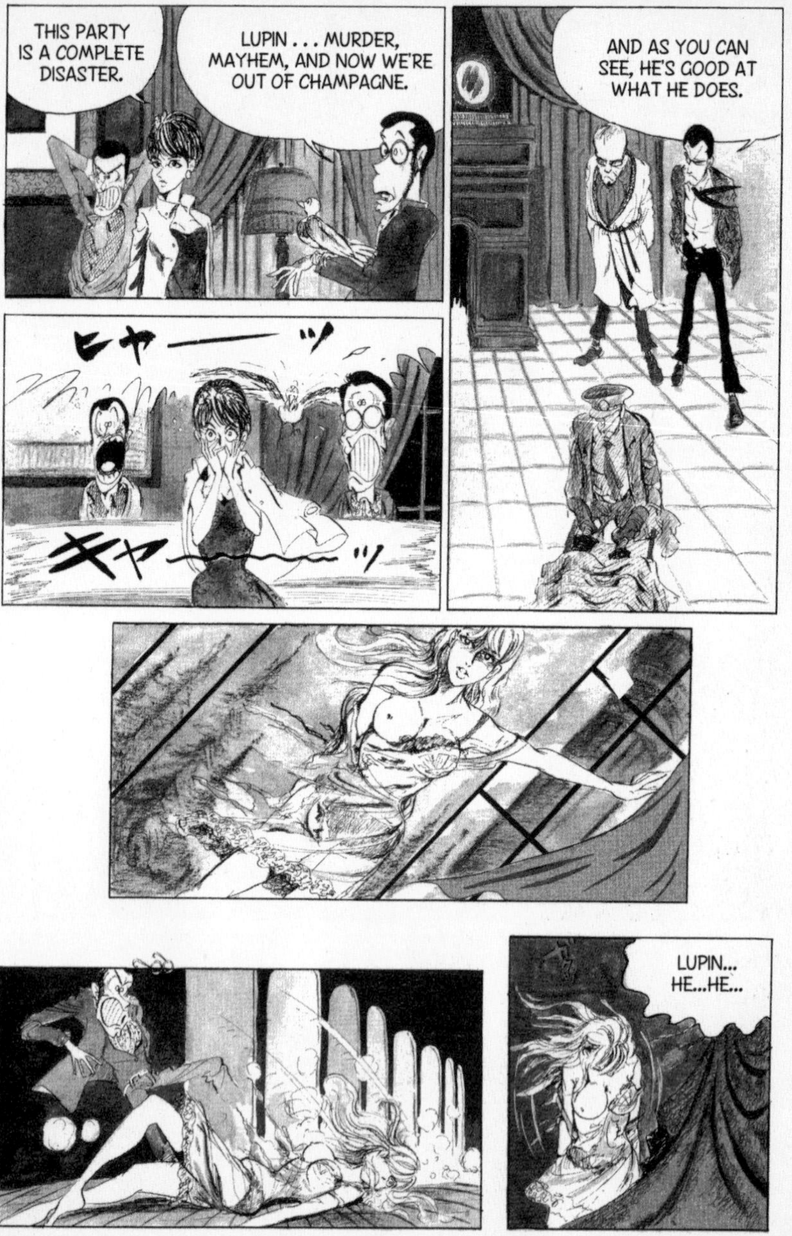
AND AS YOU CAN SEE, HE'S GOOD AT WHAT HE DOES.
LUPIN . . . MURDER, MAYHEM, AND NOW WE'RE OUT OF CHAMPAGNE.
THIS PARTY IS A COMPLETE DISASTER.
ヒャーーッ
キャーーッ
LUPIN... HE...HE...

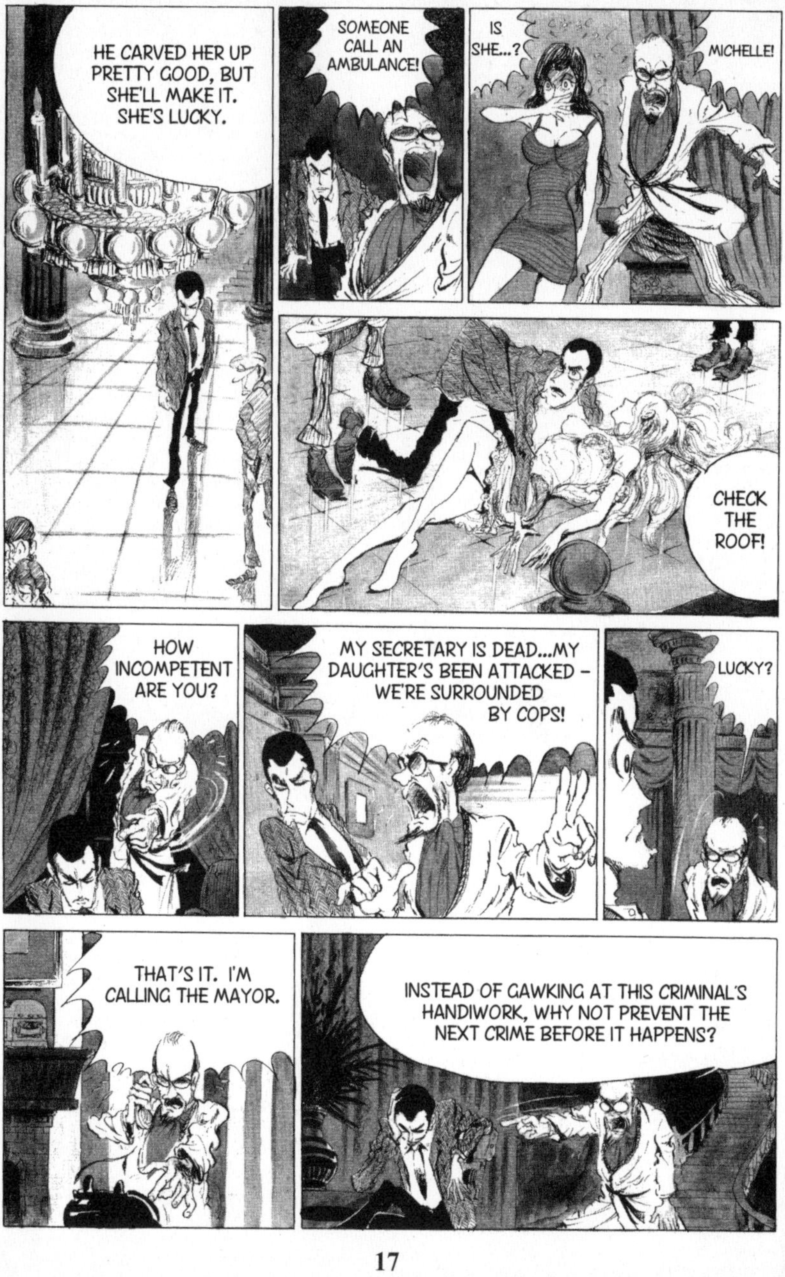
IS SHE...?
MICHELLE!
SOMEONE CALL AN AMBULANCE!
CHECK THE ROOF!
HE CARVED HER UP PRETTY GOOD, BUT SHE'LL MAKE IT. SHE'S LUCKY.
LUCKY?
MY SECRETARY IS DEAD...MY DAUGHTER'S BEEN ATTACKED – WE'RE SURROUNDED BY COPS!
HOW INCOMPETENT ARE YOU?
INSTEAD OF GAWKING AT THIS CRIMINAL'S HANDIWORK, WHY NOT PREVENT THE NEXT CRIME BEFORE IT HAPPENS?
THAT'S IT. I'M CALLING THE MAYOR.

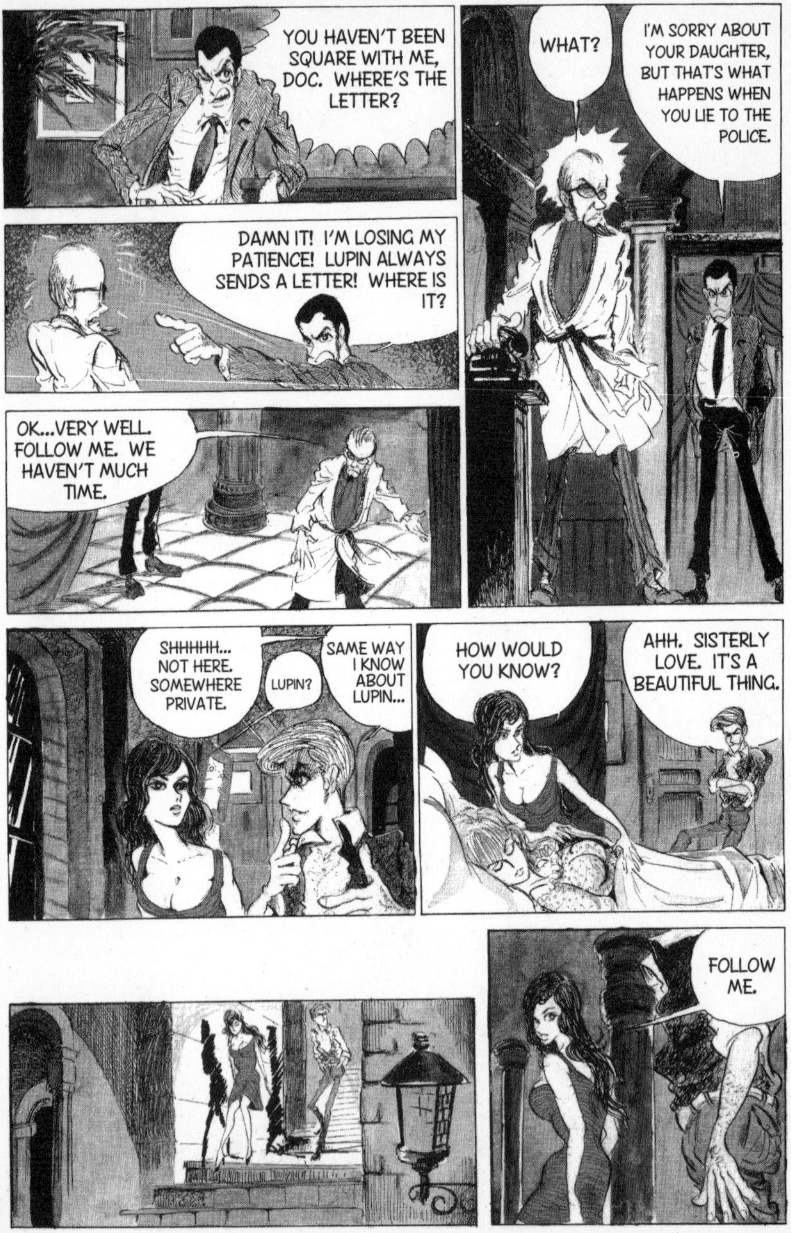
I'M SORRY ABOUT YOUR DAUGHTER, BUT THAT'S WHAT HAPPENS WHEN YOU LIE TO THE POLICE.
WHAT?
YOU HAVEN'T BEEN SQUARE WITH ME, DOC. WHERE'S THE LETTER?
DAMN IT! I'M LOSING MY PATIENCE! LUPIN ALWAYS SENDS A LETTER! WHERE IS IT?
OK...VERY WELL. FOLLOW ME. WE HAVEN'T MUCH TIME.
AHH. SISTERLY LOVE. IT'S A BEAUTIFUL THING.
HOW WOULD YOU KNOW?
SAME WAY I KNOW ABOUT LUPIN...
LUPIN?
SHHHHH... NOT HERE. SOMEWHERE PRIVATE.
FOLLOW ME.

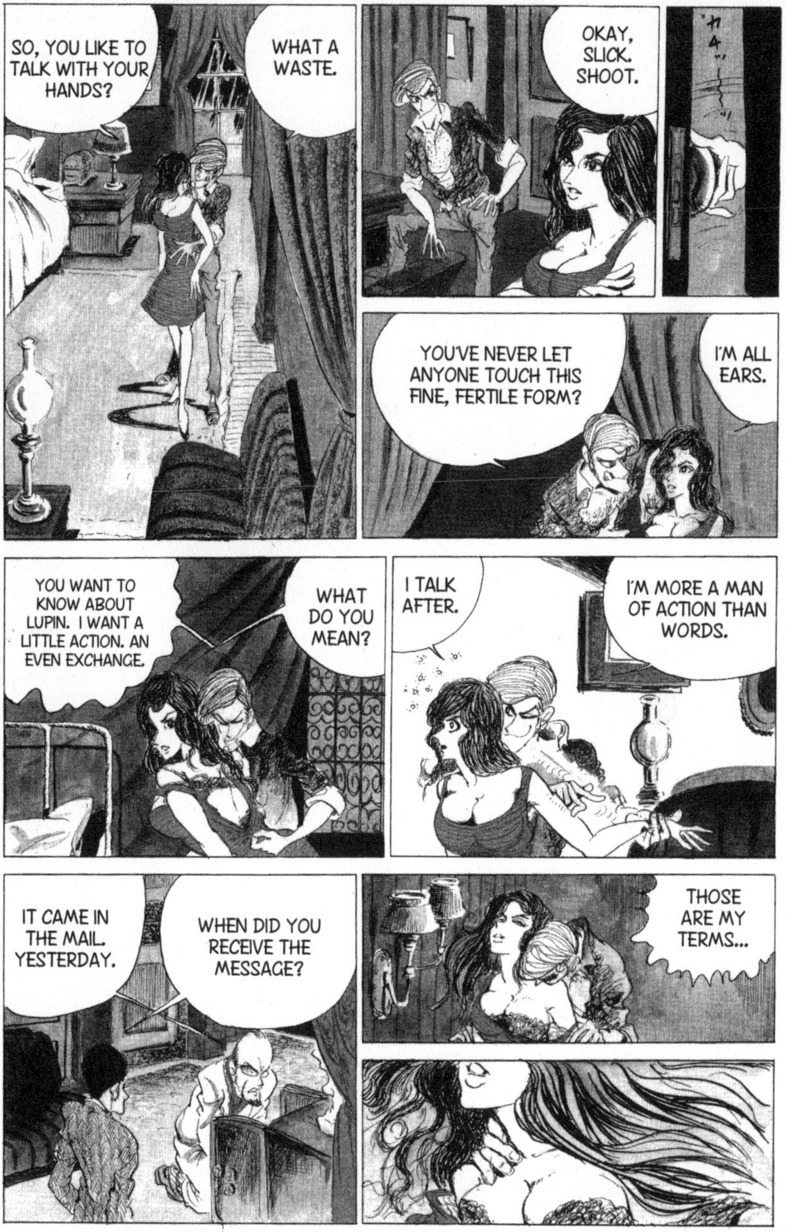
OKAY, SLICK. SHOOT.
I'M ALL EARS.
YOU'VE NEVER LET ANYONE TOUCH THIS FINE, FERTILE FORM?
WHAT A WASTE.
SO, YOU LIKE TO TALK WITH YOUR HANDS?
I'M MORE A MAN OF ACTION THAN WORDS.
I TALK AFTER.
WHAT DO YOU MEAN?
YOU WANT TO KNOW ABOUT LUPIN. I WANT A LITTLE ACTION. AN EVEN EXCHANGE.
THOSE ARE MY TERMS...
WHEN DID YOU RECEIVE THE MESSAGE?
IT CAME IN THE MAIL. YESTERDAY.

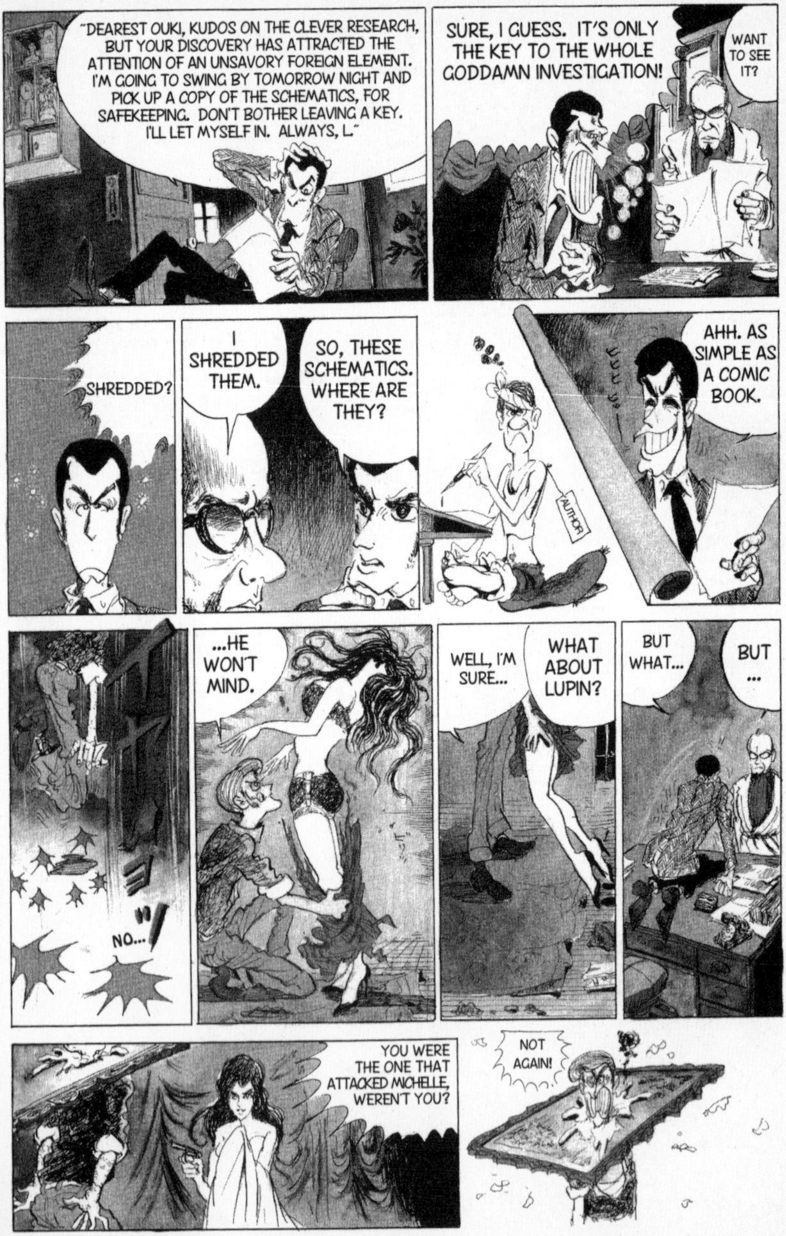
WANT TO SEE IT?
SURE, I GUESS. IT'S ONLY THE KEY TO THE WHOLE GODDAMN INVESTIGATION!
"DEAREST OUKI, KUDOS ON THE CLEVER RESEARCH, BUT YOUR DISCOVERY HAS ATTRACTED THE ATTENTION OF AN UNSAVORY FOREIGN ELEMENT. I'M GOING TO SWING BY TOMORROW NIGHT AND PICK UP A COPY OF THE SCHEMATICS, FOR SAFEKEEPING. DON'T BOTHER LEAVING A KEY. I'LL LET MYSELF IN. ALWAYS, L."
AHH. AS SIMPLE AS A COMIC BOOK.
AUTHOR
SO, THESE SCHEMATICS. WHERE ARE THEY?
I SHREDDED THEM.
SHREDDED?
BUT ...
BUT WHAT...
WHAT ABOUT LUPIN?
WELL, I'M SURE...
...HE WON'T MIND.
NO...
NOT AGAIN!
YOU WERE THE ONE THAT ATTACKED MICHELLE, WEREN'T YOU?

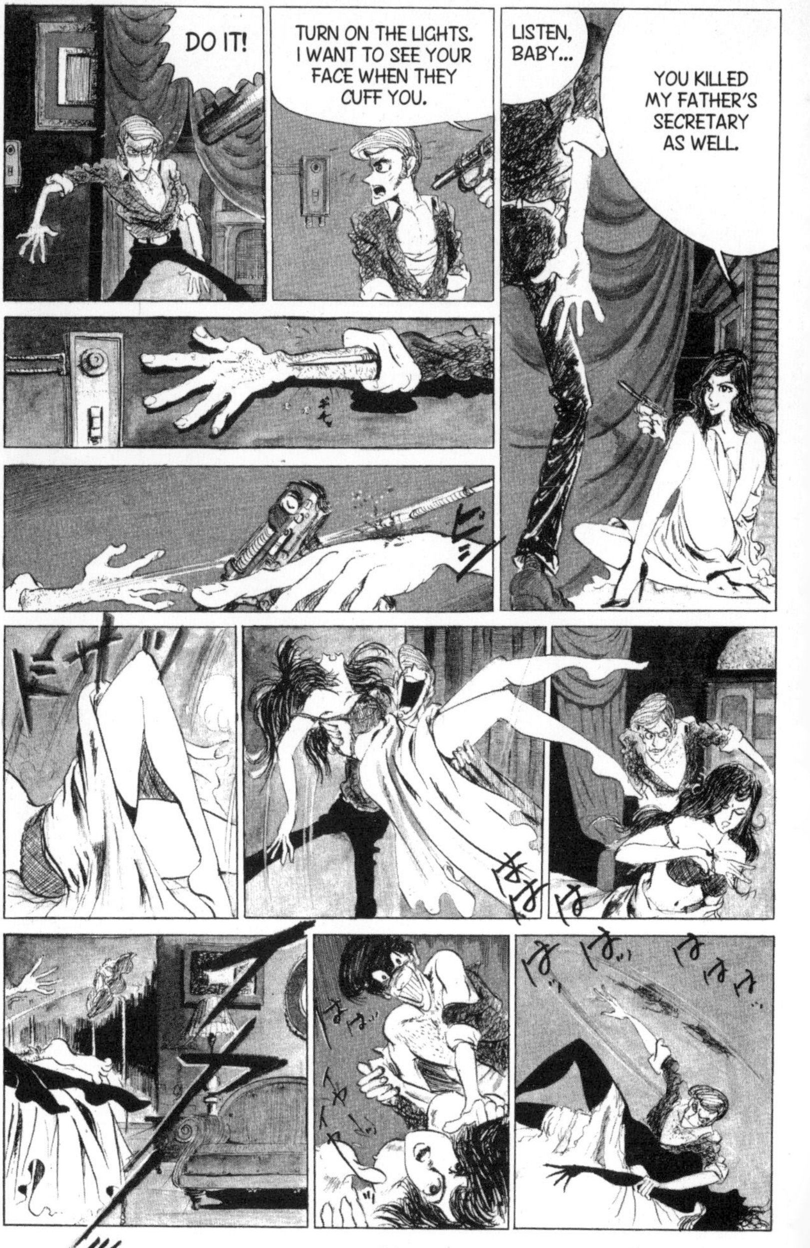
LISTEN, BABY...
YOU KILLED MY FATHER'S SECRETARY AS WELL.
TURN ON THE LIGHTS. I WANT TO SEE YOUR FACE WHEN THEY CUFF YOU.
DO IT!

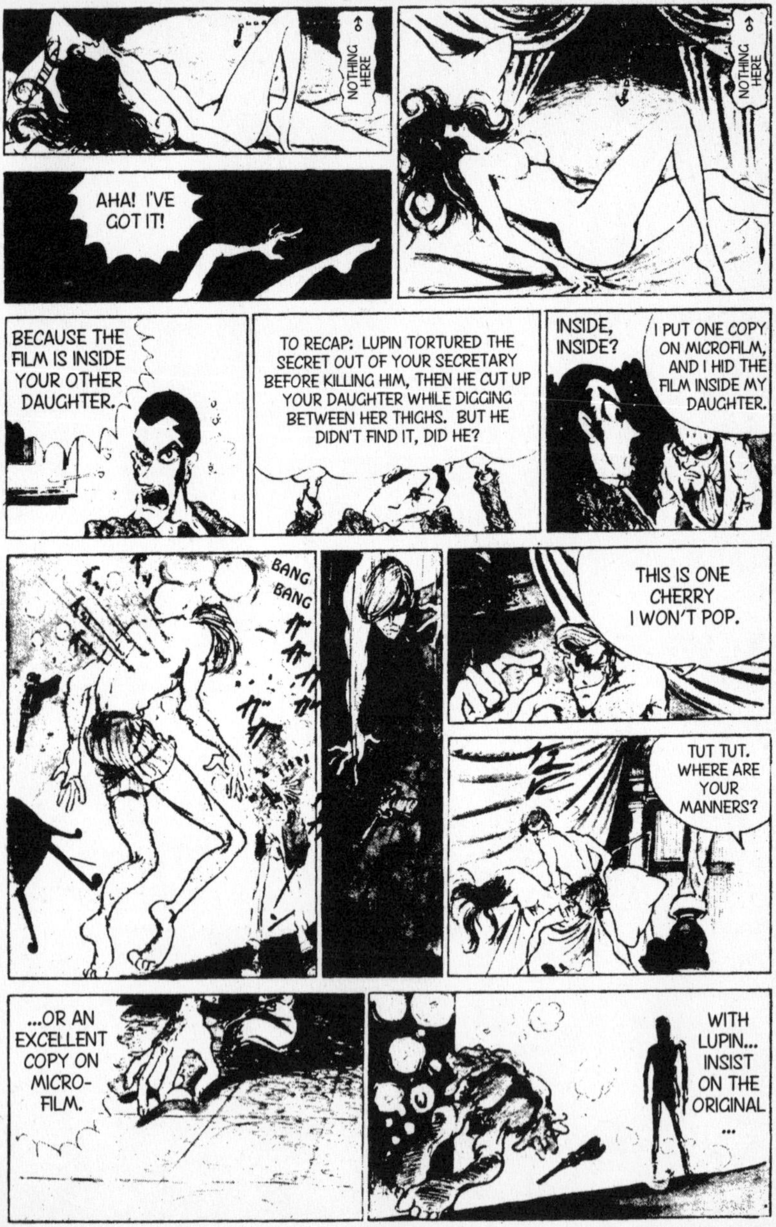
NOTHING HERE
NOTHING HERE
AHA! I'VE GOT IT!
I PUT ONE COPY ON MICROFILM, AND I HID THE FILM INSIDE MY DAUGHTER.
INSIDE, INSIDE?
TO RECAP: LUPIN TORTURED THE SECRET OUT OF YOUR SECRETARY BEFORE KILLING HIM, THEN HE CUT UP YOUR DAUGHTER WHILE DIGGING BETWEEN HER THIGHS. BUT HE DIDN'T FIND IT, DID HE?
BECAUSE THE FILM IS INSIDE YOUR OTHER DAUGHTER.
THIS IS ONE CHERRY I WON'T POP.
TUT TUT. WHERE ARE YOUR MANNERS?
BANG BANG
WITH LUPIN... INSIST ON THE ORIGINAL ...
...OR AN EXCELLENT COPY ON MICRO-FILM.

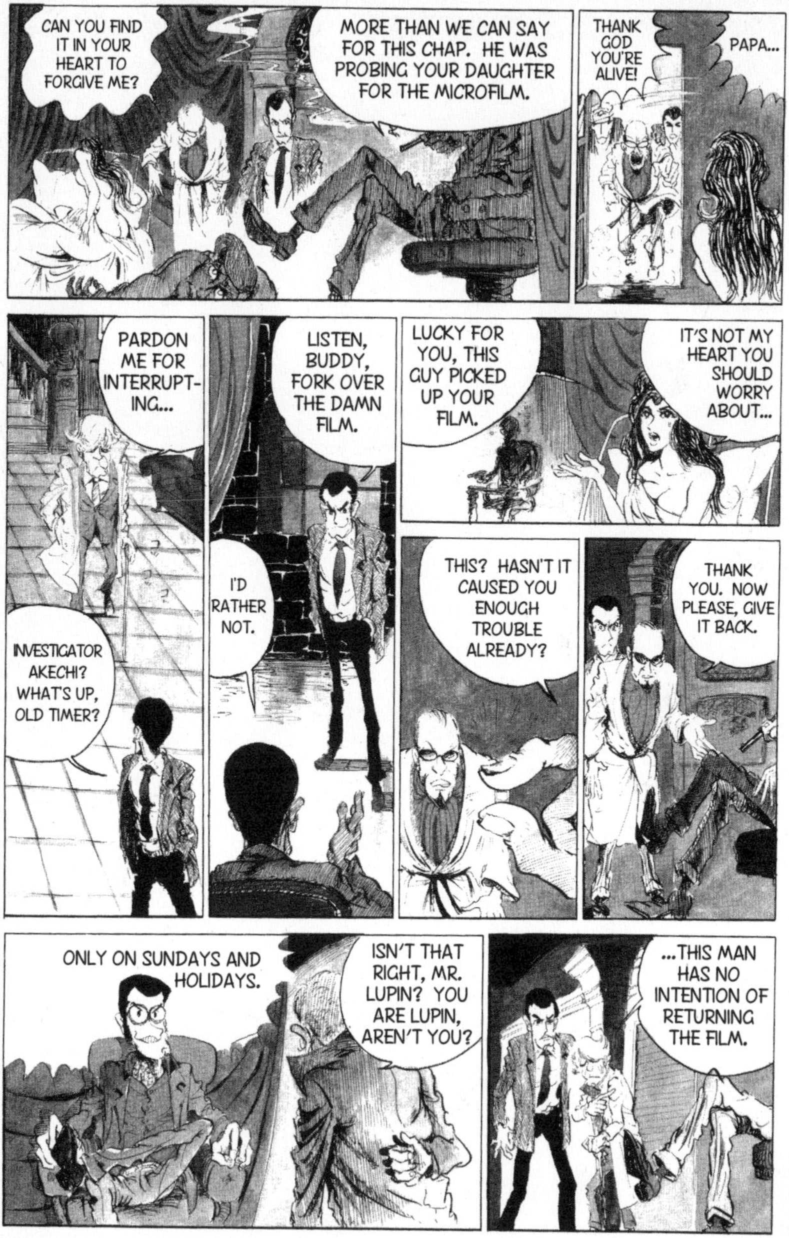
PAPA...
THANK GOD YOU'RE ALIVE!
MORE THAN WE CAN SAY FOR THIS CHAP. HE WAS PROBING YOUR DAUGHTER FOR THE MICROFILM.
CAN YOU FIND IT IN YOUR HEART TO FORGIVE ME?
IT'S NOT MY HEART YOU SHOULD WORRY ABOUT...
LUCKY FOR YOU, THIS GUY PICKED UP YOUR FILM.
THANK YOU. NOW PLEASE, GIVE IT BACK.
THIS? HASN'T IT CAUSED YOU ENOUGH TROUBLE ALREADY?
LISTEN, BUDDY, FORK OVER THE DAMN FILM.
I'D RATHER NOT.
PARDON ME FOR INTERRUPT-ING...
INVESTIGATOR AKECHI? WHAT'S UP, OLD TIMER?
...THIS MAN HAS NO INTENTION OF RETURNING THE FILM.
ISN'T THAT RIGHT, MR. LUPIN? YOU ARE LUPIN, AREN'T YOU?
ONLY ON SUNDAYS AND HOLIDAYS.

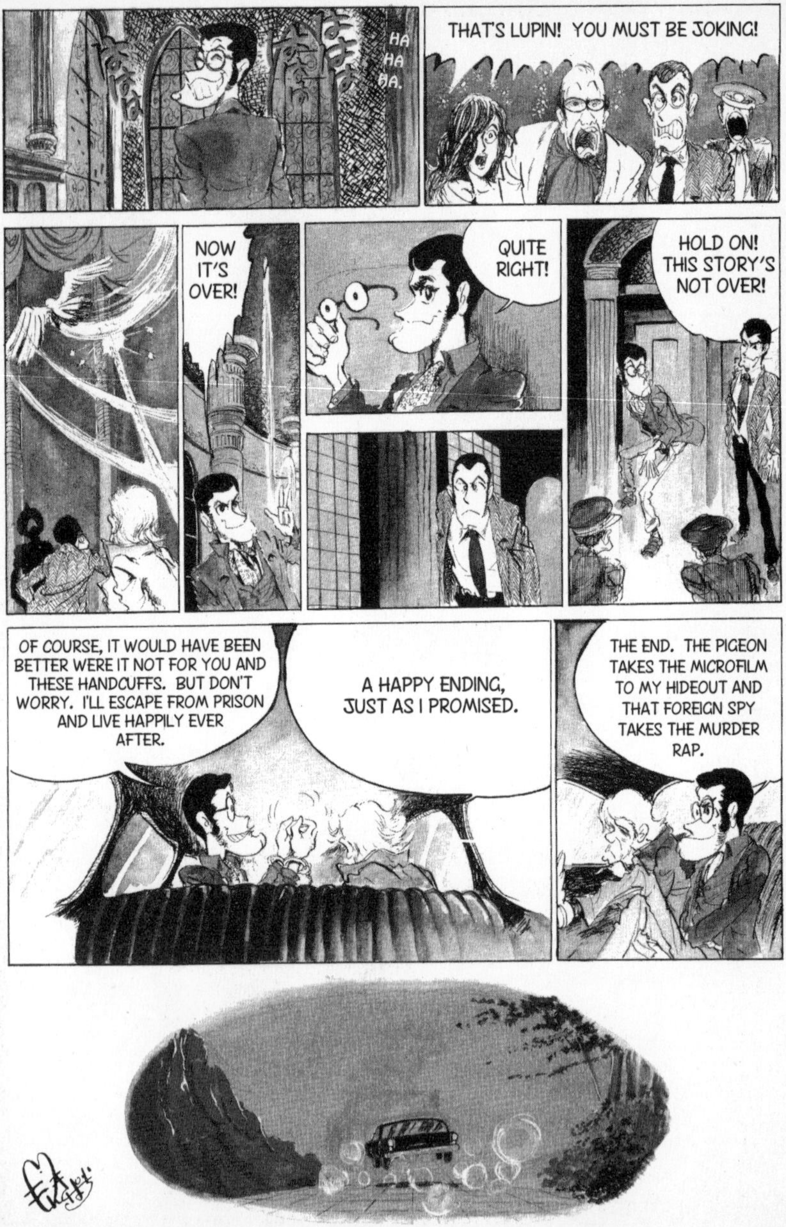
THAT'S LUPIN! YOU MUST BE JOKING!
HA HA HA.
HOLD ON! THIS STORY'S NOT OVER!
QUITE RIGHT!
NOW IT'S OVER!
THE END. THE PIGEON TAKES THE MICROFILM TO MY HIDEOUT AND THAT FOREIGN SPY TAKES THE MURDER RAP.
A HAPPY ENDING, JUST AS I PROMISED.
OF COURSE, IT WOULD HAVE BEEN BETTER WERE IT NOT FOR YOU AND THESE HANDCUFFS. BUT DON'T WORRY. I'LL ESCAPE FROM PRISON AND LIVE HAPPILY EVER AFTER.

CHAPTER 2

"THE GREAT ESCAPE"

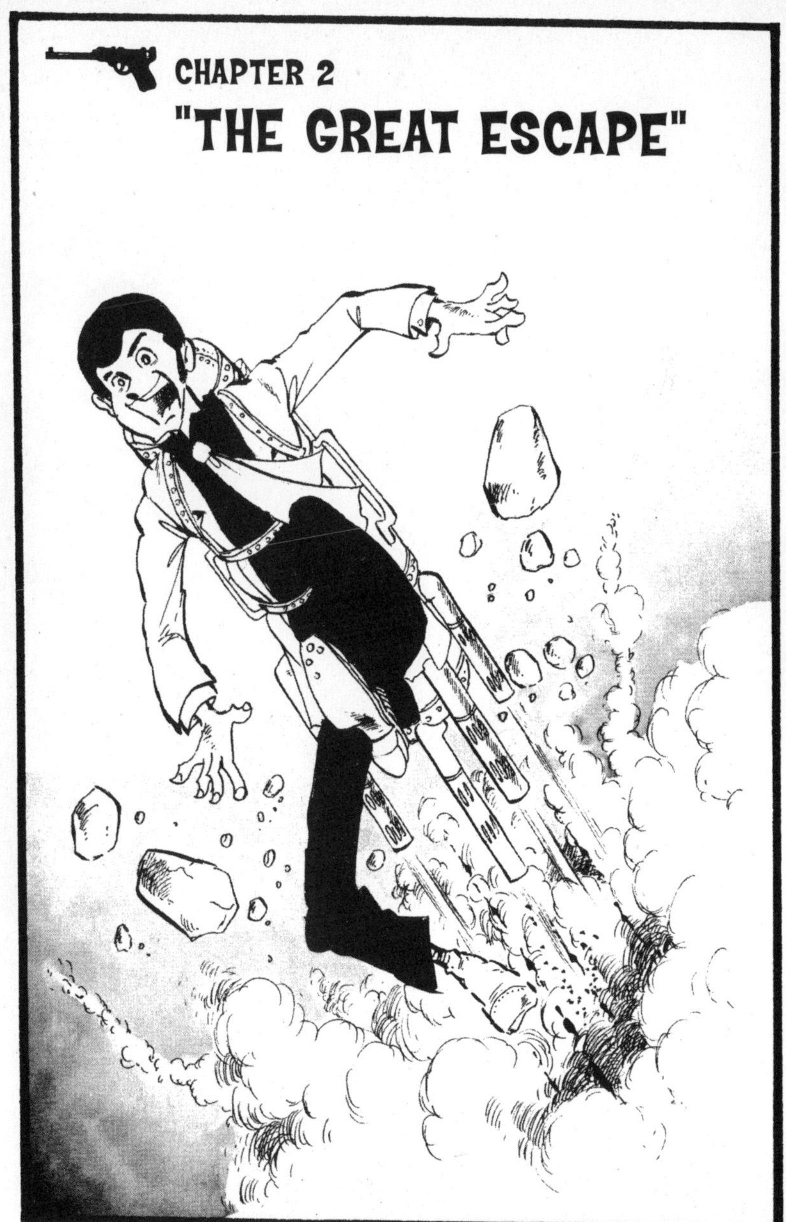

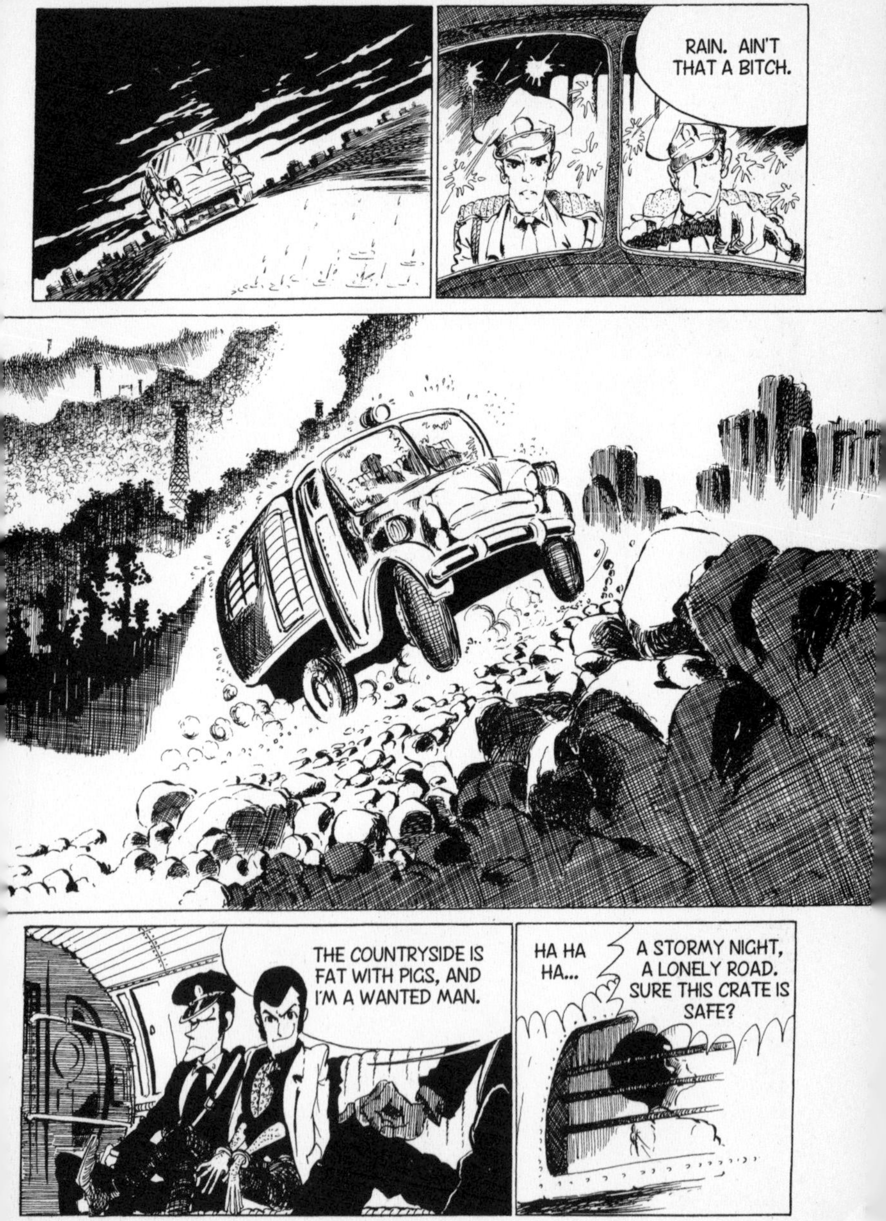
RAIN. AIN'T THAT A BITCH.
A STORMY NIGHT, A LONELY ROAD. SURE THIS CRATE IS SAFE?
HA HA HA...
THE COUNTRYSIDE IS FAT WITH PIGS, AND I'M A WANTED MAN.

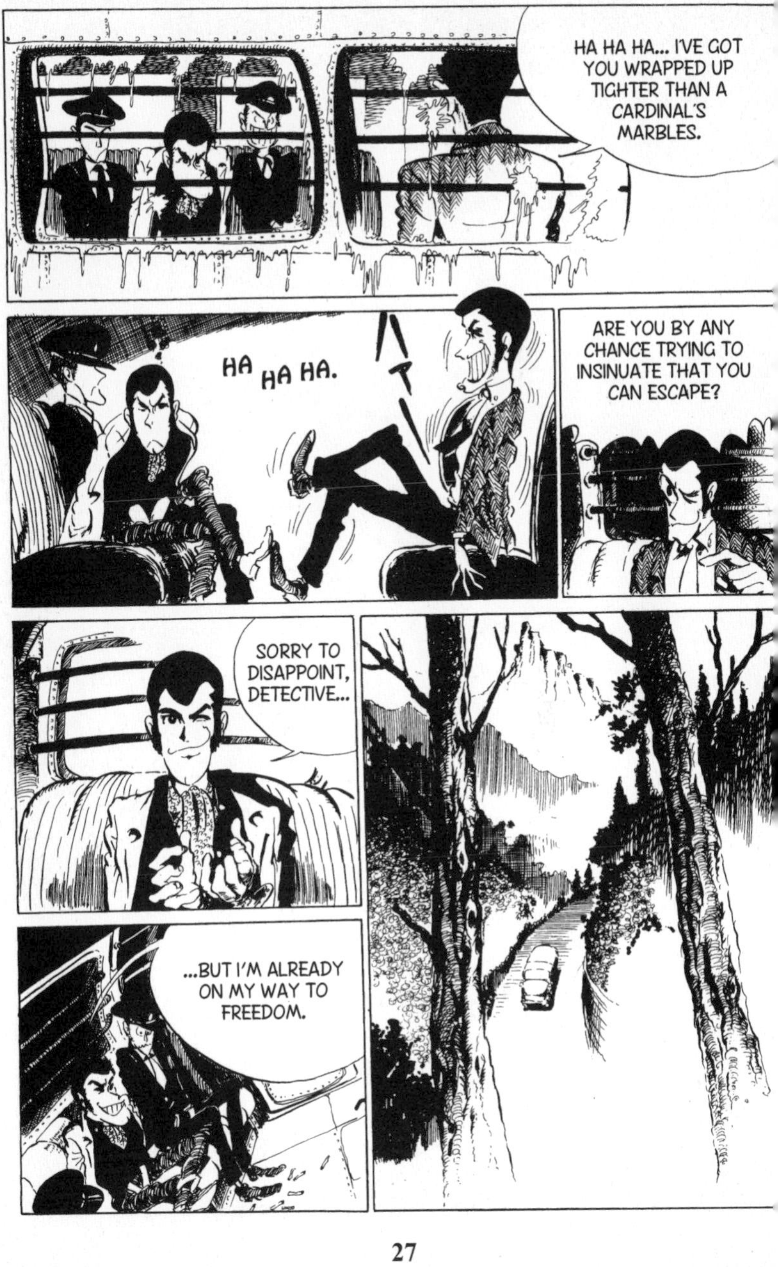
HA HA HA... I'VE GOT YOU WRAPPED UP TIGHTER THAN A CARDINAL'S MARBLES.
ARE YOU BY ANY CHANCE TRYING TO INSINUATE THAT YOU CAN ESCAPE?
HA HA HA.
SORRY TO DISAPPOINT, DETECTIVE...
...BUT I'M ALREADY ON MY WAY TO FREEDOM.

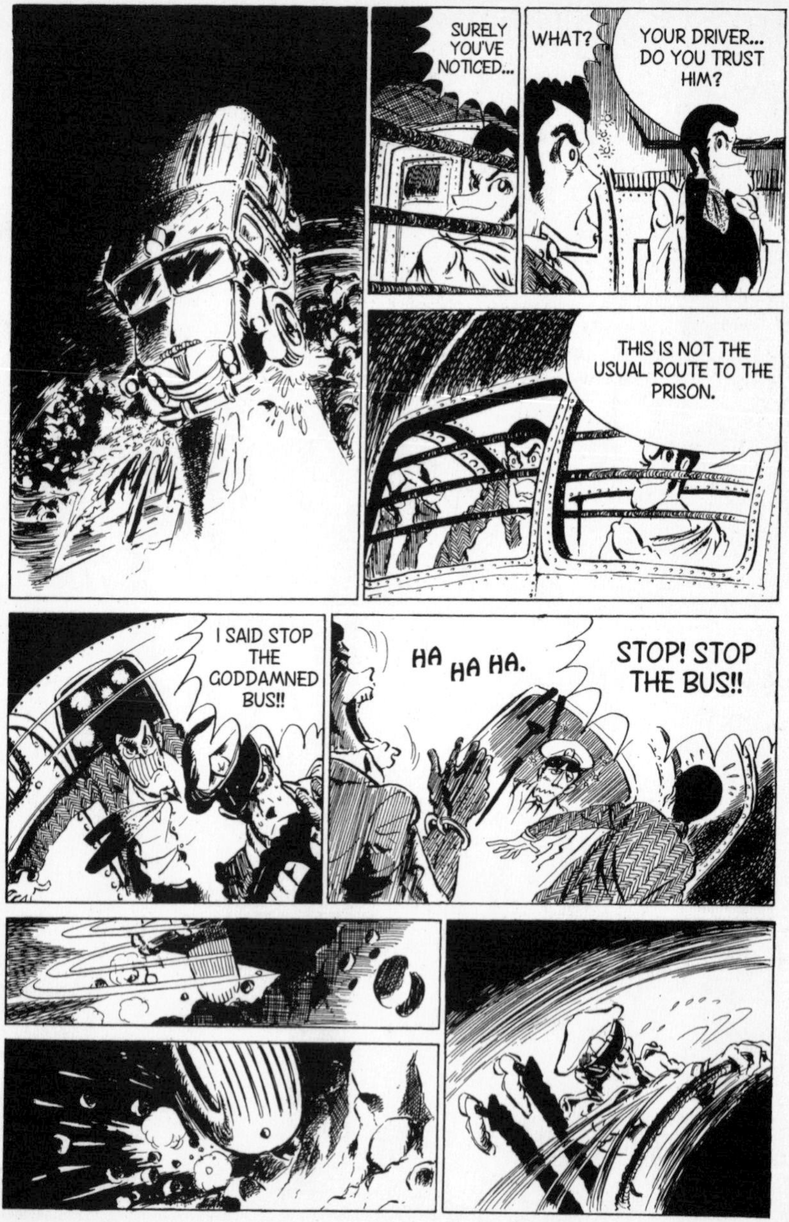
YOUR DRIVER... DO YOU TRUST HIM?
WHAT?
SURELY YOU'VE NOTICED...
THIS IS NOT THE USUAL ROUTE TO THE PRISON.
STOP! STOP THE BUS!!
HA HA HA.
I SAID STOP THE GODDAMNED BUS!!

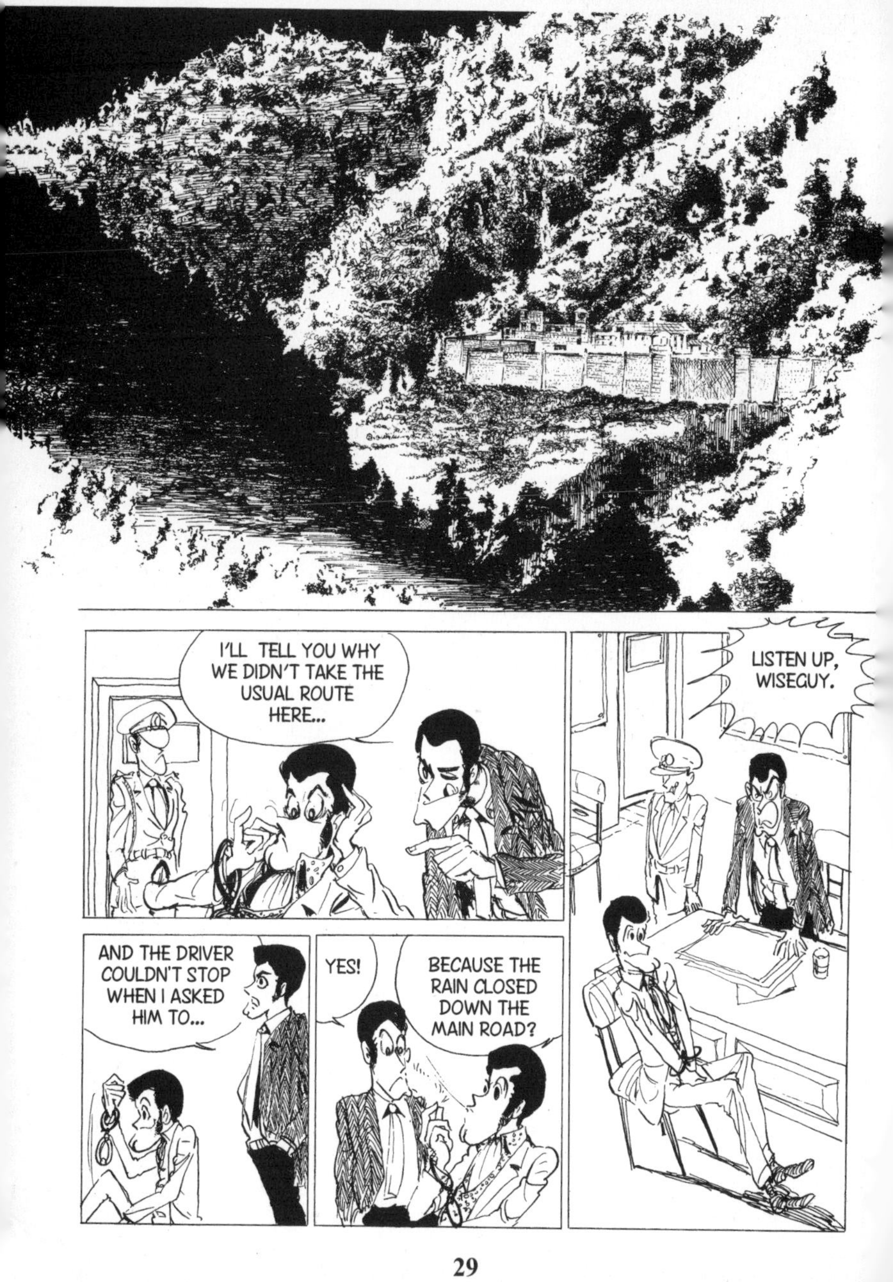
LISTEN UP, WISEGUY.
I'LL TELL YOU WHY WE DIDN'T TAKE THE USUAL ROUTE HERE...
BECAUSE THE RAIN CLOSED DOWN THE MAIN ROAD?
YES!
AND THE DRIVER COULDN'T STOP WHEN I ASKED HIM TO...

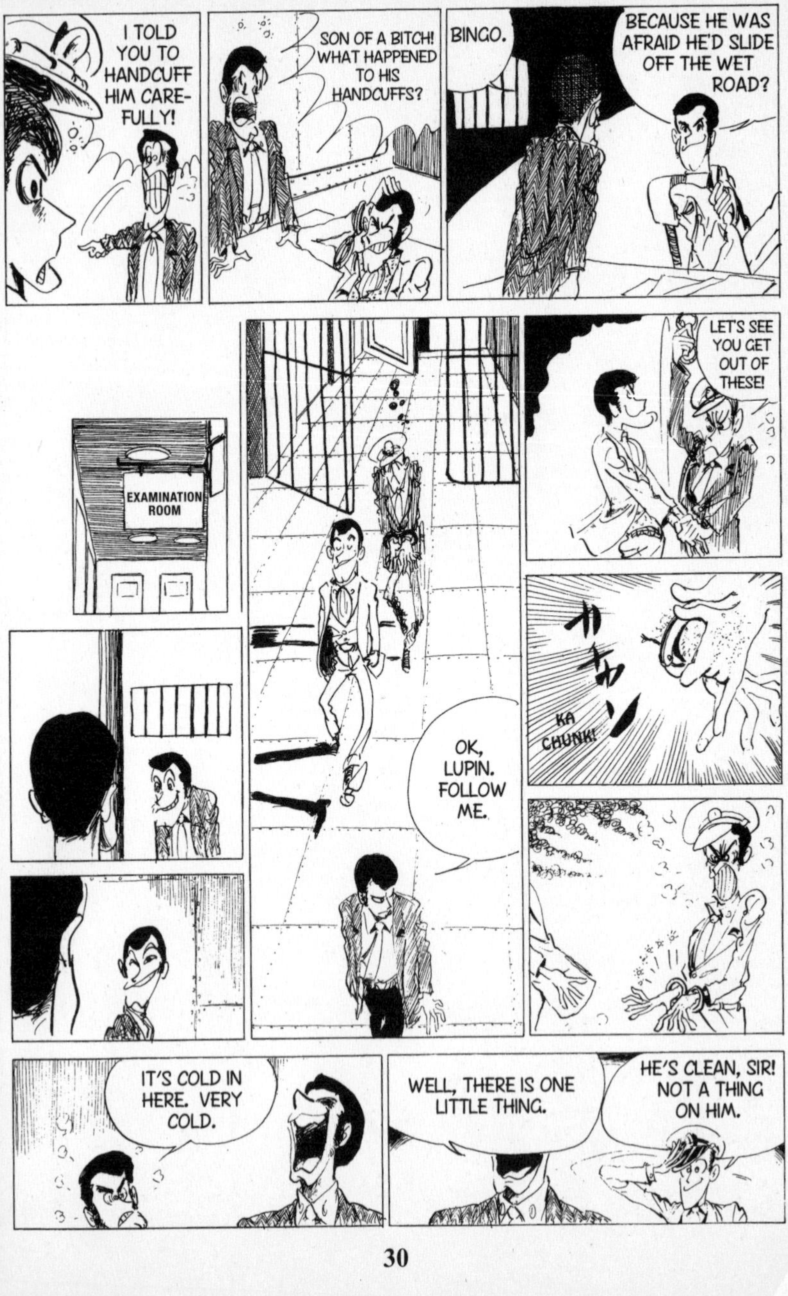
BECAUSE HE WAS AFRAID HE'D SLIDE OFF THE WET ROAD?
BINGO.
SON OF A BITCH! WHAT HAPPENED TO HIS HANDCUFFS?
I TOLD YOU TO HANDCUFF HIM CAREFULLY!
LET'S SEE YOU GET OUT OF THESE!
KA CHUNK!
OK, LUPIN. FOLLOW ME.
EXAMINATION ROOM
HE'S CLEAN, SIR! NOT A THING ON HIM.
WELL, THERE IS ONE LITTLE THING.
IT'S COLD IN HERE. VERY COLD.

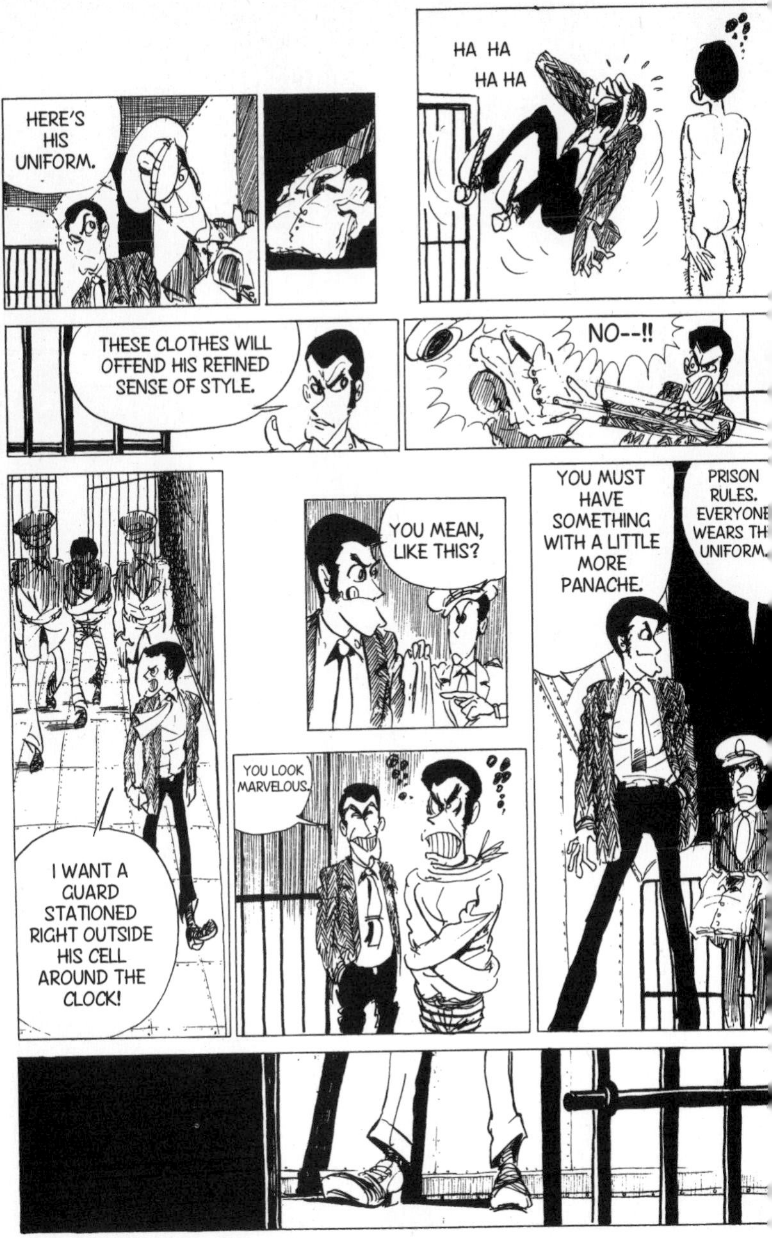
HA HA
HA HA
HERE'S HIS UNIFORM.
NO--!!
THESE CLOTHES WILL OFFEND HIS REFINED SENSE OF STYLE.
PRISON RULES. EVERYONE WEARS TH UNIFORM.
YOU MUST HAVE SOMETHING WITH A LITTLE MORE PANACHE.
YOU MEAN, LIKE THIS?
YOU LOOK MARVELOUS.
I WANT A GUARD STATIONED RIGHT OUTSIDE HIS CELL AROUND THE CLOCK!

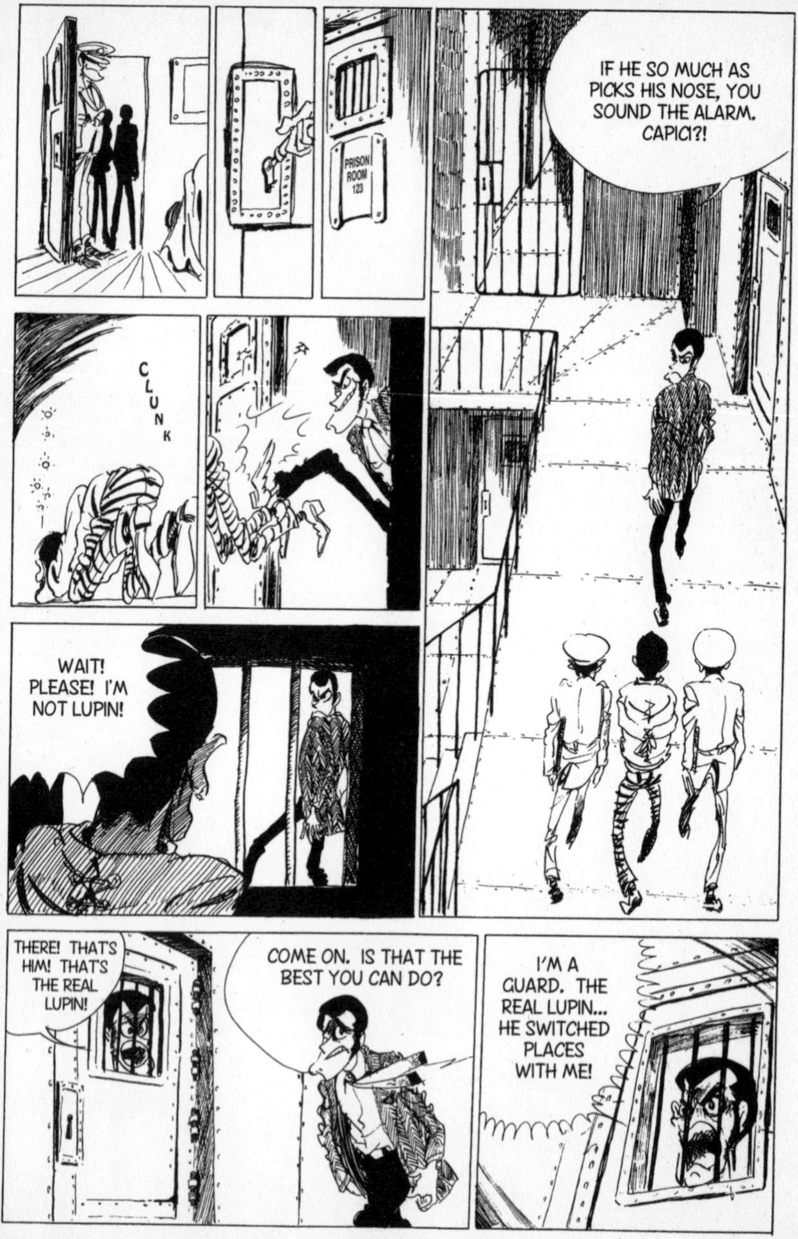
IF HE SO MUCH AS PICKS HIS NOSE, YOU SOUND THE ALARM. CAPICI?!
PRISON ROOM 123
CLUNK
WAIT! PLEASE! I'M NOT LUPIN!
I'M A GUARD. THE REAL LUPIN... HE SWITCHED PLACES WITH ME!
COME ON. IS THAT THE BEST YOU CAN DO?
THERE! THAT'S HIM! THAT'S THE REAL LUPIN!

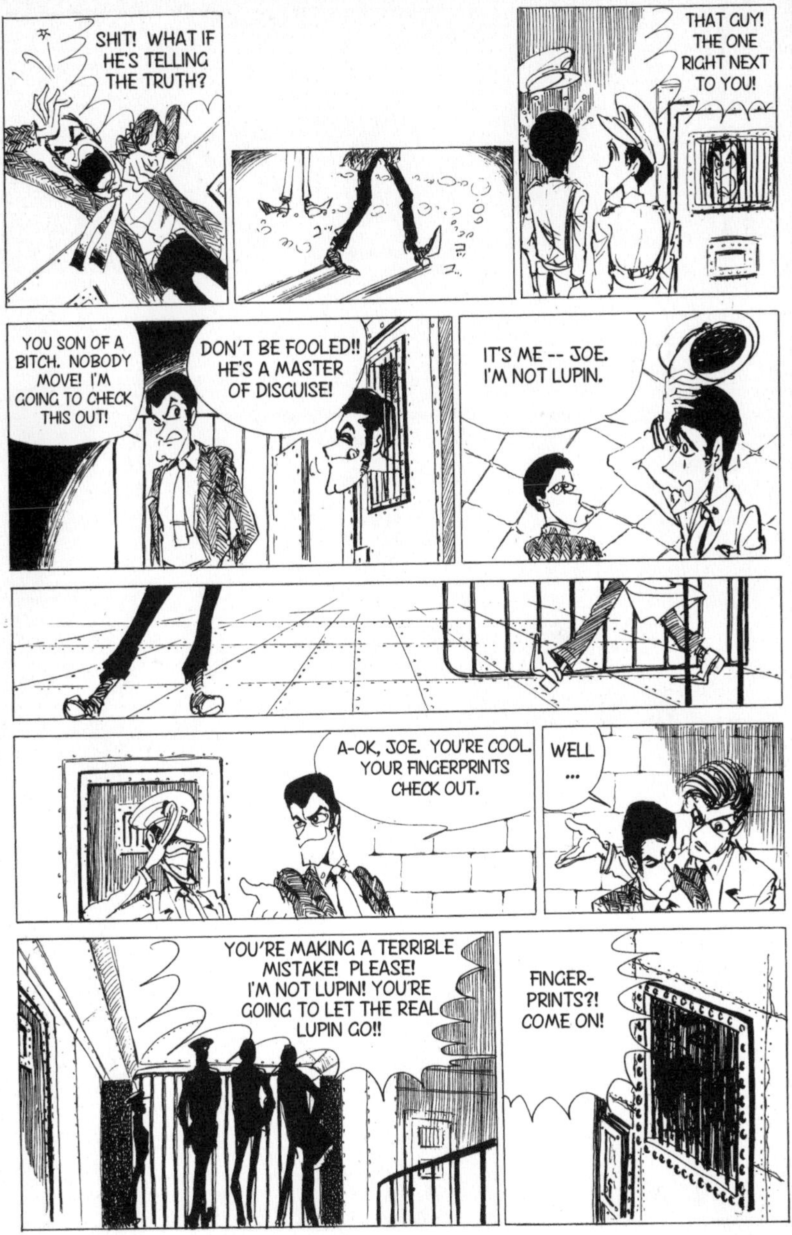
THAT GUY! THE ONE RIGHT NEXT TO YOU!
SHIT! WHAT IF HE'S TELLING THE TRUTH?
IT'S ME -- JOE. I'M NOT LUPIN.
DON'T BE FOOLED!! HE'S A MASTER OF DISGUISE!
YOU SON OF A BITCH. NOBODY MOVE! I'M GOING TO CHECK THIS OUT!
WELL ...
A-OK, JOE. YOU'RE COOL. YOUR FINGERPRINTS CHECK OUT.
FINGER-PRINTS?! COME ON!
YOU'RE MAKING A TERRIBLE MISTAKE! PLEASE! I'M NOT LUPIN! YOU'RE GOING TO LET THE REAL LUPIN GO!!

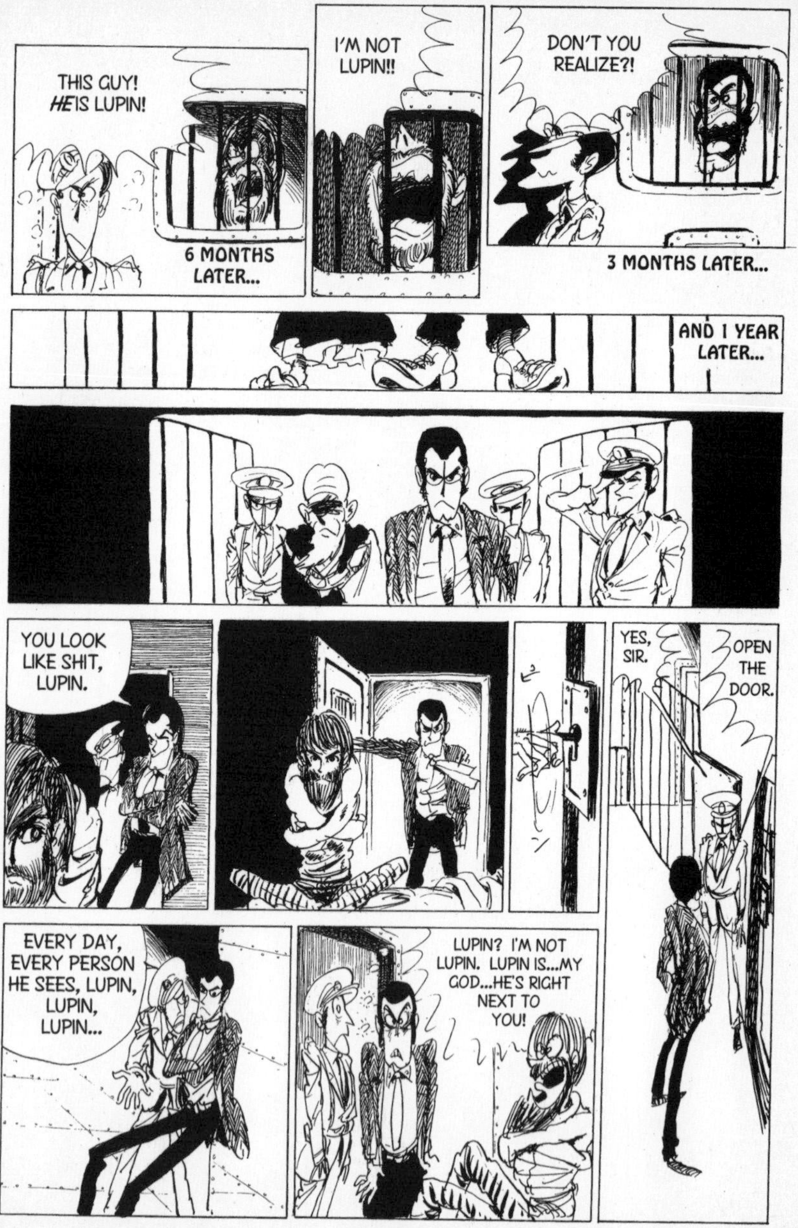
DON'T YOU REALIZE?!
3 MONTHS LATER...
I'M NOT LUPIN!!
THIS GUY! *HE* IS LUPIN!
6 MONTHS LATER...
AND 1 YEAR LATER...
OPEN THE DOOR.
YES, SIR.
YOU LOOK LIKE SHIT, LUPIN.
LUPIN? I'M NOT LUPIN. LUPIN IS...MY GOD...HE'S RIGHT NEXT TO YOU!
EVERY DAY, EVERY PERSON HE SEES, LUPIN, LUPIN, LUPIN...

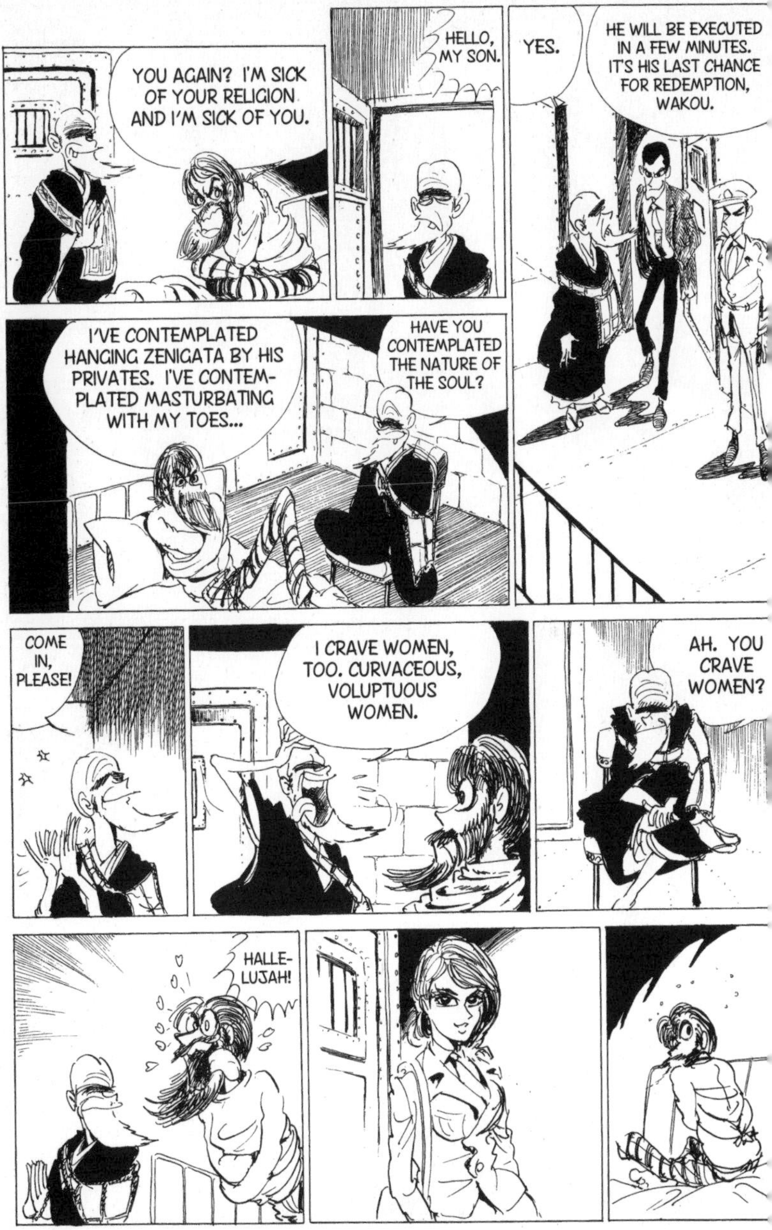
HE WILL BE EXECUTED IN A FEW MINUTES. IT'S HIS LAST CHANCE FOR REDEMPTION, WAKOU.
YES.
HELLO, MY SON.
YOU AGAIN? I'M SICK OF YOUR RELIGION AND I'M SICK OF YOU.
HAVE YOU CONTEMPLATED THE NATURE OF THE SOUL?
I'VE CONTEMPLATED HANGING ZENIGATA BY HIS PRIVATES. I'VE CONTEMPLATED MASTURBATING WITH MY TOES...
AH. YOU CRAVE WOMEN?
I CRAVE WOMEN, TOO. CURVACEOUS, VOLUPTUOUS WOMEN.
COME IN, PLEASE!
HALLELUJAH!

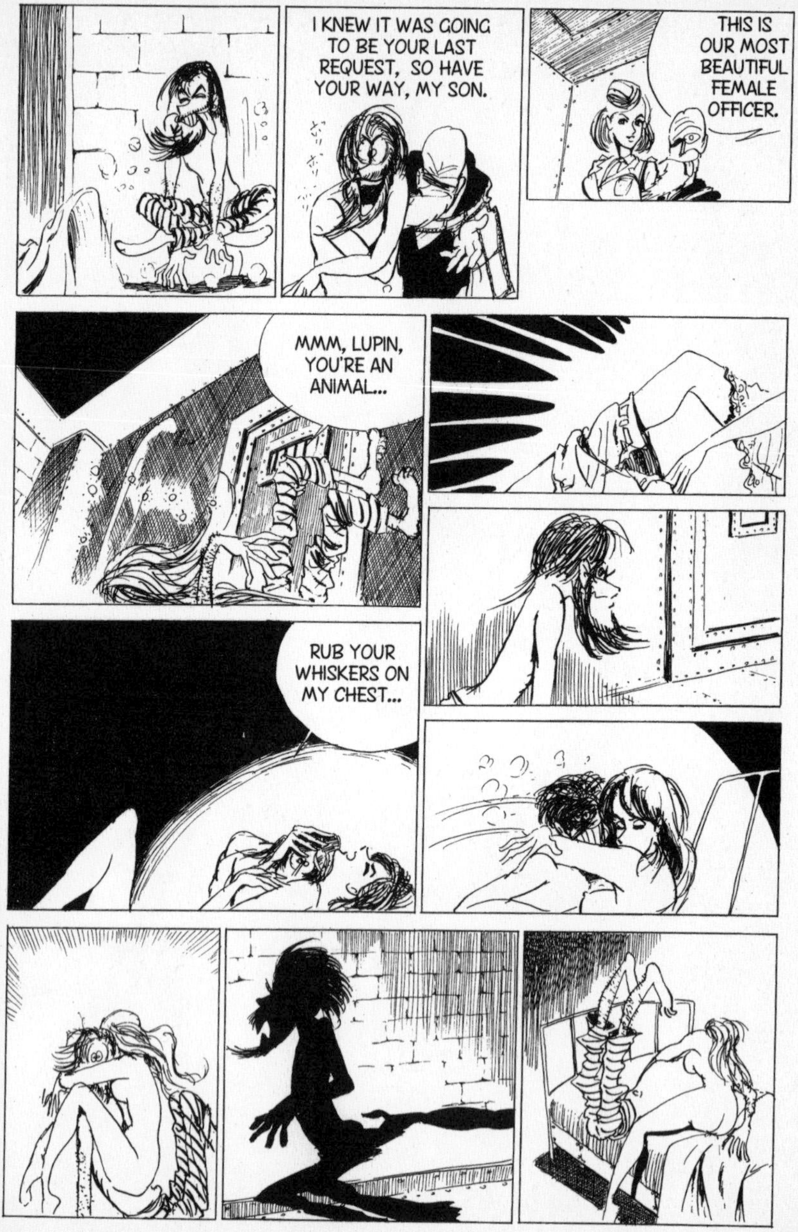
THIS IS OUR MOST BEAUTIFUL FEMALE OFFICER.
I KNEW IT WAS GOING TO BE YOUR LAST REQUEST, SO HAVE YOUR WAY, MY SON.
MMM, LUPIN, YOU'RE AN ANIMAL...
RUB YOUR WHISKERS ON MY CHEST...

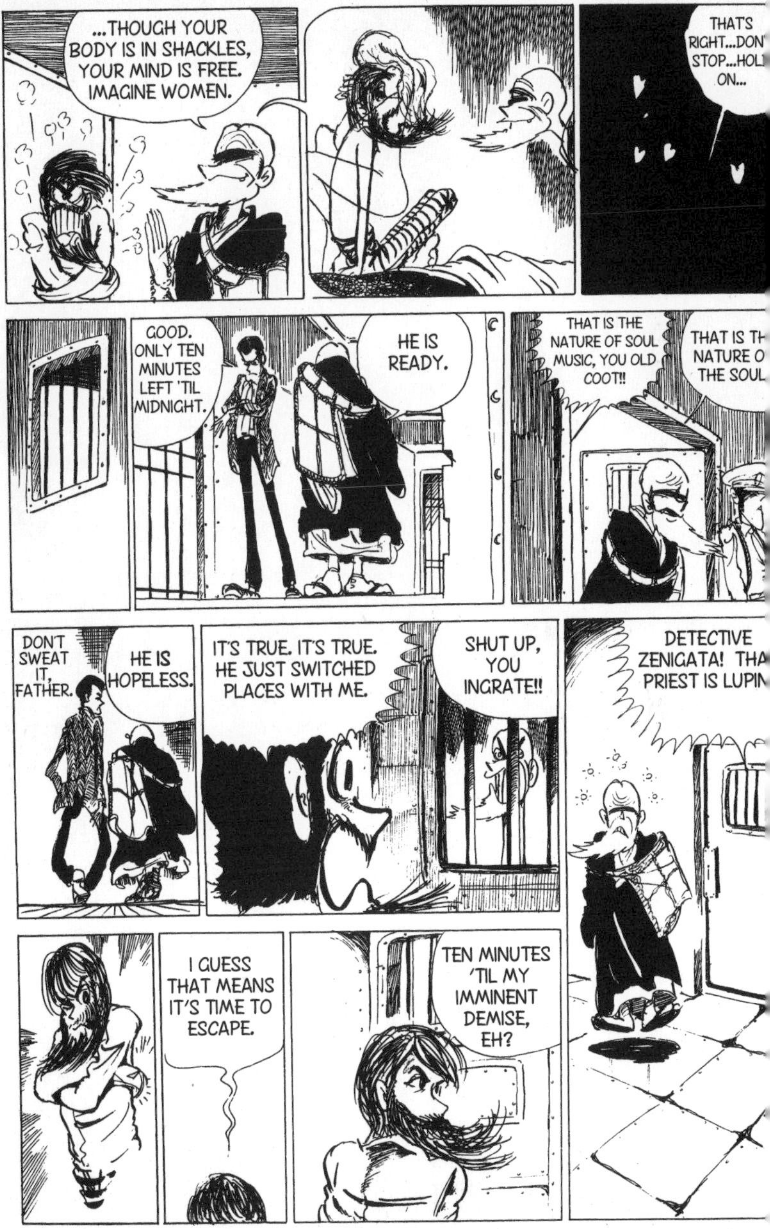
THAT'S RIGHT...DON' STOP...HOL ON...
...THOUGH YOUR BODY IS IN SHACKLES, YOUR MIND IS FREE. IMAGINE WOMEN.
THAT IS TH NATURE O THE SOUL
THAT IS THE NATURE OF SOUL MUSIC, YOU OLD COOT!!
HE IS READY.
GOOD. ONLY TEN MINUTES LEFT 'TIL MIDNIGHT.
DETECTIVE ZENIGATA! THA PRIEST IS LUPIN
SHUT UP, YOU INGRATE!!
IT'S TRUE. IT'S TRUE. HE JUST SWITCHED PLACES WITH ME.
HE IS HOPELESS.
DON'T SWEAT IT, FATHER.
TEN MINUTES 'TIL MY IMMINENT DEMISE, EH?
I GUESS THAT MEANS IT'S TIME TO ESCAPE.

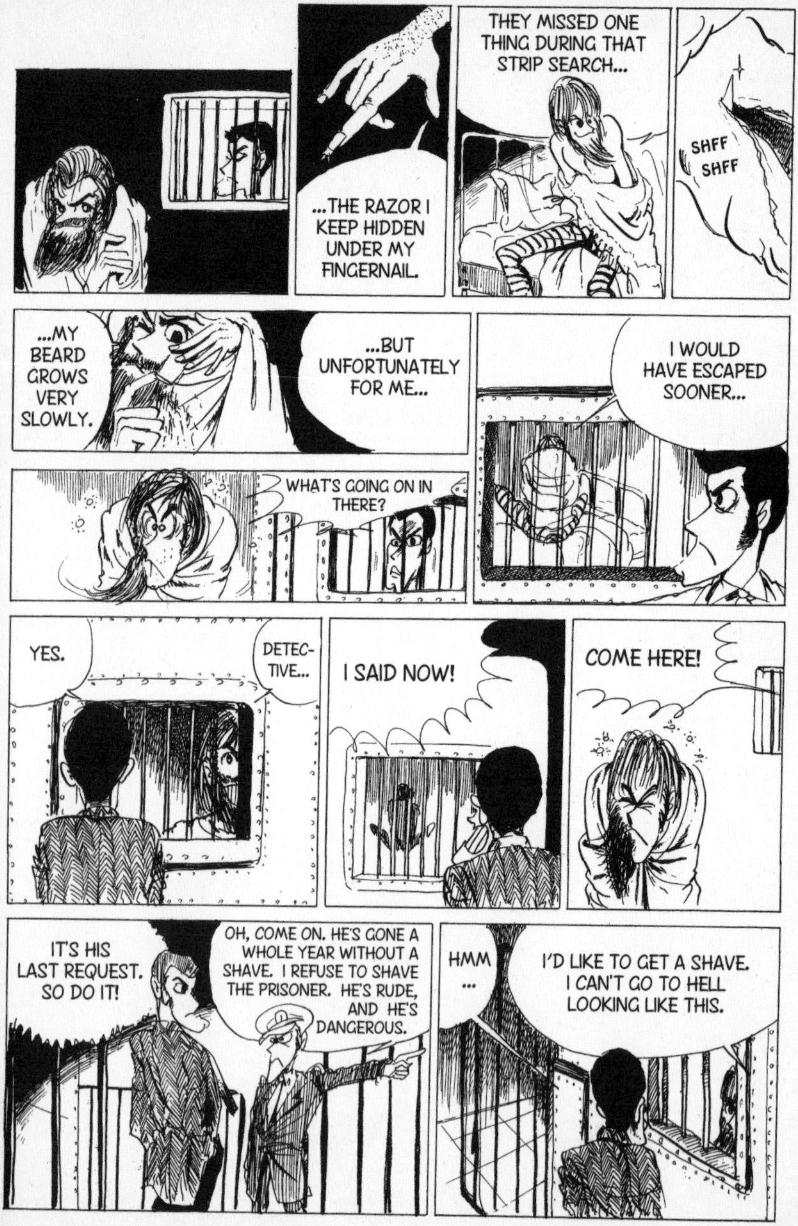
SHFF
SHFF
THEY MISSED ONE THING DURING THAT STRIP SEARCH...
...THE RAZOR I KEEP HIDDEN UNDER MY FINGERNAIL.
I WOULD HAVE ESCAPED SOONER...
...BUT UNFORTUNATELY FOR ME...
...MY BEARD GROWS VERY SLOWLY.
WHAT'S GOING ON IN THERE?
COME HERE!
I SAID NOW!
DETECTIVE...
YES.
I'D LIKE TO GET A SHAVE. I CAN'T GO TO HELL LOOKING LIKE THIS.
HMM ...
OH, COME ON. HE'S GONE A WHOLE YEAR WITHOUT A SHAVE. I REFUSE TO SHAVE THE PRISONER. HE'S RUDE, AND HE'S DANGEROUS.
IT'S HIS LAST REQUEST. SO DO IT!

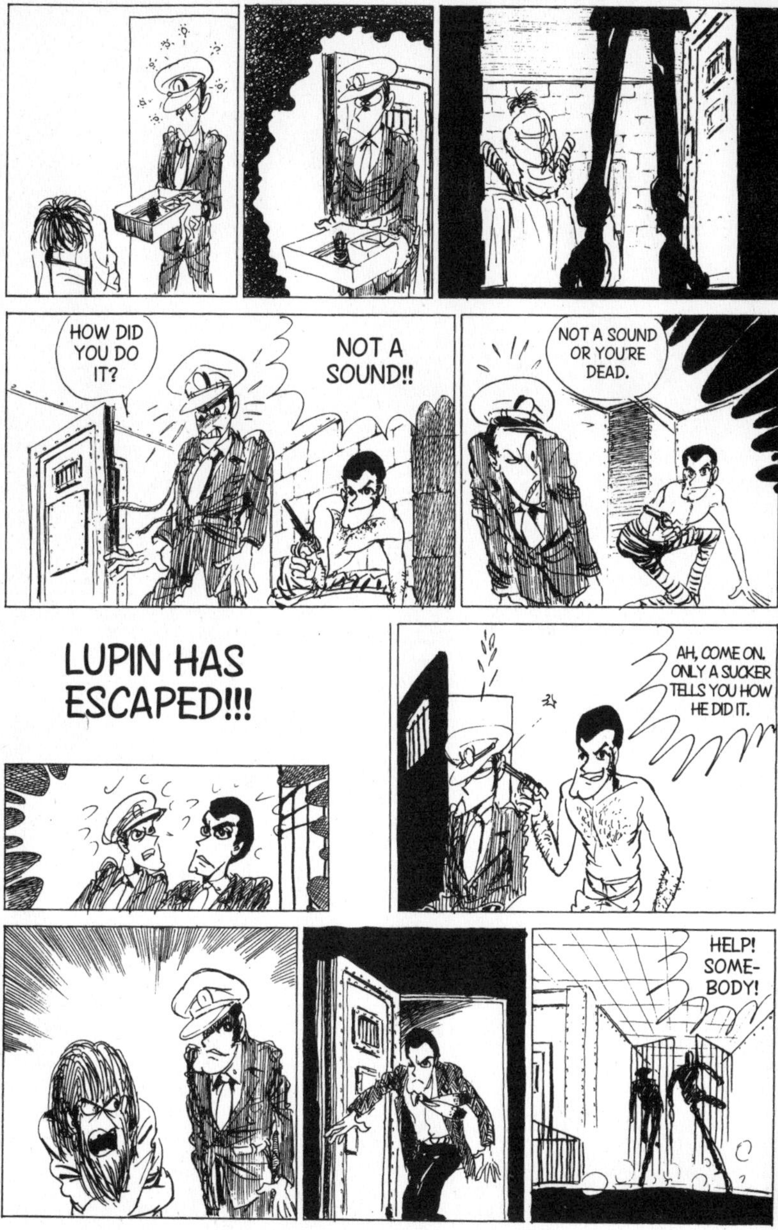
NOT A SOUND OR YOU'RE DEAD.
HOW DID YOU DO IT?
NOT A SOUND!!
AH, COME ON. ONLY A SUCKER TELLS YOU HOW HE DID IT.
LUPIN HAS ESCAPED!!!
HELP! SOME-BODY!

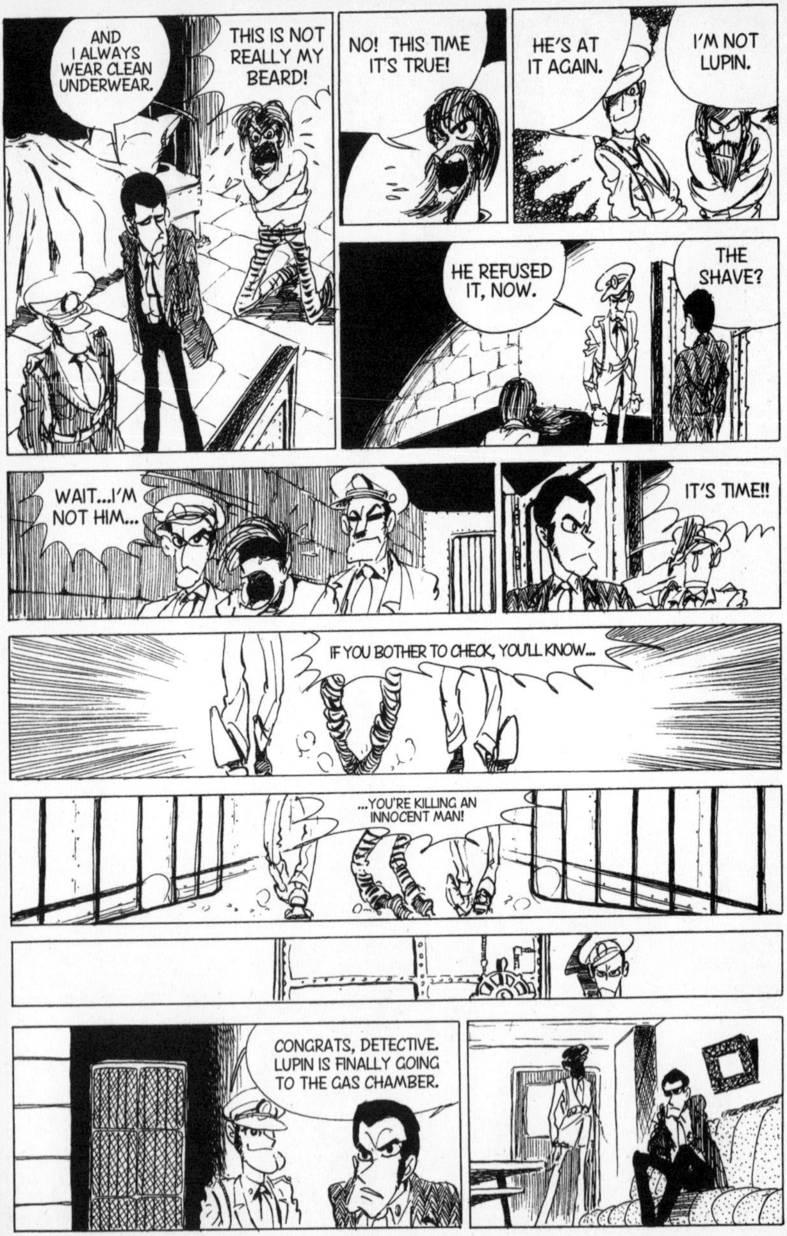
I'M NOT LUPIN.
HE'S AT IT AGAIN.
NO! THIS TIME IT'S TRUE!
THE SHAVE?
HE REFUSED IT, NOW.
THIS IS NOT REALLY MY BEARD!
AND I ALWAYS WEAR CLEAN UNDERWEAR.
IT'S TIME!!
WAIT...I'M NOT HIM...
IF YOU BOTHER TO CHECK, YOU'LL KNOW...
...YOU'RE KILLING AN INNOCENT MAN!
CONGRATS, DETECTIVE. LUPIN IS FINALLY GOING TO THE GAS CHAMBER.

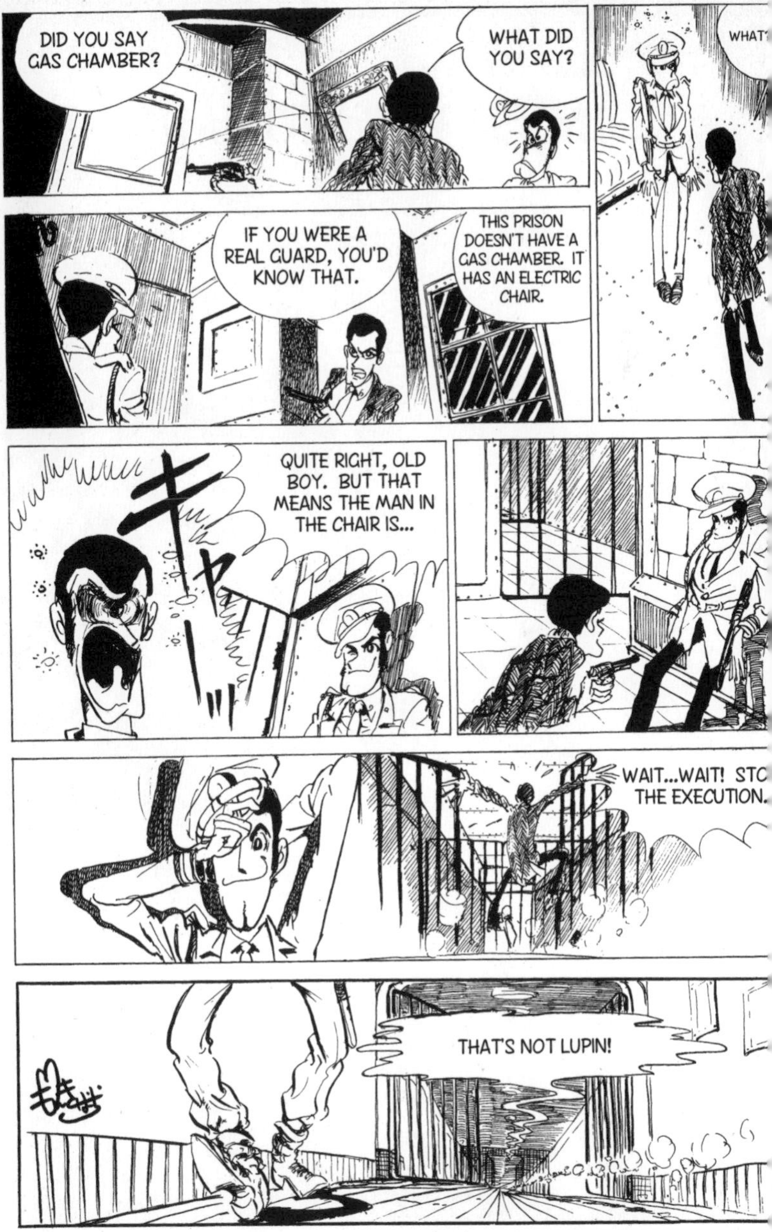
WHAT
WHAT DID YOU SAY?
DID YOU SAY GAS CHAMBER?
THIS PRISON DOESN'T HAVE A GAS CHAMBER. IT HAS AN ELECTRIC CHAIR.
IF YOU WERE A REAL GUARD, YOU'D KNOW THAT.
QUITE RIGHT, OLD BOY. BUT THAT MEANS THE MAN IN THE CHAIR IS...
キャーッ
WAIT...WAIT! STO
THE EXECUTION.
THAT'S NOT LUPIN!

CHAPTER 3
"MYSTERY WOMAN"

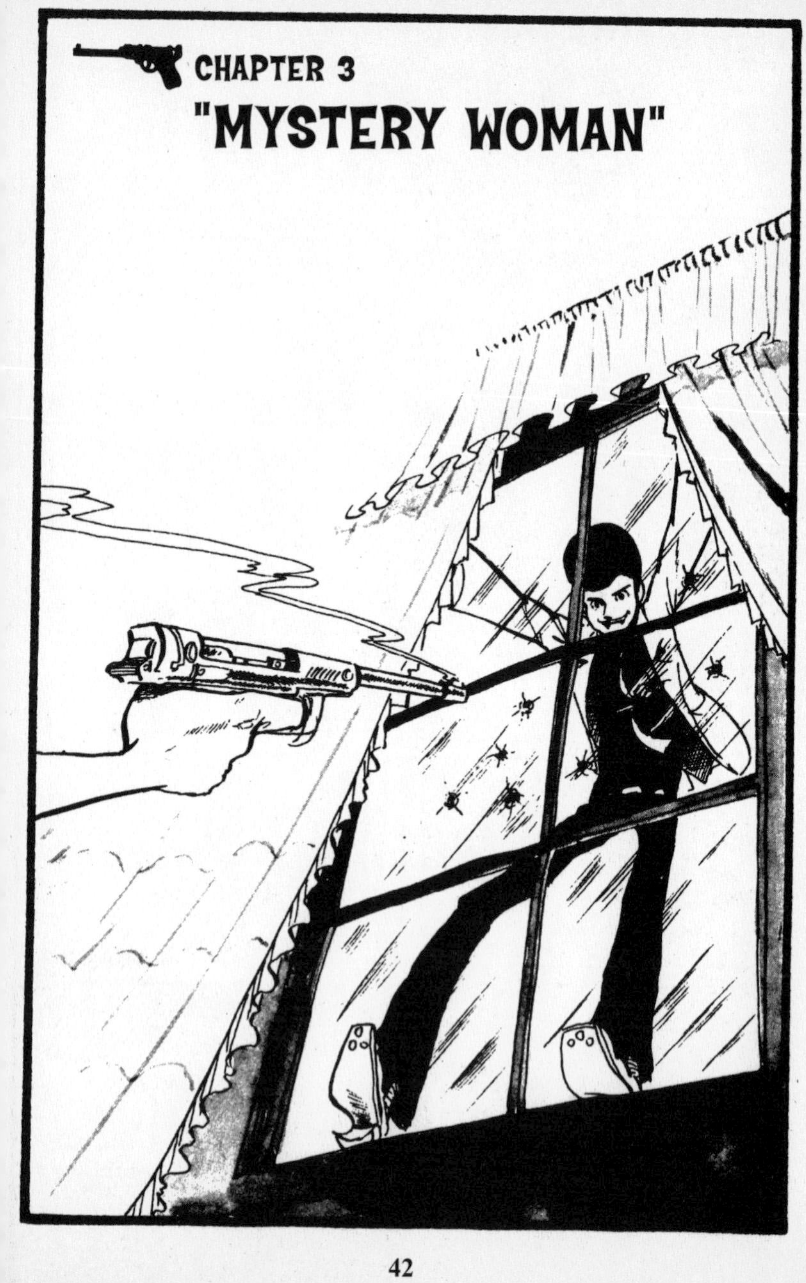

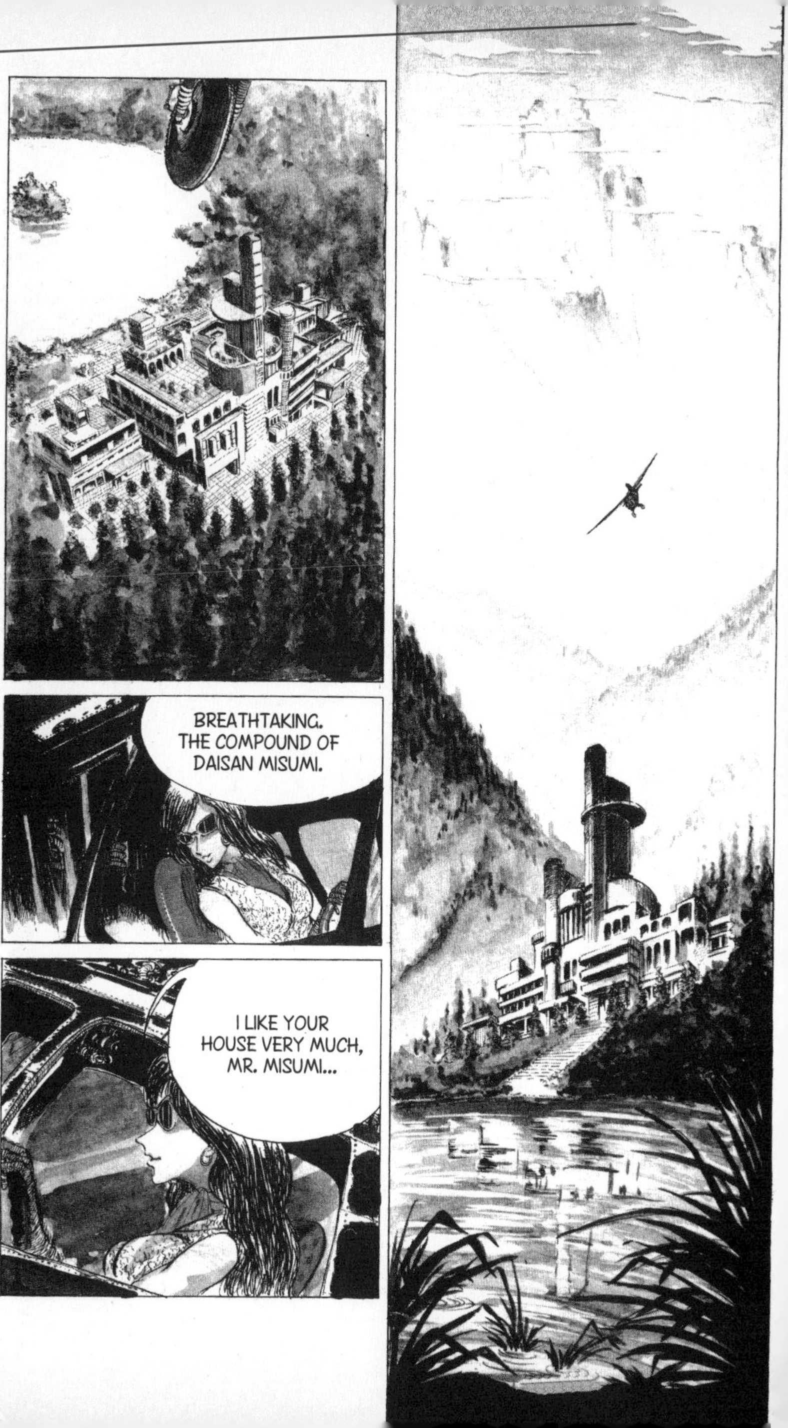
BREATHTAKING. THE COMPOUND OF DAISAN MISUMI.
I LIKE YOUR HOUSE VERY MUCH, MR. MISUMI...

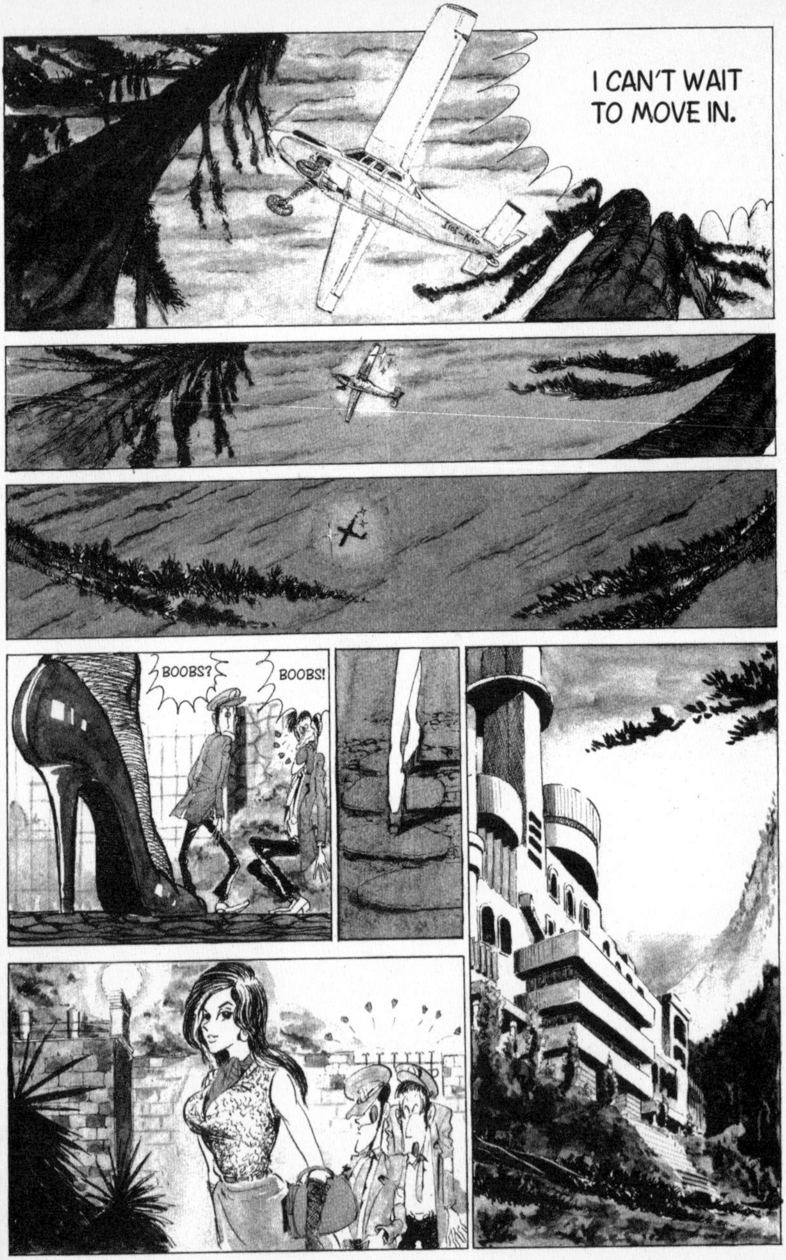
I CAN'T WAIT TO MOVE IN.
BOOBS!
BOOBS?

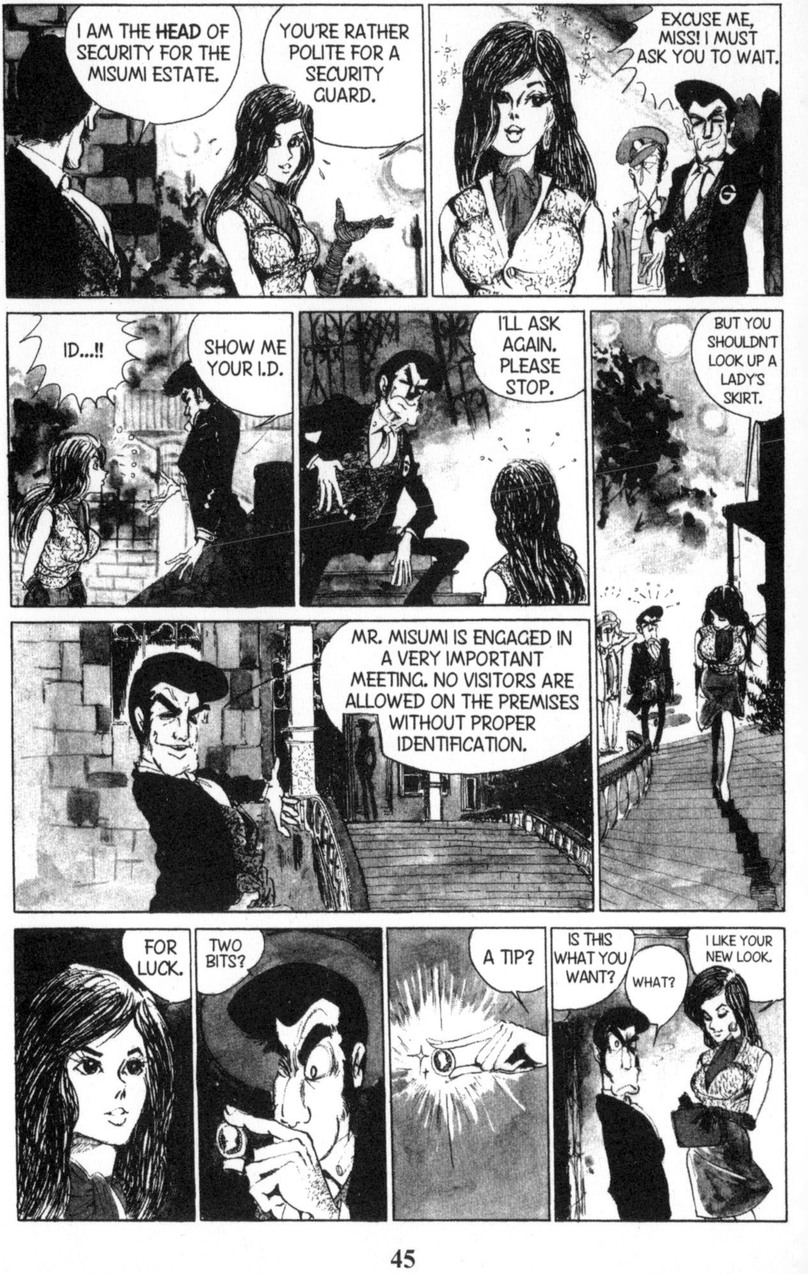
EXCUSE ME, MISS! I MUST ASK YOU TO WAIT.
YOU'RE RATHER POLITE FOR A SECURITY GUARD.
I AM THE **HEAD** OF SECURITY FOR THE MISUMI ESTATE.
BUT YOU SHOULDN'T LOOK UP A LADY'S SKIRT.
I'LL ASK AGAIN. PLEASE STOP.
SHOW ME YOUR I.D.
ID...!!
MR. MISUMI IS ENGAGED IN A VERY IMPORTANT MEETING. NO VISITORS ARE ALLOWED ON THE PREMISES WITHOUT PROPER IDENTIFICATION.
I LIKE YOUR NEW LOOK.
IS THIS WHAT YOU WANT?
WHAT?
A TIP?
TWO BITS?
FOR LUCK.

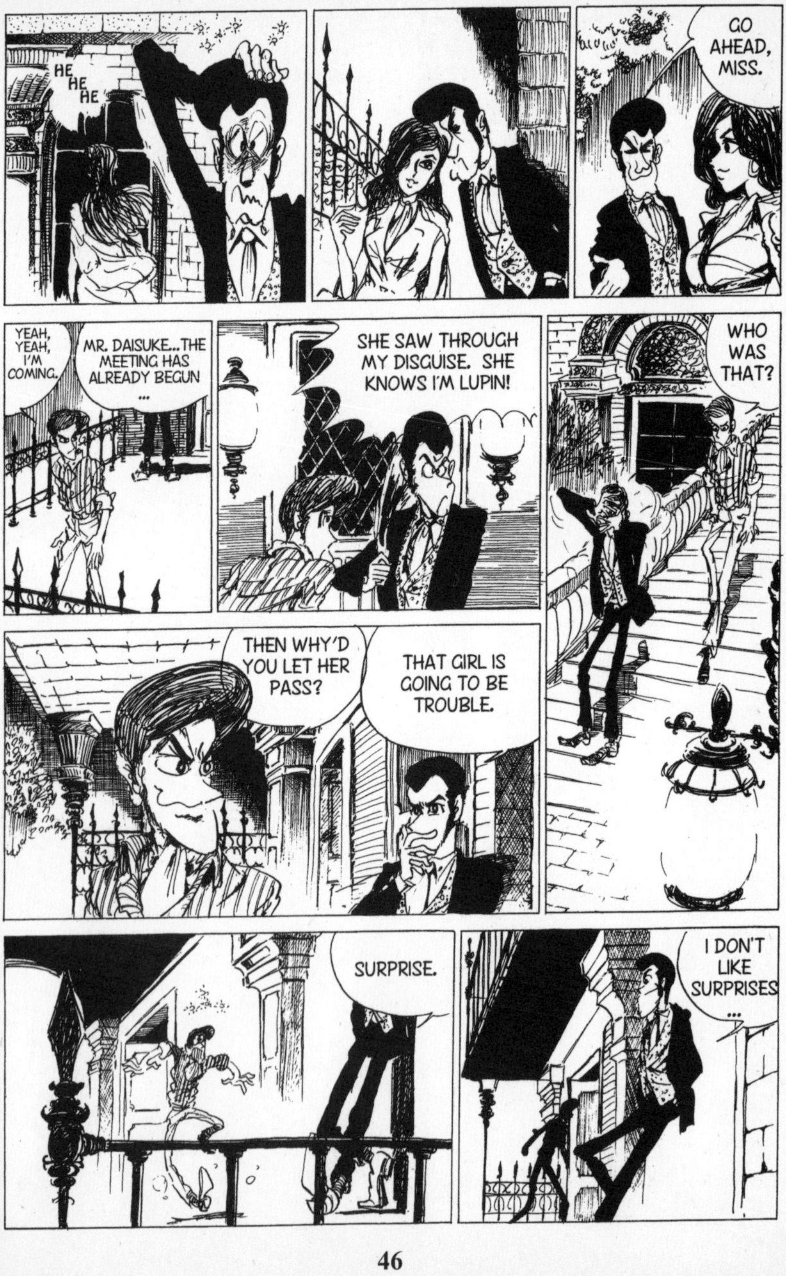
GO AHEAD, MISS.
HE HE HE
WHO WAS THAT?
SHE SAW THROUGH MY DISGUISE. SHE KNOWS I'M LUPIN!
MR. DAISUKE...THE MEETING HAS ALREADY BEGUN ...
YEAH, YEAH, I'M COMING.
THAT GIRL IS GOING TO BE TROUBLE.
THEN WHY'D YOU LET HER PASS?
I DON'T LIKE SURPRISES ...
SURPRISE.

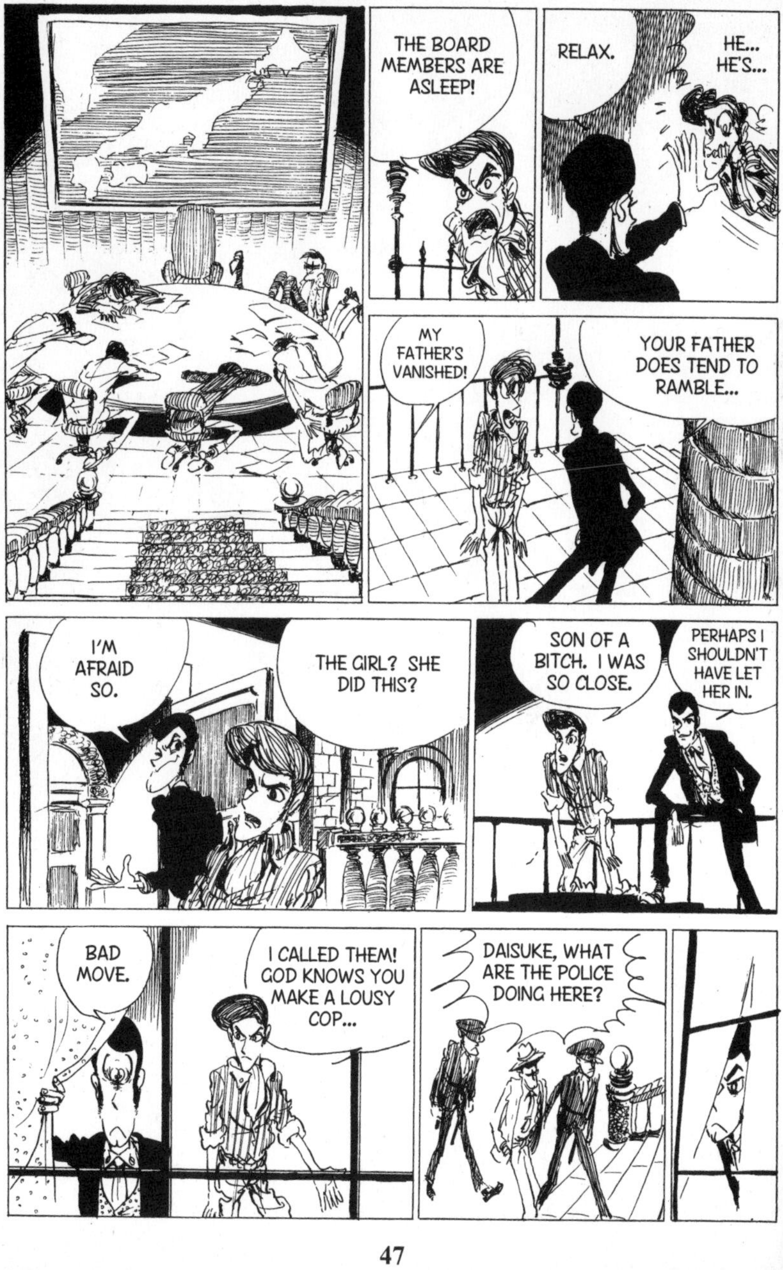
HE... HE'S...
RELAX.
THE BOARD MEMBERS ARE ASLEEP!
YOUR FATHER DOES TEND TO RAMBLE...
MY FATHER'S VANISHED!
PERHAPS I SHOULDN'T HAVE LET HER IN.
SON OF A BITCH. I WAS SO CLOSE.
THE GIRL? SHE DID THIS?
I'M AFRAID SO.
DAISUKE, WHAT ARE THE POLICE DOING HERE?
I CALLED THEM! GOD KNOWS YOU MAKE A LOUSY COP...
BAD MOVE.

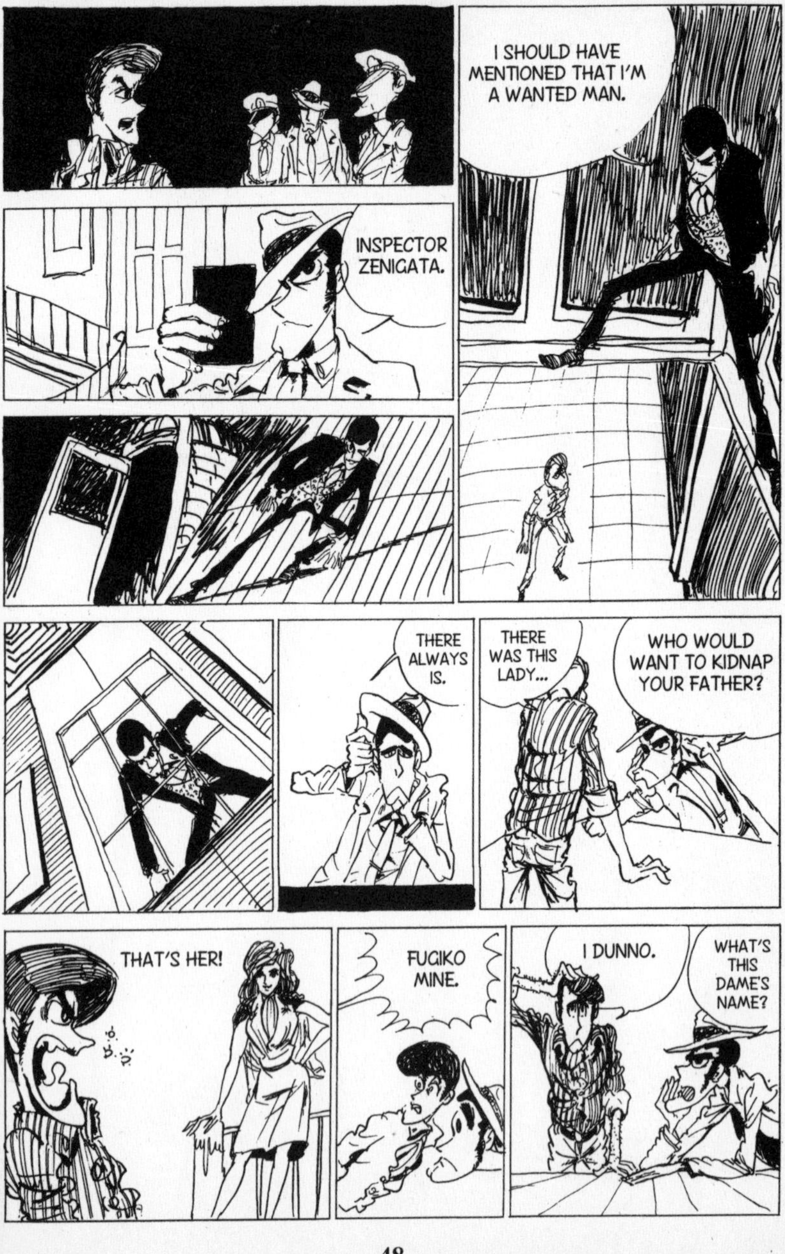
I SHOULD HAVE MENTIONED THAT I'M A WANTED MAN.
INSPECTOR ZENIGATA.
WHO WOULD WANT TO KIDNAP YOUR FATHER?
THERE WAS THIS LADY...
THERE ALWAYS IS.
WHAT'S THIS DAME'S NAME?
I DUNNO.
FUGIKO MINE.
THAT'S HER!

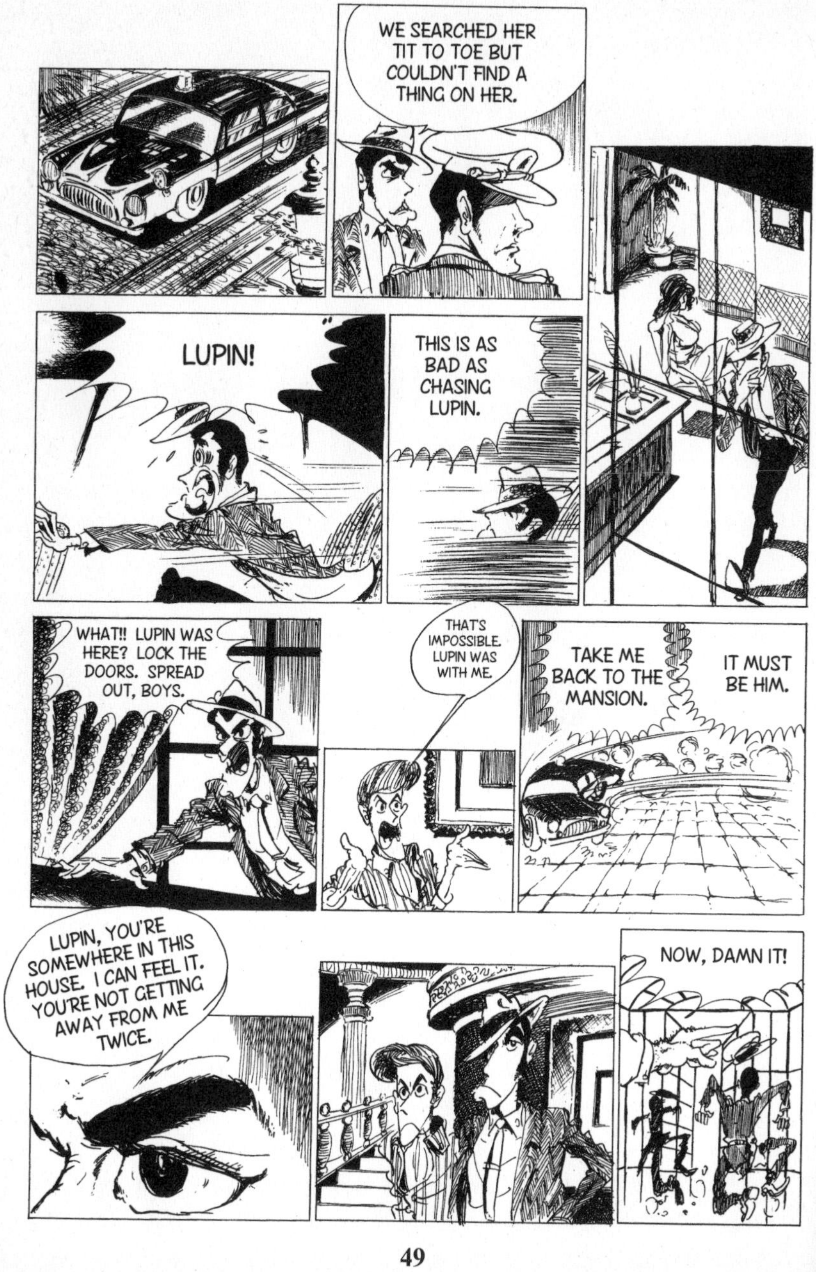
WE SEARCHED HER TIT TO TOE BUT COULDN'T FIND A THING ON HER.
THIS IS AS BAD AS CHASING LUPIN.
LUPIN!
IT MUST BE HIM.
TAKE ME BACK TO THE MANSION.
THAT'S IMPOSSIBLE. LUPIN WAS WITH ME.
WHAT!! LUPIN WAS HERE? LOCK THE DOORS. SPREAD OUT, BOYS.
NOW, DAMN IT!
LUPIN, YOU'RE SOMEWHERE IN THIS HOUSE. I CAN FEEL IT. YOU'RE NOT GETTING AWAY FROM ME TWICE.

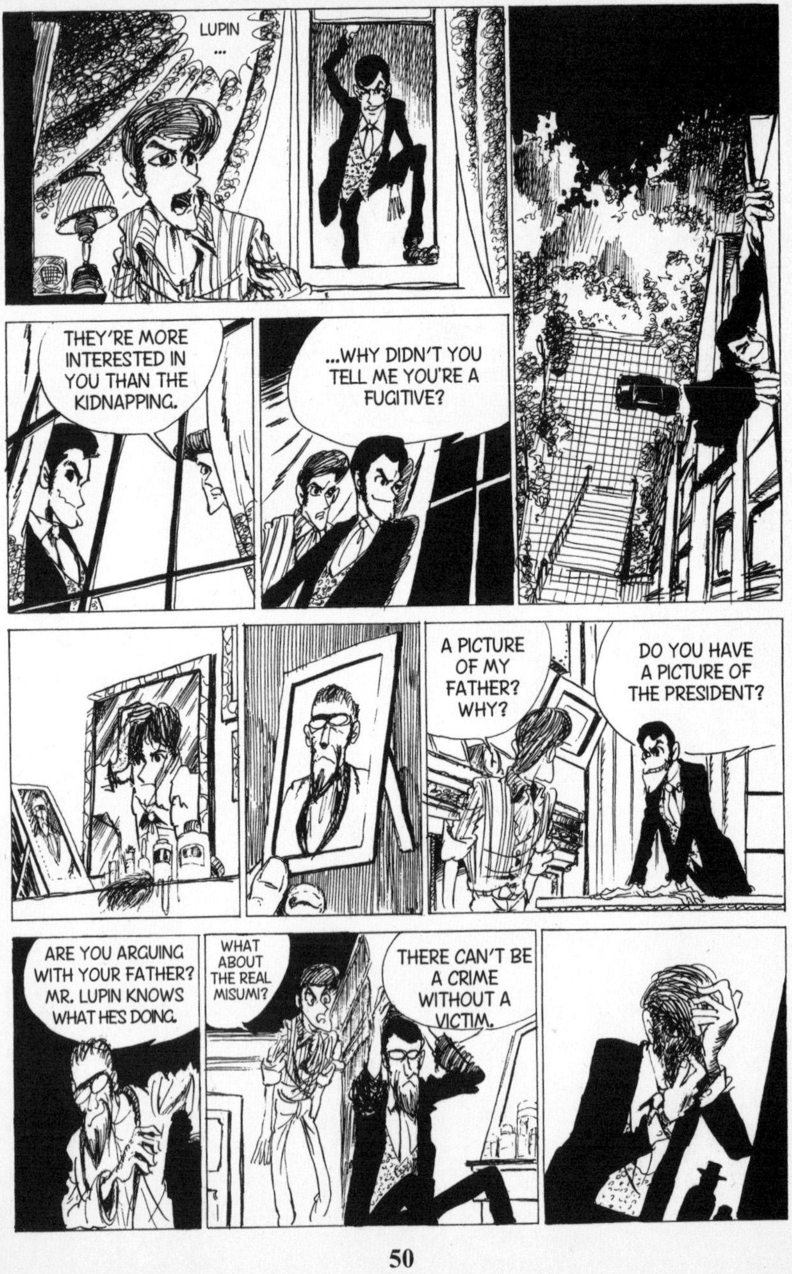
LUPIN ...
...WHY DIDN'T YOU TELL ME YOU'RE A FUGITIVE?
THEY'RE MORE INTERESTED IN YOU THAN THE KIDNAPPING.
DO YOU HAVE A PICTURE OF THE PRESIDENT?
A PICTURE OF MY FATHER? WHY?
THERE CAN'T BE A CRIME WITHOUT A VICTIM.
WHAT ABOUT THE REAL MISUMI?
ARE YOU ARGUING WITH YOUR FATHER? MR. LUPIN KNOWS WHAT HE'S DOING.

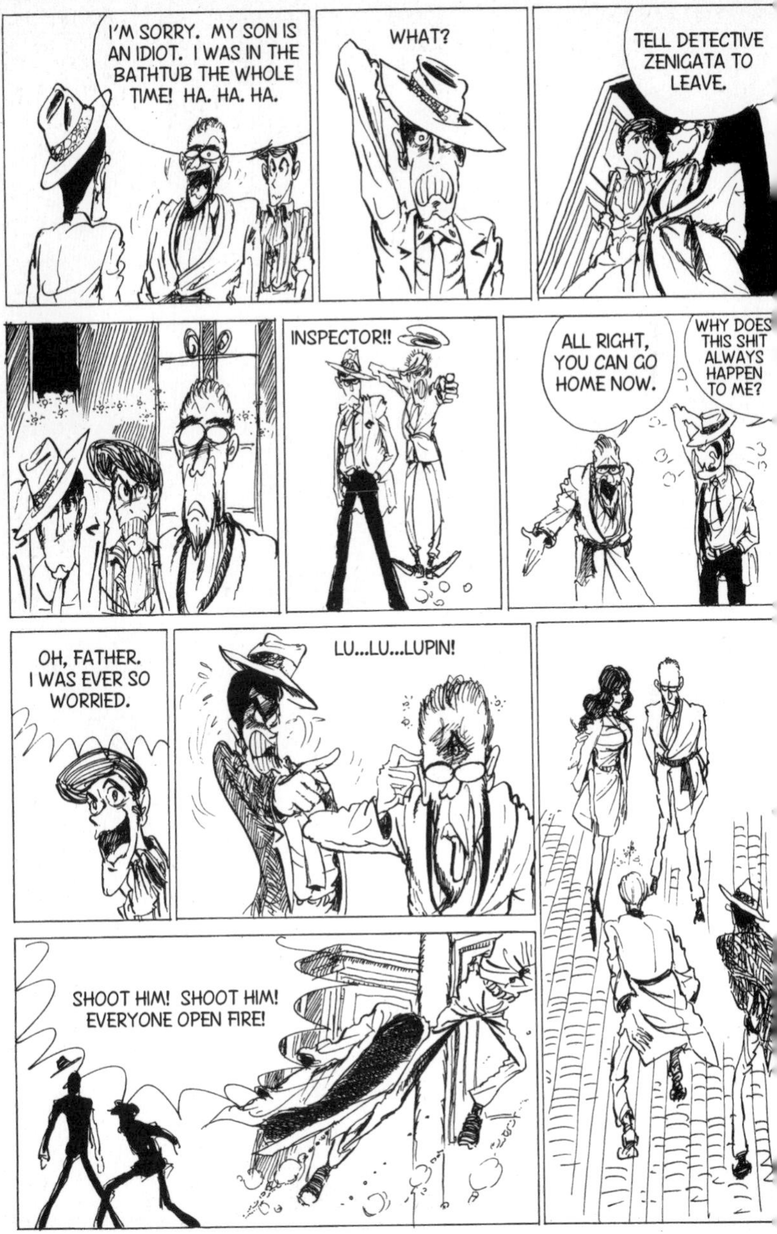
TELL DETECTIVE ZENIGATA TO LEAVE.
WHAT?
I'M SORRY. MY SON IS AN IDIOT. I WAS IN THE BATHTUB THE WHOLE TIME! HA. HA. HA.
WHY DOES THIS SHIT ALWAYS HAPPEN TO ME?
ALL RIGHT, YOU CAN GO HOME NOW.
INSPECTOR!!
LU...LU...LUPIN!
OH, FATHER. I WAS EVER SO WORRIED.
SHOOT HIM! SHOOT HIM! EVERYONE OPEN FIRE!

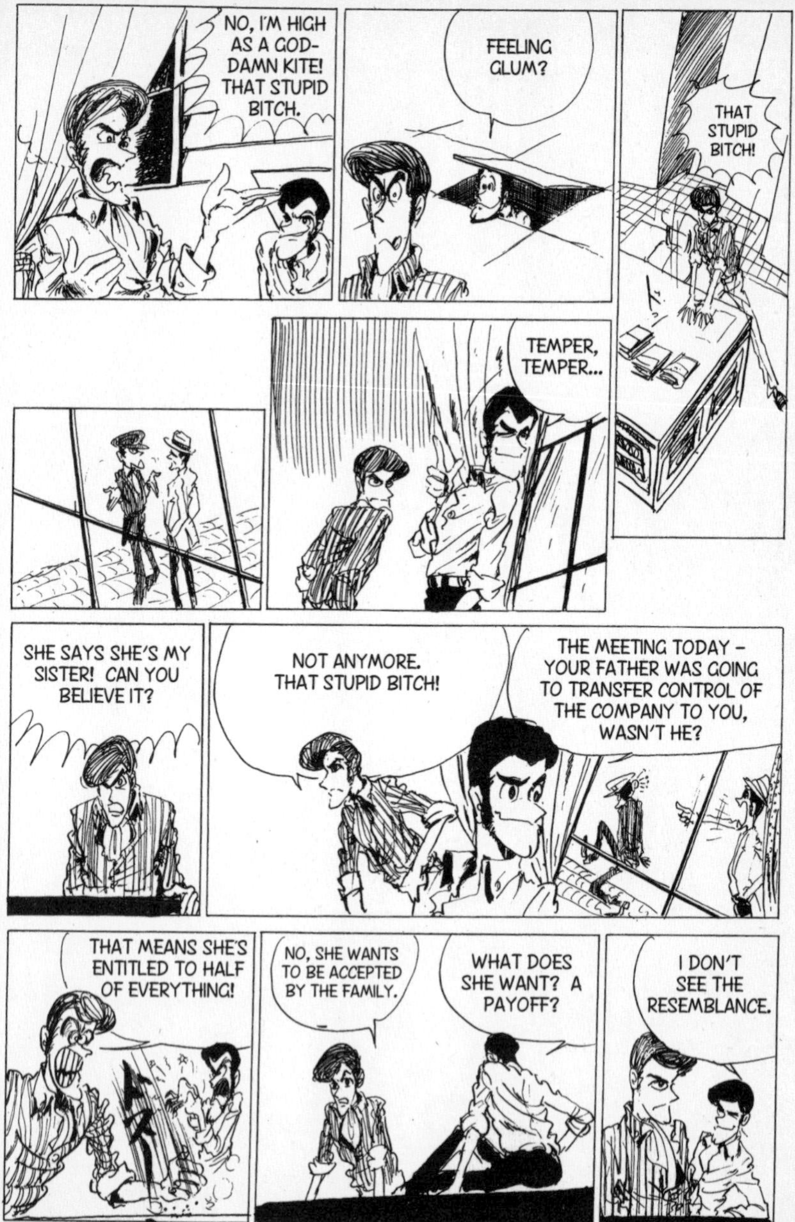
THAT STUPID BITCH!
FEELING GLUM?
NO, I'M HIGH AS A GOD-DAMN KITE! THAT STUPID BITCH.
TEMPER, TEMPER...
THE MEETING TODAY - YOUR FATHER WAS GOING TO TRANSFER CONTROL OF THE COMPANY TO YOU, WASN'T HE?
NOT ANYMORE. THAT STUPID BITCH!
SHE SAYS SHE'S MY SISTER! CAN YOU BELIEVE IT?
I DON'T SEE THE RESEMBLANCE.
WHAT DOES SHE WANT? A PAYOFF?
NO, SHE WANTS TO BE ACCEPTED BY THE FAMILY.
THAT MEANS SHE'S ENTITLED TO HALF OF EVERYTHING!

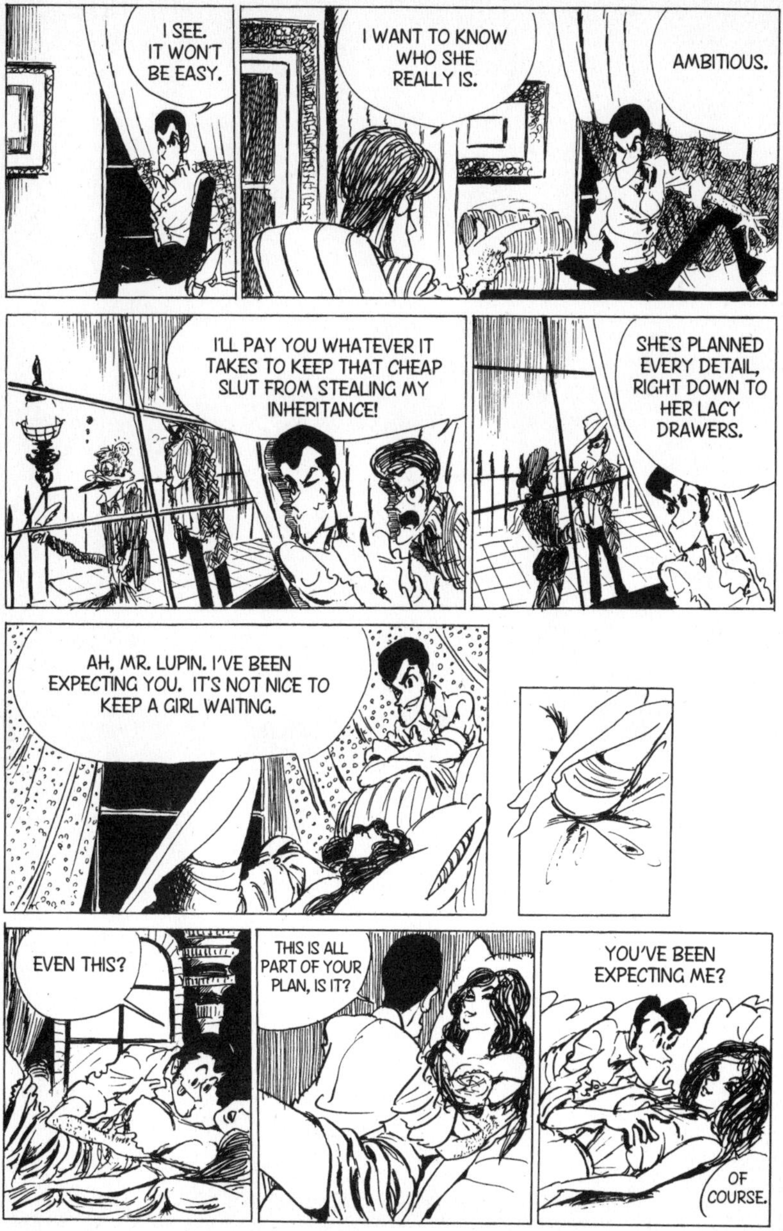
AMBITIOUS.
I WANT TO KNOW WHO SHE REALLY IS.
I SEE. IT WON'T BE EASY.
SHE'S PLANNED EVERY DETAIL, RIGHT DOWN TO HER LACY DRAWERS.
I'LL PAY YOU WHATEVER IT TAKES TO KEEP THAT CHEAP SLUT FROM STEALING MY INHERITANCE!
AH, MR. LUPIN. I'VE BEEN EXPECTING YOU. IT'S NOT NICE TO KEEP A GIRL WAITING.
YOU'VE BEEN EXPECTING ME?
OF COURSE.
THIS IS ALL PART OF YOUR PLAN, IS IT?
EVEN THIS?

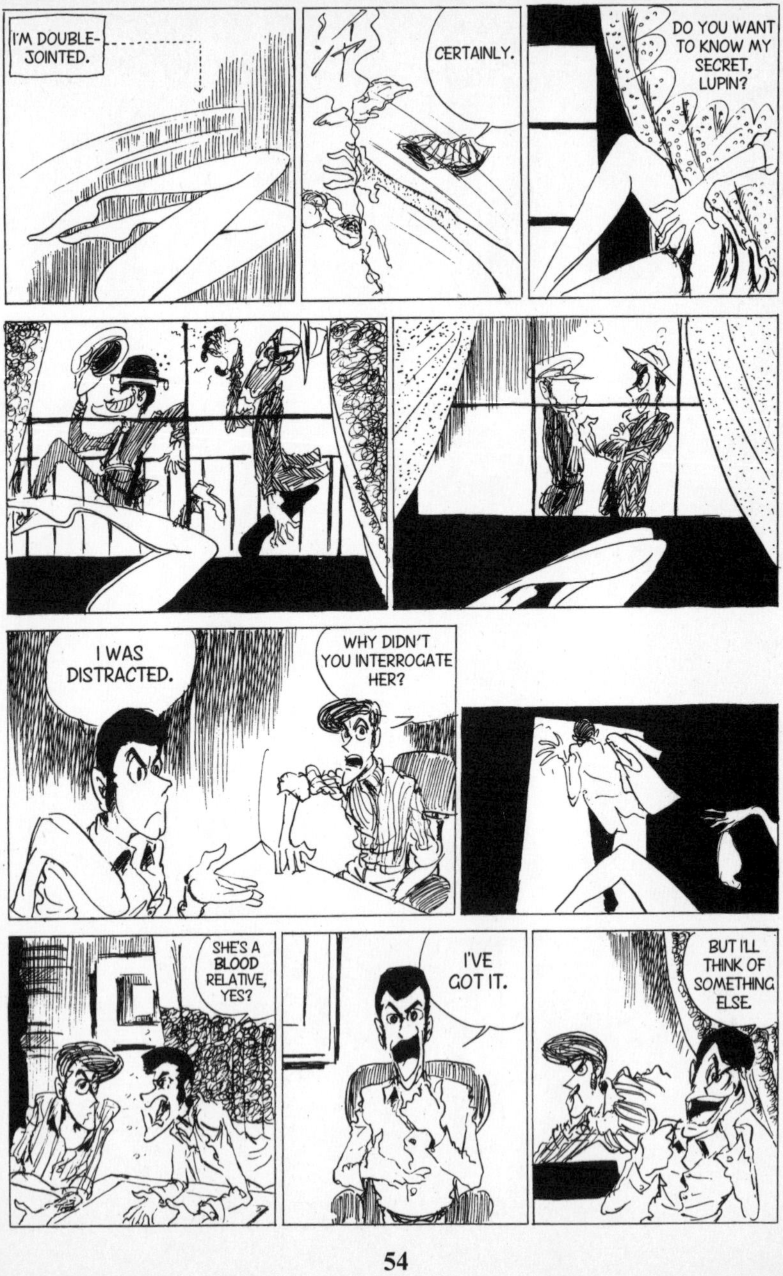
DO YOU WANT TO KNOW MY SECRET, LUPIN?
CERTAINLY.
I'M DOUBLE-JOINTED.
WHY DIDN'T YOU INTERROGATE HER?
I WAS DISTRACTED.
BUT I'LL THINK OF SOMETHING ELSE.
I'VE GOT IT.
SHE'S A BLOOD RELATIVE, YES?

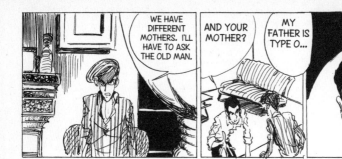

SO, LET'S CHECK HER BLOOD TYPE.
MY FATHER IS TYPE O...
AND YOUR MOTHER?
WE HAVE DIFFERENT MOTHERS. I'LL HAVE TO ASK THE OLD MAN.
HER BLOOD TYPE?
I'LL BE HONEST WITH YOU. I'VE HAD DOZENS OF AFFAIRS. FUGIKO'S MOTHER WAS A GIRL IN THE SECRETARY POOL. I BARELY KNEW HER.
I **BARELY** KNEW THE BABY WAS EVEN BORN. LUCKY FOR ME, SHE DIED BEFORE SHE COULD TELL ANYONE. OH, YEAH! I REMEMBER! SHE WAS TYPE O.
THAT'S CONVENIENT. IF FUGIKO IS TELLING THE TRUTH, SHE MUST BE TYPE O AS WELL.

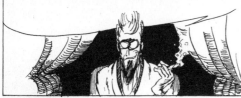

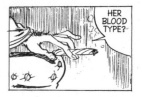

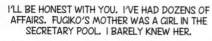

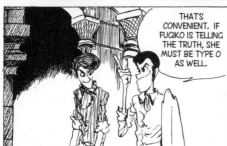

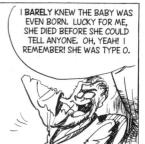

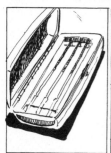

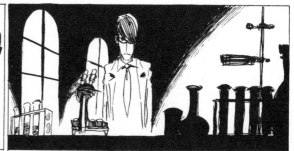

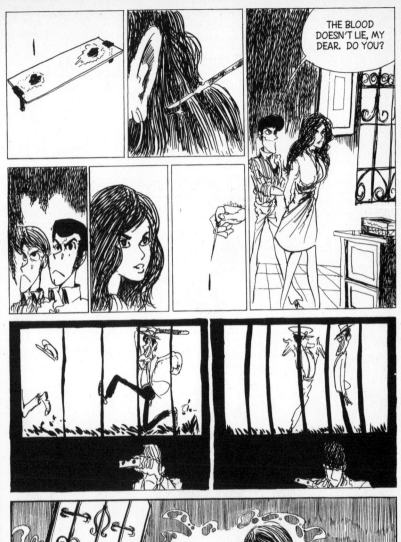

THE BLOOD DOESN'T LIE, MY DEAR. DO YOU?

CHAPTER 4

"TO CATCH A WEASEL"

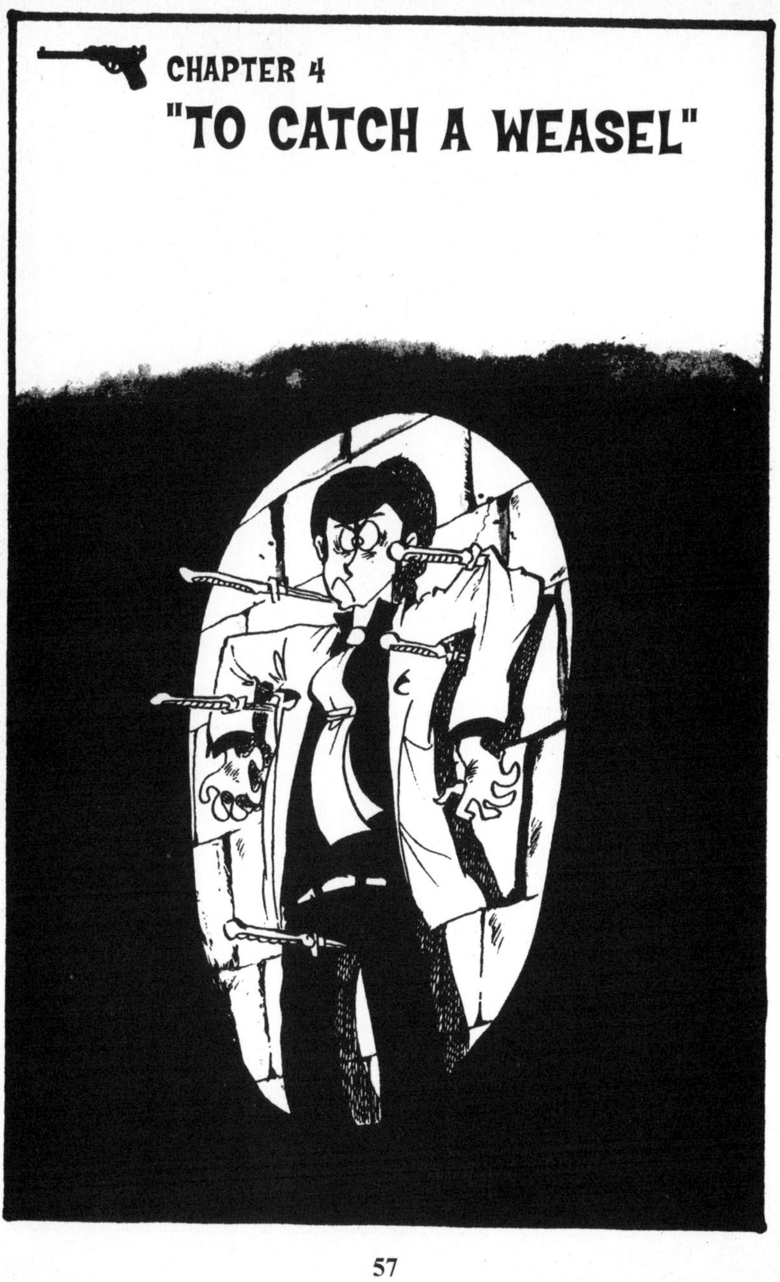

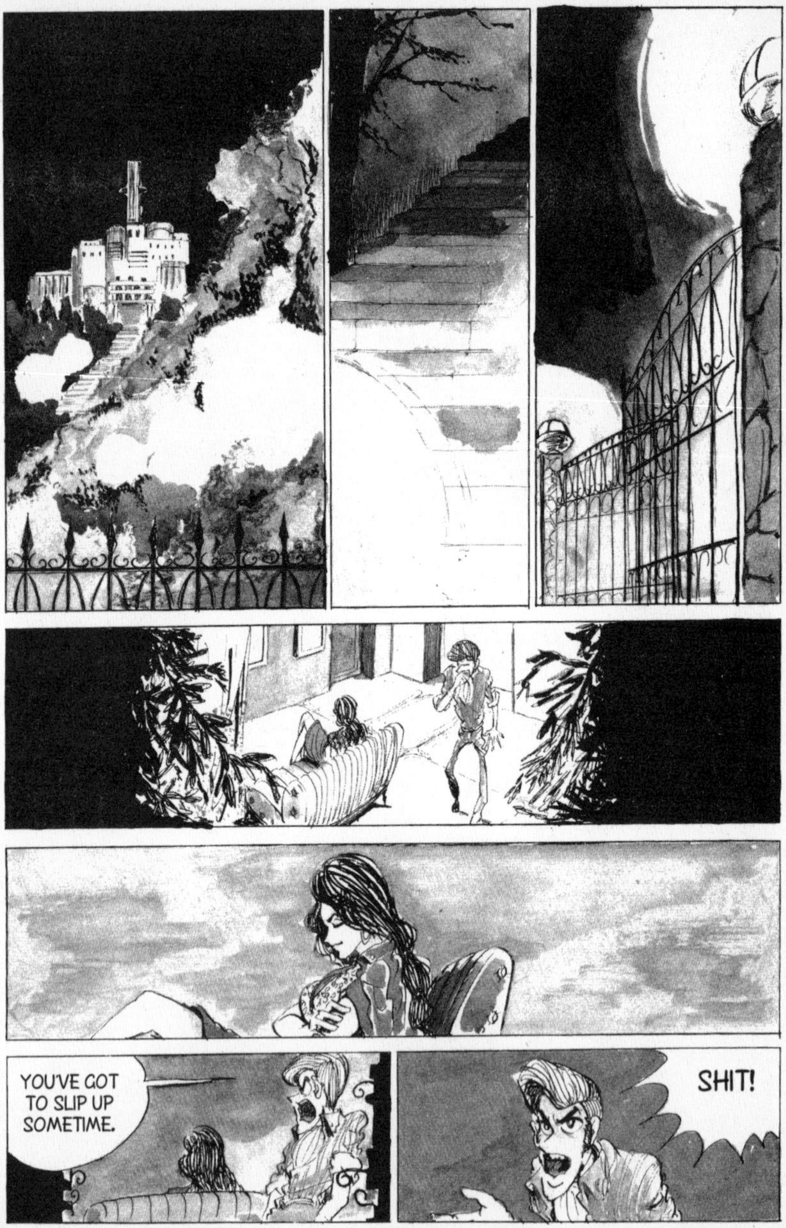
SHIT!
YOU'VE GOT TO SLIP UP SOMETIME.

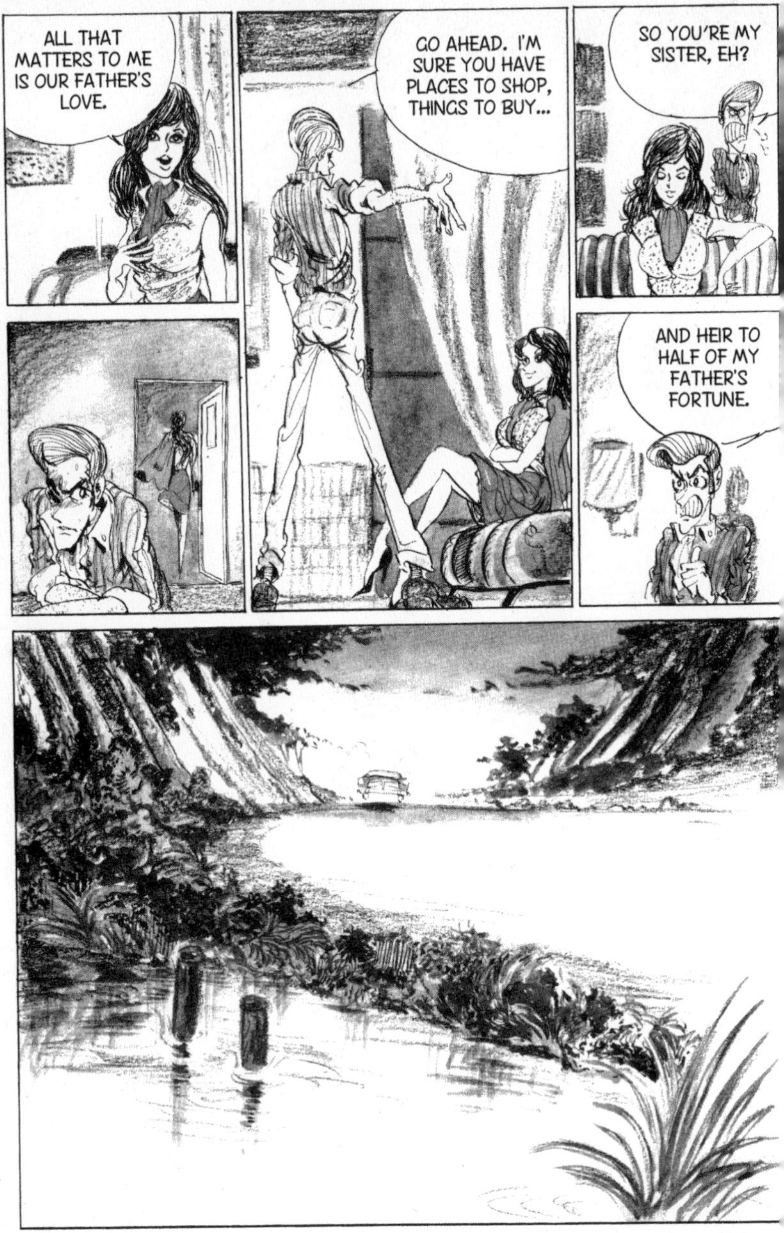
SO YOU'RE MY SISTER, EH?
AND HEIR TO HALF OF MY FATHER'S FORTUNE.
GO AHEAD. I'M SURE YOU HAVE PLACES TO SHOP, THINGS TO BUY...
ALL THAT MATTERS TO ME IS OUR FATHER'S LOVE.

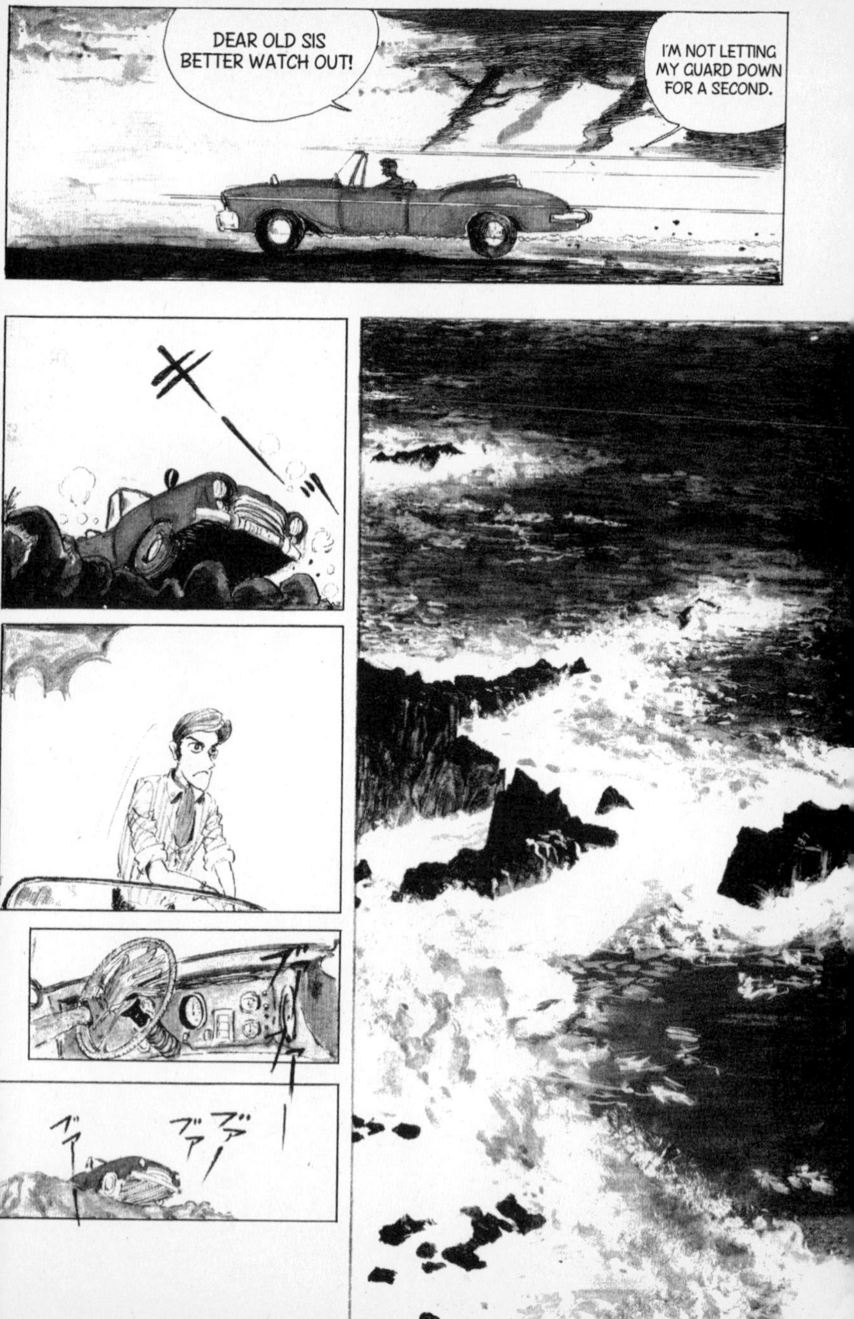
I'M NOT LETTING MY GUARD DOWN FOR A SECOND.
DEAR OLD SIS BETTER WATCH OUT!
ブァーー
ブァ
ブァ
ブァー

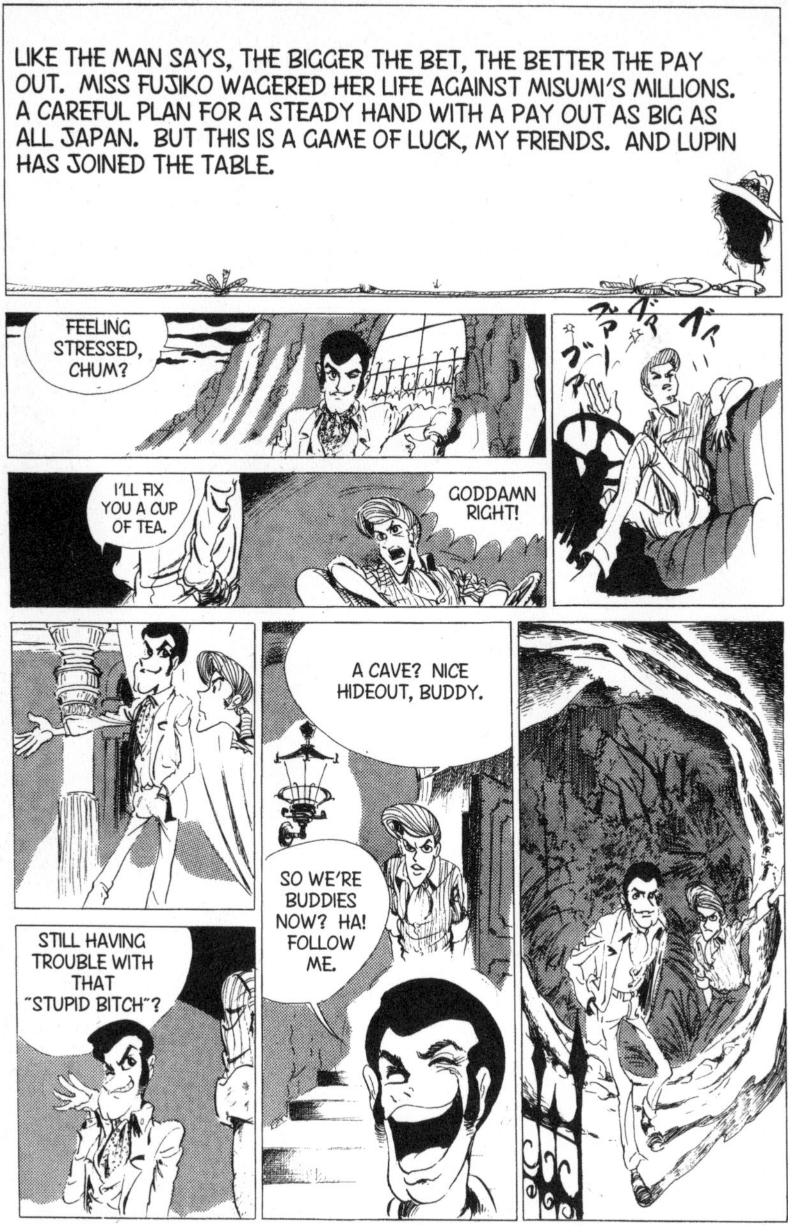
LIKE THE MAN SAYS, THE BIGGER THE BET, THE BETTER THE PAY OUT. MISS FUJIKO WAGERED HER LIFE AGAINST MISUMI'S MILLIONS. A CAREFUL PLAN FOR A STEADY HAND WITH A PAY OUT AS BIG AS ALL JAPAN. BUT THIS IS A GAME OF LUCK, MY FRIENDS. AND LUPIN HAS JOINED THE TABLE.
FEELING STRESSED, CHUM?
GODDAMN RIGHT!
I'LL FIX YOU A CUP OF TEA.
A CAVE? NICE HIDEOUT, BUDDY.
SO WE'RE BUDDIES NOW? HA! FOLLOW ME.
STILL HAVING TROUBLE WITH THAT "STUPID BITCH"?

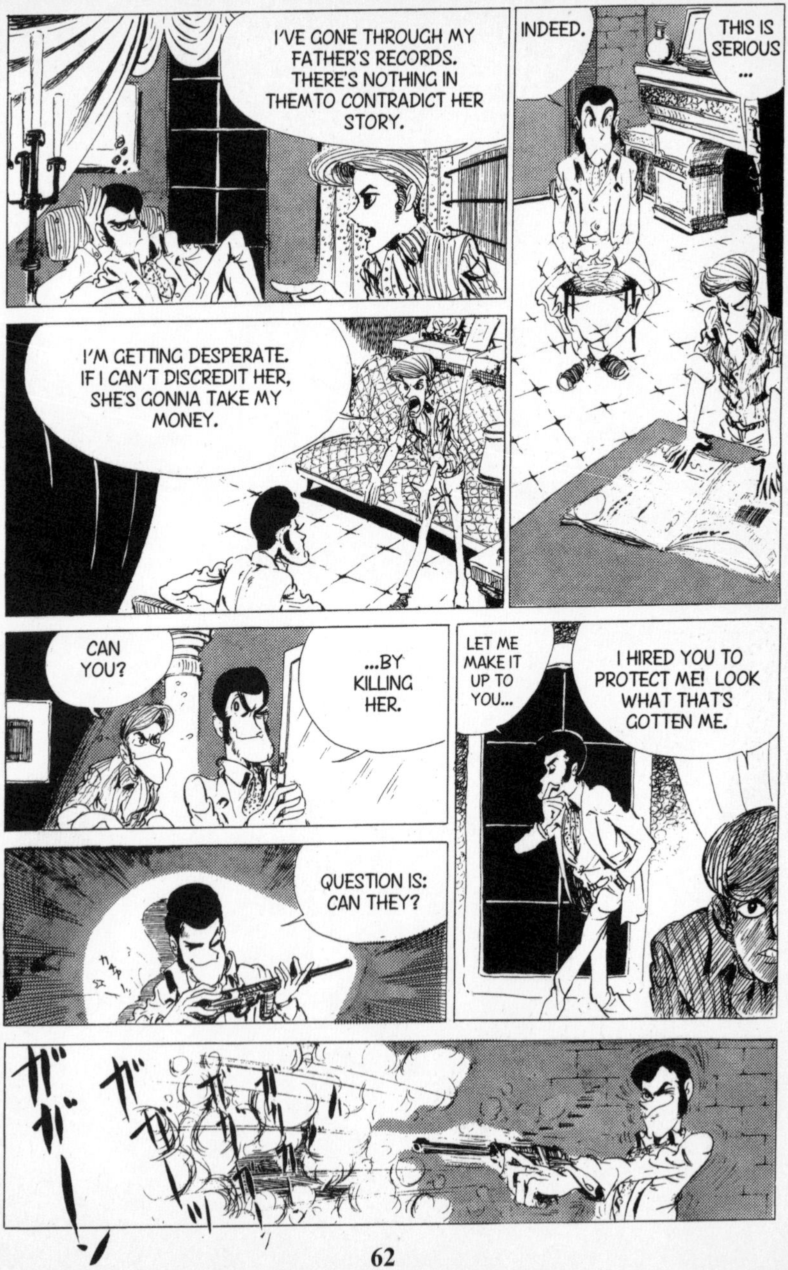
THIS IS SERIOUS ...
INDEED.
I'VE GONE THROUGH MY FATHER'S RECORDS. THERE'S NOTHING IN THEMTO CONTRADICT HER STORY.
I'M GETTING DESPERATE. IF I CAN'T DISCREDIT HER, SHE'S GONNA TAKE MY MONEY.
I HIRED YOU TO PROTECT ME! LOOK WHAT THAT'S GOTTEN ME.
LET ME MAKE IT UP TO YOU...
...BY KILLING HER.
CAN YOU?
QUESTION IS: CAN THEY?

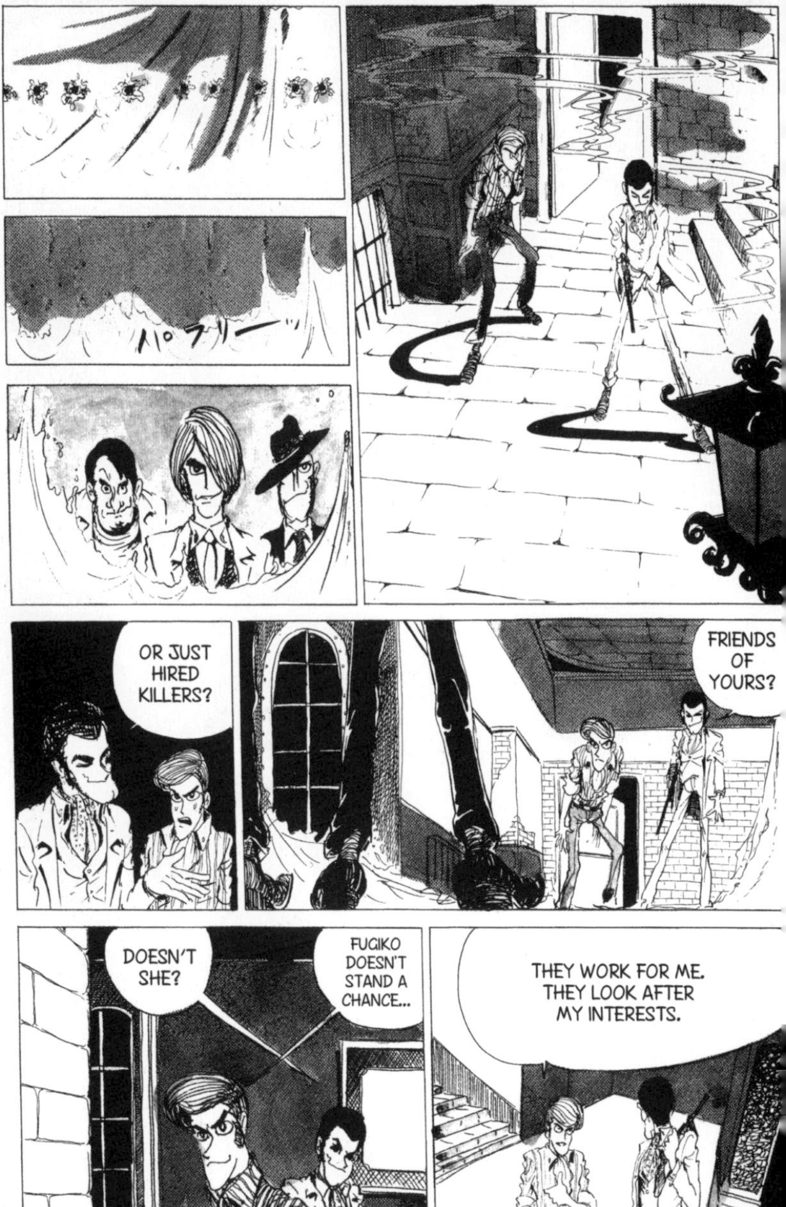
パフリーッ
FRIENDS OF YOURS?
OR JUST HIRED KILLERS?
THEY WORK FOR ME. THEY LOOK AFTER MY INTERESTS.
FUGIKO DOESN'T STAND A CHANCE...
DOESN'T SHE?

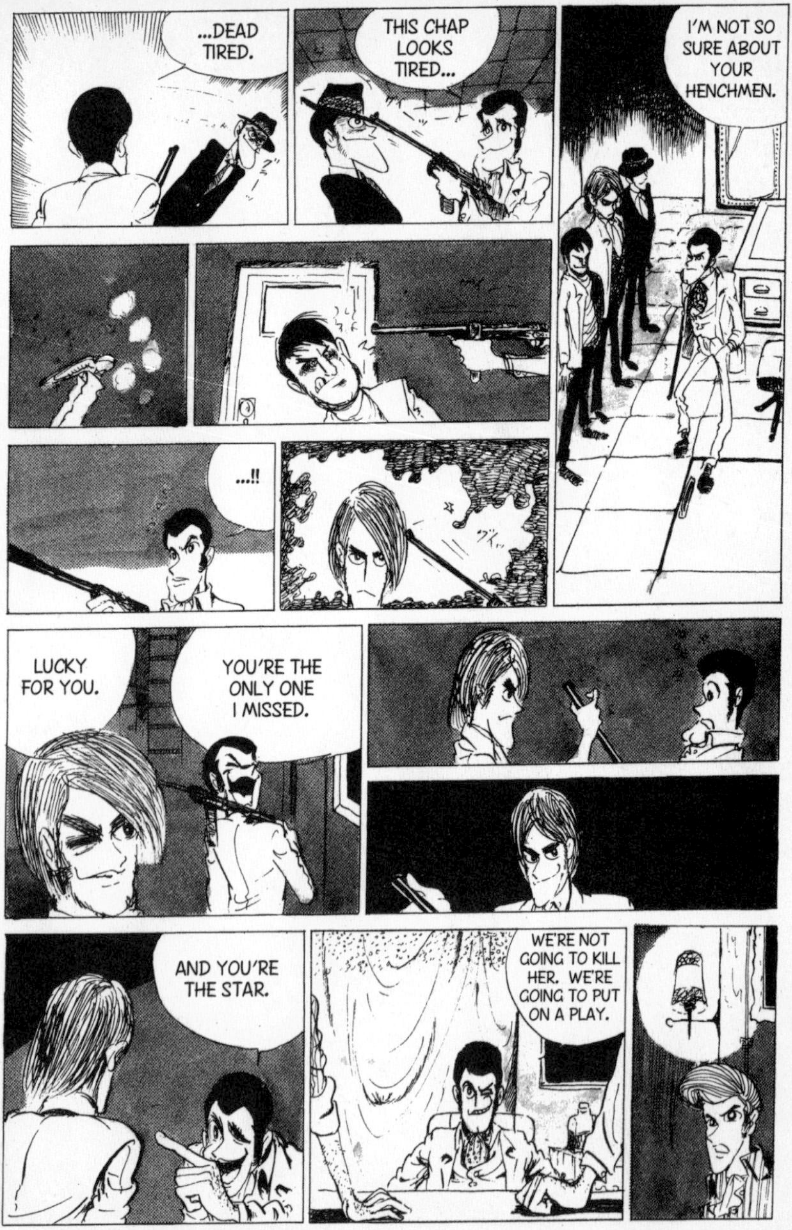
I'M NOT SO SURE ABOUT YOUR HENCHMEN.
THIS CHAP LOOKS TIRED...
...DEAD TIRED.
...!!
YOU'RE THE ONLY ONE I MISSED.
LUCKY FOR YOU.
WE'RE NOT GOING TO KILL HER. WE'RE GOING TO PUT ON A PLAY.
AND YOU'RE THE STAR.

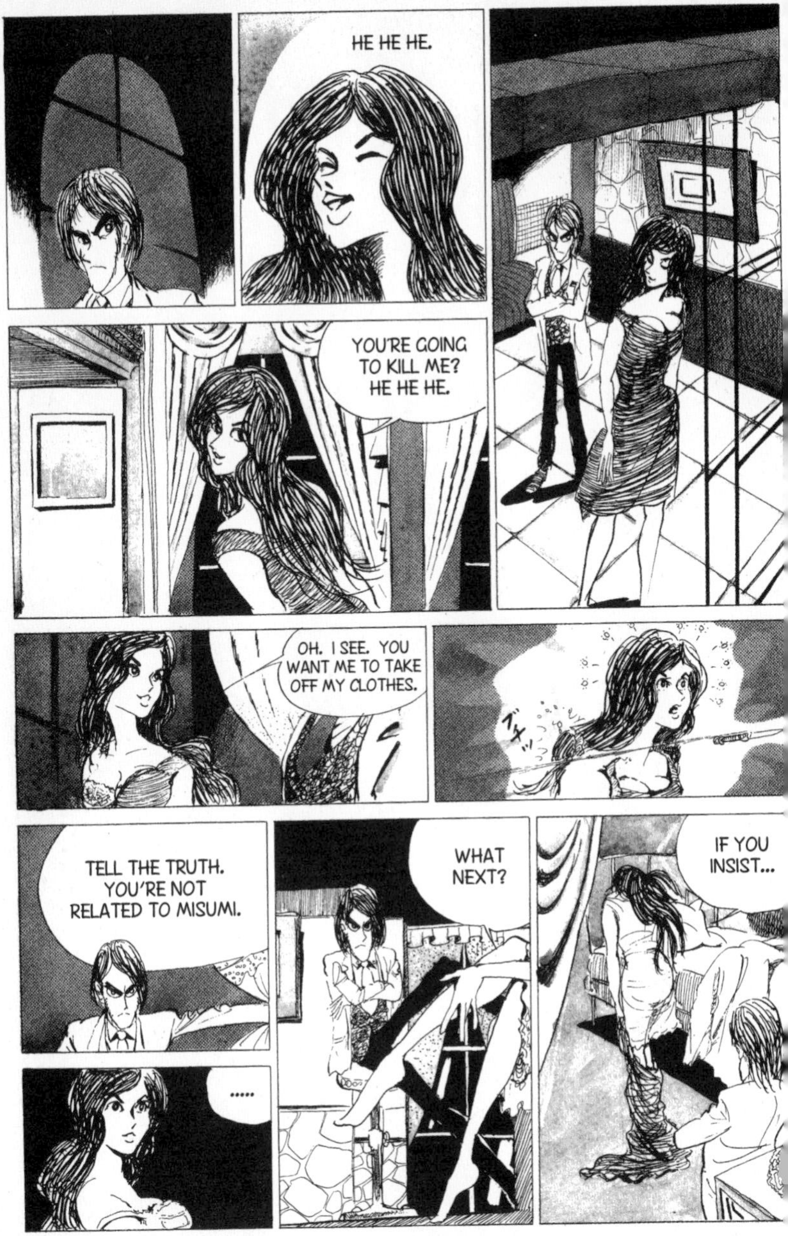
HE HE HE.
YOU'RE GOING TO KILL ME? HE HE HE.
OH. I SEE. YOU WANT ME TO TAKE OFF MY CLOTHES.
IF YOU INSIST...
WHAT NEXT?
TELL THE TRUTH. YOU'RE NOT RELATED TO MISUMI.
......

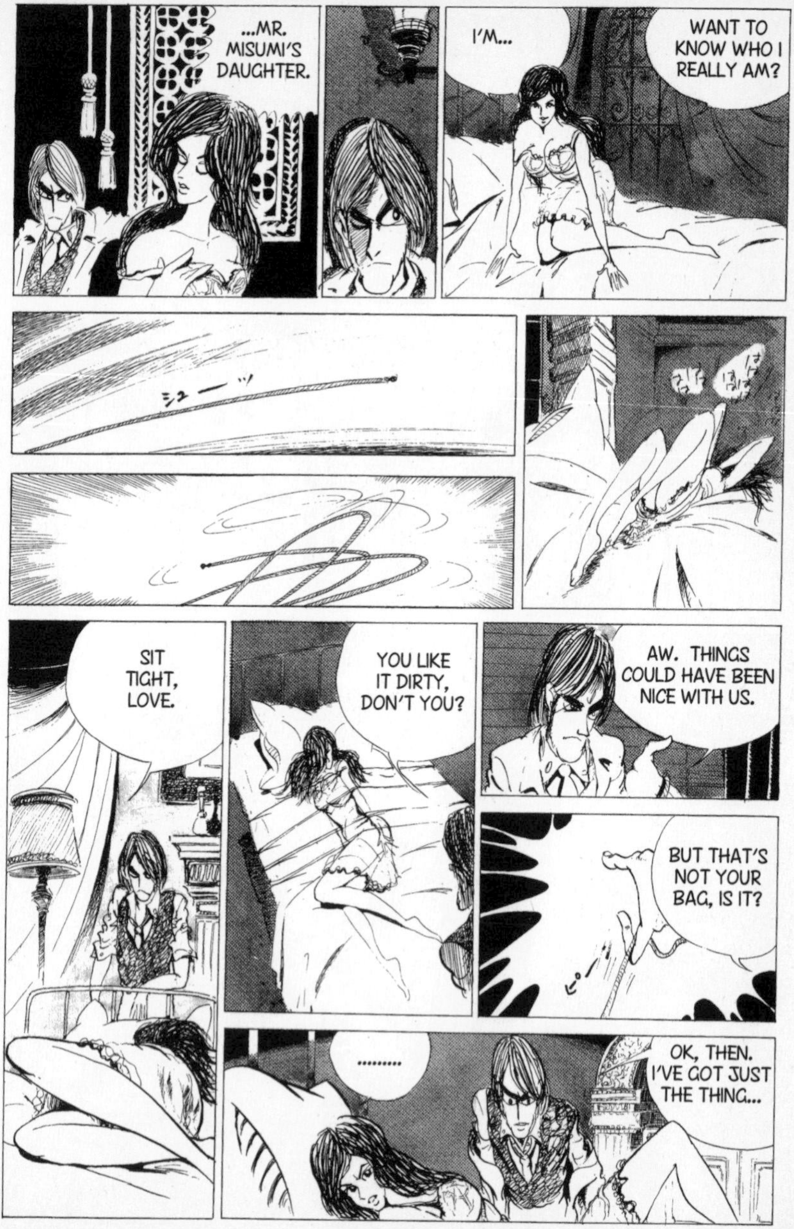
WANT TO KNOW WHO I REALLY AM?
I'M...
...MR. MISUMI'S DAUGHTER.
シューッ
AW. THINGS COULD HAVE BEEN NICE WITH US.
BUT THAT'S NOT YOUR BAG, IS IT?
YOU LIKE IT DIRTY, DON'T YOU?
OK, THEN. I'VE GOT JUST THE THING...
....
SIT TIGHT, LOVE.

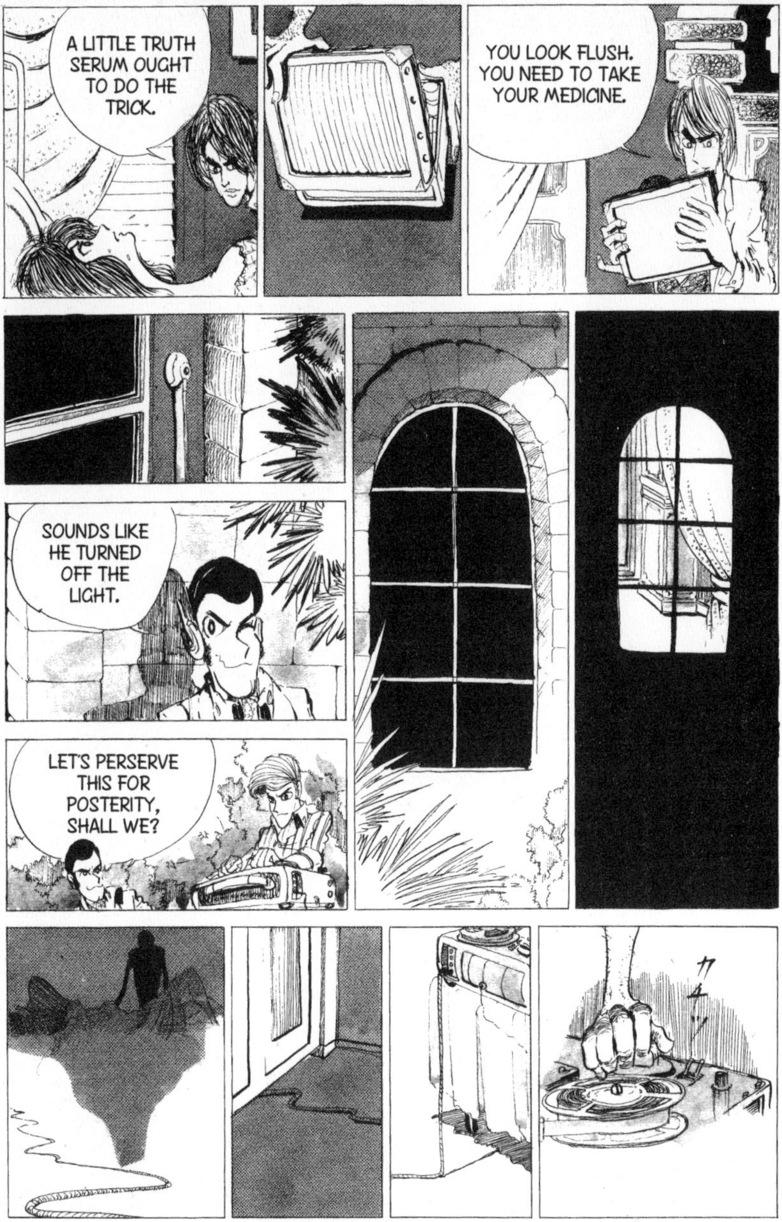
YOU LOOK FLUSH. YOU NEED TO TAKE YOUR MEDICINE.
A LITTLE TRUTH SERUM OUGHT TO DO THE TRICK.
SOUNDS LIKE HE TURNED OFF THE LIGHT.
LET'S PERSERVE THIS FOR POSTERITY, SHALL WE?

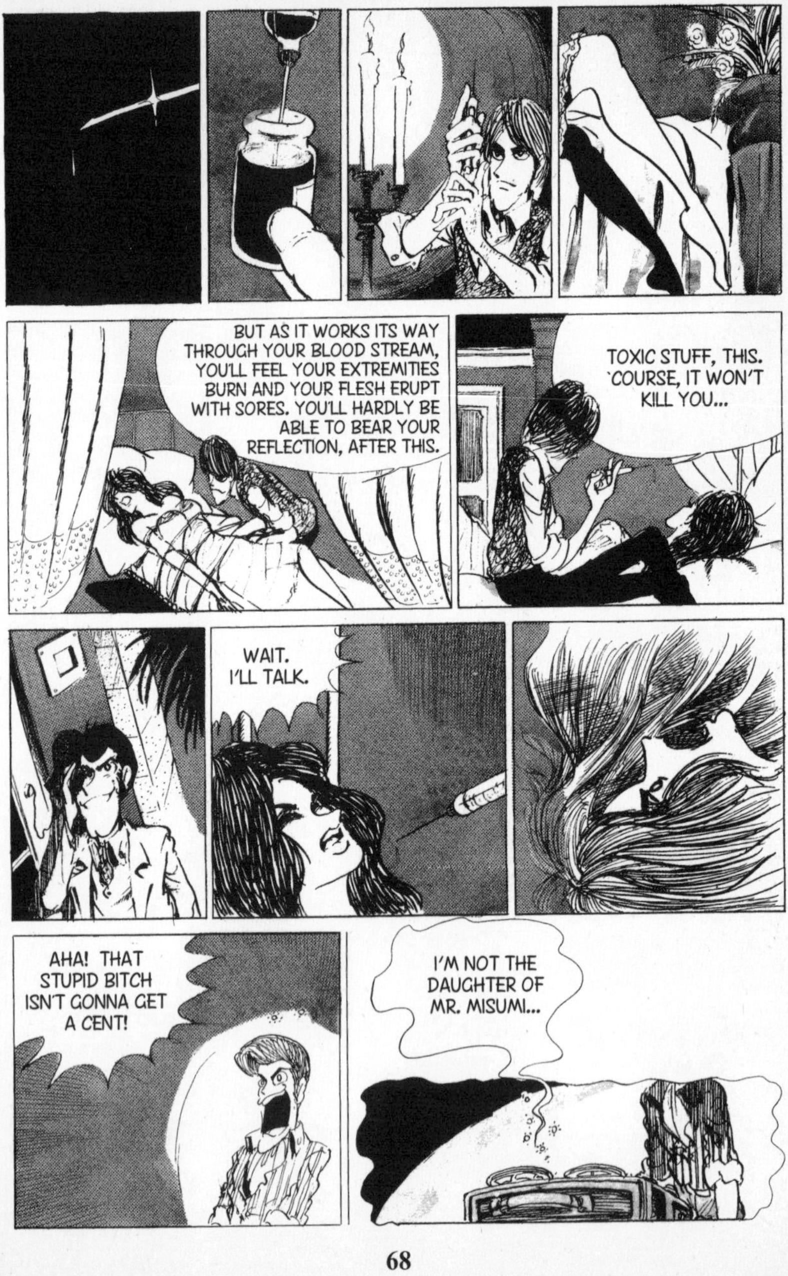
TOXIC STUFF, THIS. `COURSE, IT WON'T KILL YOU...
BUT AS IT WORKS ITS WAY THROUGH YOUR BLOOD STREAM, YOU'LL FEEL YOUR EXTREMITIES BURN AND YOUR FLESH ERUPT WITH SORES. YOU'LL HARDLY BE ABLE TO BEAR YOUR REFLECTION, AFTER THIS.
WAIT. I'LL TALK.
I'M NOT THE DAUGHTER OF MR. MISUMI...
AHA! THAT STUPID BITCH ISN'T GONNA GET A CENT!

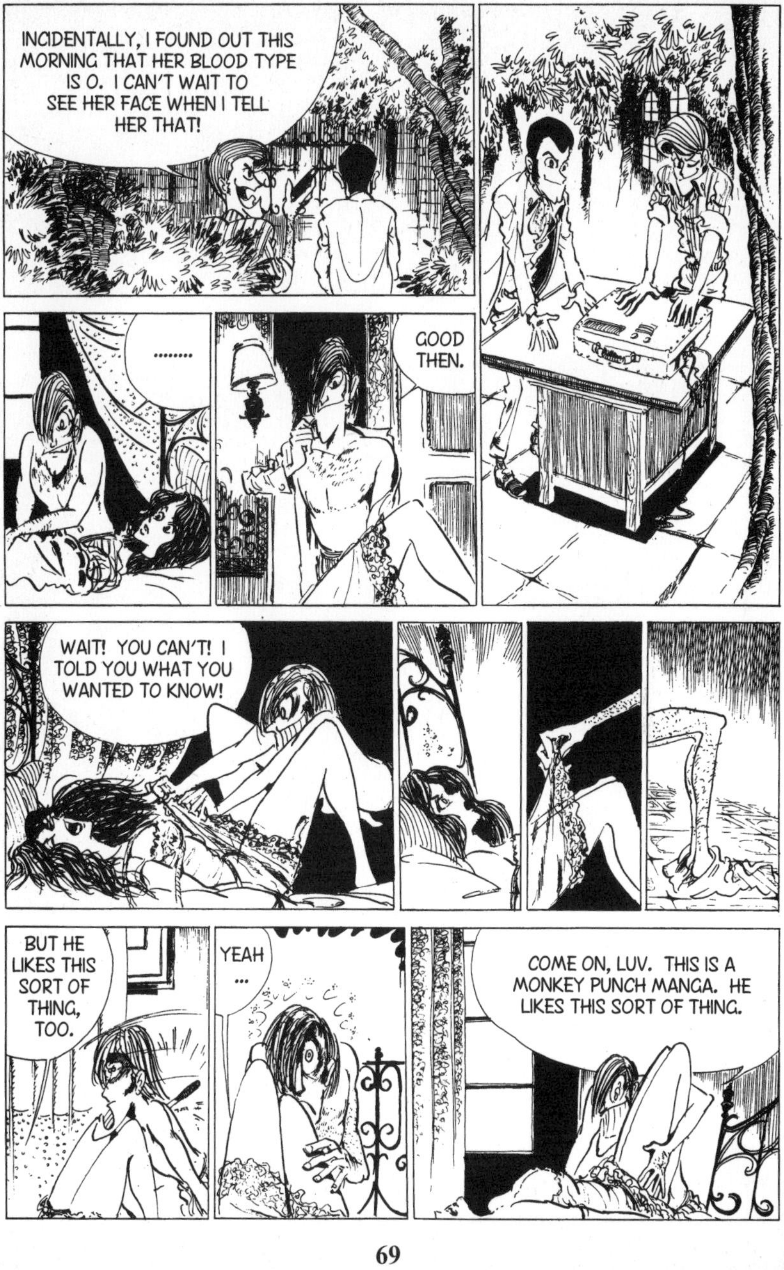
INCIDENTALLY, I FOUND OUT THIS MORNING THAT HER BLOOD TYPE IS O. I CAN'T WAIT TO SEE HER FACE WHEN I TELL HER THAT!
GOOD THEN.
....
WAIT! YOU CAN'T! I TOLD YOU WHAT YOU WANTED TO KNOW!
COME ON, LUV. THIS IS A MONKEY PUNCH MANGA. HE LIKES THIS SORT OF THING.
YEAH ...
BUT HE LIKES THIS SORT OF THING, TOO.

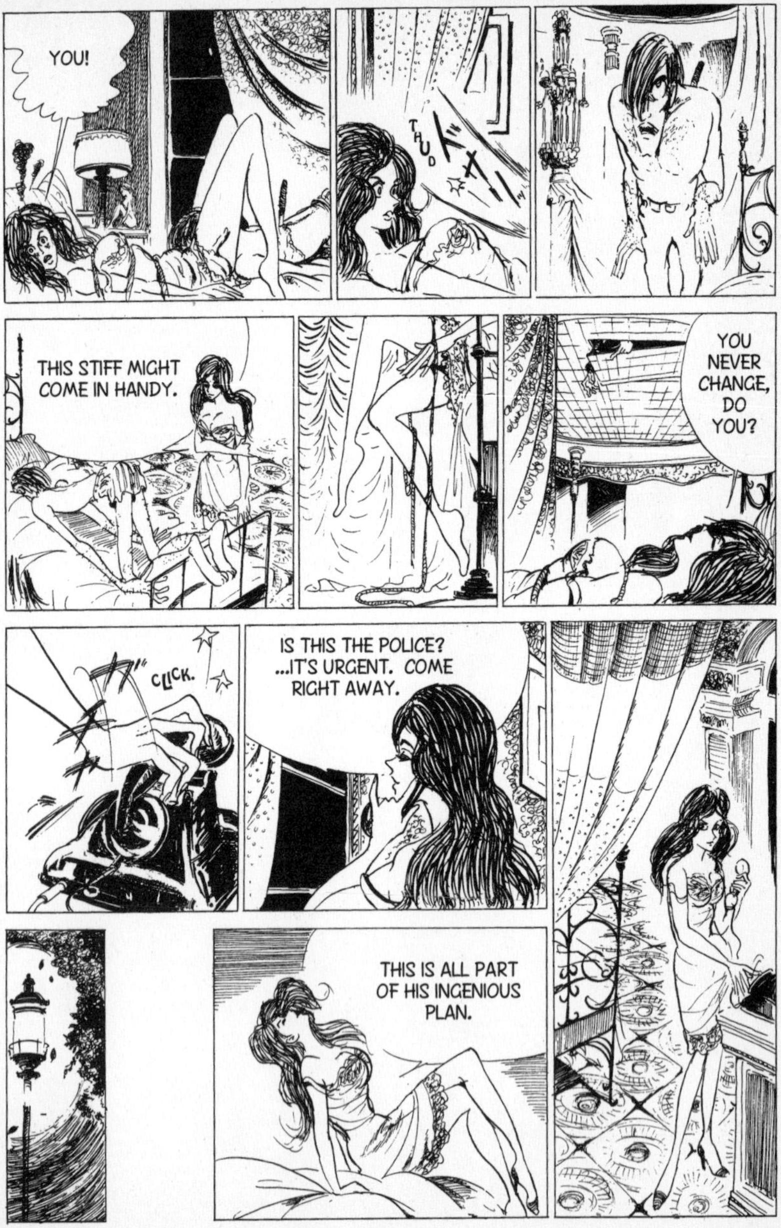
THUD
YOU!
YOU NEVER CHANGE, DO YOU?
THIS STIFF MIGHT COME IN HANDY.
IS THIS THE POLICE? ...IT'S URGENT. COME RIGHT AWAY.
CLICK.
THIS IS ALL PART OF HIS INGENIOUS PLAN.

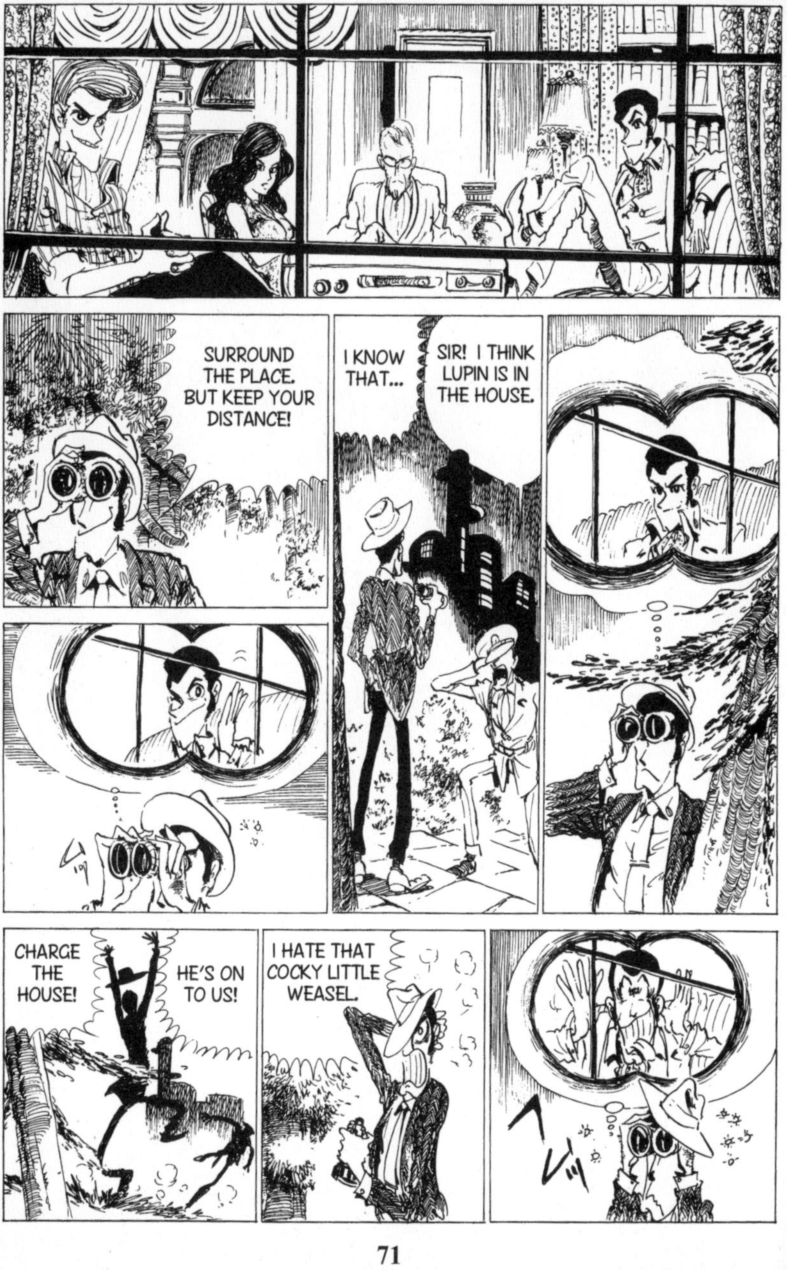
SIR! I THINK LUPIN IS IN THE HOUSE.
I KNOW THAT...
SURROUND THE PLACE. BUT KEEP YOUR DISTANCE!
I HATE THAT COCKY LITTLE WEASEL.
HE'S ON TO US!
CHARGE THE HOUSE!

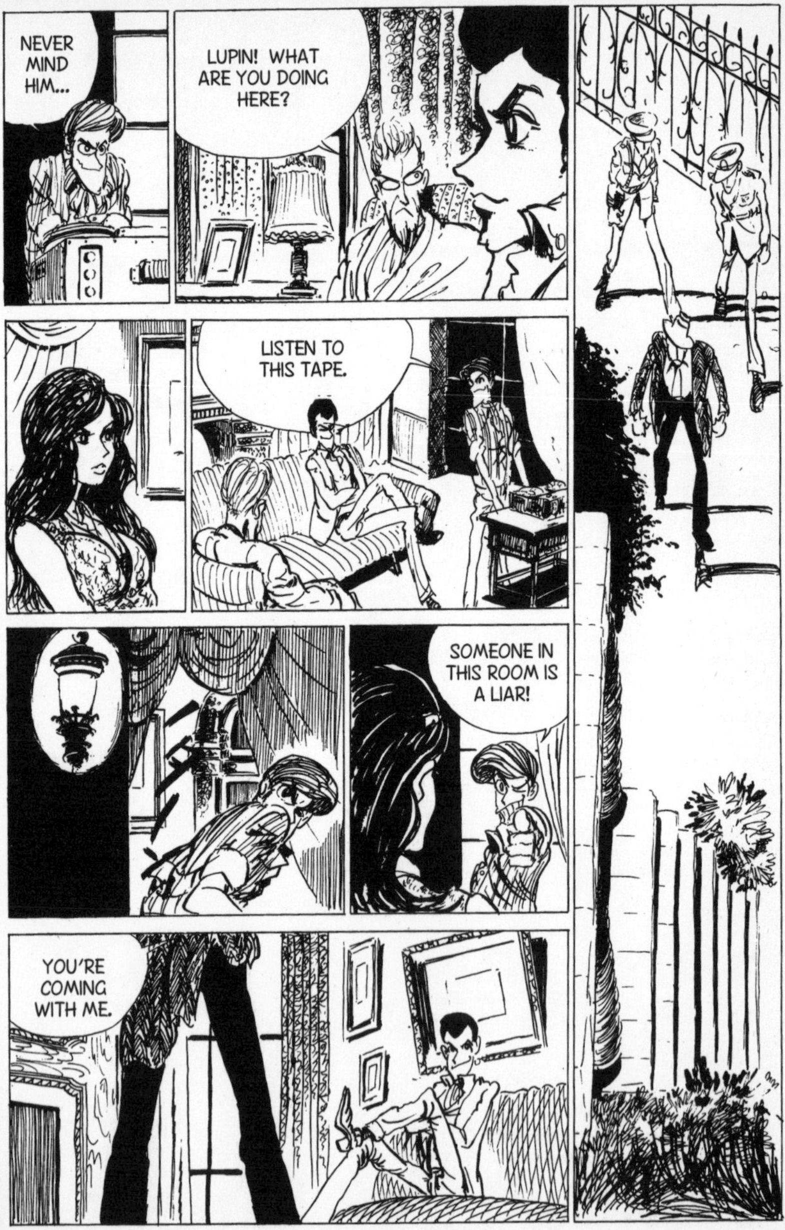
LUPIN! WHAT ARE YOU DOING HERE?
NEVER MIND HIM...
LISTEN TO THIS TAPE.
SOMEONE IN THIS ROOM IS A LIAR!
YOU'RE COMING WITH ME.

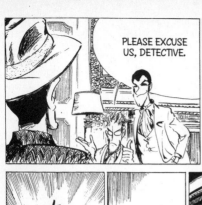

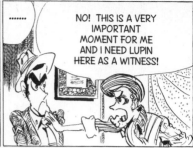

NO! THIS IS A VERY IMPORTANT MOMENT FOR ME AND I NEED LUPIN HERE AS A WITNESS!
....
PLEASE EXCUSE US, DETECTIVE.
LISTEN UP, SIS. YOU'LL FIND THIS VERY INTERESTING.
カチッ
~~~~
~~~~~~
I CAN'T HEAR. TURN IT UP.
I'M HERE TO...
私は
I'M GOING TO MAKE A CONFESSION.

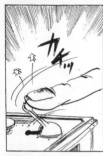

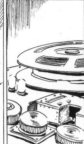

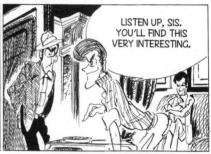

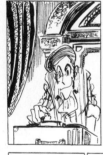

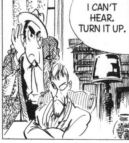

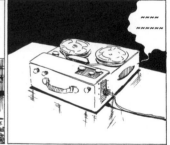

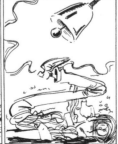

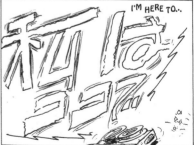

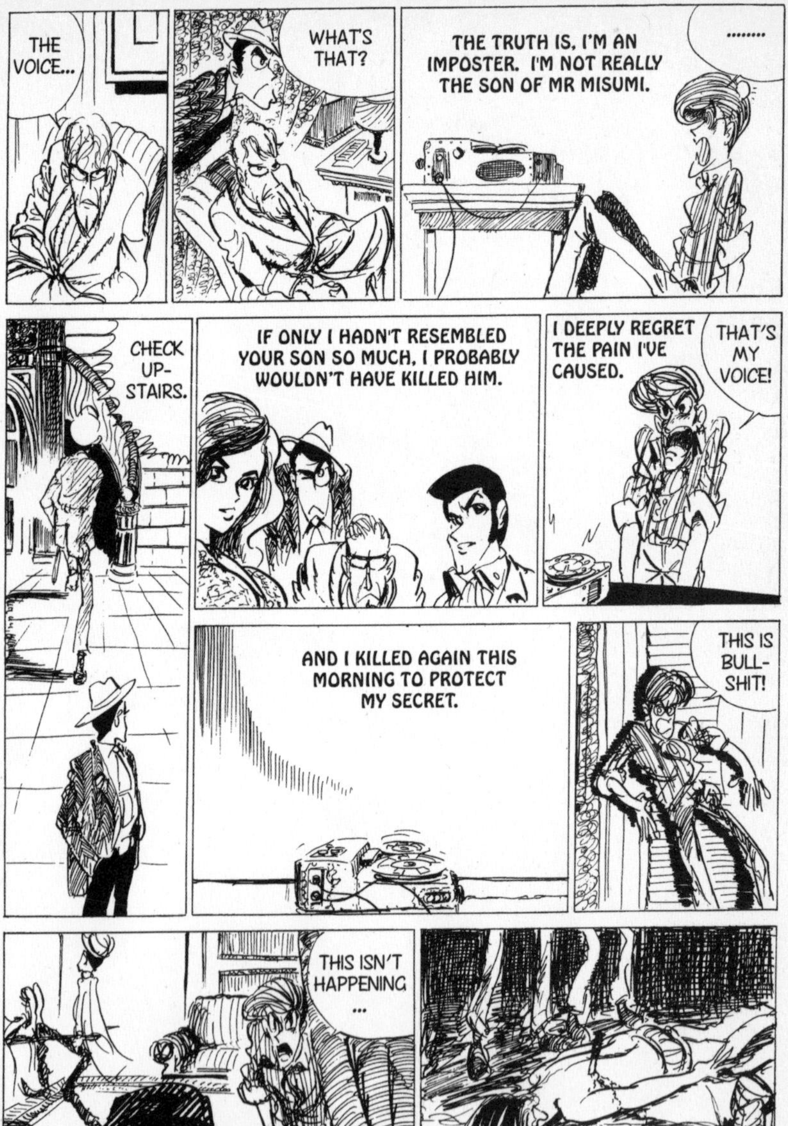
....
THE TRUTH IS, I'M AN IMPOSTER. I'M NOT REALLY THE SON OF MR MISUMI.
WHAT'S THAT?
THE VOICE...
THAT'S MY VOICE!
I DEEPLY REGRET THE PAIN I'VE CAUSED.
IF ONLY I HADN'T RESEMBLED YOUR SON SO MUCH, I PROBABLY WOULDN'T HAVE KILLED HIM.
THIS IS BULL-SHIT!
AND I KILLED AGAIN THIS MORNING TO PROTECT MY SECRET.
CHECK UP-STAIRS.
THIS ISN'T HAPPENING ...

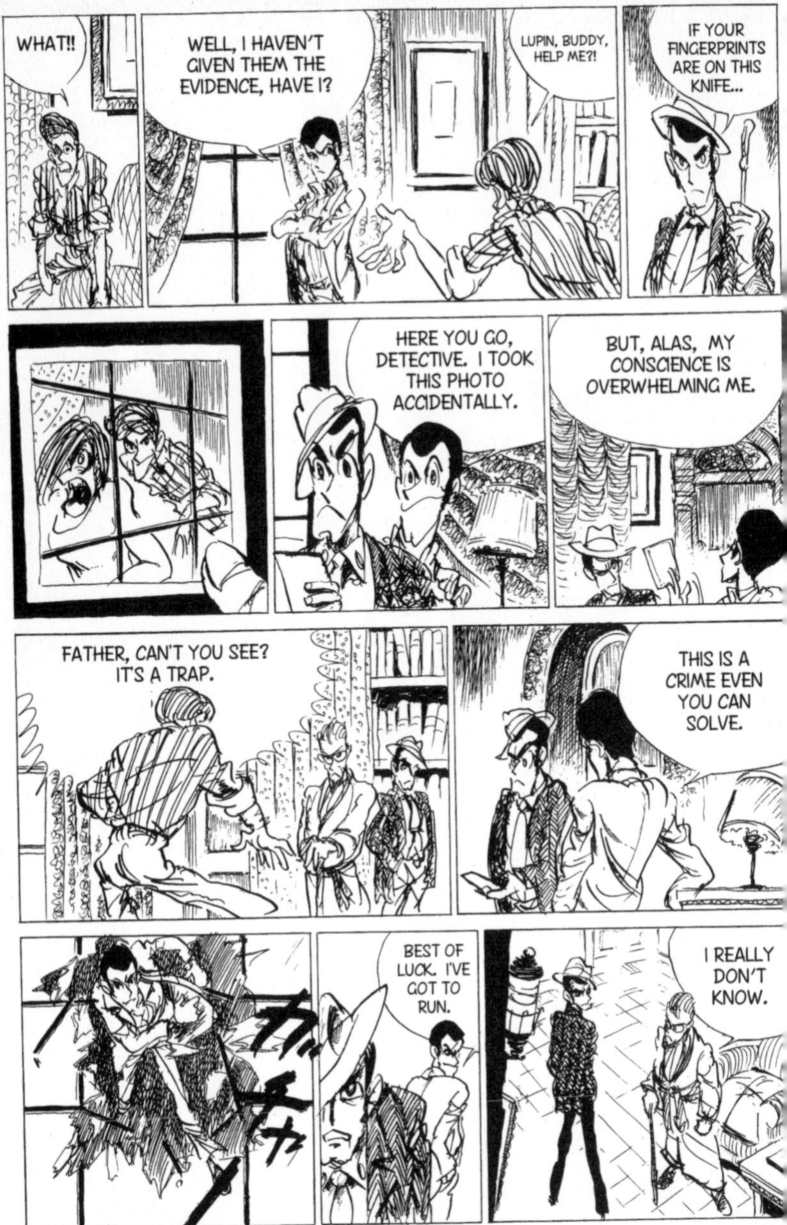
IF YOUR FINGERPRINTS ARE ON THIS KNIFE...
LUPIN, BUDDY, HELP ME?!
WELL, I HAVEN'T GIVEN THEM THE EVIDENCE, HAVE I?
WHAT!!
BUT, ALAS, MY CONSCIENCE IS OVERWHELMING ME.
HERE YOU GO, DETECTIVE. I TOOK THIS PHOTO ACCIDENTALLY.
THIS IS A CRIME EVEN YOU CAN SOLVE.
FATHER, CAN'T YOU SEE? IT'S A TRAP.
I REALLY DON'T KNOW.
BEST OF LUCK. I'VE GOT TO RUN.

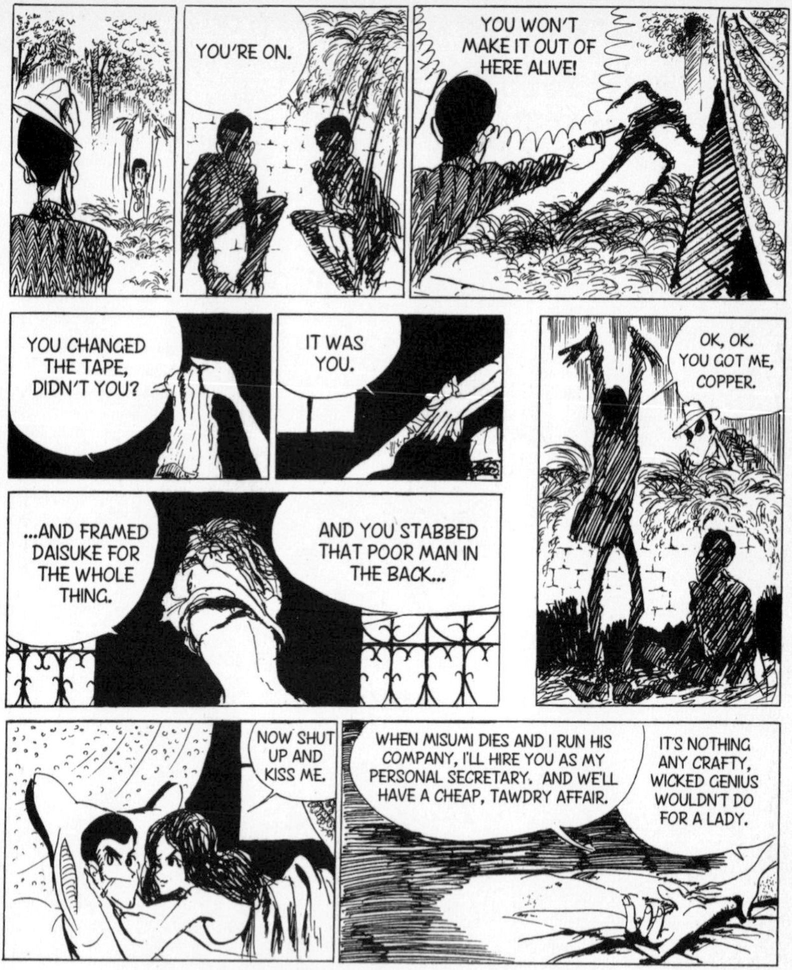
YOU WON'T MAKE IT OUT OF HERE ALIVE!
YOU'RE ON.
OK, OK. YOU GOT ME, COPPER.
IT WAS YOU.
YOU CHANGED THE TAPE, DIDN'T YOU?
AND YOU STABBED THAT POOR MAN IN THE BACK...
...AND FRAMED DAISUKE FOR THE WHOLE THING.
IT'S NOTHING ANY CRAFTY, WICKED GENIUS WOULDN'T DO FOR A LADY.
WHEN MISUMI DIES AND I RUN HIS COMPANY, I'LL HIRE YOU AS MY PERSONAL SECRETARY. AND WE'LL HAVE A CHEAP, TAWDRY AFFAIR.
NOW SHUT UP AND KISS ME.

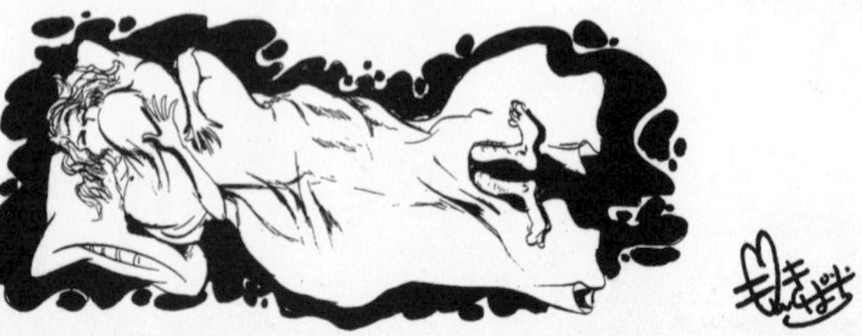

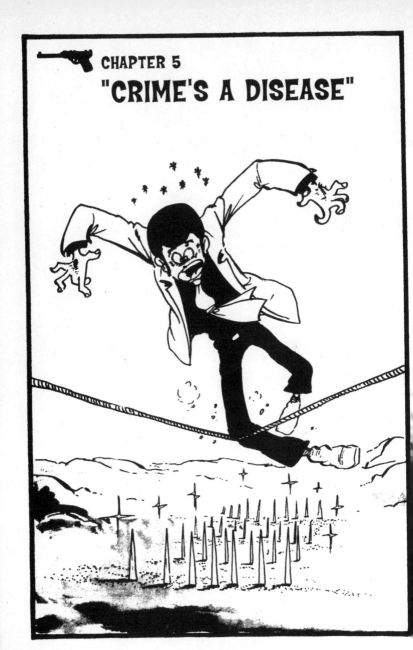

CHAPTER 5

"CRIME'S A DISEASE"

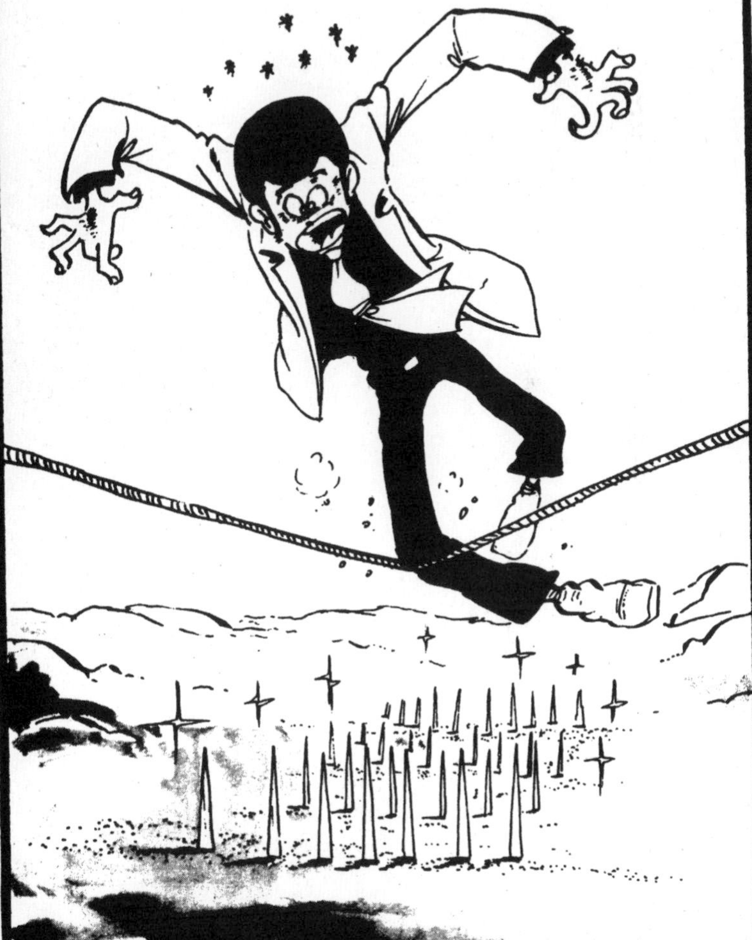

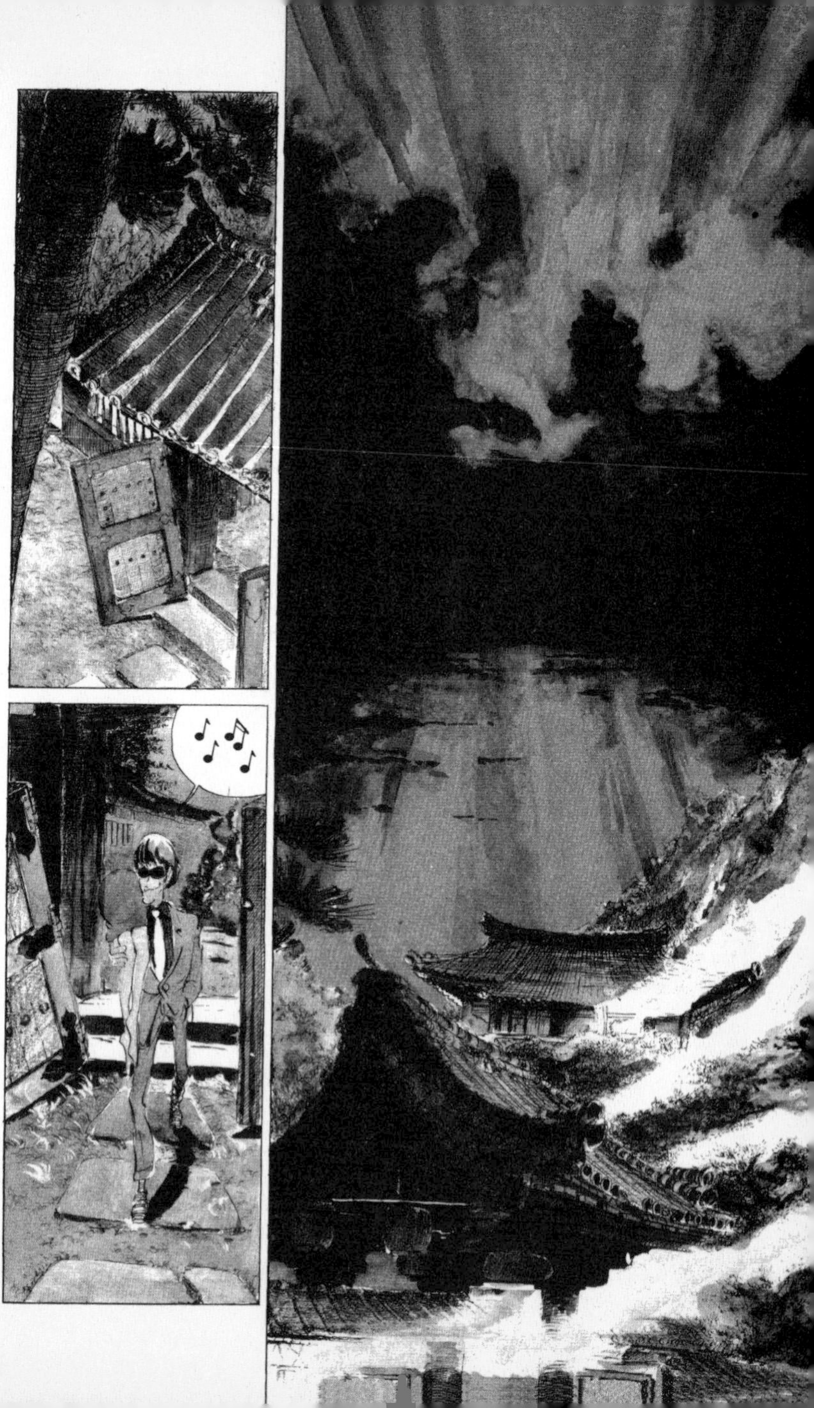

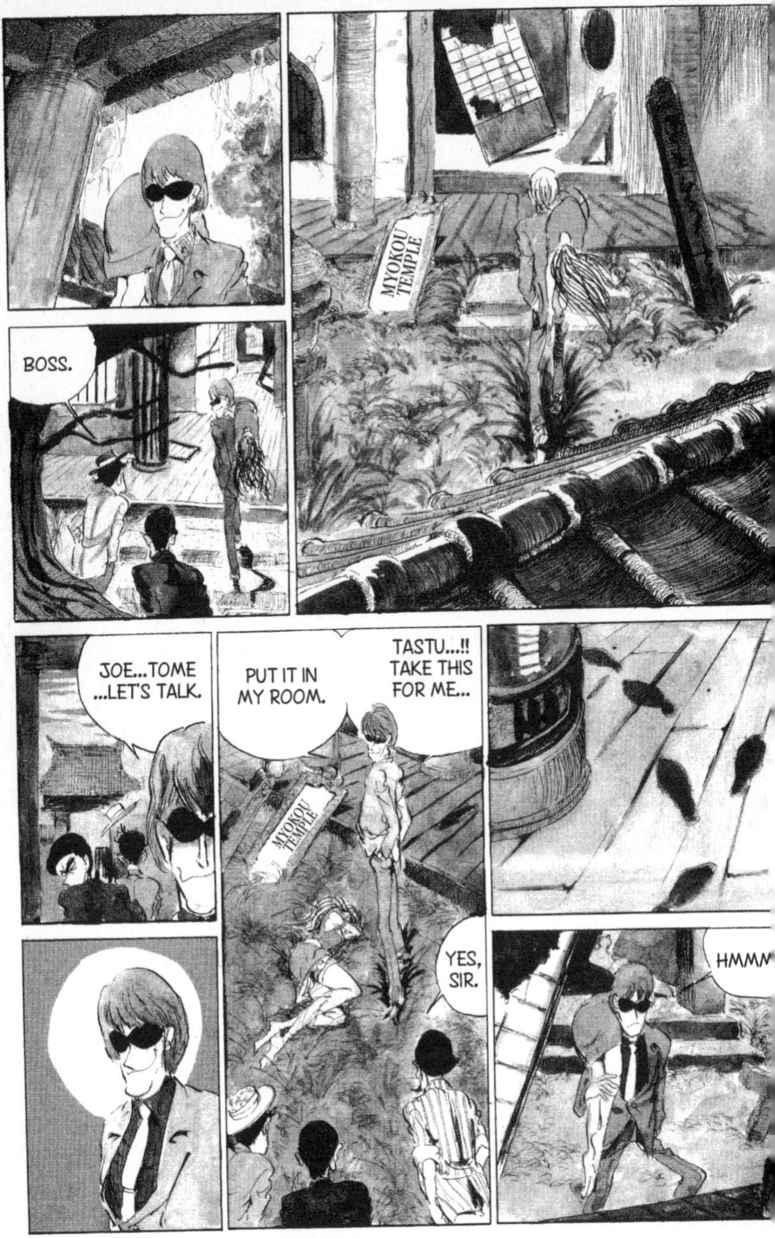
MYOKOU TEMPLE
BOSS.
HMMM
TASTU...!! TAKE THIS FOR ME...
PUT IT IN MY ROOM.
MYOKOU TEMPLE
YES, SIR.
JOE...TOME ...LET'S TALK.

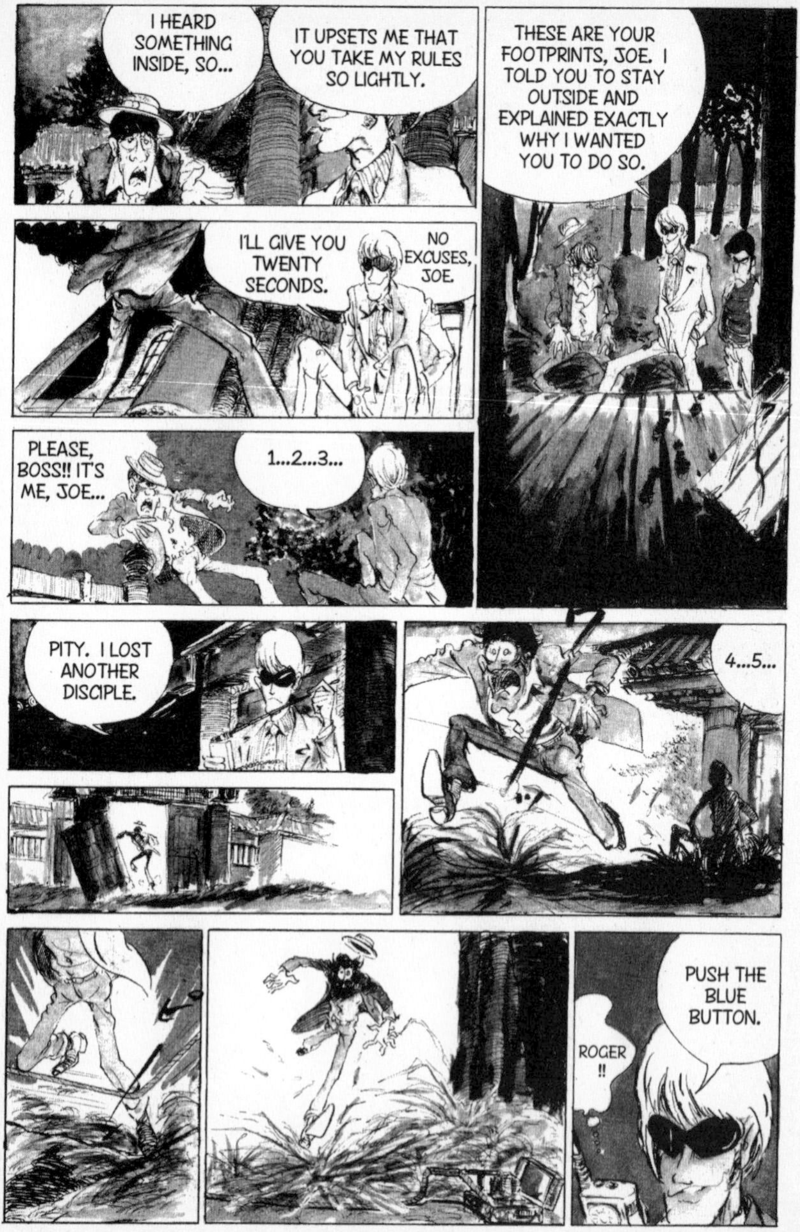
THESE ARE YOUR FOOTPRINTS, JOE. I TOLD YOU TO STAY OUTSIDE AND EXPLAINED EXACTLY WHY I WANTED YOU TO DO SO.
IT UPSETS ME THAT YOU TAKE MY RULES SO LIGHTLY.
I HEARD SOMETHING INSIDE, SO...
NO EXCUSES, JOE.
I'LL GIVE YOU TWENTY SECONDS.
1...2...3...
PLEASE, BOSS!! IT'S ME, JOE...
4...5...
PITY. I LOST ANOTHER DISCIPLE.
PUSH THE BLUE BUTTON.
ROGER !!

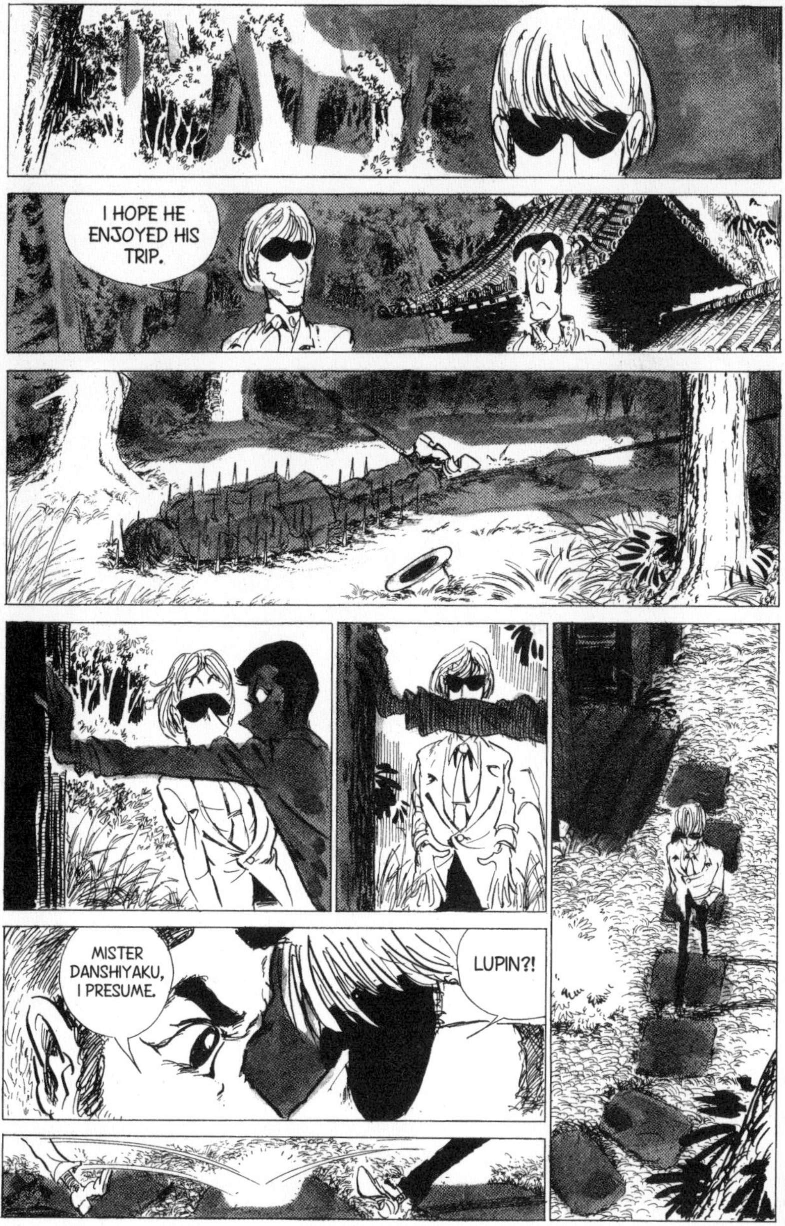
I HOPE HE ENJOYED HIS TRIP.
LUPIN?!
MISTER DANSHIYAKU, I PRESUME.

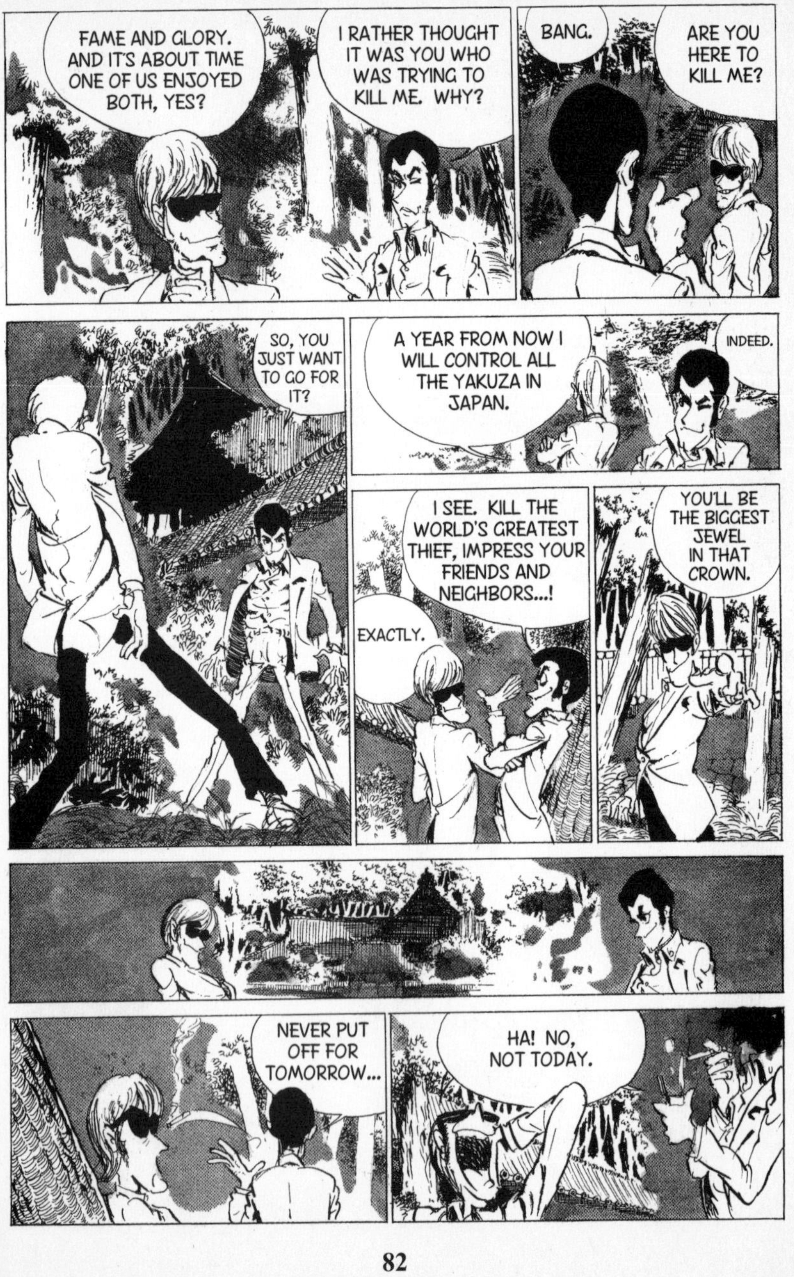
ARE YOU HERE TO KILL ME?
BANG.
I RATHER THOUGHT IT WAS YOU WHO WAS TRYING TO KILL ME. WHY?
FAME AND GLORY. AND IT'S ABOUT TIME ONE OF US ENJOYED BOTH, YES?
INDEED.
A YEAR FROM NOW I WILL CONTROL ALL THE YAKUZA IN JAPAN.
YOU'LL BE THE BIGGEST JEWEL IN THAT CROWN.
I SEE. KILL THE WORLD'S GREATEST THIEF, IMPRESS YOUR FRIENDS AND NEIGHBORS...!
EXACTLY.
SO, YOU JUST WANT TO GO FOR IT?
HA! NO, NOT TODAY.
NEVER PUT OFF FOR TOMORROW...

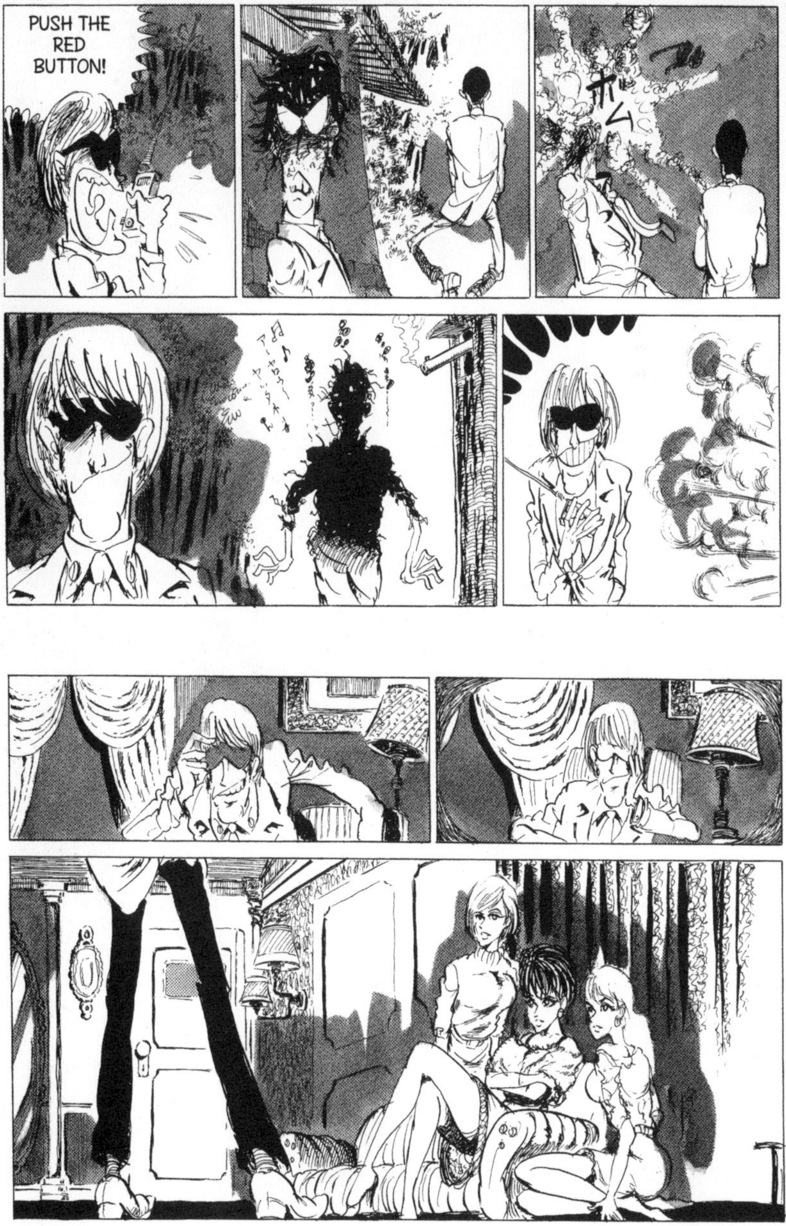
ボム
PUSH THE RED BUTTON!

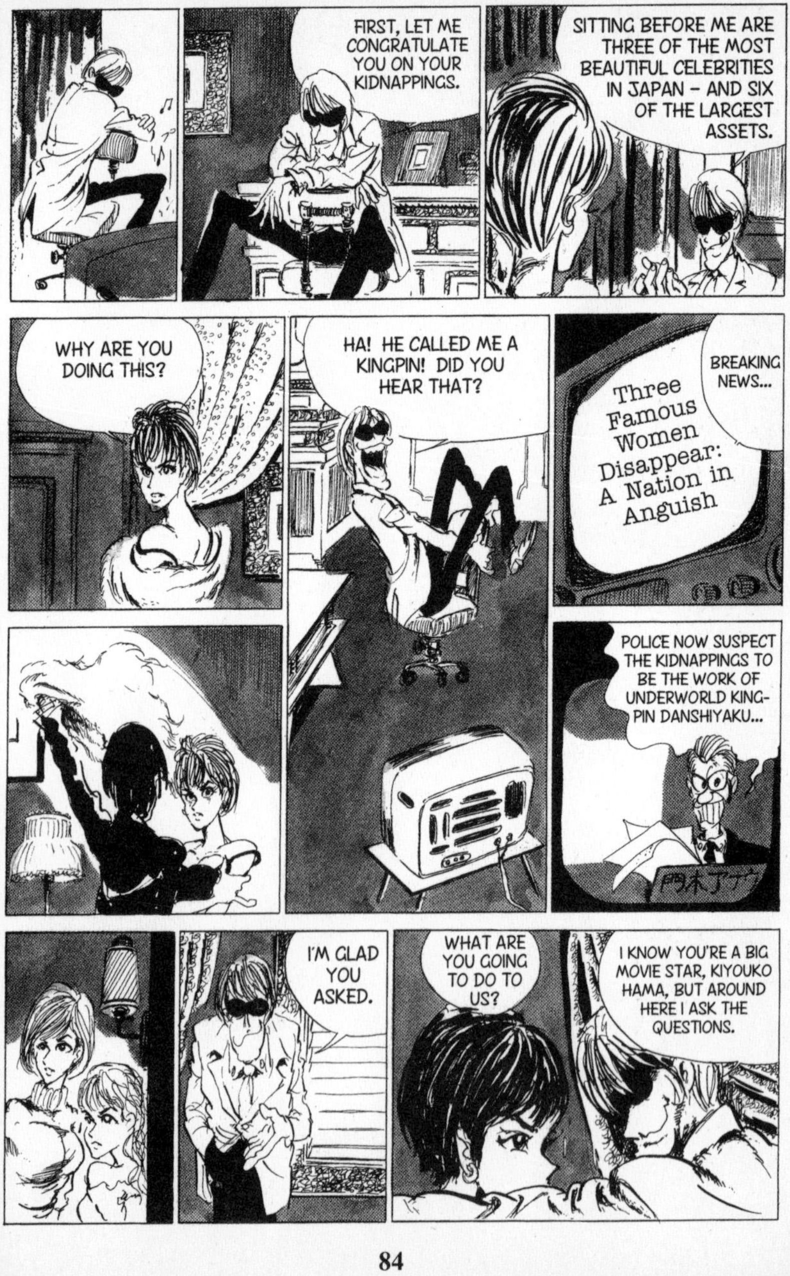
SITTING BEFORE ME ARE THREE OF THE MOST BEAUTIFUL CELEBRITIES IN JAPAN – AND SIX OF THE LARGEST ASSETS.
FIRST, LET ME CONGRATULATE YOU ON YOUR KIDNAPPINGS.
BREAKING NEWS...
Three Famous Women Disappear: A Nation in Anguish
POLICE NOW SUSPECT THE KIDNAPPINGS TO BE THE WORK OF UNDERWORLD KING-PIN DANSHIYAKU...
HA! HE CALLED ME A KINGPIN! DID YOU HEAR THAT?
WHY ARE YOU DOING THIS?
I KNOW YOU'RE A BIG MOVIE STAR, KIYOUKO HAMA, BUT AROUND HERE I ASK THE QUESTIONS.
WHAT ARE YOU GOING TO DO TO US?
I'M GLAD YOU ASKED.

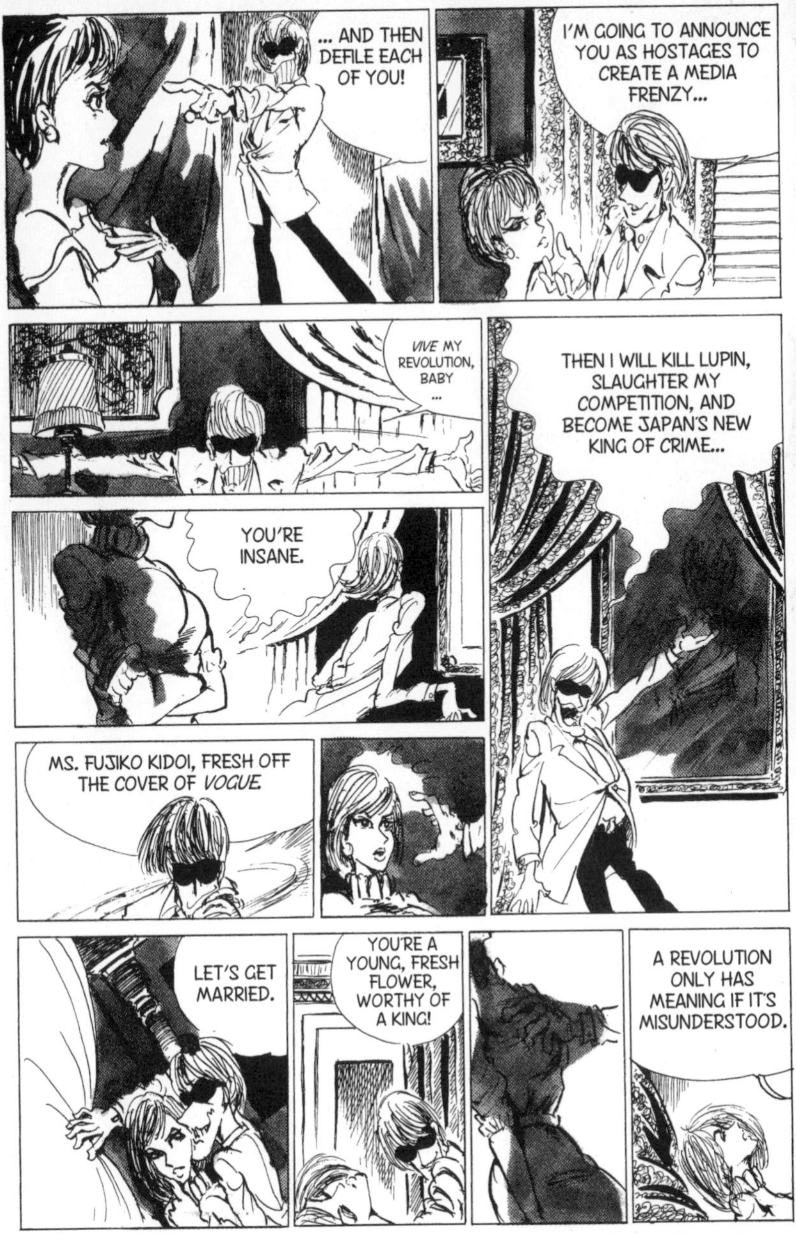
I'M GOING TO ANNOUNCE YOU AS HOSTAGES TO CREATE A MEDIA FRENZY...
... AND THEN DEFILE EACH OF YOU!
THEN I WILL KILL LUPIN, SLAUGHTER MY COMPETITION, AND BECOME JAPAN'S NEW KING OF CRIME...
VIVE MY REVOLUTION, BABY ...
YOU'RE INSANE.
MS. FUJIKO KIDOI, FRESH OFF THE COVER OF *VOGUE*.
A REVOLUTION ONLY HAS MEANING IF IT'S MISUNDERSTOOD.
YOU'RE A YOUNG, FRESH FLOWER, WORTHY OF A KING!
LET'S GET MARRIED.

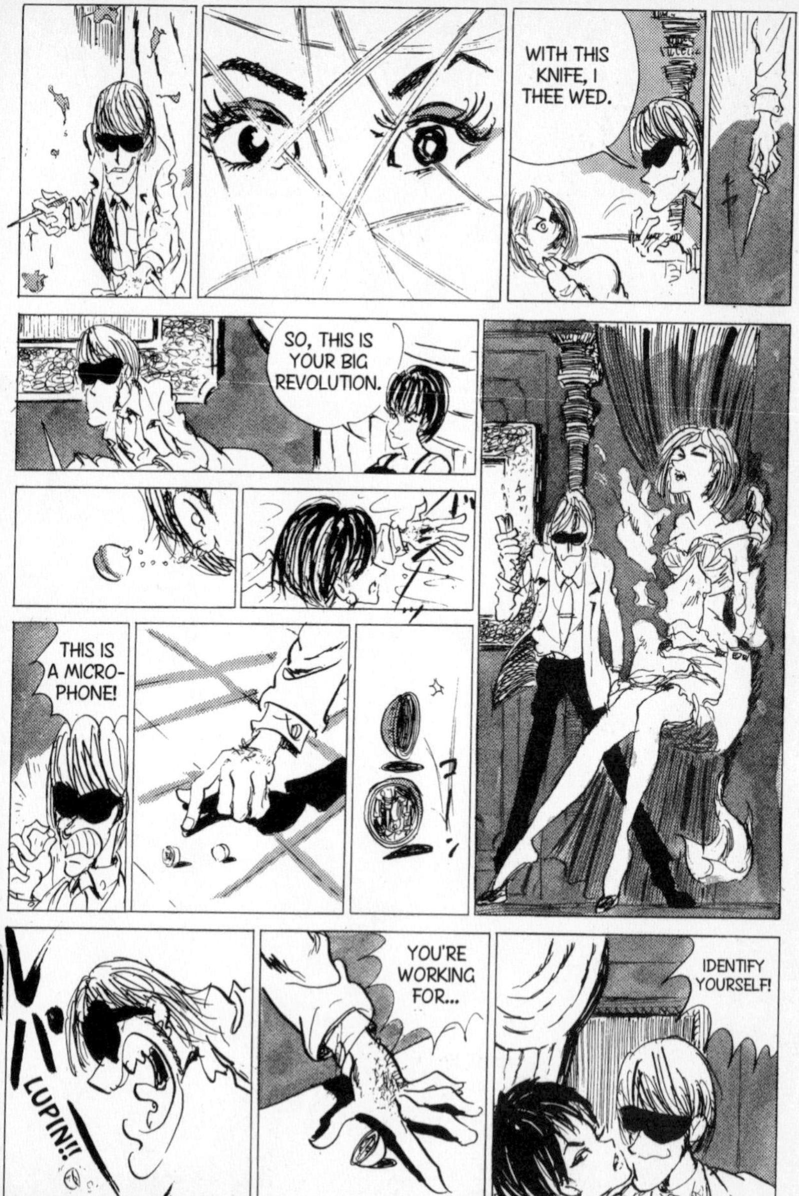
WITH THIS KNIFE, I THEE WED.
SO, THIS IS YOUR BIG REVOLUTION.
THIS IS A MICROPHONE!
IDENTIFY YOURSELF!
YOU'RE WORKING FOR...
LUPIN!!

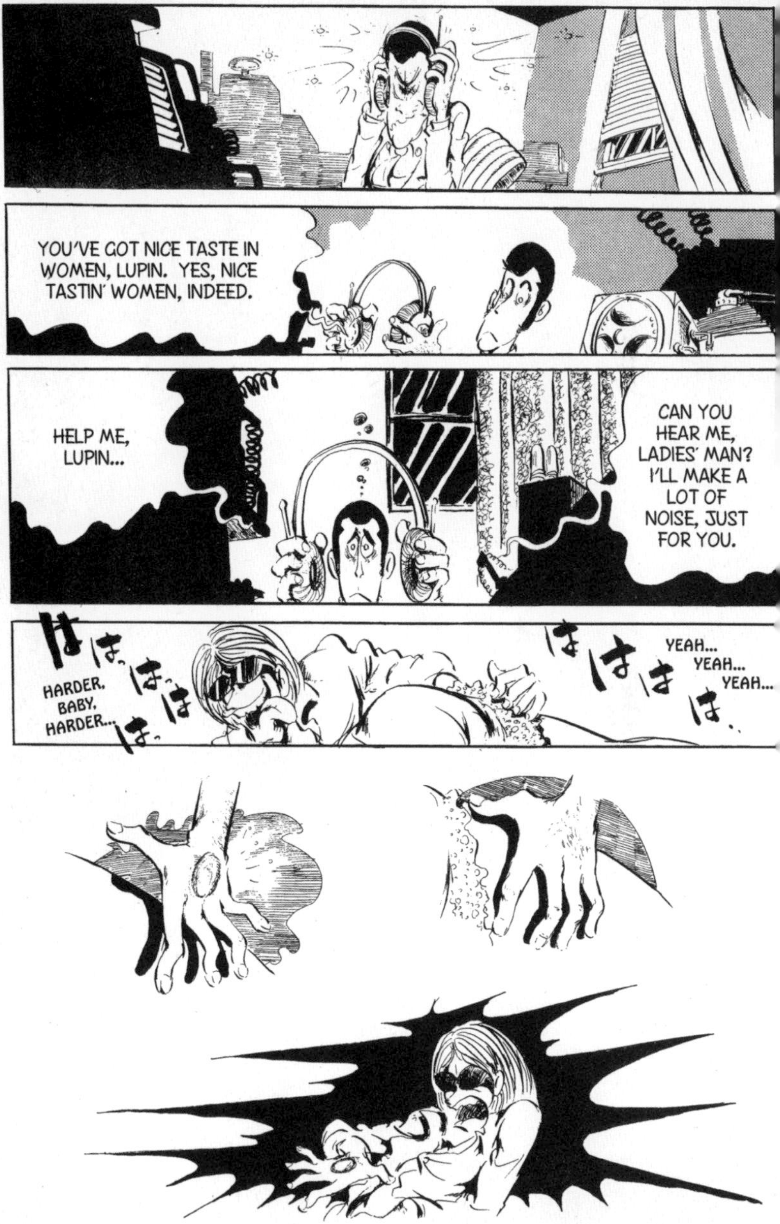
YOU'VE GOT NICE TASTE IN WOMEN, LUPIN. YES, NICE TASTIN' WOMEN, INDEED.
CAN YOU HEAR ME, LADIES' MAN? I'LL MAKE A LOT OF NOISE, JUST FOR YOU.
HELP ME, LUPIN...
YEAH... YEAH... YEAH...
はははは
ははははは
HARDER, BABY, HARDER...

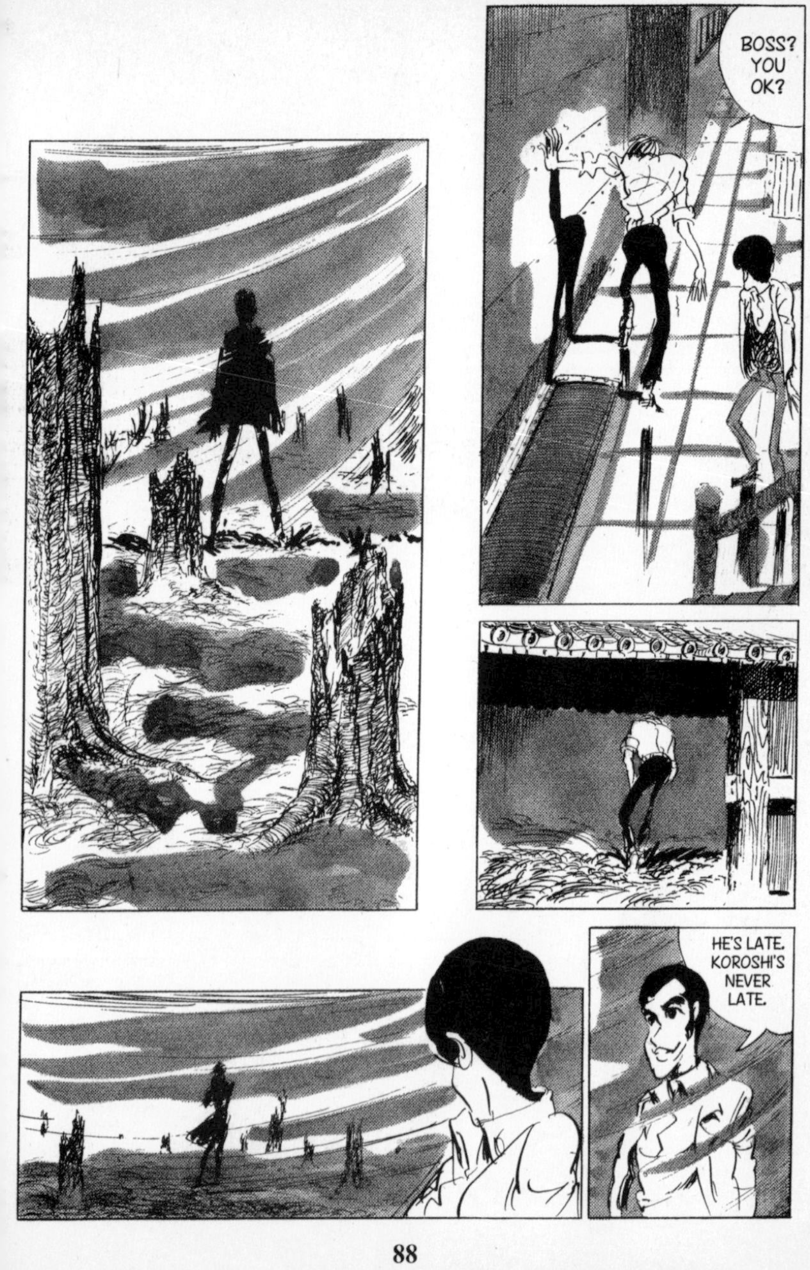
BOSS? YOU OK?
HE'S LATE. KOROSHI'S NEVER LATE.

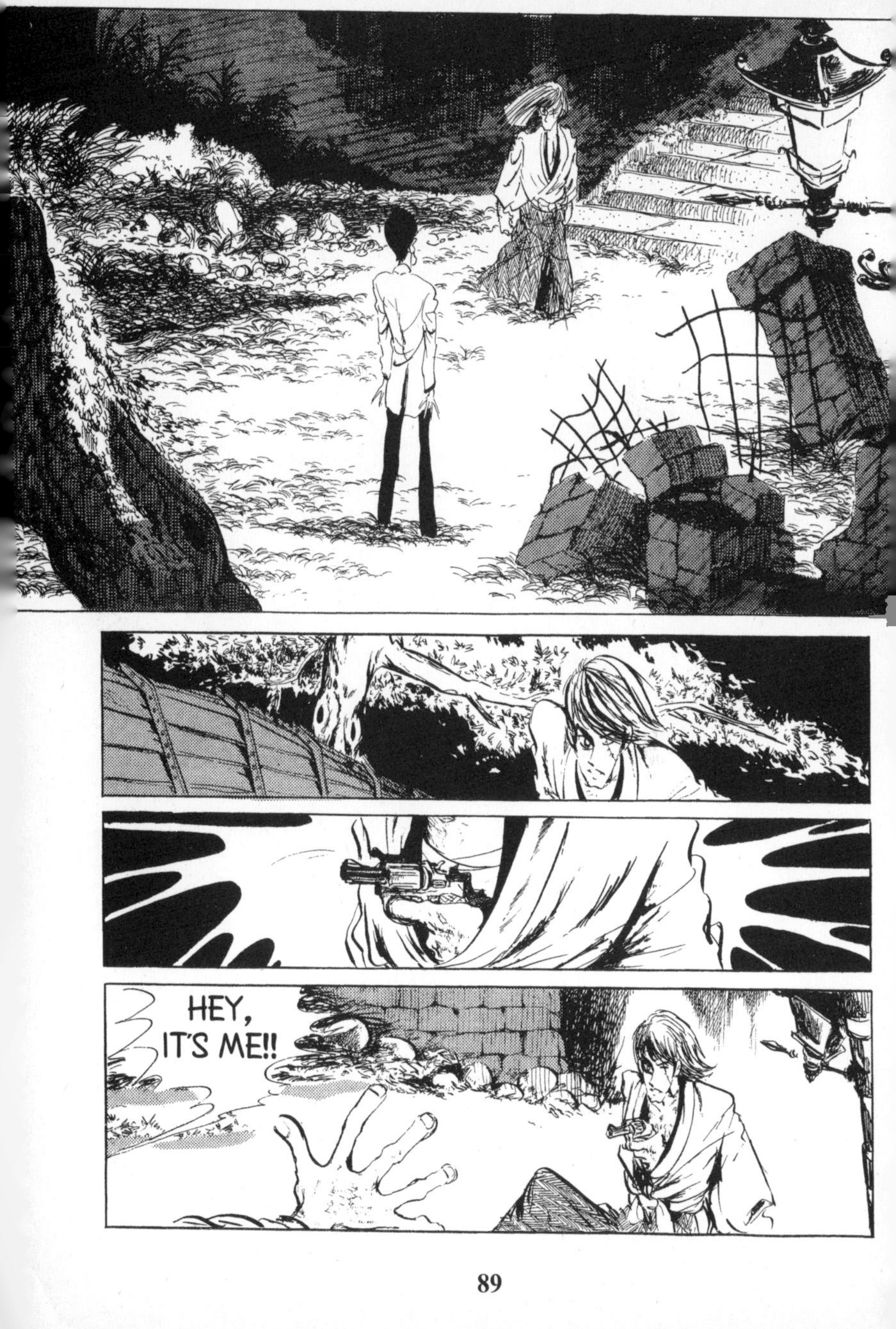
HEY, IT'S ME!!

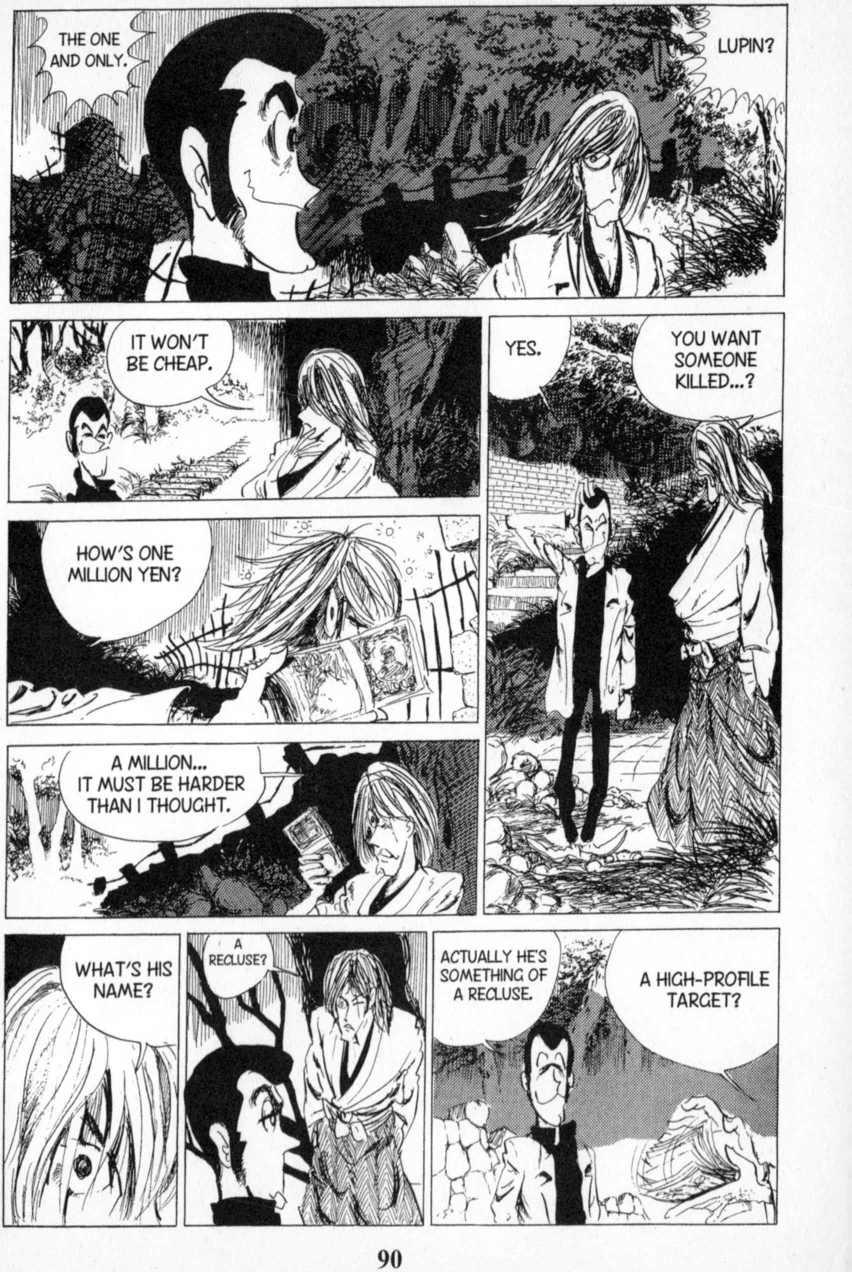

LUPIN?
THE ONE AND ONLY.
YOU WANT SOMEONE KILLED...?
YES.
IT WON'T BE CHEAP.
HOW'S ONE MILLION YEN?
A MILLION... IT MUST BE HARDER THAN I THOUGHT.
A HIGH-PROFILE TARGET?
ACTUALLY HE'S SOMETHING OF A RECLUSE.
A RECLUSE?
WHAT'S HIS NAME?

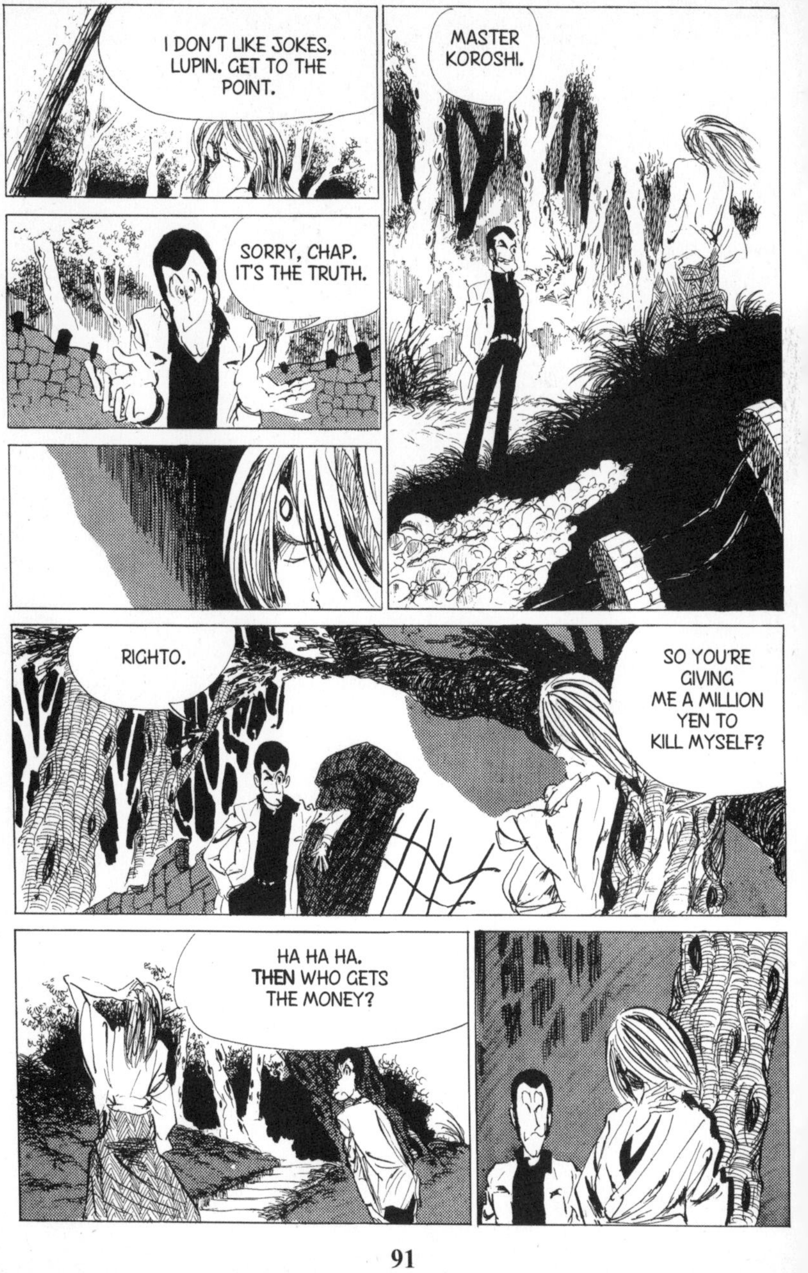
MASTER KOROSHI.
I DON'T LIKE JOKES, LUPIN. GET TO THE POINT.
SORRY, CHAP. IT'S THE TRUTH.
SO YOU'RE GIVING ME A MILLION YEN TO KILL MYSELF?
RIGHTO.
HA HA HA. THEN WHO GETS THE MONEY?

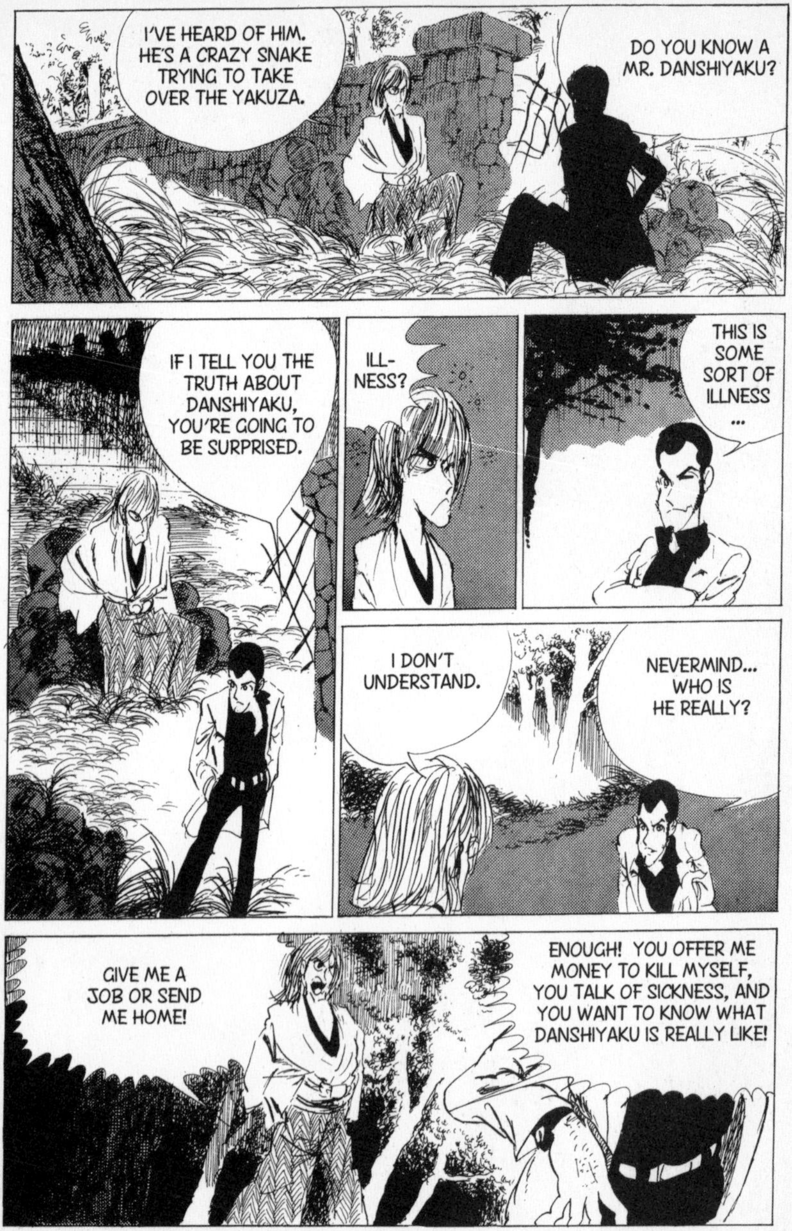
DO YOU KNOW A MR. DANSHIYAKU?
I'VE HEARD OF HIM. HE'S A CRAZY SNAKE TRYING TO TAKE OVER THE YAKUZA.
THIS IS SOME SORT OF ILLNESS ...
ILL-NESS?
NEVERMIND... WHO IS HE REALLY?
I DON'T UNDERSTAND.
IF I TELL YOU THE TRUTH ABOUT DANSHIYAKU, YOU'RE GOING TO BE SURPRISED.
ENOUGH! YOU OFFER ME MONEY TO KILL MYSELF, YOU TALK OF SICKNESS, AND YOU WANT TO KNOW WHAT DANSHIYAKU IS REALLY LIKE!
GIVE ME A JOB OR SEND ME HOME!

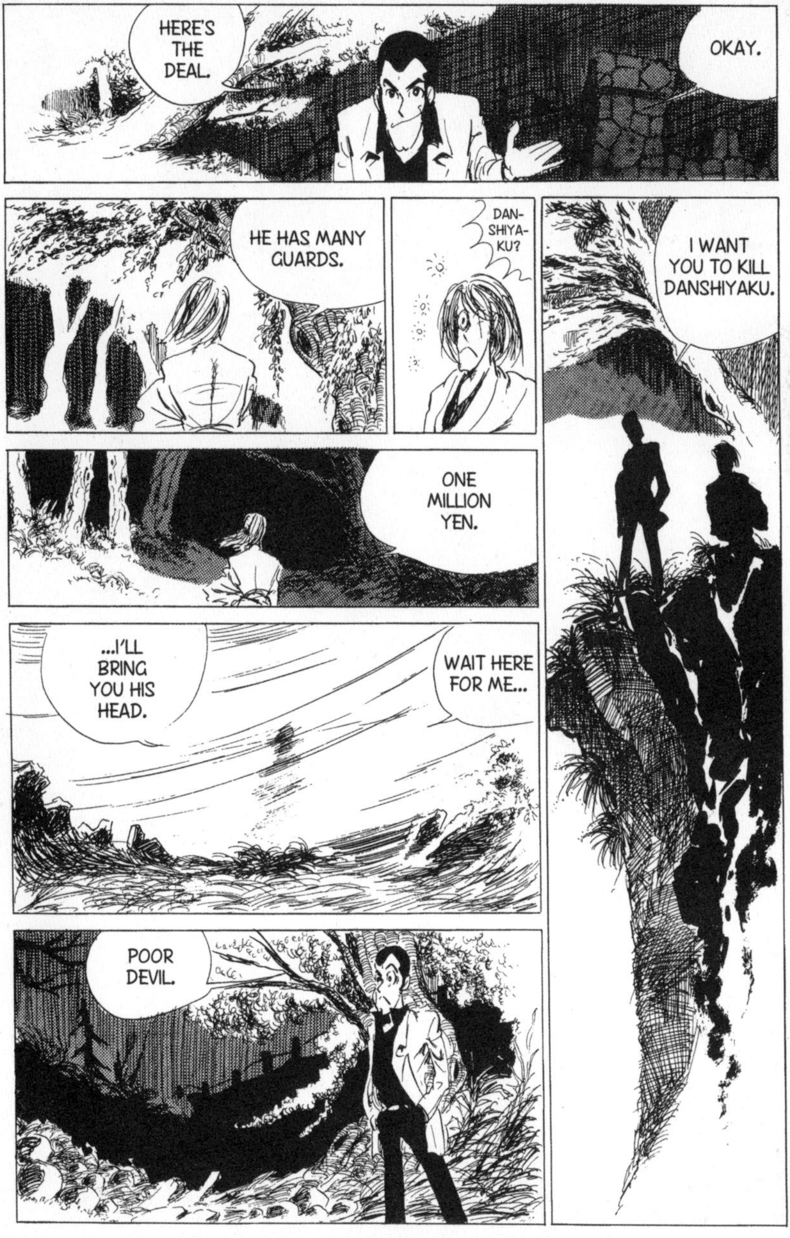
OKAY.
HERE'S THE DEAL.
I WANT YOU TO KILL DANSHIYAKU.
DAN-SHIYA-KU?
HE HAS MANY GUARDS.
ONE MILLION YEN.
WAIT HERE FOR ME...
...I'LL BRING YOU HIS HEAD.
POOR DEVIL.

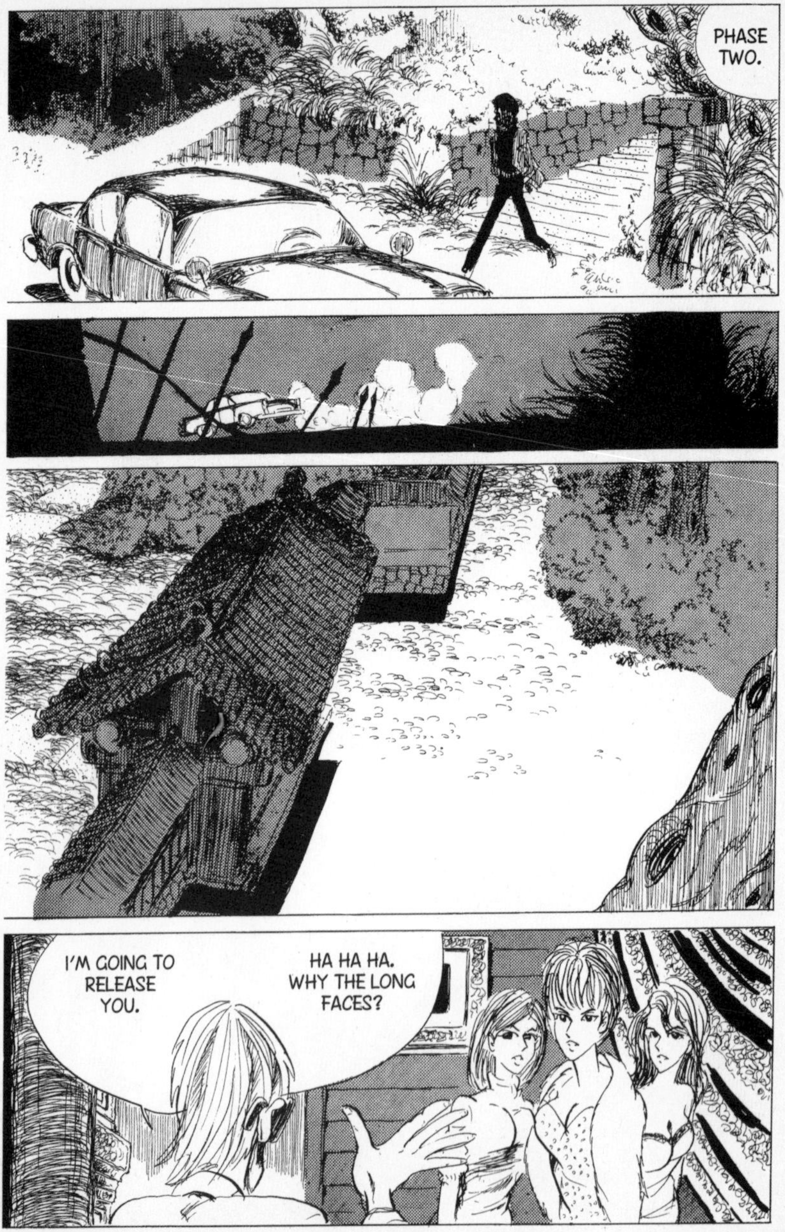
PHASE TWO.
HA HA HA. WHY THE LONG FACES?
I'M GOING TO RELEASE YOU.

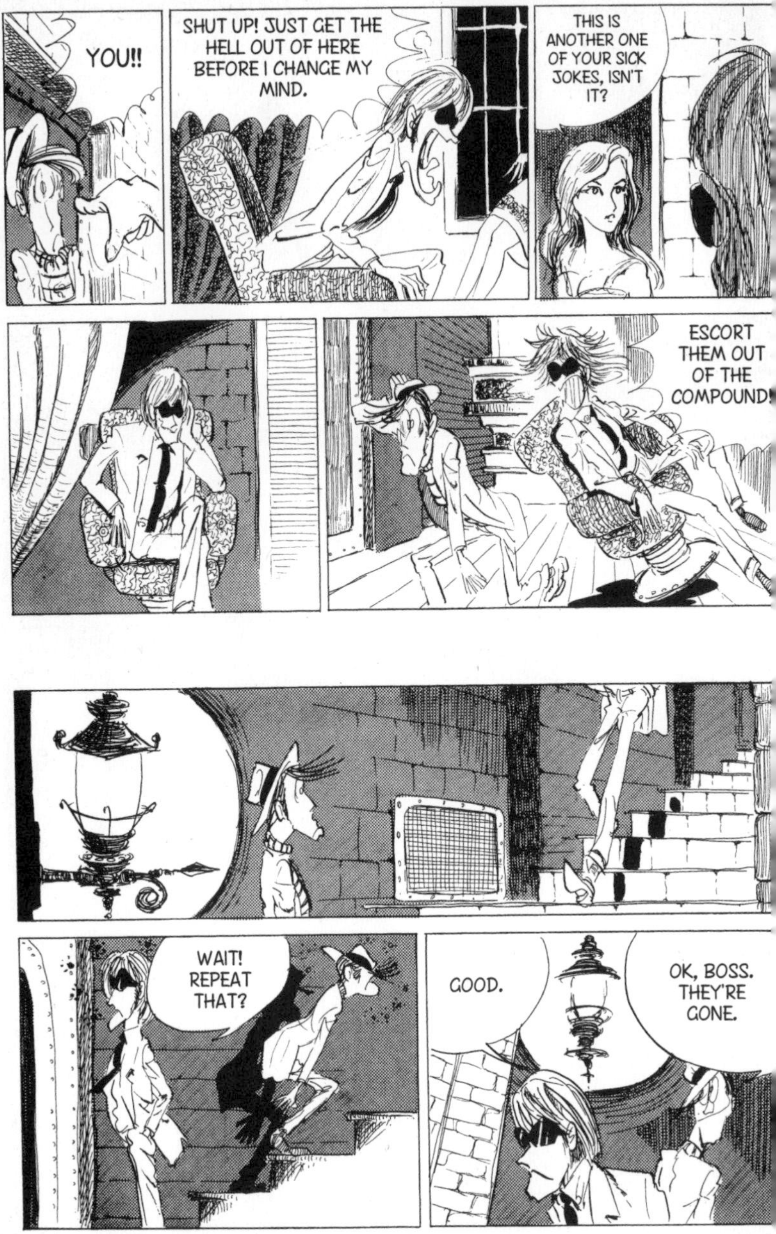
THIS IS ANOTHER ONE OF YOUR SICK JOKES, ISN'T IT?
SHUT UP! JUST GET THE HELL OUT OF HERE BEFORE I CHANGE MY MIND.
YOU!!
ESCORT THEM OUT OF THE COMPOUND!
OK, BOSS. THEY'RE GONE.
GOOD.
WAIT! REPEAT THAT?

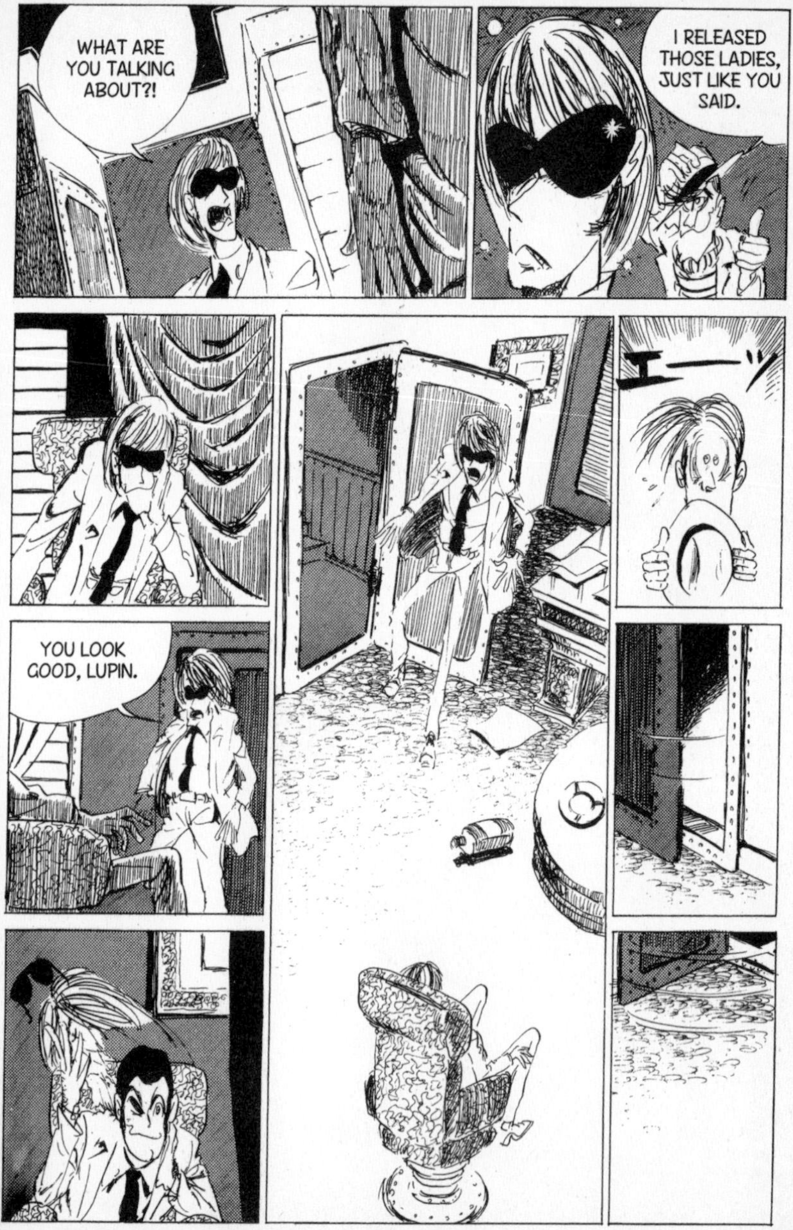
I RELEASED THOSE LADIES, JUST LIKE YOU SAID.
WHAT ARE YOU TALKING ABOUT?!
エーッ
YOU LOOK GOOD, LUPIN.

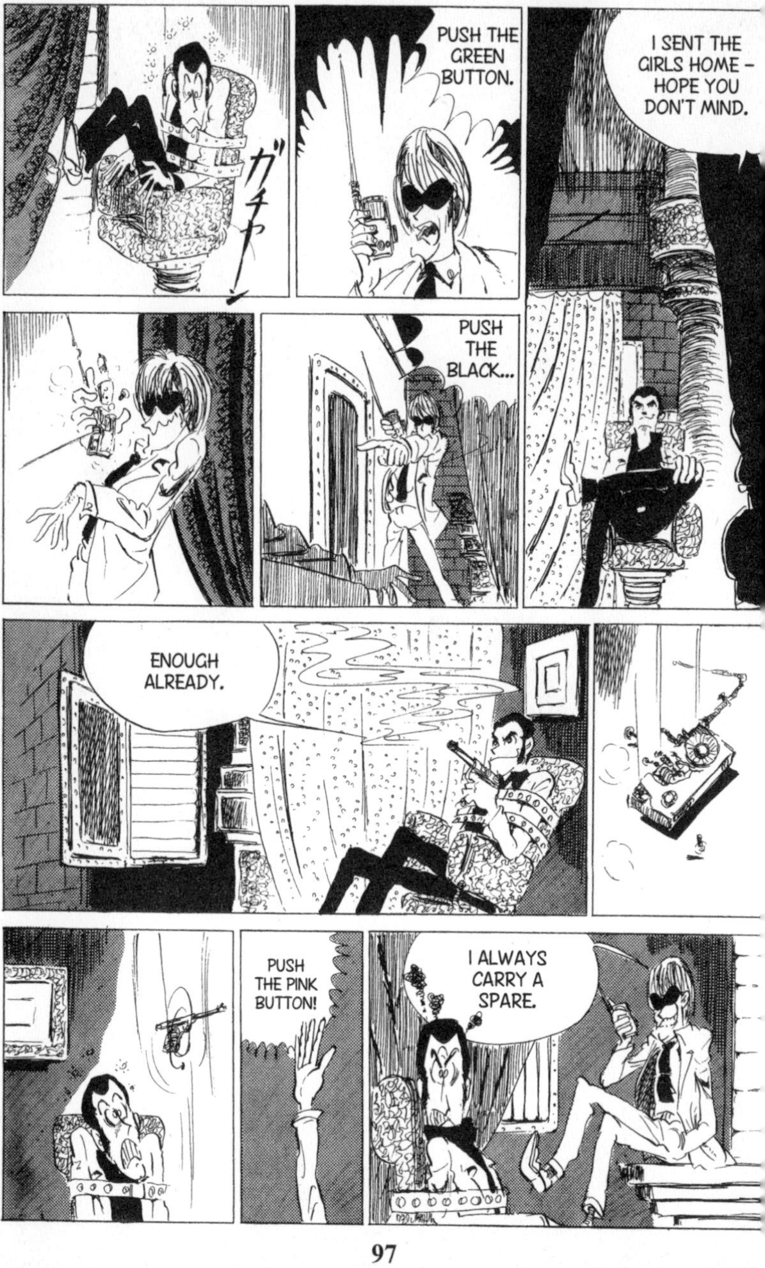
I SENT THE GIRLS HOME – HOPE YOU DON'T MIND.
PUSH THE GREEN BUTTON.
ガチャーン
PUSH THE BLACK...
ENOUGH ALREADY.
I ALWAYS CARRY A SPARE.
PUSH THE PINK BUTTON!

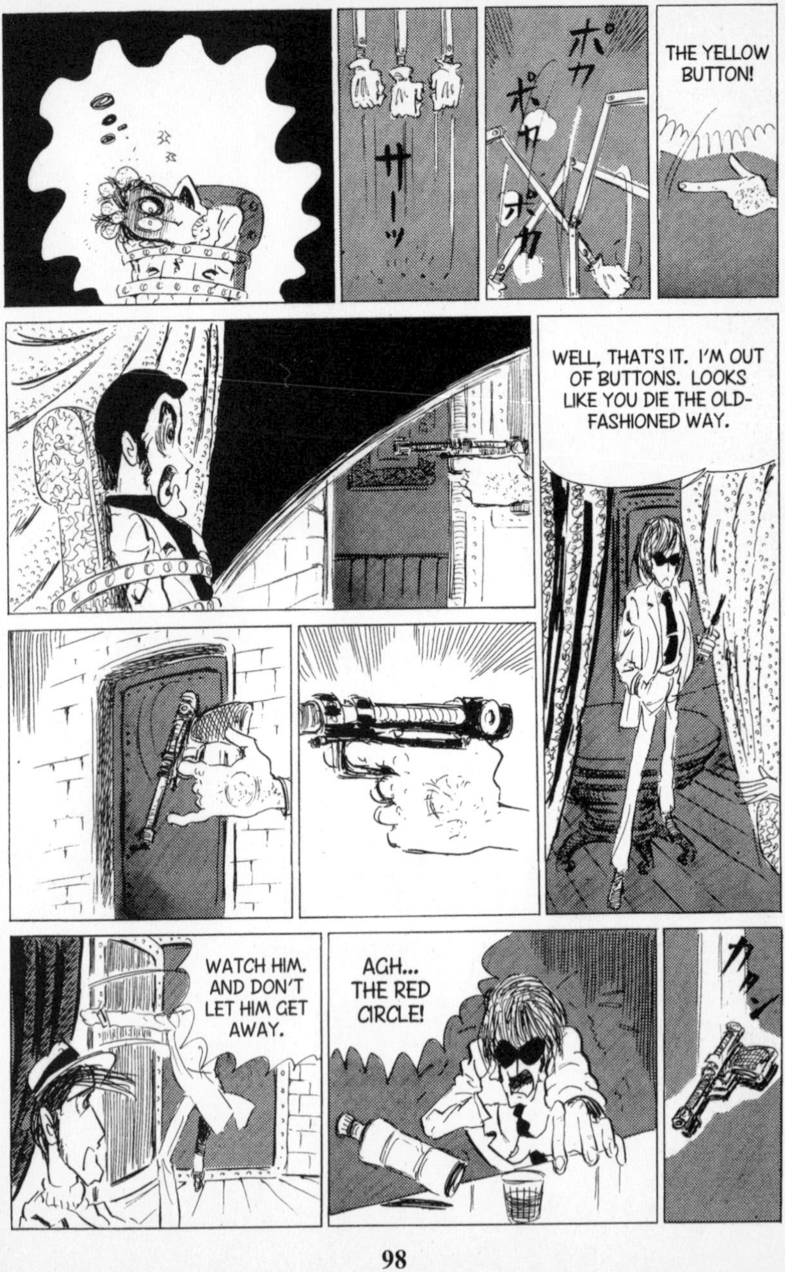
THE YELLOW BUTTON!
ポカ ポカ ポカ
サーッ
WELL, THAT'S IT. I'M OUT OF BUTTONS. LOOKS LIKE YOU DIE THE OLD-FASHIONED WAY.
AGH... THE RED CIRCLE!
WATCH HIM. AND DON'T LET HIM GET AWAY.

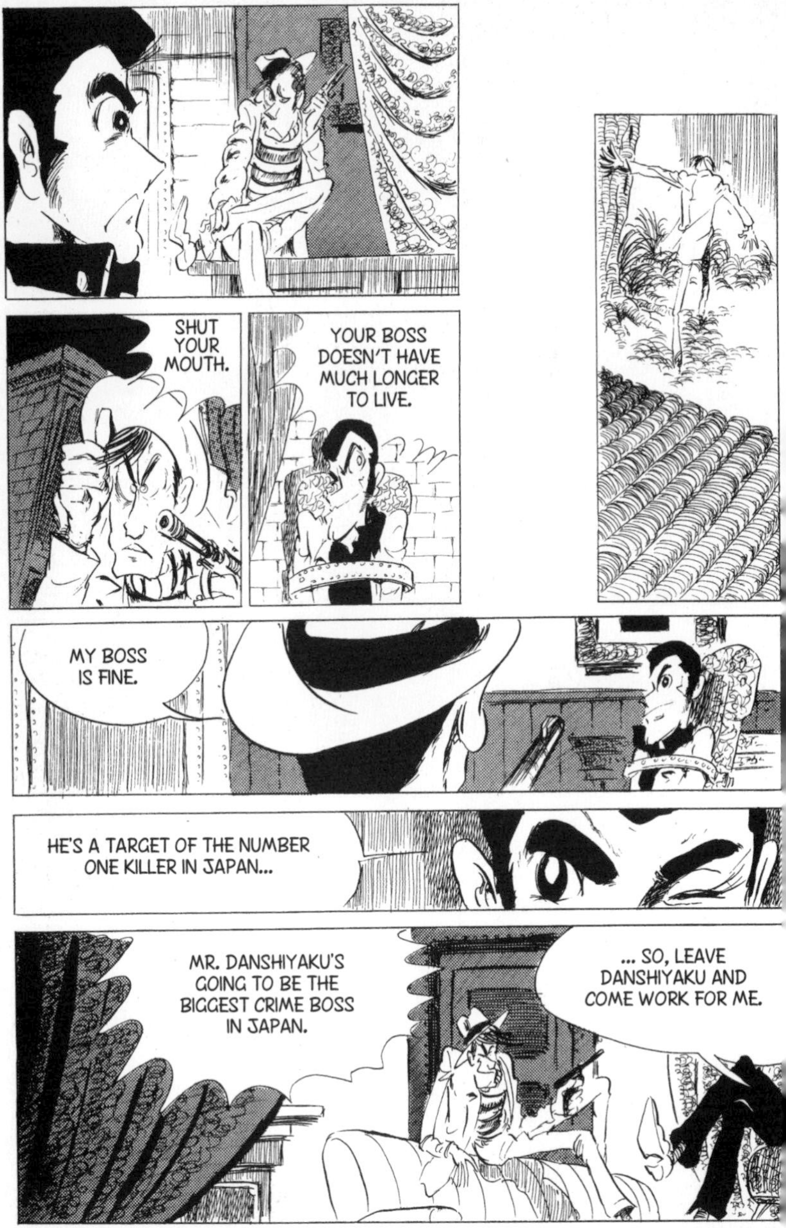
YOUR BOSS DOESN'T HAVE MUCH LONGER TO LIVE.
SHUT YOUR MOUTH.
MY BOSS IS FINE.
HE'S A TARGET OF THE NUMBER ONE KILLER IN JAPAN...
... SO, LEAVE DANSHIYAKU AND COME WORK FOR ME.
MR. DANSHIYAKU'S GOING TO BE THE BIGGEST CRIME BOSS IN JAPAN.

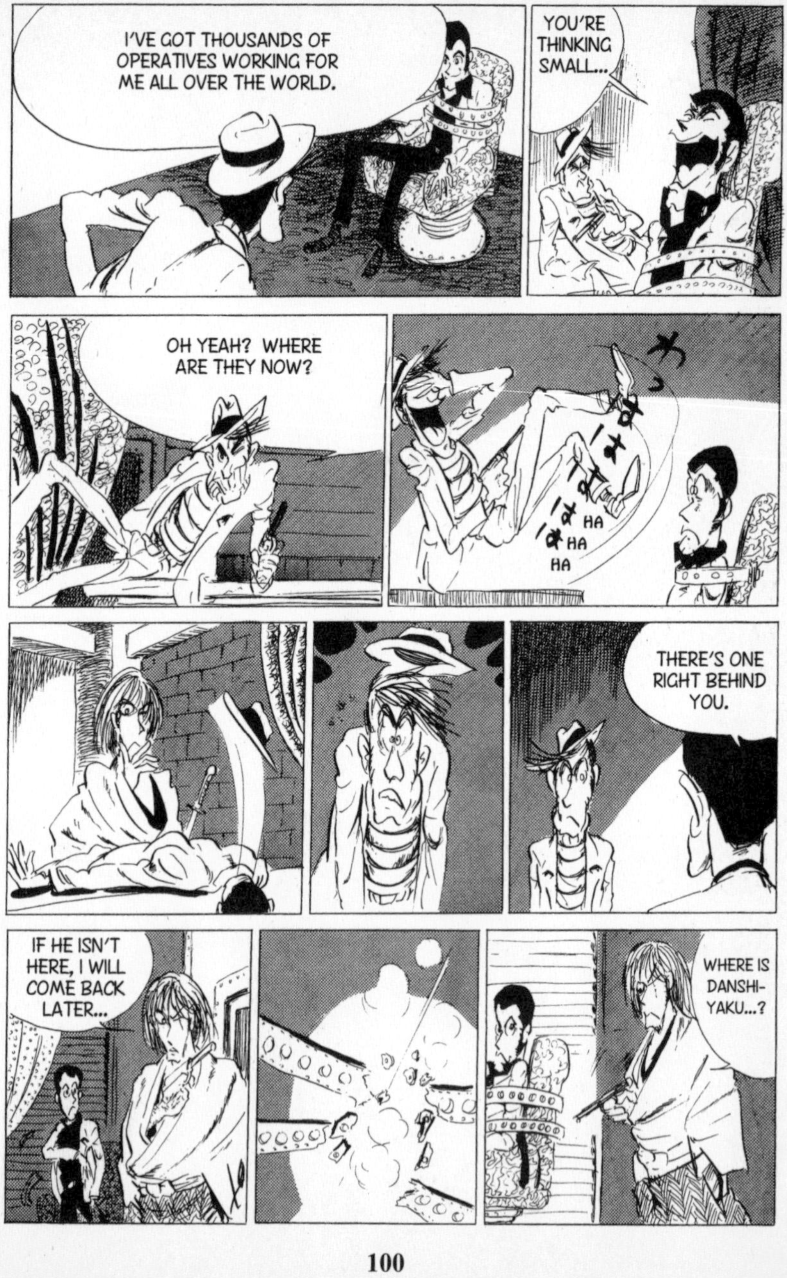

YOU'RE THINKING SMALL...
I'VE GOT THOUSANDS OF OPERATIVES WORKING FOR ME ALL OVER THE WORLD.
わっ
はははは
HA HA HA
OH YEAH? WHERE ARE THEY NOW?
THERE'S ONE RIGHT BEHIND YOU.
WHERE IS DANSHI-YAKU...?
IF HE ISN'T HERE, I WILL COME BACK LATER...

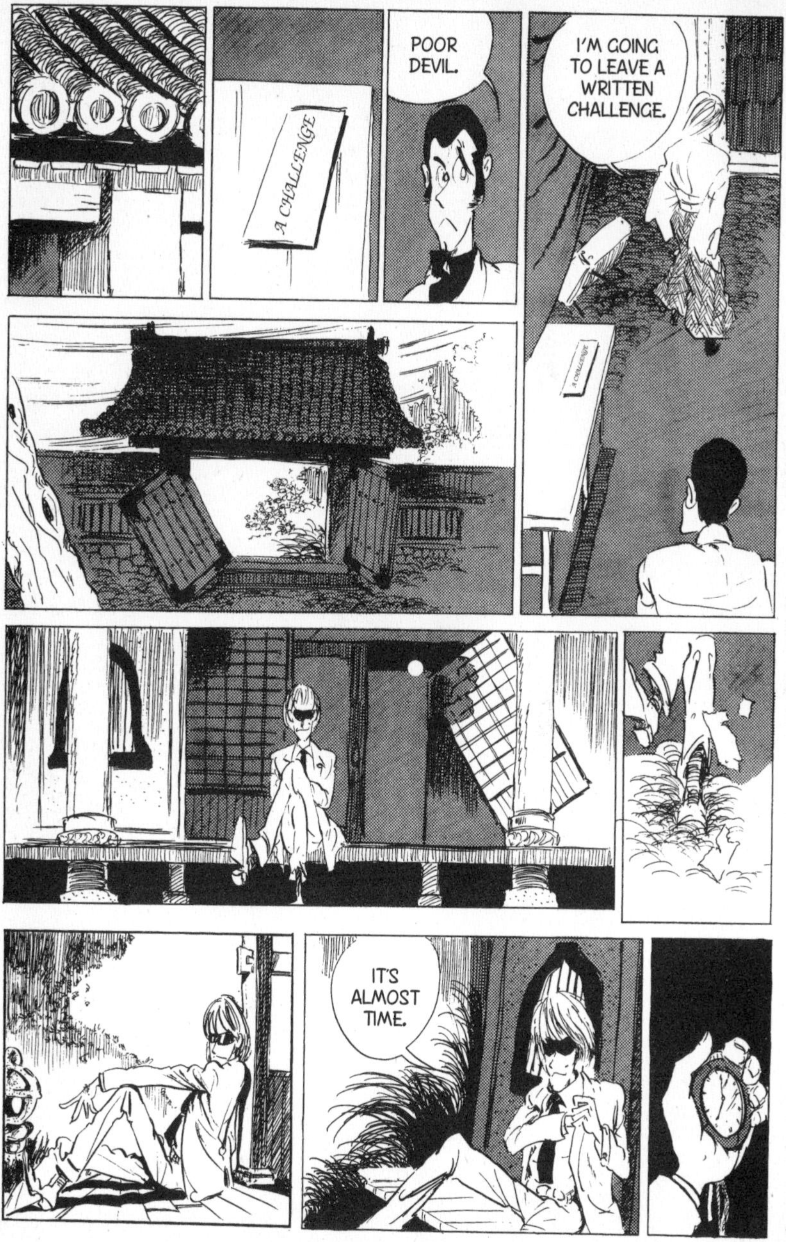
I'M GOING TO LEAVE A WRITTEN CHALLENGE.
A CHALLENGE
POOR DEVIL.
A CHALLENGE
IT'S ALMOST TIME.

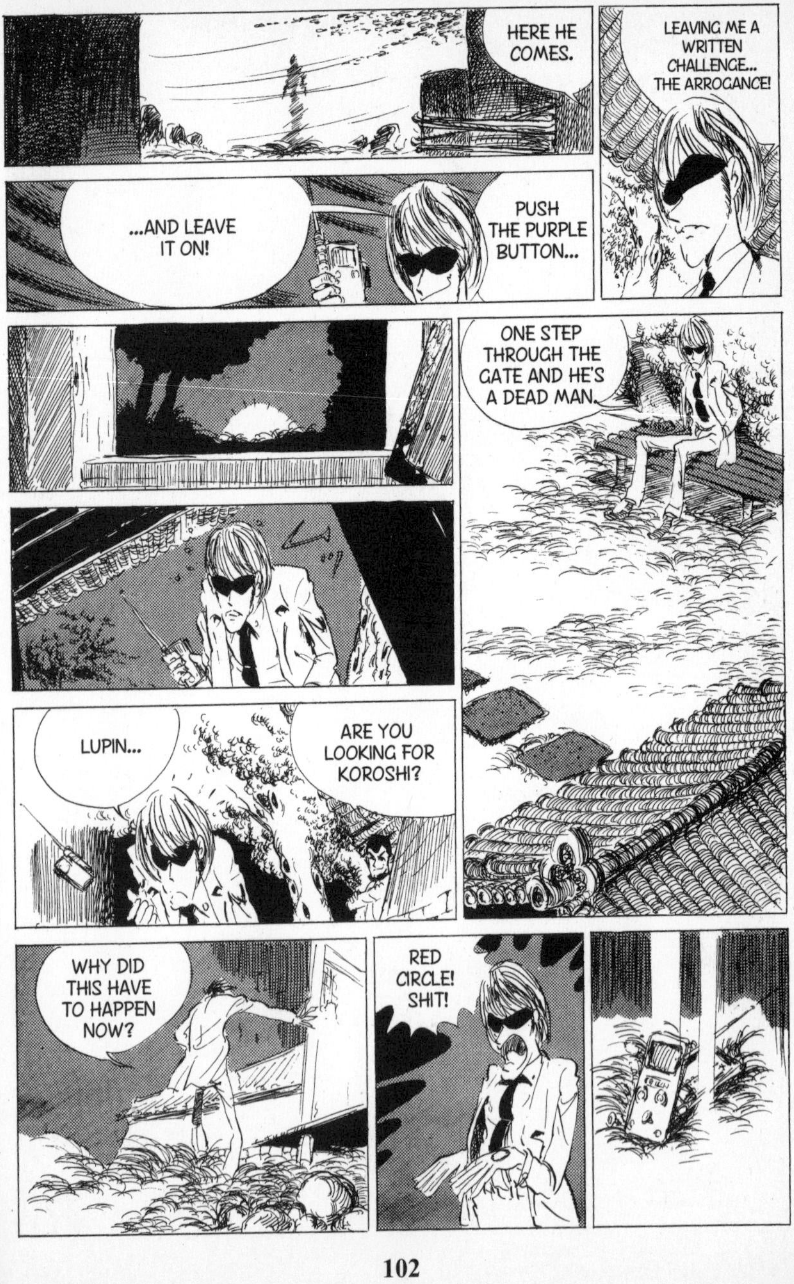
LEAVING ME A WRITTEN CHALLENGE.. THE ARROGANCE!
HERE HE COMES.
PUSH THE PURPLE BUTTON...
...AND LEAVE IT ON!
ONE STEP THROUGH THE GATE AND HE'S A DEAD MAN.
ARE YOU LOOKING FOR KOROSHI?
LUPIN...
RED CIRCLE! SHIT!
WHY DID THIS HAVE TO HAPPEN NOW?

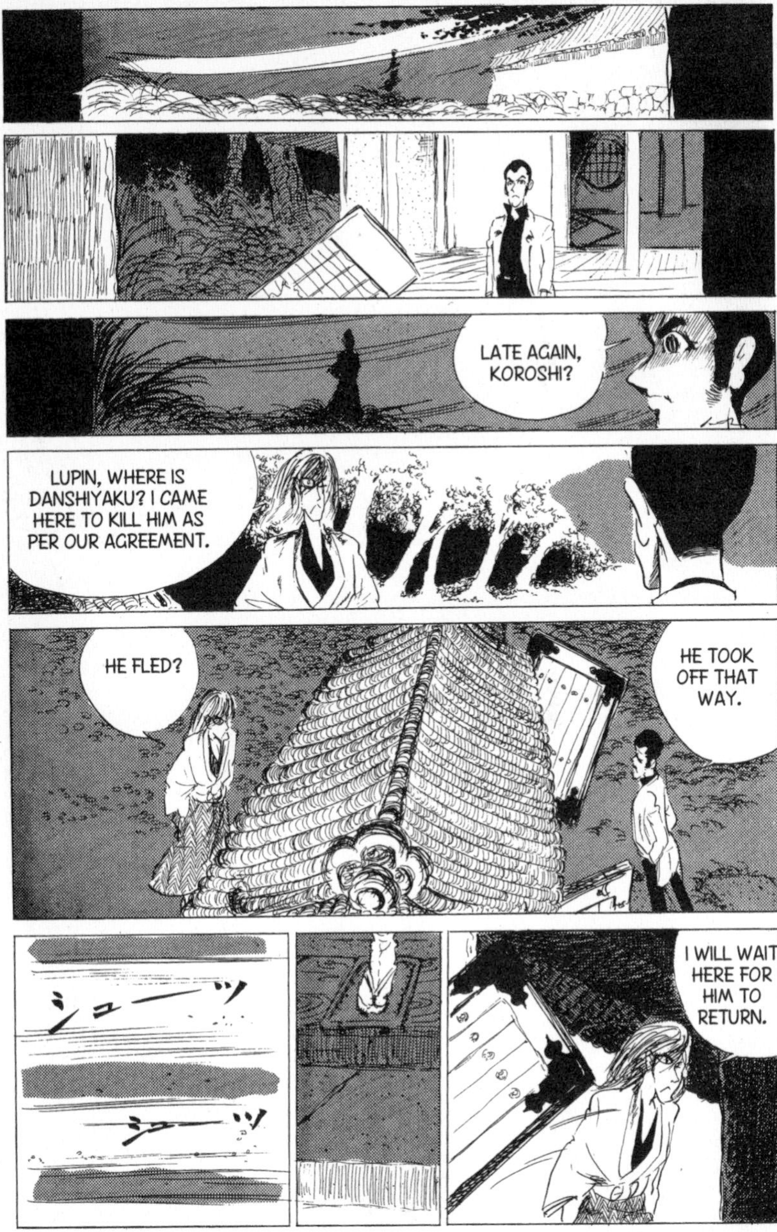
LATE AGAIN, KOROSHI?
LUPIN, WHERE IS DANSHIYAKU? I CAME HERE TO KILL HIM AS PER OUR AGREEMENT.
HE TOOK OFF THAT WAY.
HE FLED?
I WILL WAIT HERE FOR HIM TO RETURN.
シューッ
シューッ

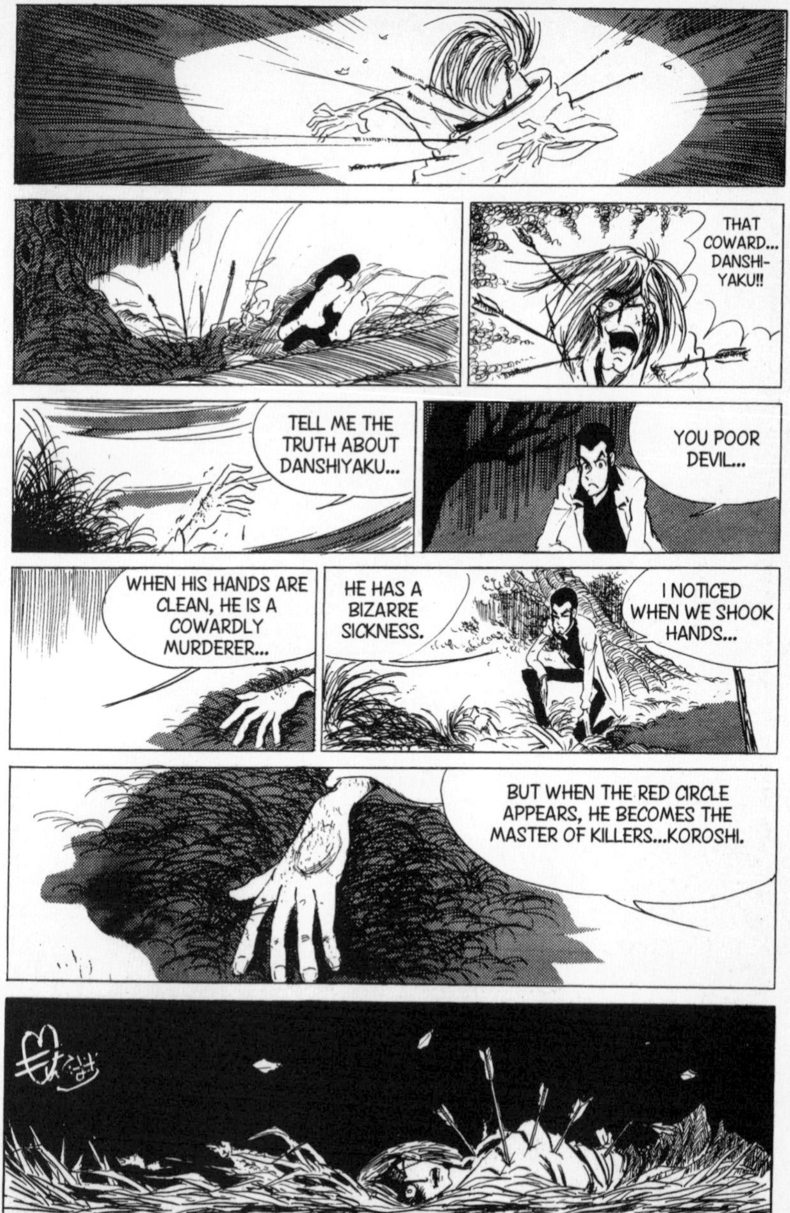
THAT COWARD... DANSHI-YAKU!!
YOU POOR DEVIL...
TELL ME THE TRUTH ABOUT DANSHIYAKU...
I NOTICED WHEN WE SHOOK HANDS...
HE HAS A BIZARRE SICKNESS.
WHEN HIS HANDS ARE CLEAN, HE IS A COWARDLY MURDERER...
BUT WHEN THE RED CIRCLE APPEARS, HE BECOMES THE MASTER OF KILLERS...KOROSHI.

CHAPTER 6
"IMPRESSION IMPOSSIBLE"

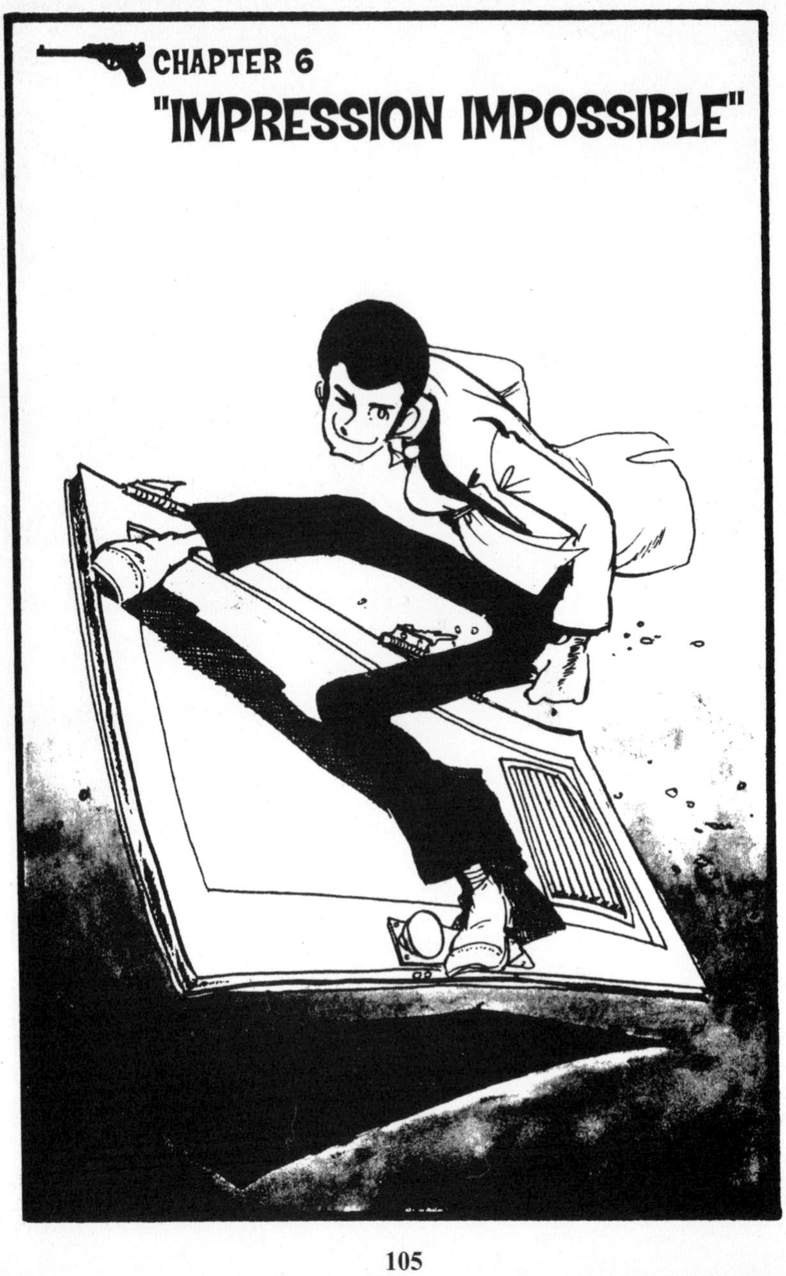

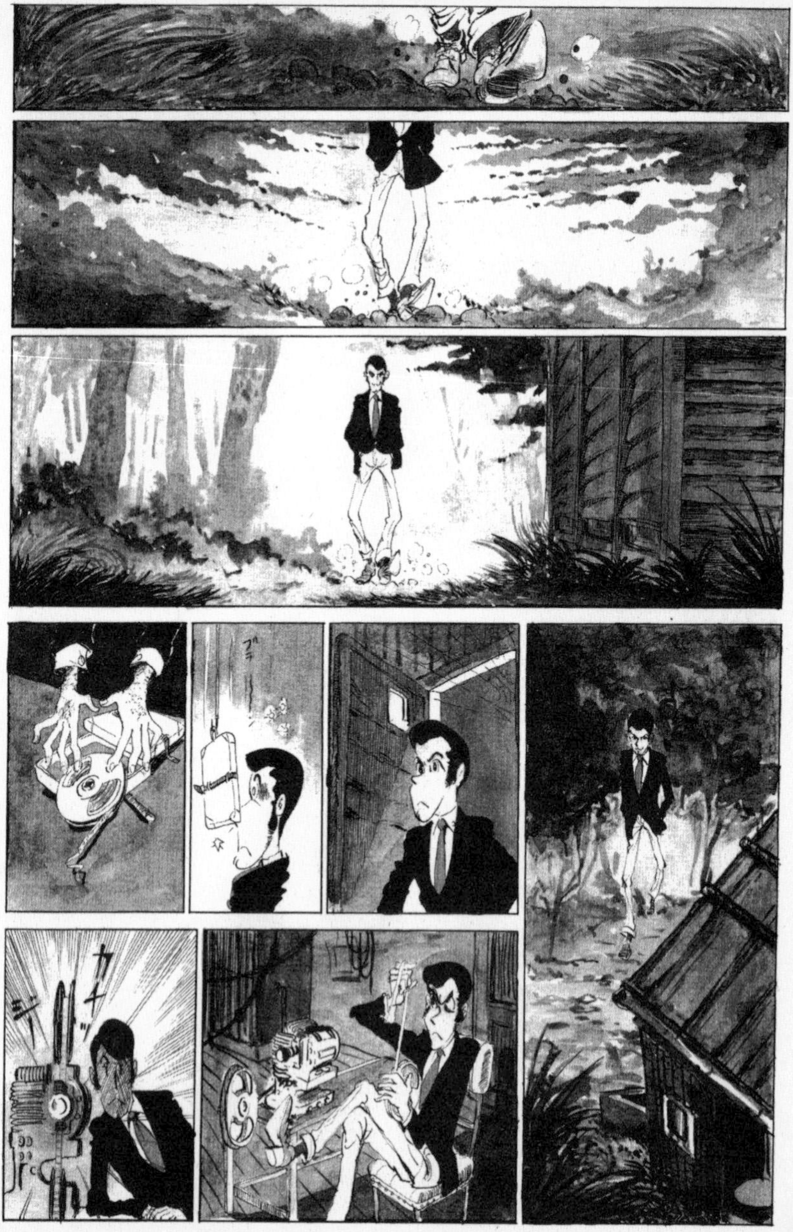
ブラー
カチッ
ジー

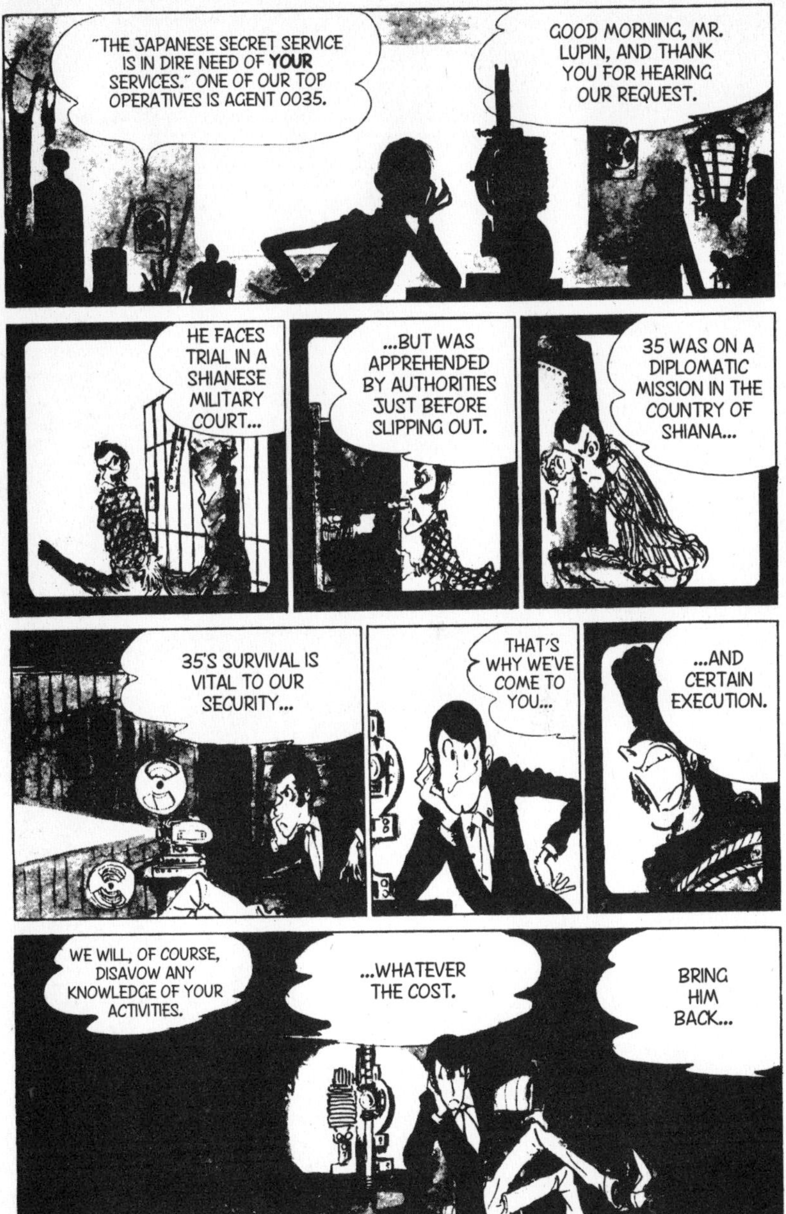

GOOD MORNING, MR. LUPIN, AND THANK YOU FOR HEARING OUR REQUEST.
"THE JAPANESE SECRET SERVICE IS IN DIRE NEED OF **YOUR** SERVICES." ONE OF OUR TOP OPERATIVES IS AGENT 0035.
35 WAS ON A DIPLOMATIC MISSION IN THE COUNTRY OF SHIANA...
...BUT WAS APPREHENDED BY AUTHORITIES JUST BEFORE SLIPPING OUT.
HE FACES TRIAL IN A SHIANESE MILITARY COURT...
...AND CERTAIN EXECUTION.
THAT'S WHY WE'VE COME TO YOU...
35'S SURVIVAL IS VITAL TO OUR SECURITY...
BRING HIM BACK...
...WHATEVER THE COST.
WE WILL, OF COURSE, DISAVOW ANY KNOWLEDGE OF YOUR ACTIVITIES.

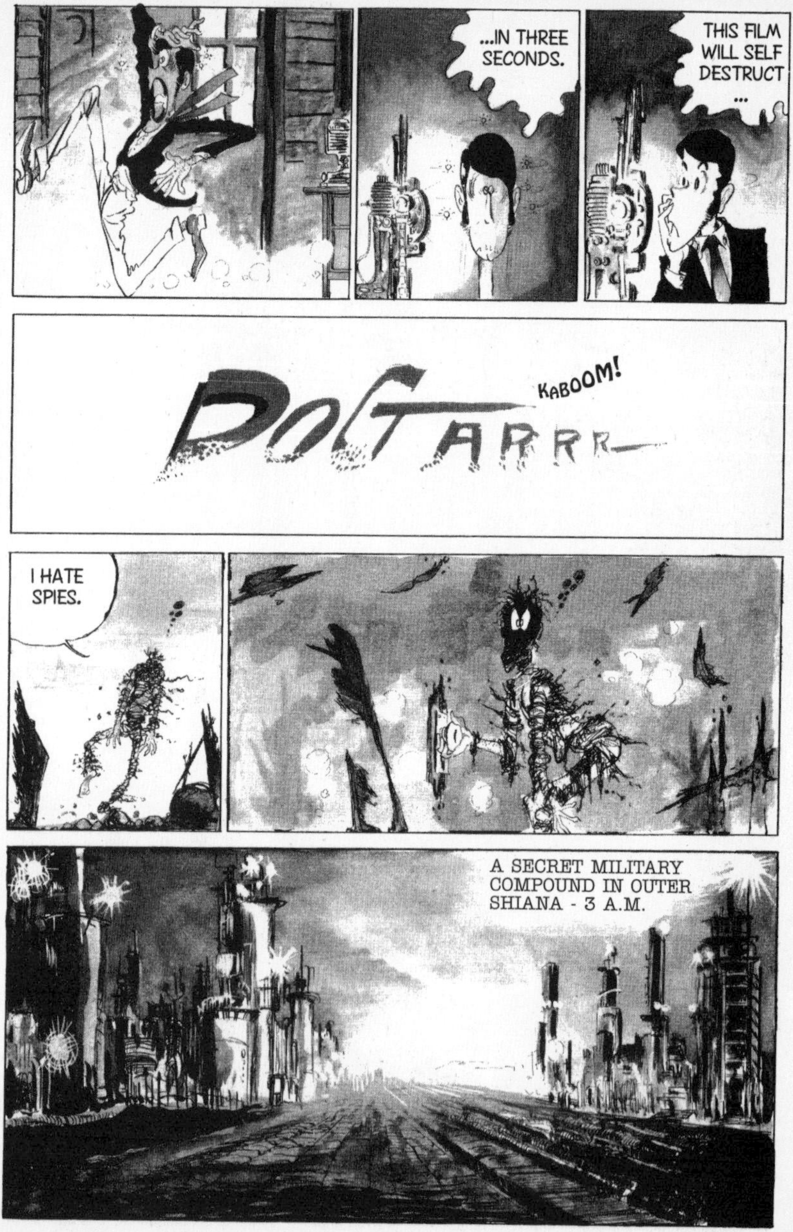
THIS FILM WILL SELF DESTRUCT ...
...IN THREE SECONDS.
DOGARRR
KABOOM!
I HATE SPIES.
A SECRET MILITARY COMPOUND IN OUTER SHIANA - 3 A.M.

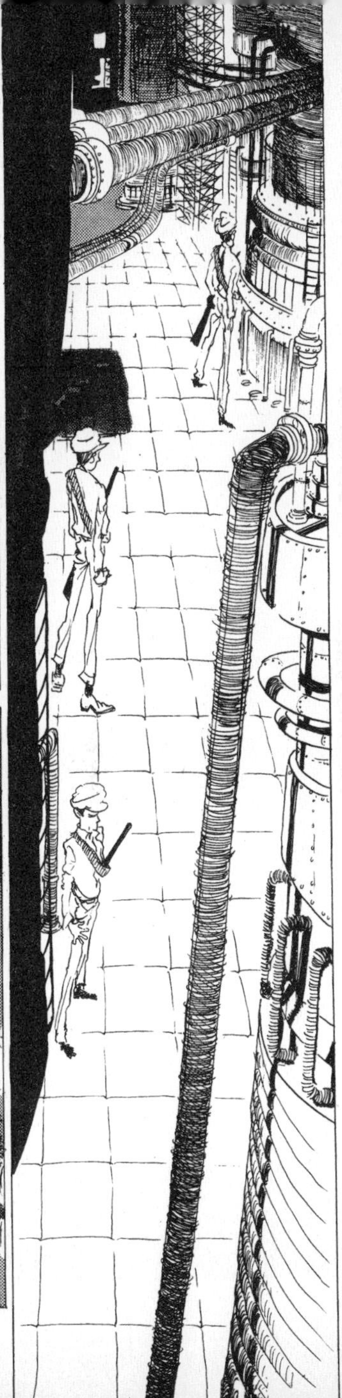

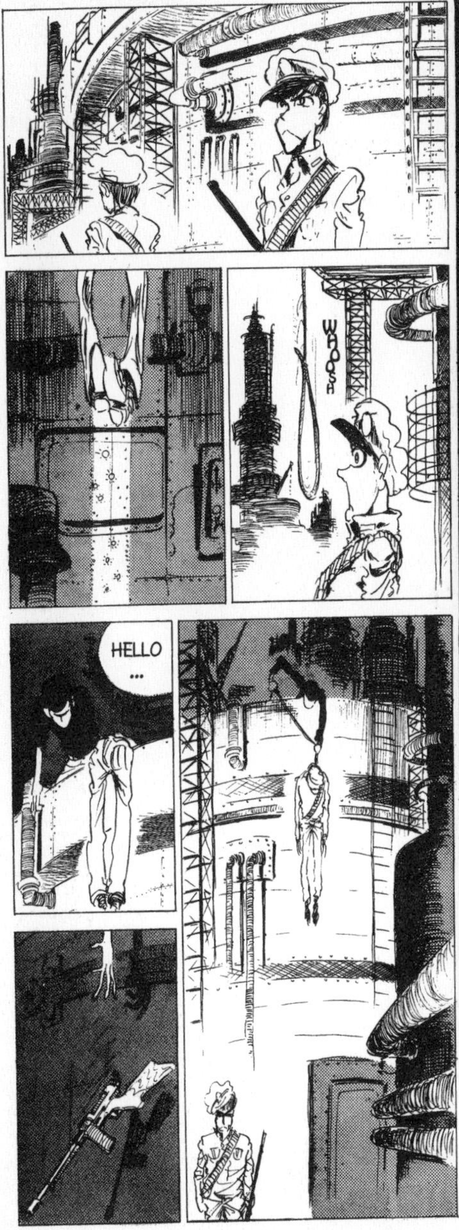
WHOOSH
HELLO ...

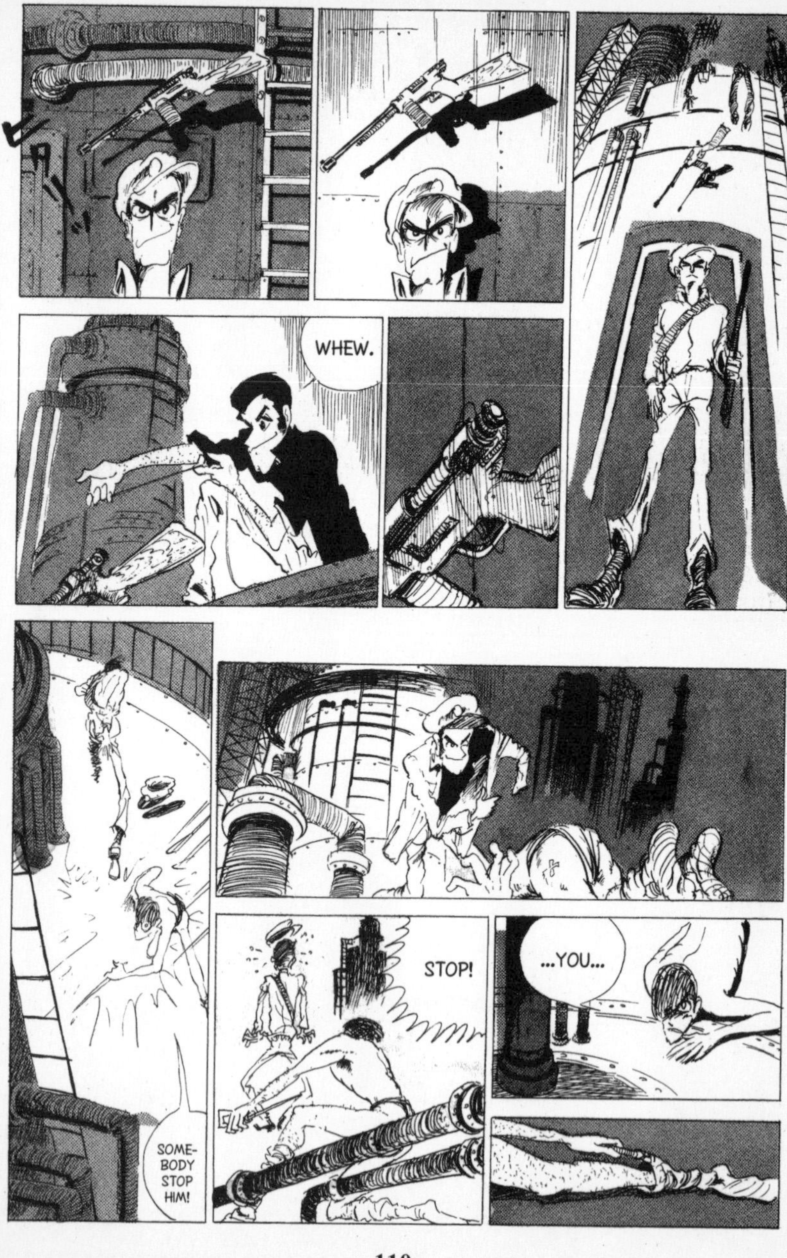
WHEW.
...YOU...
STOP!
SOME-BODY STOP HIM!

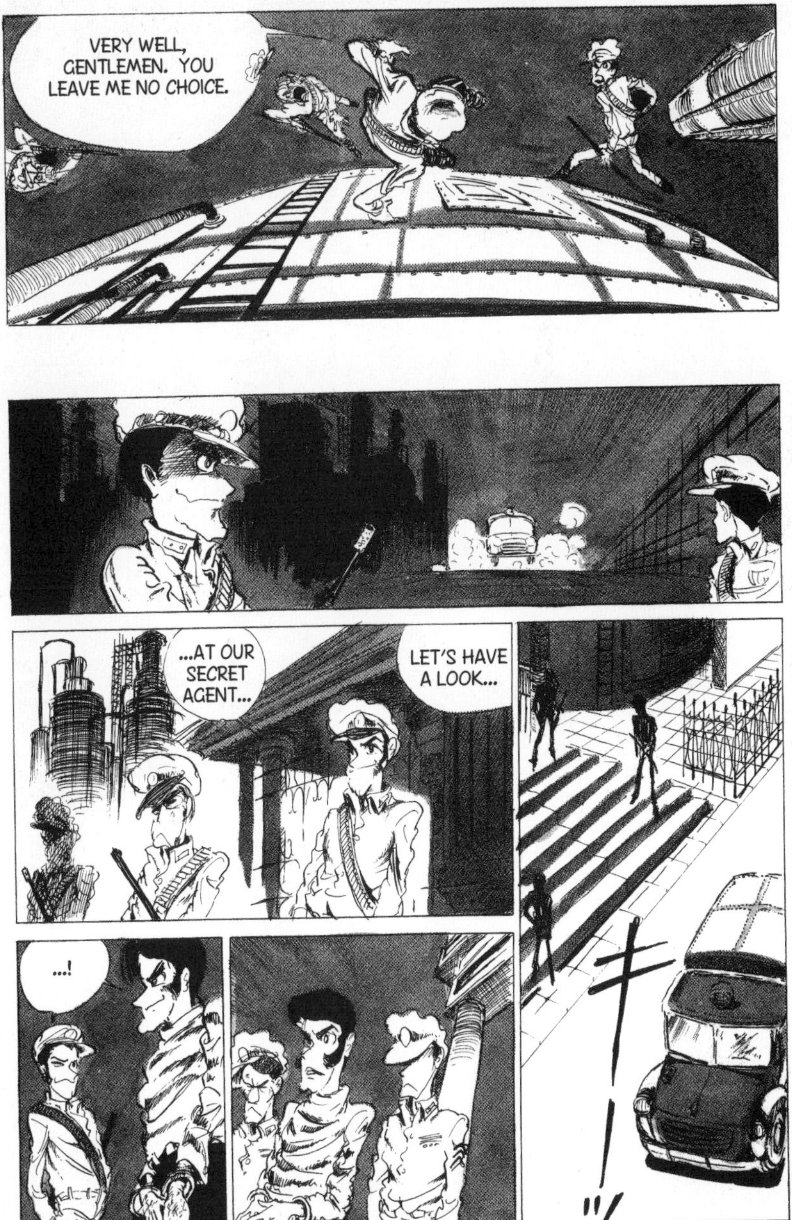
VERY WELL, GENTLEMEN. YOU LEAVE ME NO CHOICE.
キーーッ
LET'S HAVE A LOOK...
...AT OUR SECRET AGENT...
...!

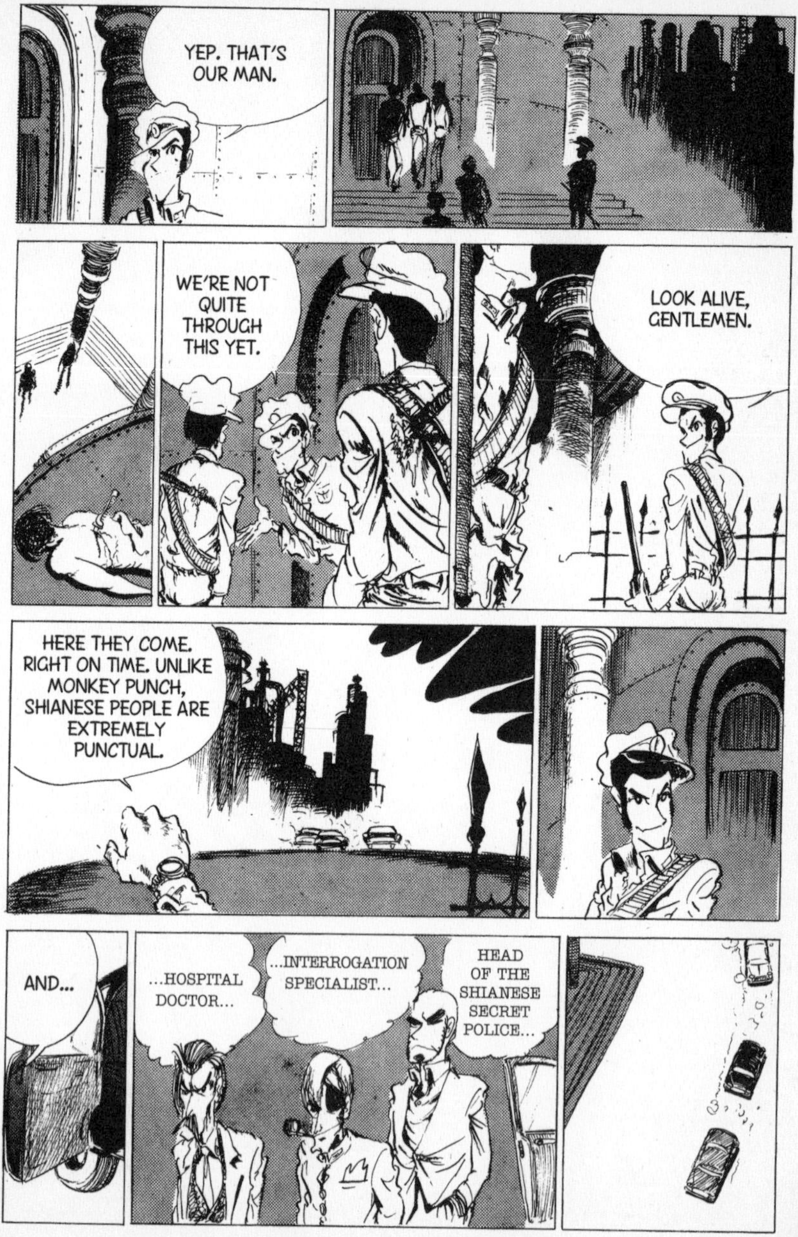
YEP. THAT'S OUR MAN.
LOOK ALIVE, GENTLEMEN.
WE'RE NOT QUITE THROUGH THIS YET.
HERE THEY COME. RIGHT ON TIME. UNLIKE MONKEY PUNCH, SHIANESE PEOPLE ARE EXTREMELY PUNCTUAL.
HEAD OF THE SHIANESE SECRET POLICE...
...INTERROGATION SPECIALIST...
...HOSPITAL DOCTOR...
AND...

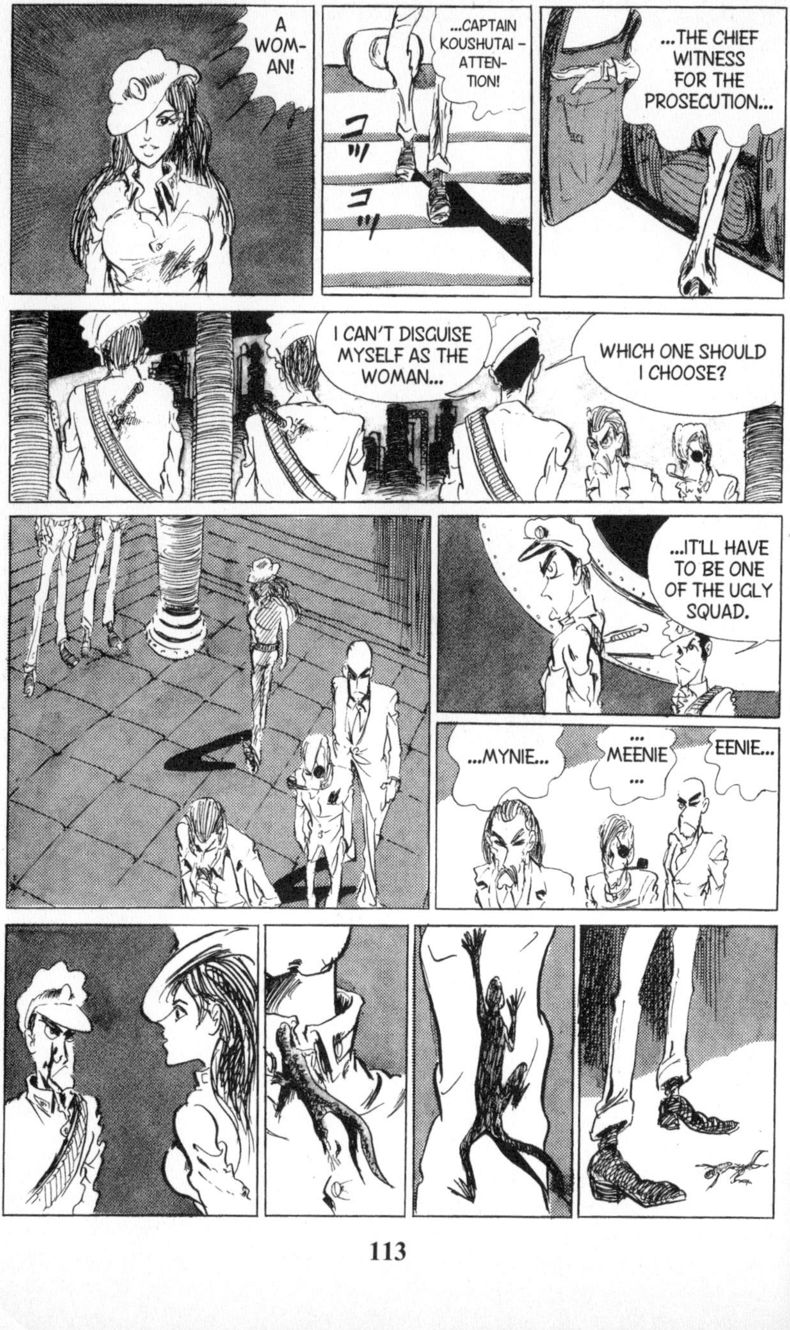
...THE CHIEF WITNESS FOR THE PROSECUTION...
...CAPTAIN KOUSHUTAI – ATTEN-TION!
コツ
コツ
A WOM-AN!
WHICH ONE SHOULD I CHOOSE?
I CAN'T DISGUISE MYSELF AS THE WOMAN...
...IT'LL HAVE TO BE ONE OF THE UGLY SQUAD.
EENIE...
...MEENIE...
...MYNIE...

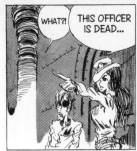

OH NO ...
THIS OFFICER IS DEAD...
WHAT?!
I'M NOT DEAD.
THIS LIZARD IS A BELOVED PET OF MINE.
DEAD MEN TELL NO TALES... AND THEY DON'T KEEP PETS.
THEN HOW DID HE SPEAK, YOU ASK? I'LL TELL YOU LATER SO AS TO KEEP THE AIR THICK WITH SUSPENSE. UNLESS YOU ALREADY KNOW THAT LUPIN IS NOT ONLY A MASTER THIEF, BUT A VENTRILOQUIST AS WELL... OOPS...
DON'T WASTE SPACE WITH LONG EXPLANATIONS!
THIS MANGA IS VERY THRILLING...!!

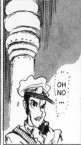

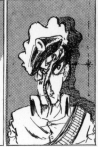

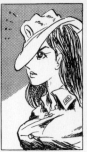

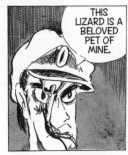

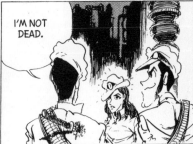

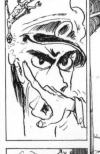

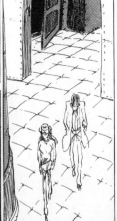

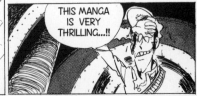

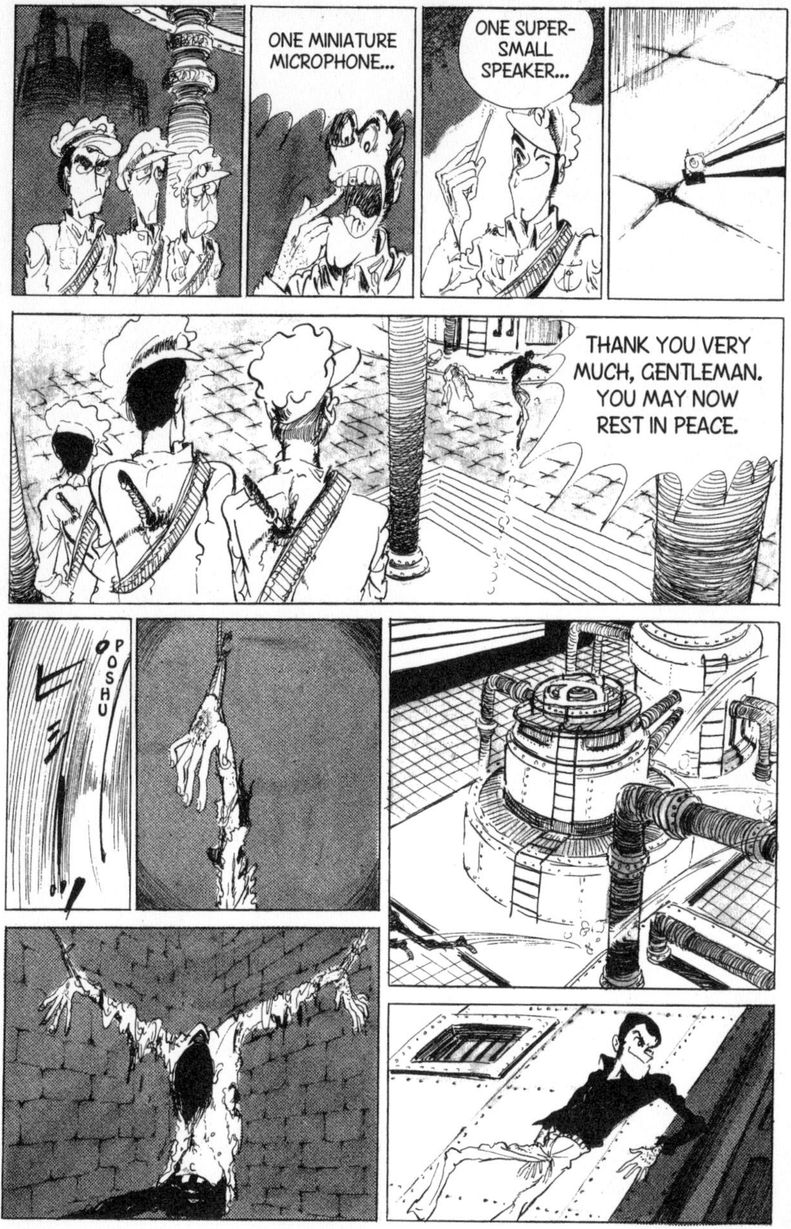
ONE SUPER-SMALL SPEAKER...
ONE MINIATURE MICROPHONE...
THANK YOU VERY MUCH, GENTLEMAN. YOU MAY NOW REST IN PEACE.
POSHU

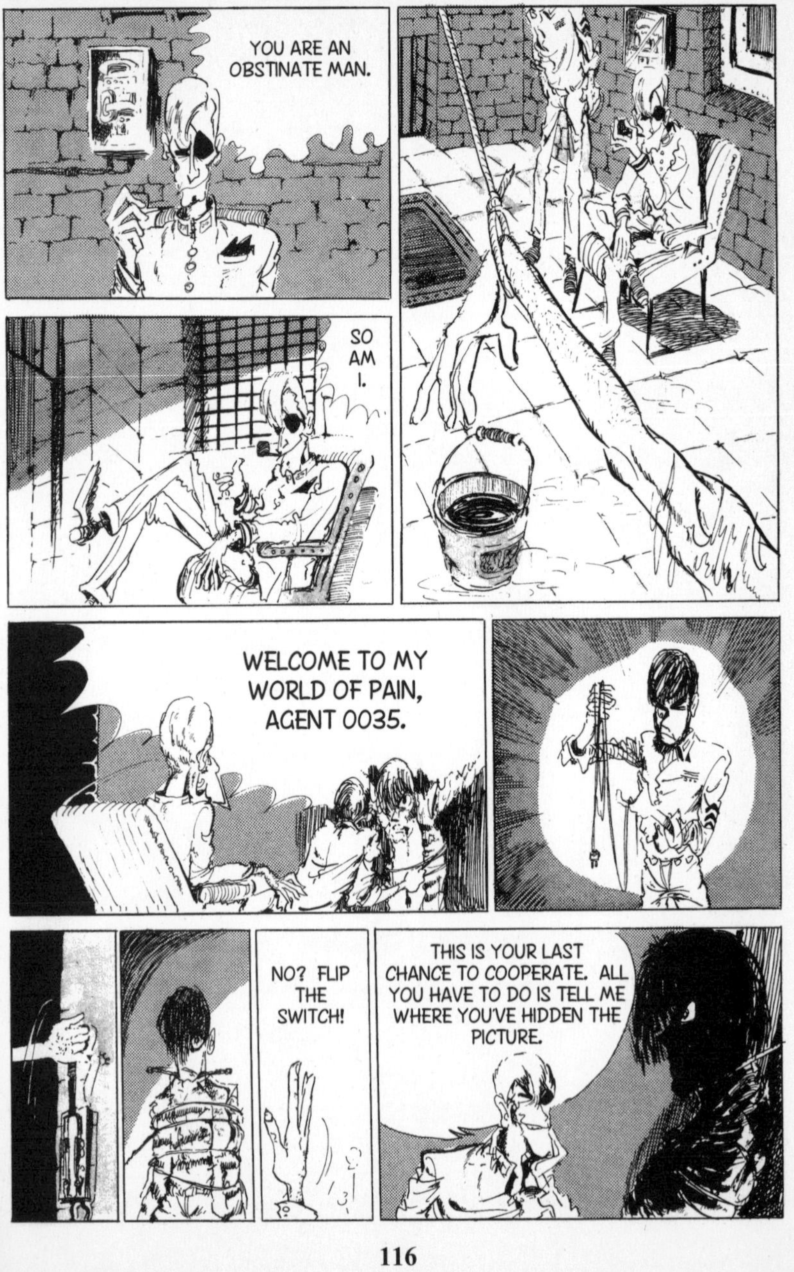
YOU ARE AN OBSTINATE MAN.
SO AM I.
WELCOME TO MY WORLD OF PAIN, AGENT 0035.
THIS IS YOUR LAST CHANCE TO COOPERATE. ALL YOU HAVE TO DO IS TELL ME WHERE YOU'VE HIDDEN THE PICTURE.
NO? FLIP THE SWITCH!

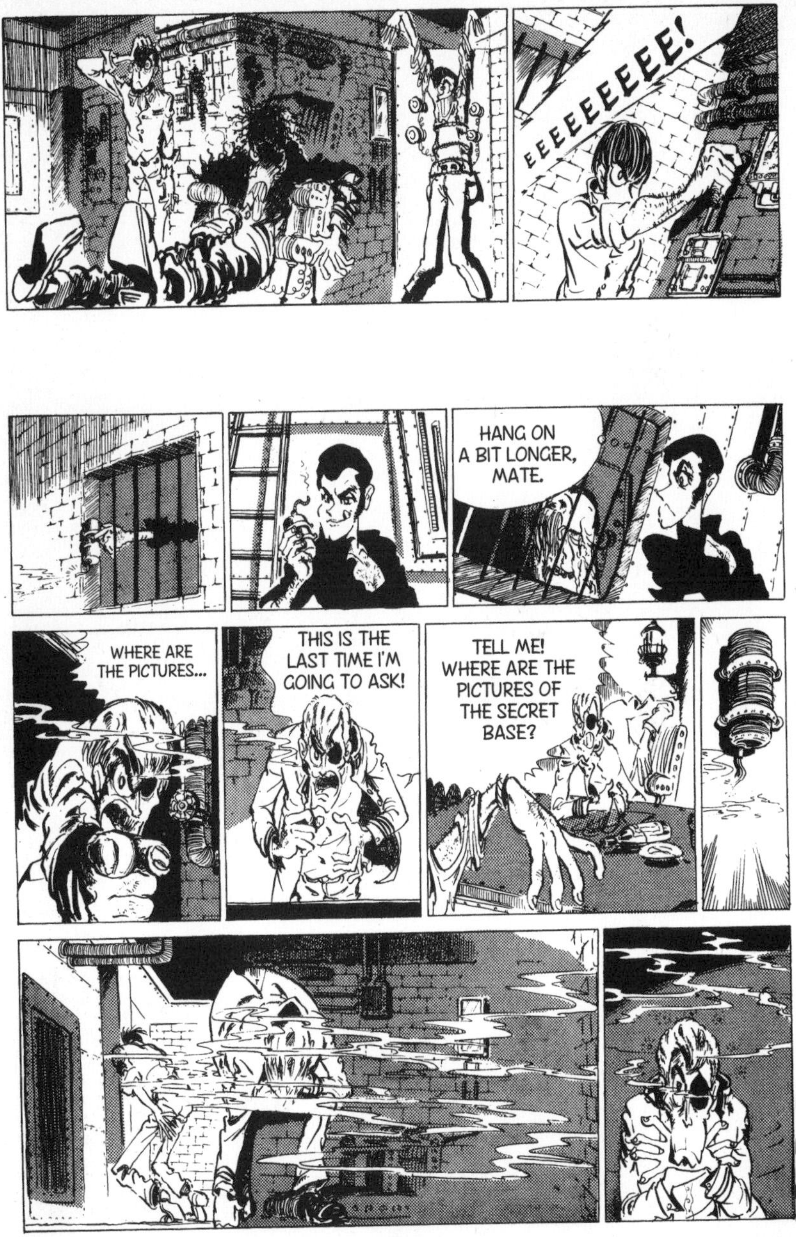
EEEEEEEEE!
HANG ON A BIT LONGER, MATE.
TELL ME! WHERE ARE THE PICTURES OF THE SECRET BASE?
THIS IS THE LAST TIME I'M GOING TO ASK!
WHERE ARE THE PICTURES...

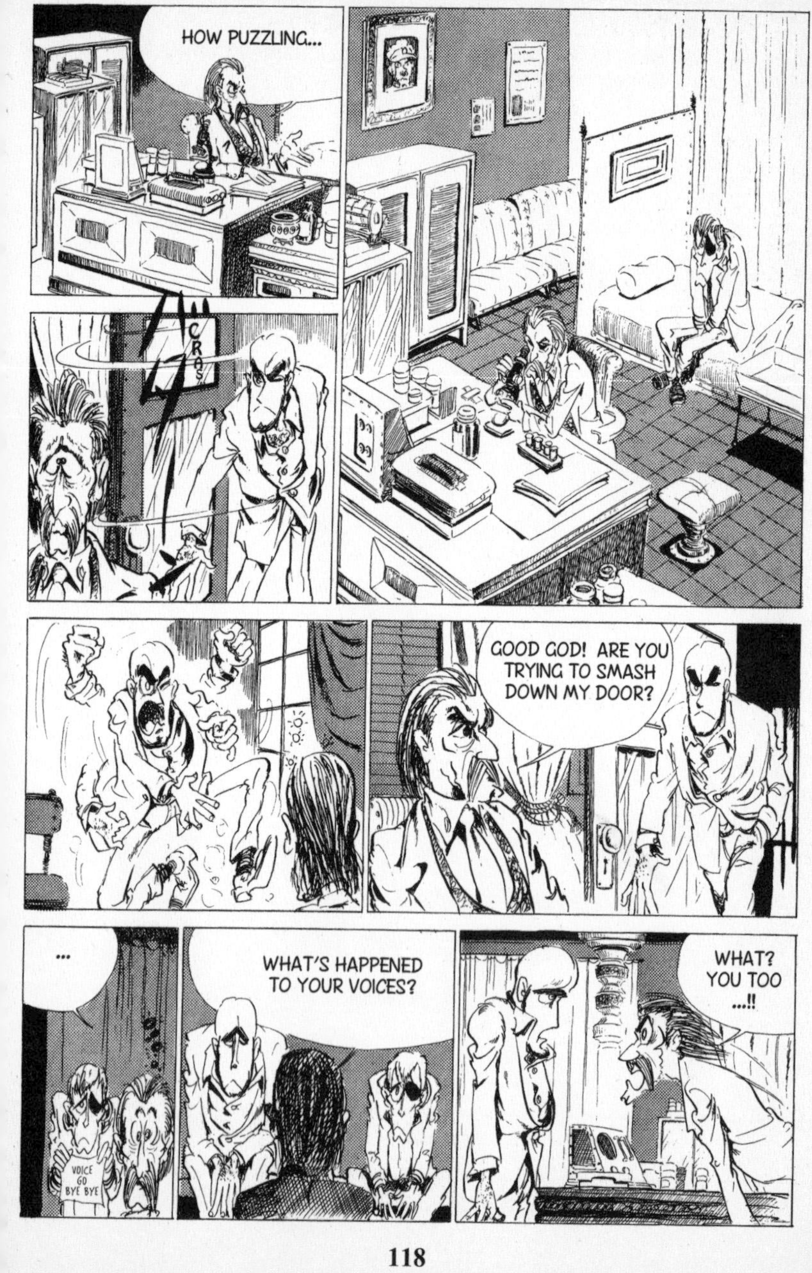
HOW PUZZLING...
CRAS
GOOD GOD! ARE YOU TRYING TO SMASH DOWN MY DOOR?
WHAT? YOU TOO ...!!
WHAT'S HAPPENED TO YOUR VOICES?
...
VOICE GO BYE BYE

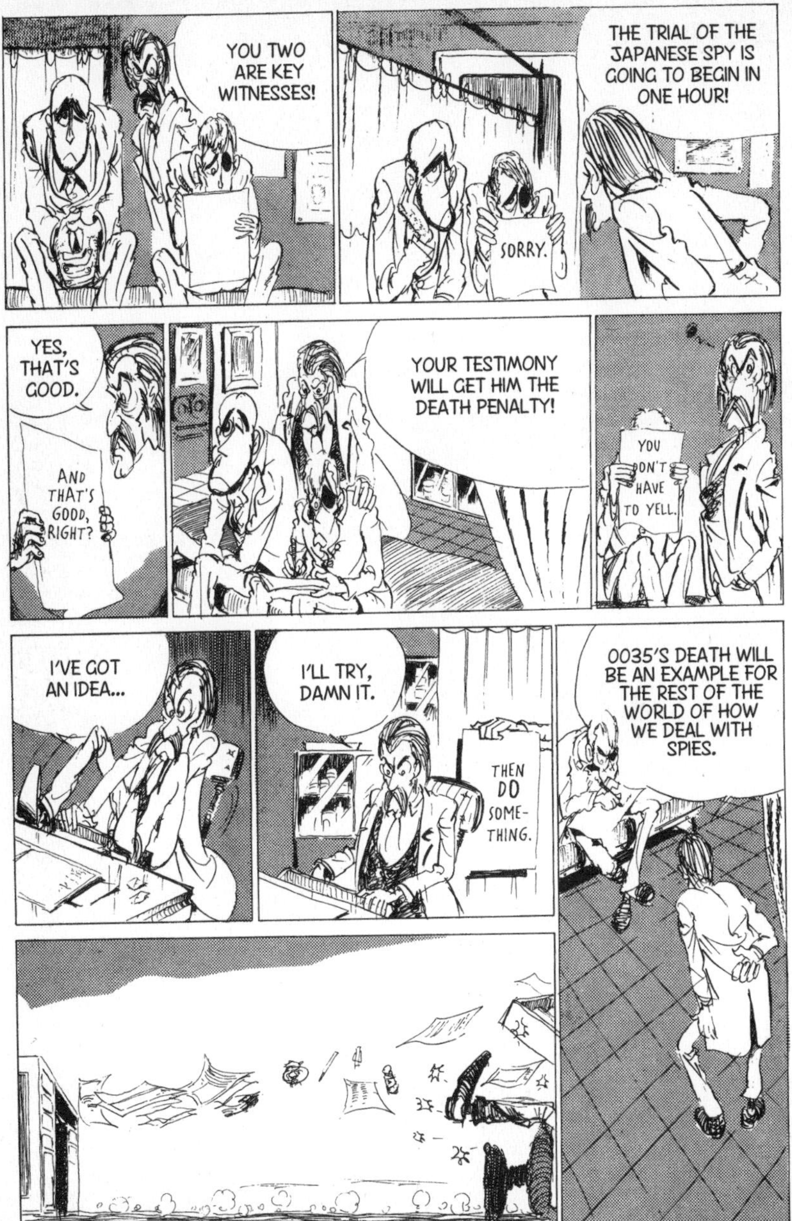
THE TRIAL OF THE JAPANESE SPY IS GOING TO BEGIN IN ONE HOUR!
SORRY.
YOU TWO ARE KEY WITNESSES!
YOU DON'T HAVE TO YELL.
YOUR TESTIMONY WILL GET HIM THE DEATH PENALTY!
YES, THAT'S GOOD.
AND THAT'S GOOD, RIGHT?
0035'S DEATH WILL BE AN EXAMPLE FOR THE REST OF THE WORLD OF HOW WE DEAL WITH SPIES.
I'LL TRY, DAMN IT.
THEN DO SOMETHING.
I'VE GOT AN IDEA...

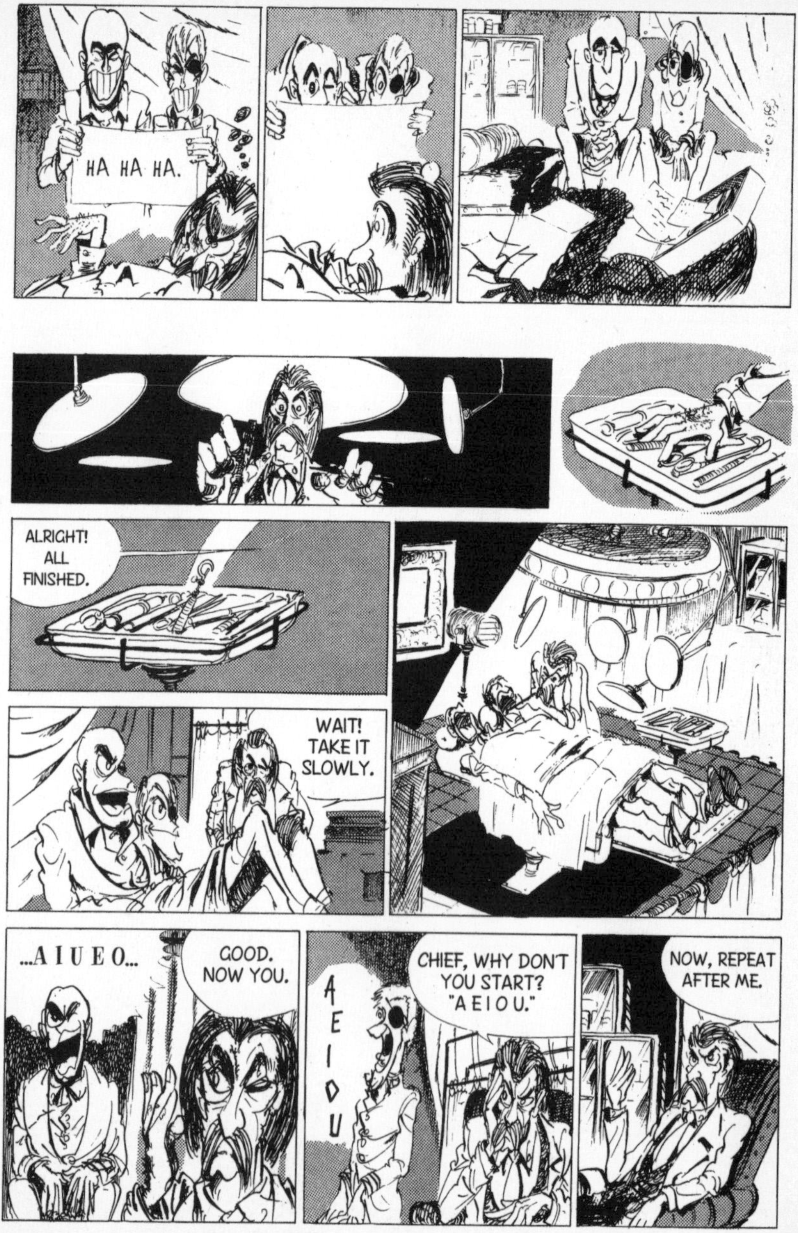
HA HA HA.
ALRIGHT! ALL FINISHED.
WAIT! TAKE IT SLOWLY.
NOW, REPEAT AFTER ME.
CHIEF, WHY DON'T YOU START? "A E I O U."
A E I O U
GOOD. NOW YOU.
...A I U E O...

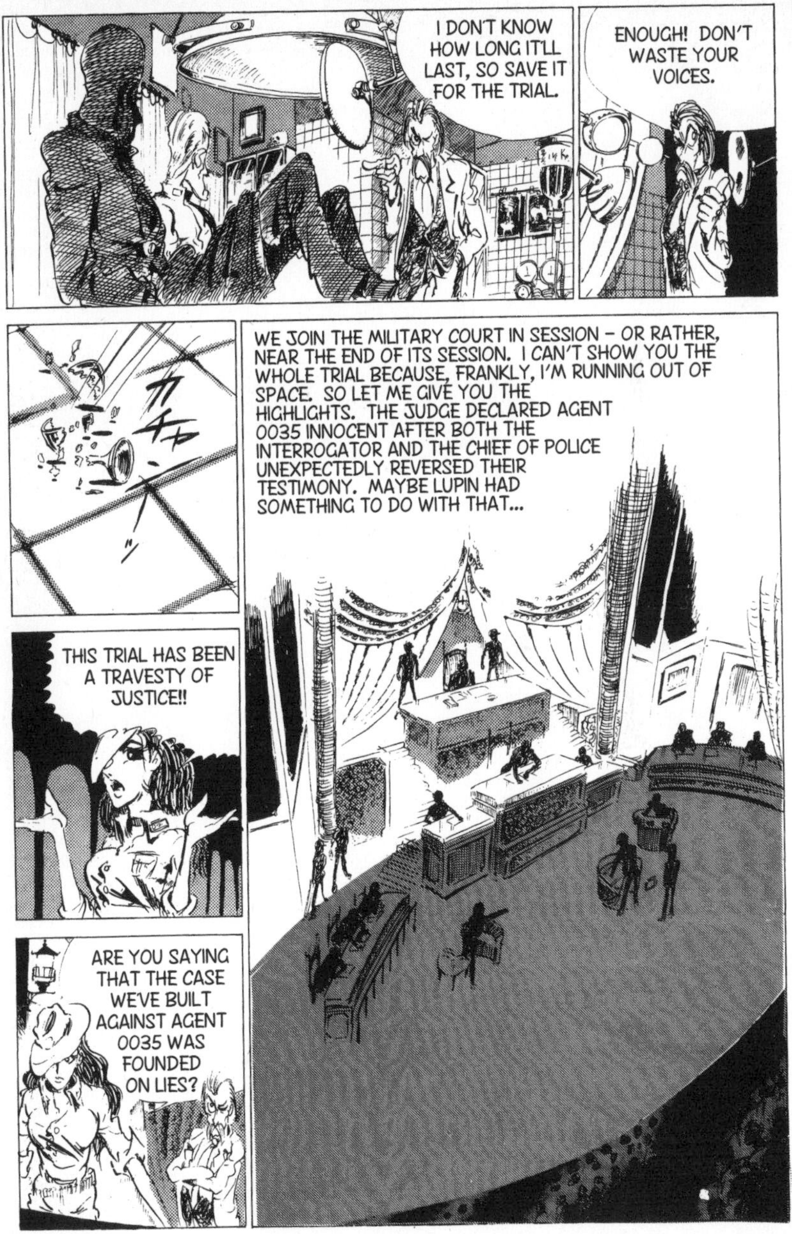
ENOUGH! DON'T WASTE YOUR VOICES.
I DON'T KNOW HOW LONG IT'LL LAST, SO SAVE IT FOR THE TRIAL.
WE JOIN THE MILITARY COURT IN SESSION – OR RATHER, NEAR THE END OF ITS SESSION. I CAN'T SHOW YOU THE WHOLE TRIAL BECAUSE, FRANKLY, I'M RUNNING OUT OF SPACE. SO LET ME GIVE YOU THE HIGHLIGHTS. THE JUDGE DECLARED AGENT 0035 INNOCENT AFTER BOTH THE INTERROGATOR AND THE CHIEF OF POLICE UNEXPECTEDLY REVERSED THEIR TESTIMONY. MAYBE LUPIN HAD SOMETHING TO DO WITH THAT...
THIS TRIAL HAS BEEN A TRAVESTY OF JUSTICE!!
ARE YOU SAYING THAT THE CASE WE'VE BUILT AGAINST AGENT 0035 WAS FOUNDED ON LIES?

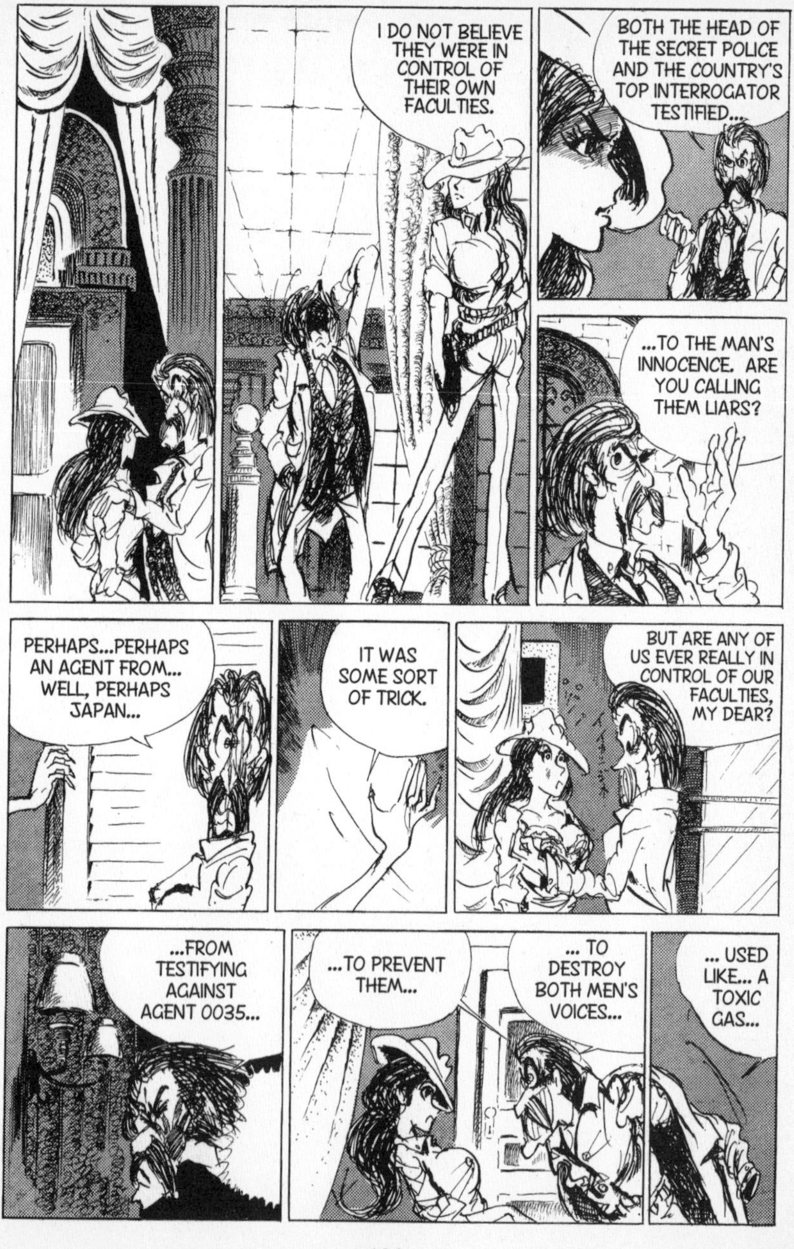
BOTH THE HEAD OF THE SECRET POLICE AND THE COUNTRY'S TOP INTERROGATOR TESTIFIED...
...TO THE MAN'S INNOCENCE. ARE YOU CALLING THEM LIARS?
I DO NOT BELIEVE THEY WERE IN CONTROL OF THEIR OWN FACULTIES.
BUT ARE ANY OF US EVER REALLY IN CONTROL OF OUR FACULTIES, MY DEAR?
IT WAS SOME SORT OF TRICK.
PERHAPS...PERHAPS AN AGENT FROM... WELL, PERHAPS JAPAN...
... USED LIKE... A TOXIC GAS...
... TO DESTROY BOTH MEN'S VOICES...
...TO PREVENT THEM...
...FROM TESTIFYING AGAINST AGENT 0035...

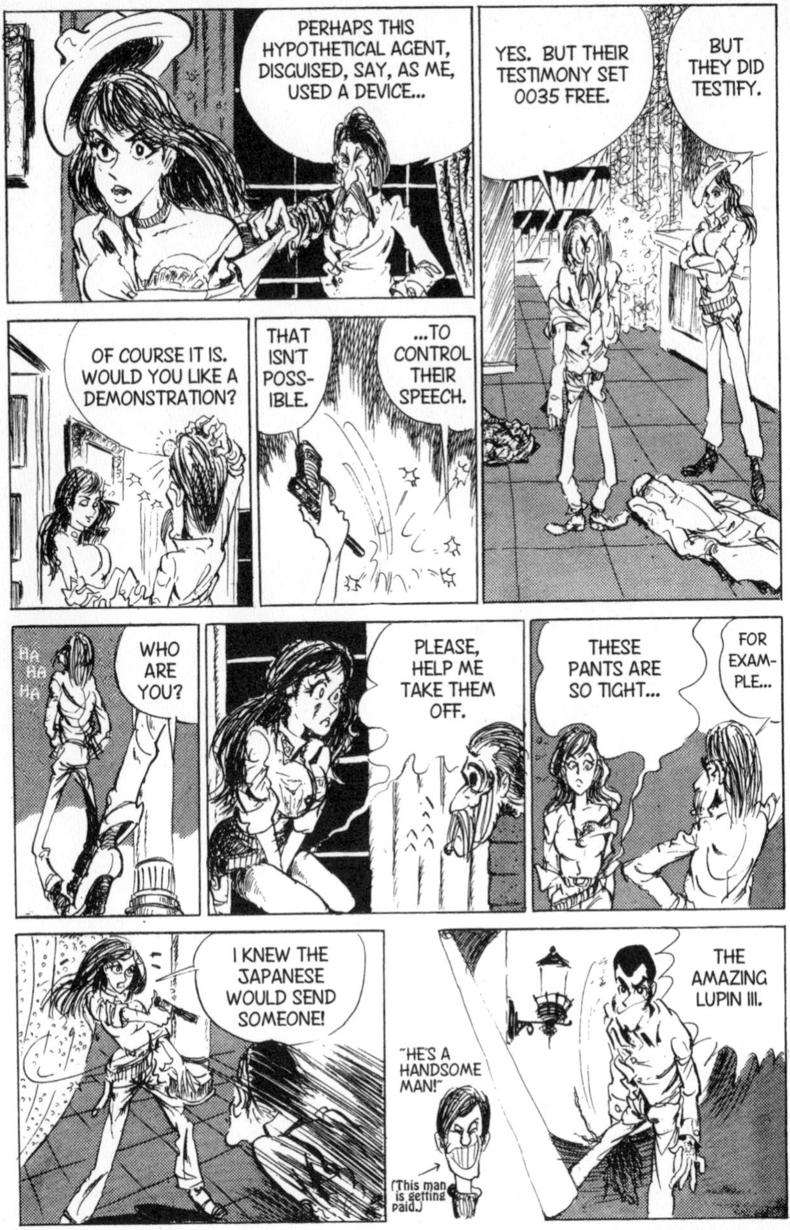
BUT THEY DID TESTIFY.
YES. BUT THEIR TESTIMONY SET 0035 FREE.
PERHAPS THIS HYPOTHETICAL AGENT, DISGUISED, SAY, AS ME, USED A DEVICE...
...TO CONTROL THEIR SPEECH.
THAT ISN'T POSS-IBLE.
OF COURSE IT IS. WOULD YOU LIKE A DEMONSTRATION?
FOR EXAM-PLE...
THESE PANTS ARE SO TIGHT...
PLEASE, HELP ME TAKE THEM OFF.
WHO ARE YOU?
HA HA HA
THE AMAZING LUPIN III.
"HE'S A HANDSOME MAN!"
(This man is getting paid.)
I KNEW THE JAPANESE WOULD SEND SOMEONE!

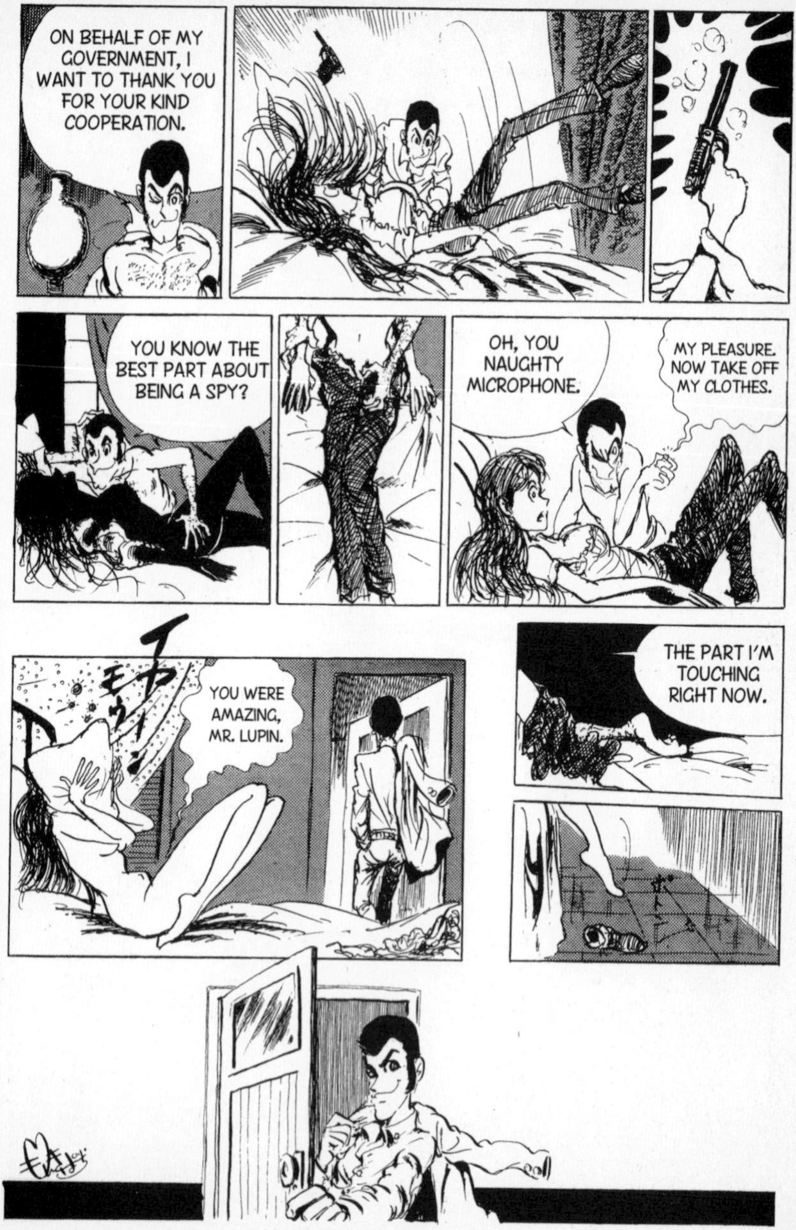
ON BEHALF OF MY GOVERNMENT, I WANT TO THANK YOU FOR YOUR KIND COOPERATION.
MY PLEASURE. NOW TAKE OFF MY CLOTHES.
OH, YOU NAUGHTY MICROPHONE.
YOU KNOW THE BEST PART ABOUT BEING A SPY?
THE PART I'M TOUCHING RIGHT NOW.
YOU WERE AMAZING, MR. LUPIN.

CHAPTER 7

"THE HAND IS QUICKER THAN THE SPY"

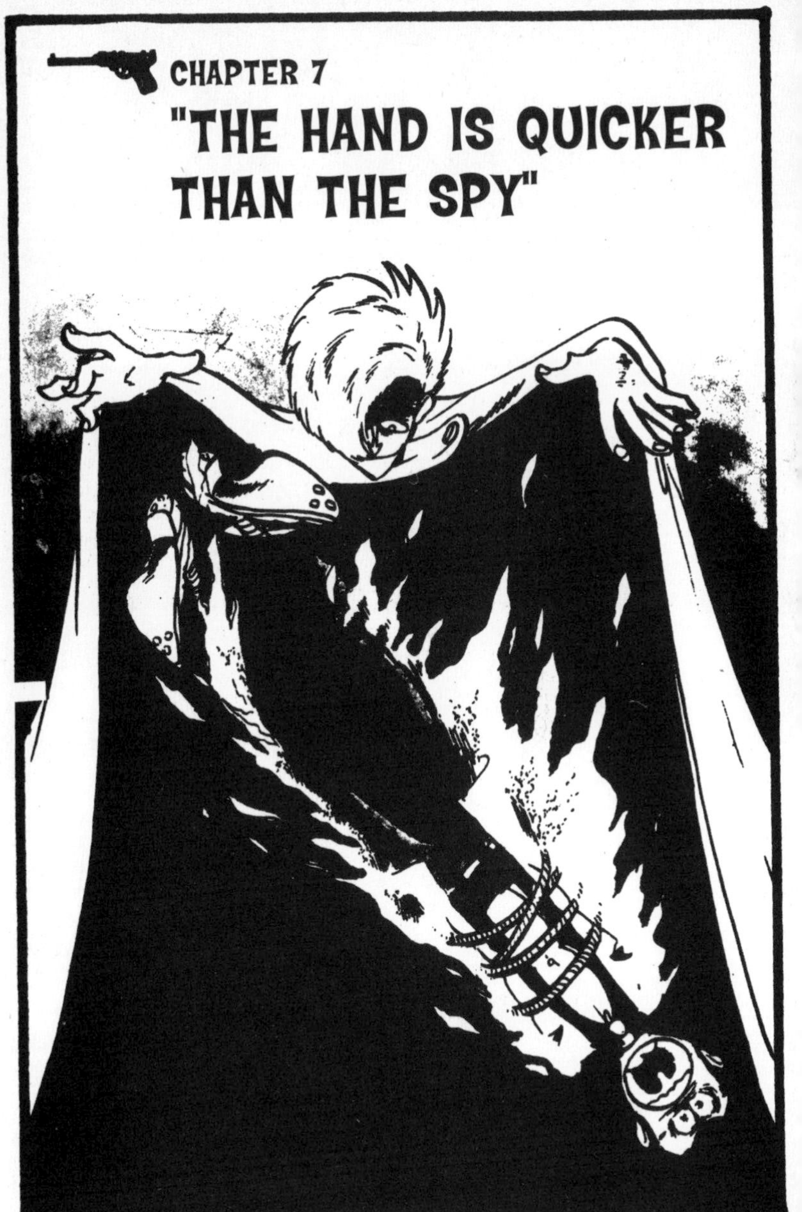

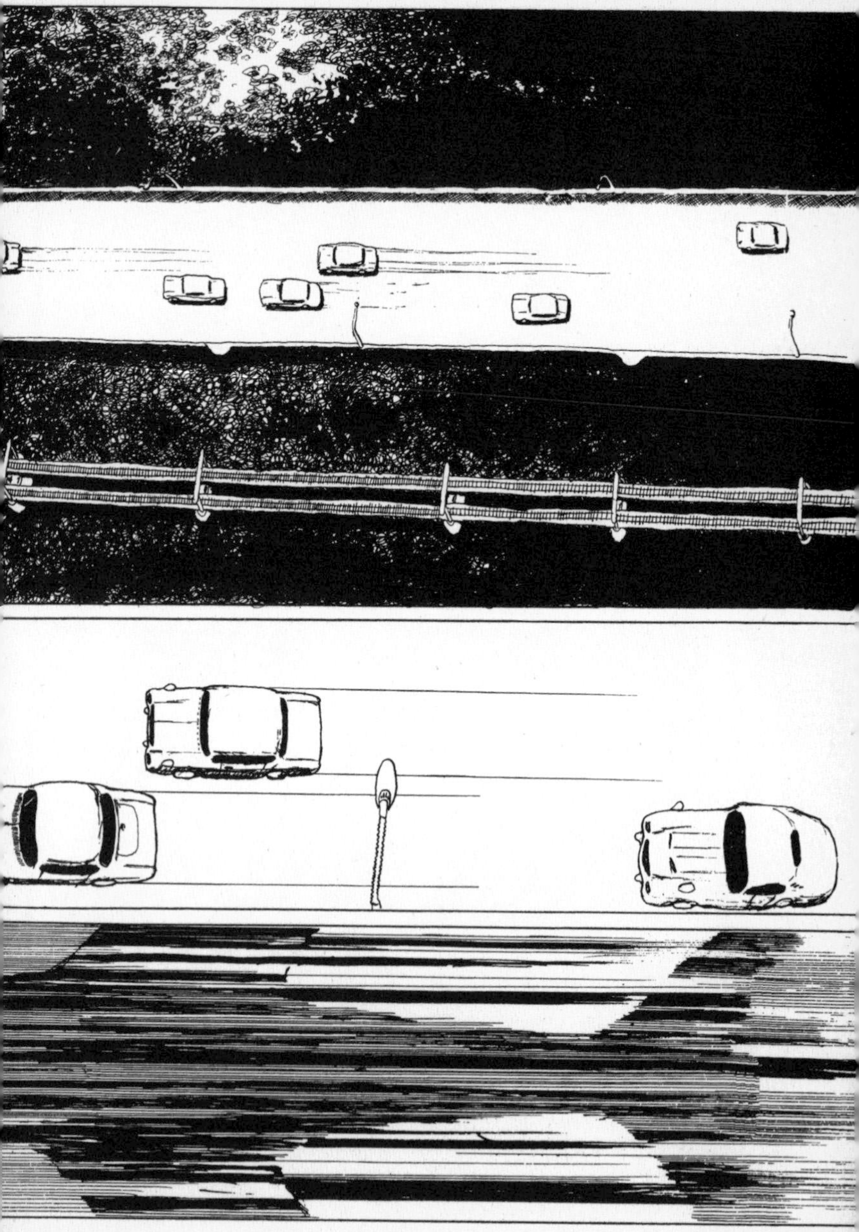

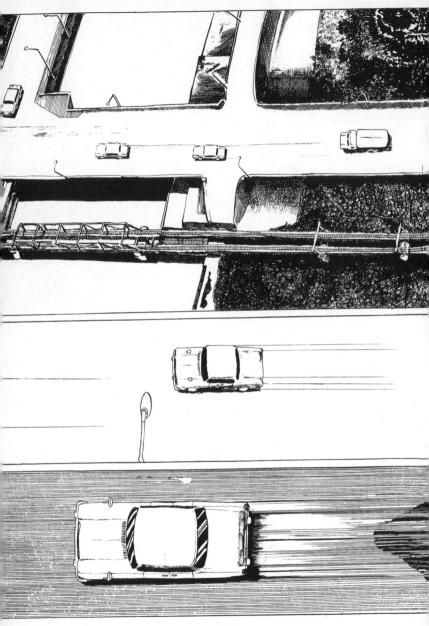

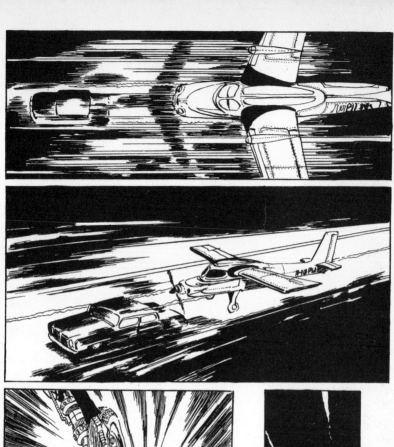

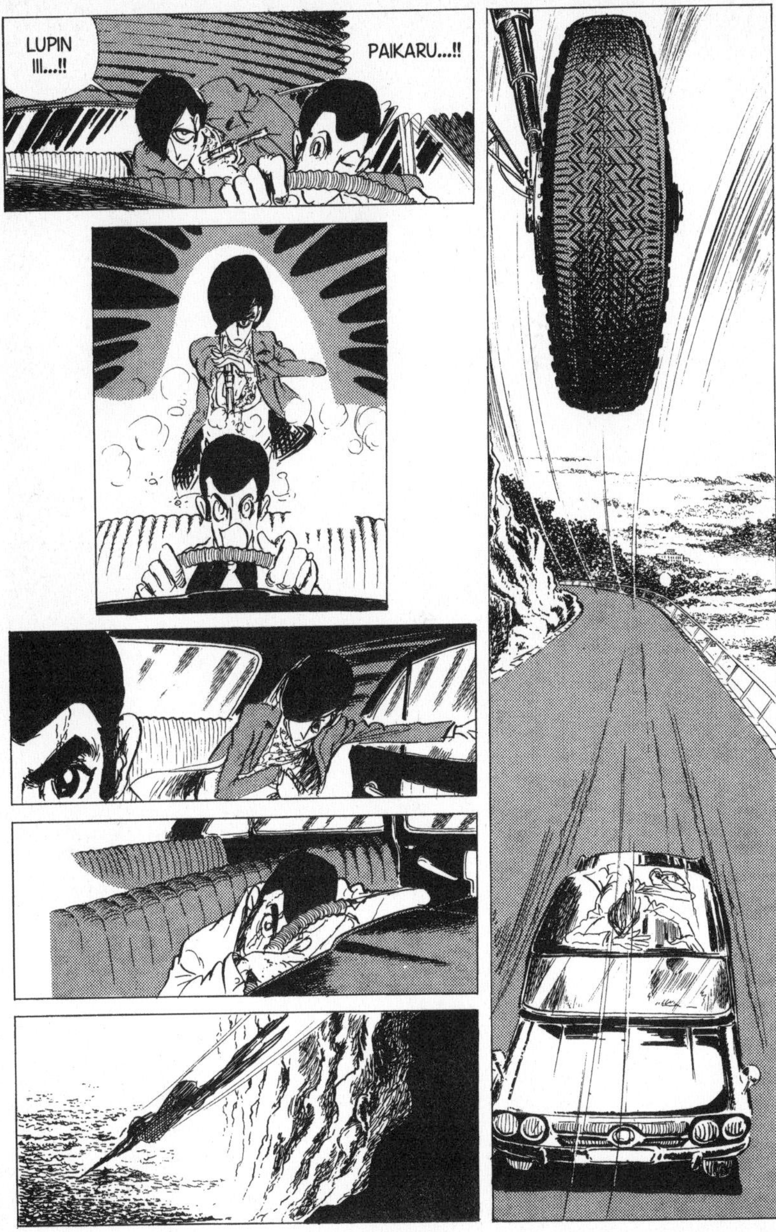
PAIKARU...!!
LUPIN III...!!

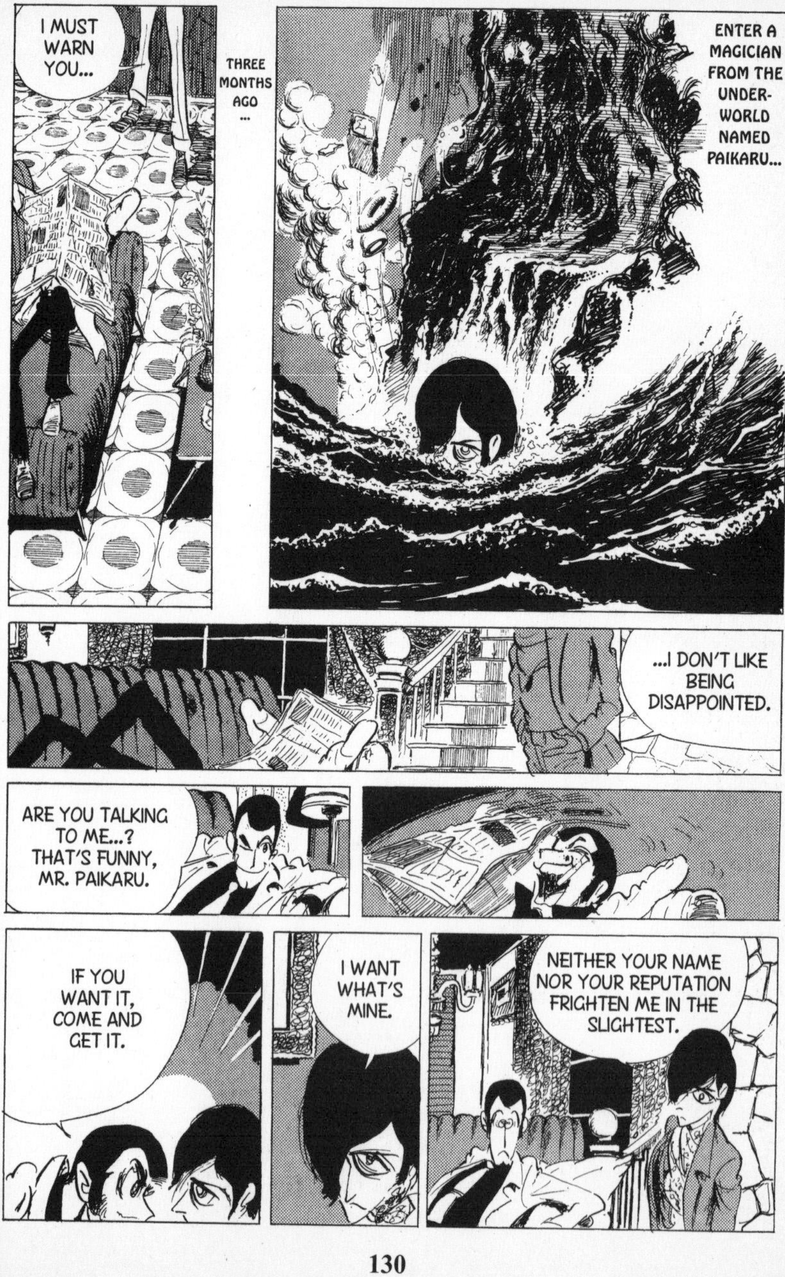
ENTER A MAGICIAN FROM THE UNDER-WORLD NAMED PAIKARU...
THREE MONTHS AGO ...
I MUST WARN YOU...
...I DON'T LIKE BEING DISAPPOINTED.
ARE YOU TALKING TO ME...? THAT'S FUNNY, MR. PAIKARU.
NEITHER YOUR NAME NOR YOUR REPUTATION FRIGHTEN ME IN THE SLIGHTEST.
I WANT WHAT'S MINE.
IF YOU WANT IT, COME AND GET IT.

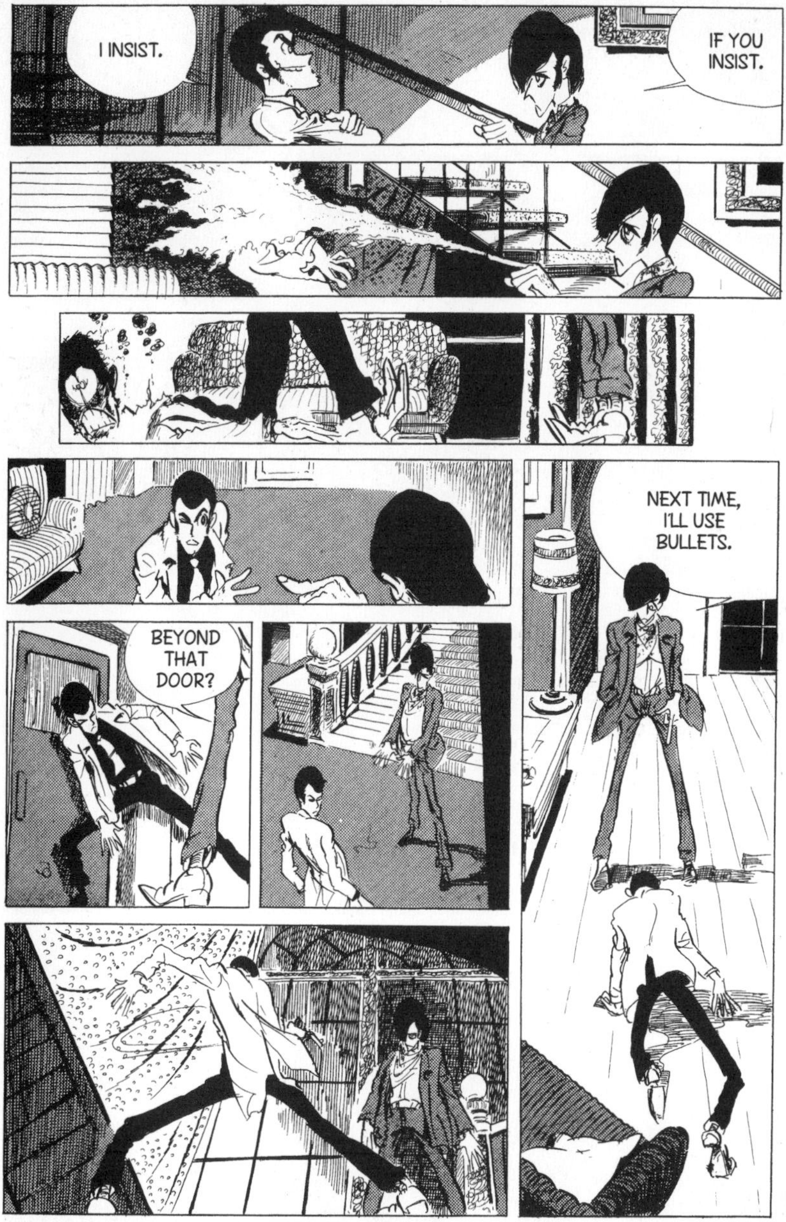
IF YOU INSIST.
I INSIST.
NEXT TIME, I'LL USE BULLETS.
BEYOND THAT DOOR?

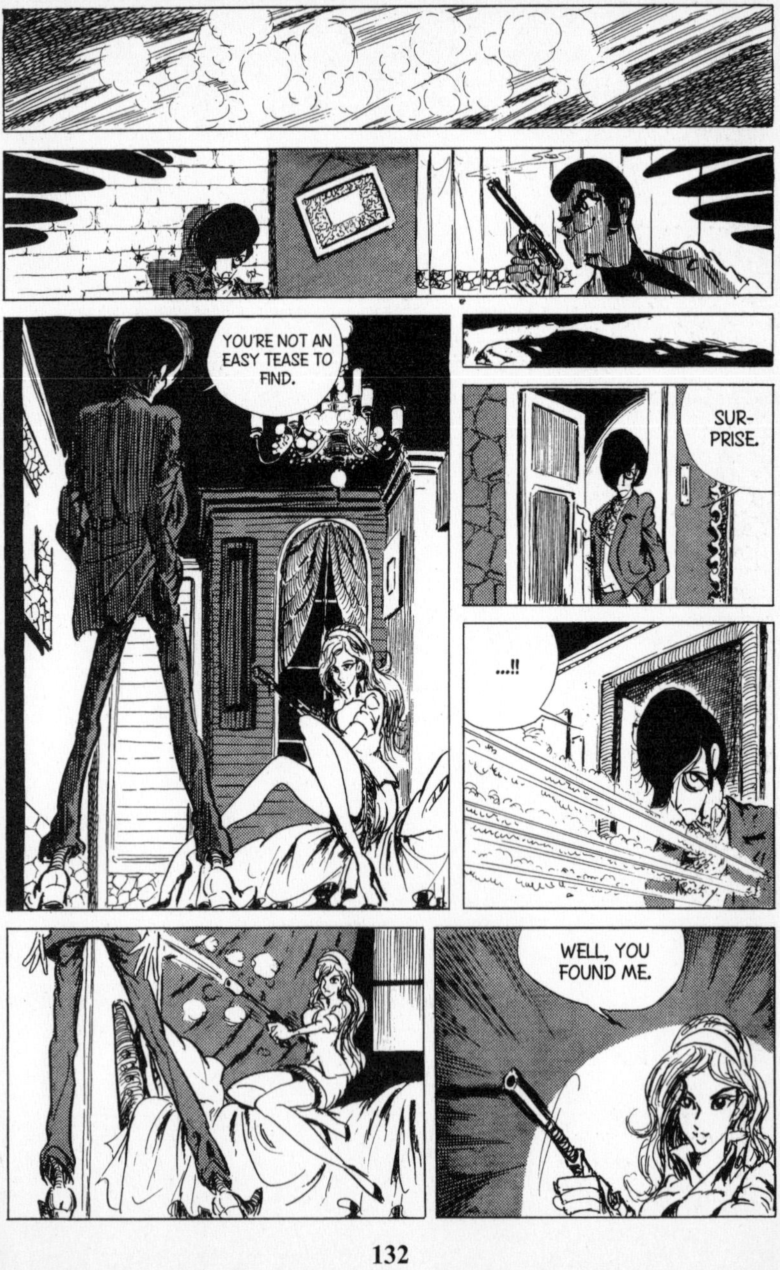
SUR-
PRISE.
...!!
YOU'RE NOT AN EASY TEASE TO FIND.
WELL, YOU FOUND ME.

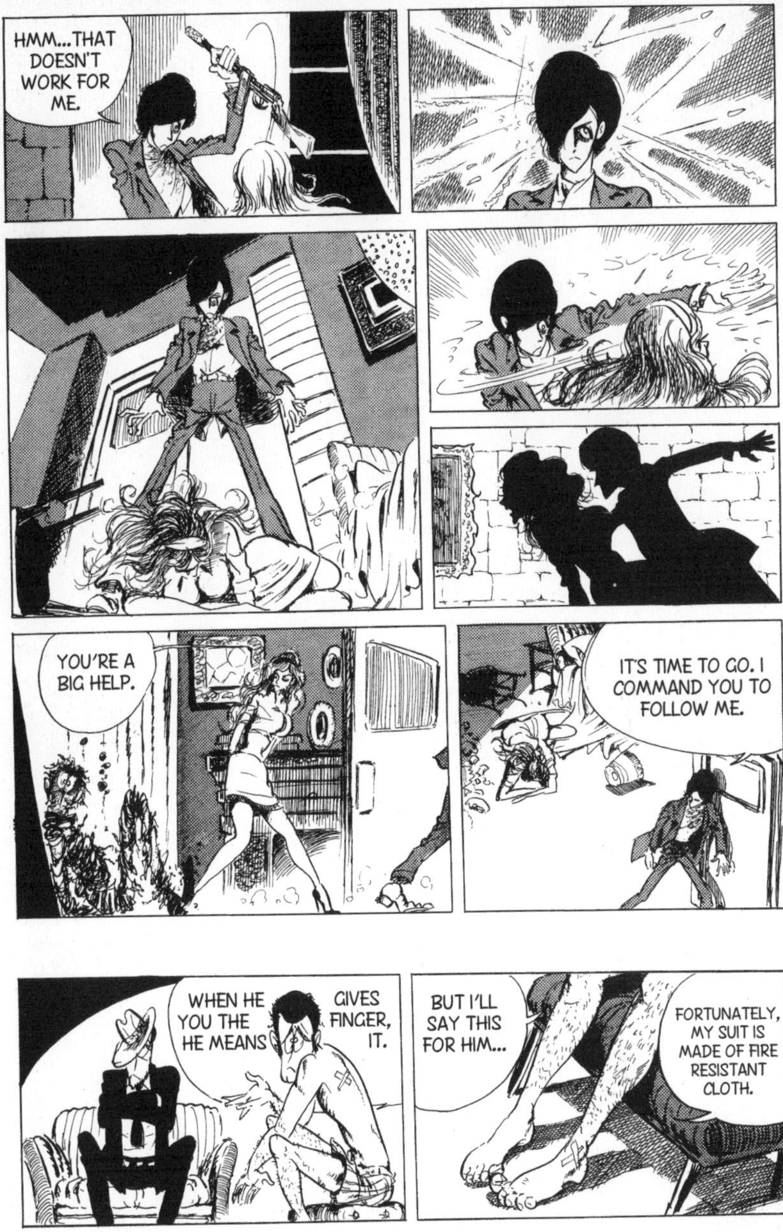
HMM...THAT DOESN'T WORK FOR ME.
IT'S TIME TO GO. I COMMAND YOU TO FOLLOW ME.
YOU'RE A BIG HELP.
FORTUNATELY, MY SUIT IS MADE OF FIRE RESISTANT CLOTH.
BUT I'LL SAY THIS FOR HIM...
WHEN HE GIVES YOU THE FINGER, HE MEANS IT.

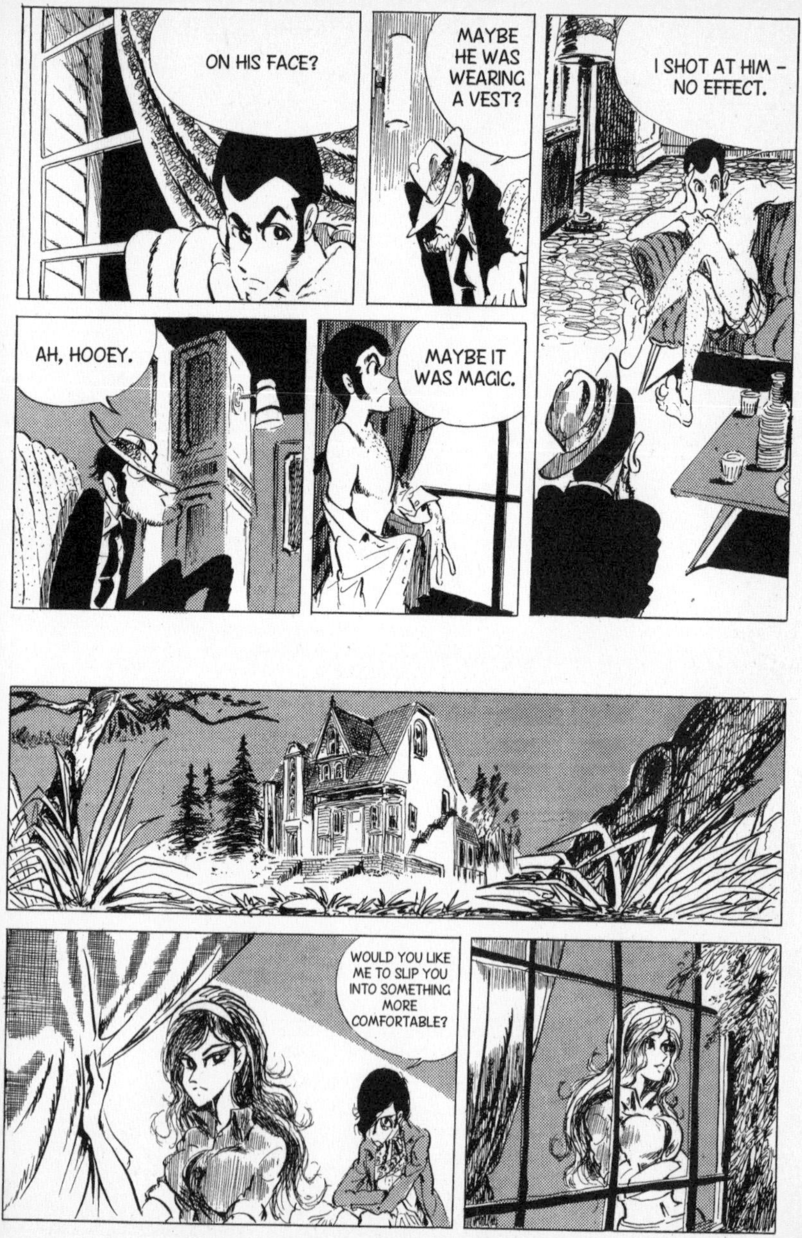
I SHOT AT HIM - NO EFFECT.
MAYBE HE WAS WEARING A VEST?
ON HIS FACE?
MAYBE IT WAS MAGIC.
AH, HOOEY.
WOULD YOU LIKE ME TO SLIP YOU INTO SOMETHING MORE COMFORTABLE?

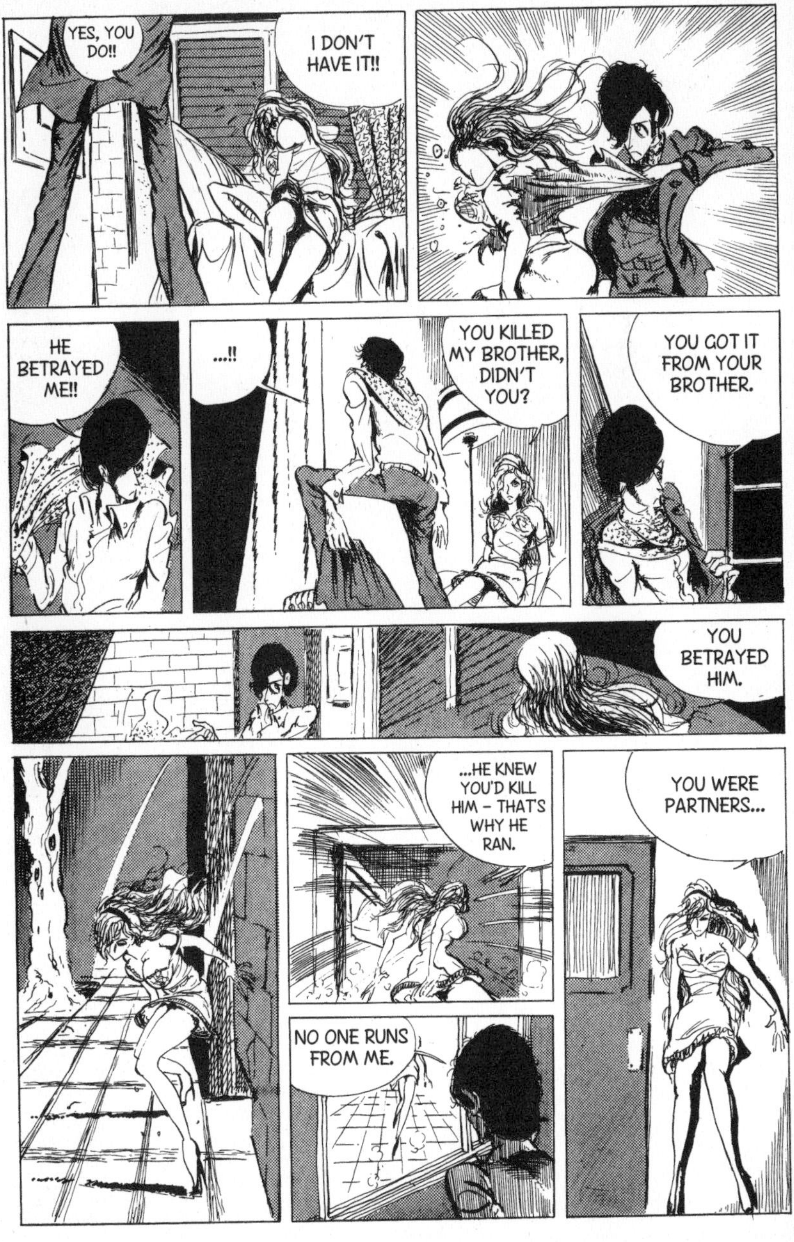
I DON'T HAVE IT!!
YES, YOU DO!!
YOU GOT IT FROM YOUR BROTHER.
YOU KILLED MY BROTHER, DIDN'T YOU?
...!!
HE BETRAYED ME!!
YOU BETRAYED HIM.
YOU WERE PARTNERS...
...HE KNEW YOU'D KILL HIM – THAT'S WHY HE RAN.
NO ONE RUNS FROM ME.

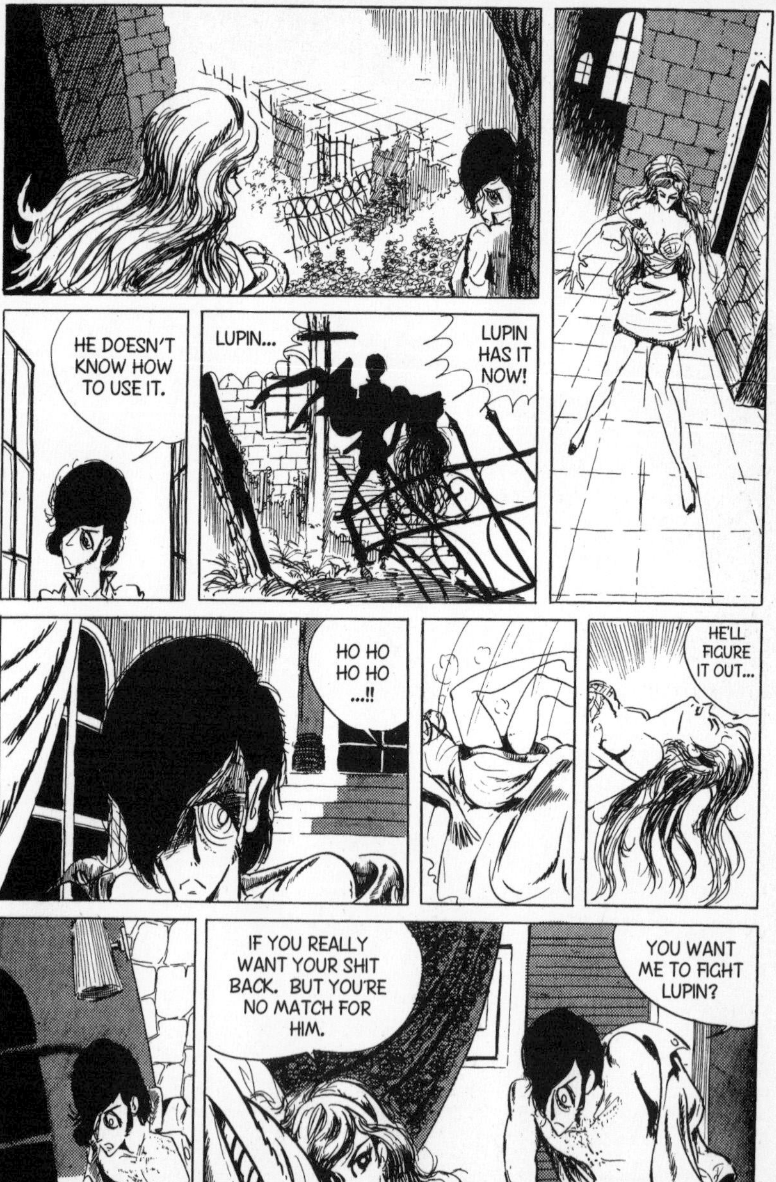
LUPIN HAS IT NOW!
LUPIN...
HE DOESN'T KNOW HOW TO USE IT.
HE'LL FIGURE IT OUT...
HO HO HO HO ...!!
YOU WANT ME TO FIGHT LUPIN?
IF YOU REALLY WANT YOUR SHIT BACK. BUT YOU'RE NO MATCH FOR HIM.

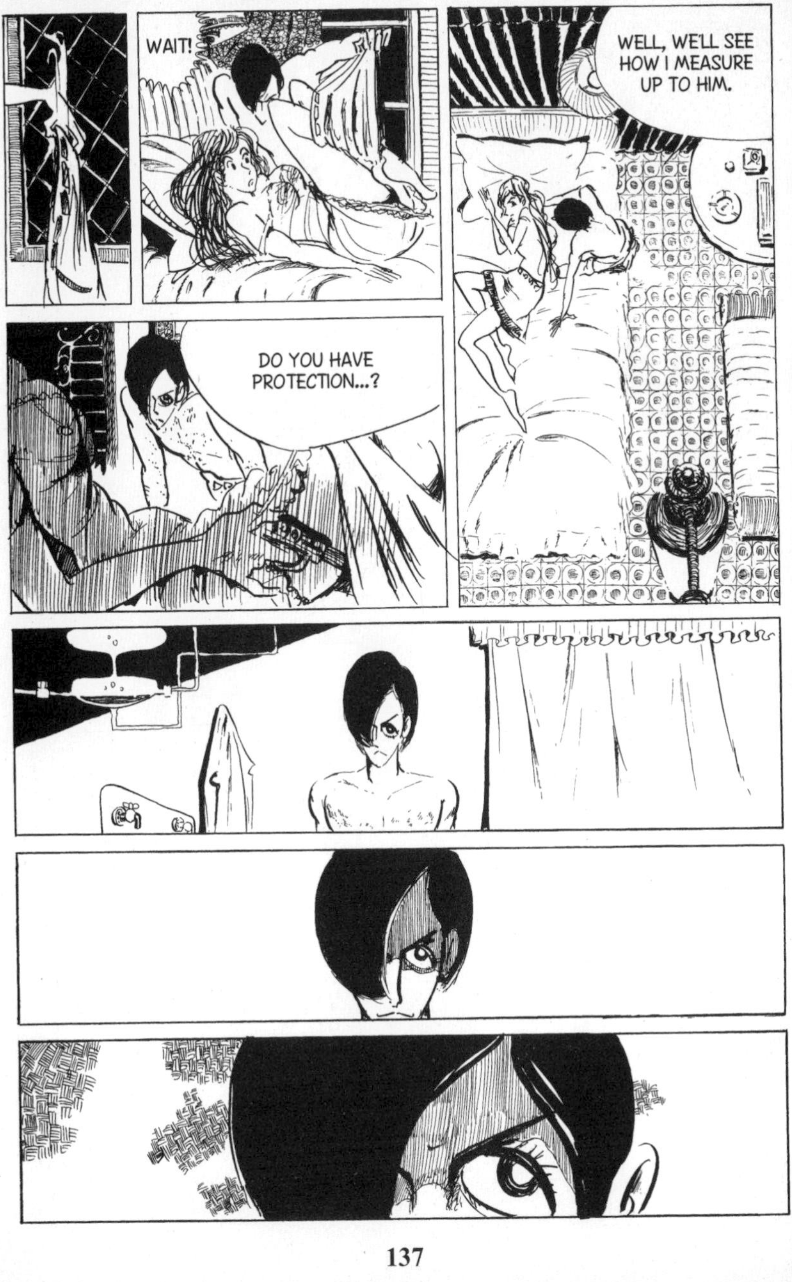
WELL, WE'LL SEE HOW I MEASURE UP TO HIM.
WAIT!
DO YOU HAVE PROTECTION...?

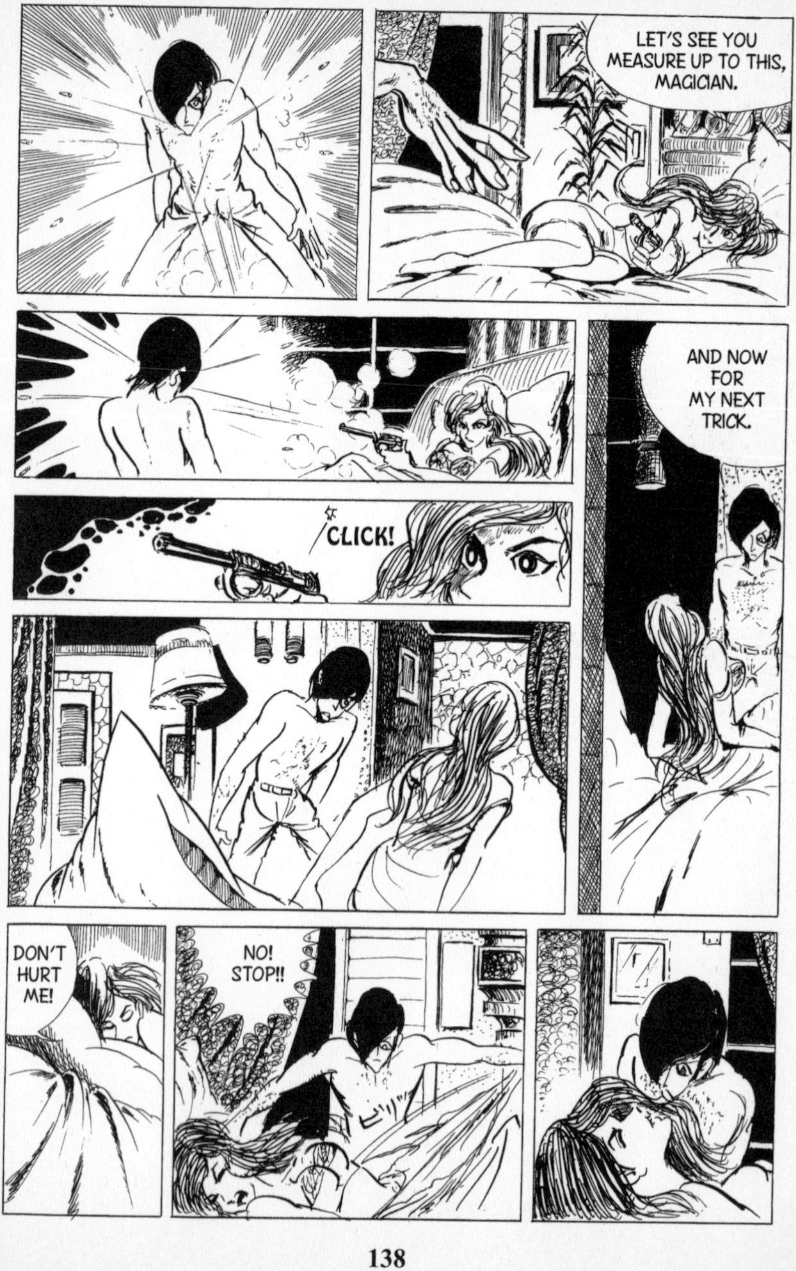
LET'S SEE YOU MEASURE UP TO THIS, MAGICIAN.
AND NOW FOR MY NEXT TRICK.
CLICK!
NO! STOP!!
DON'T HURT ME!

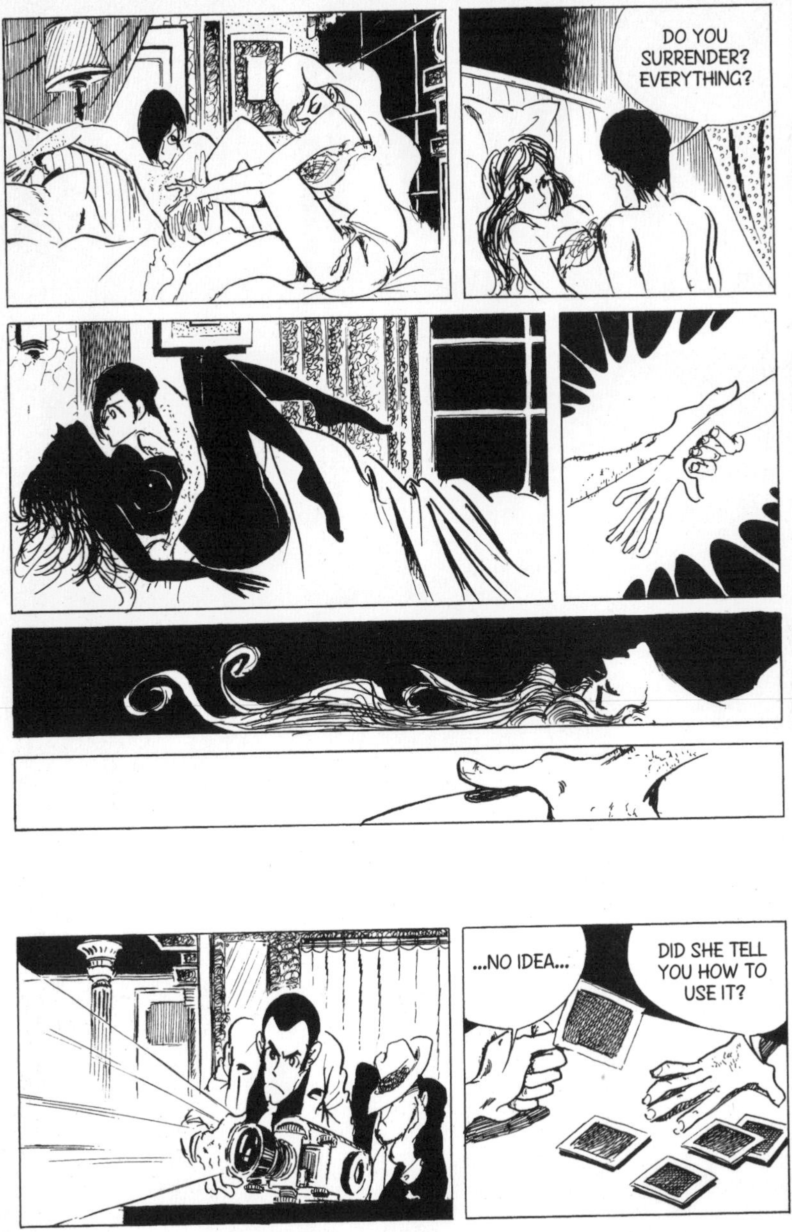
DO YOU SURRENDER? EVERYTHING?
DID SHE TELL YOU HOW TO USE IT?
...NO IDEA...

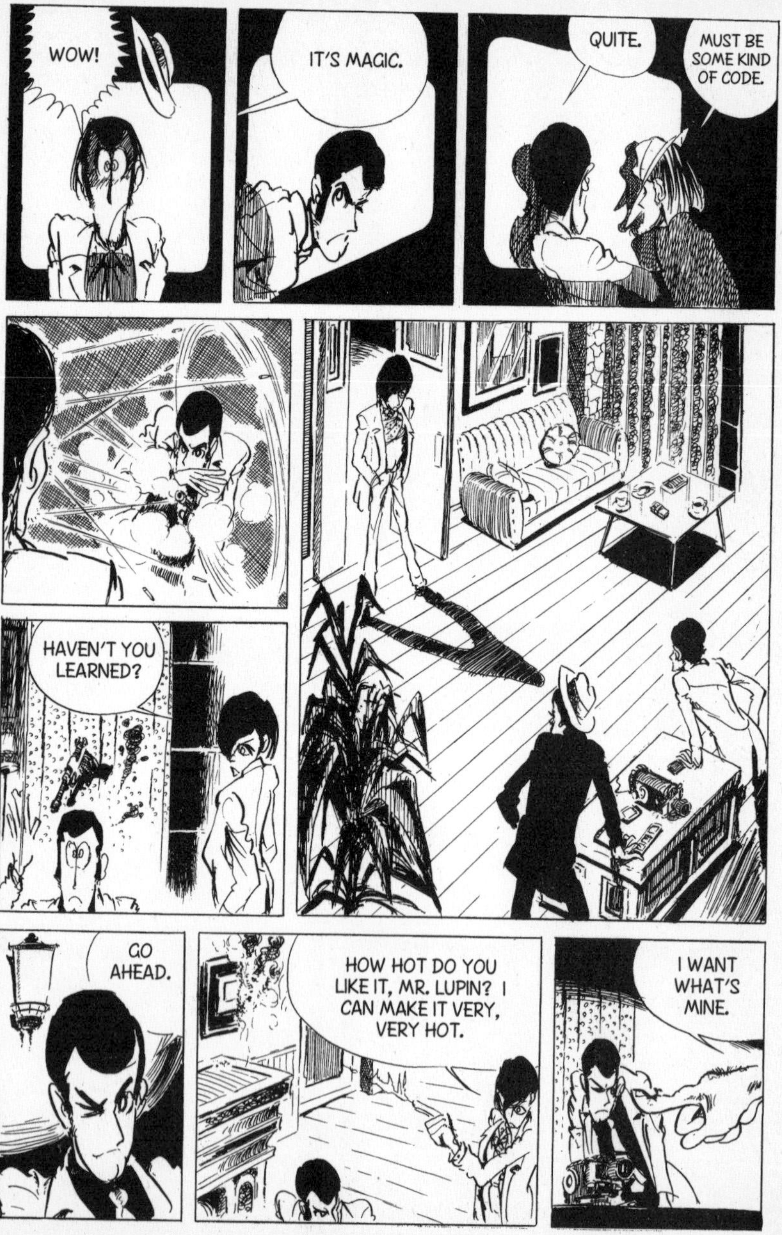
MUST BE SOME KIND OF CODE.
QUITE.
IT'S MAGIC.
WOW!
HAVEN'T YOU LEARNED?
I WANT WHAT'S MINE.
HOW HOT DO YOU LIKE IT, MR. LUPIN? I CAN MAKE IT VERY, VERY HOT.
GO AHEAD.

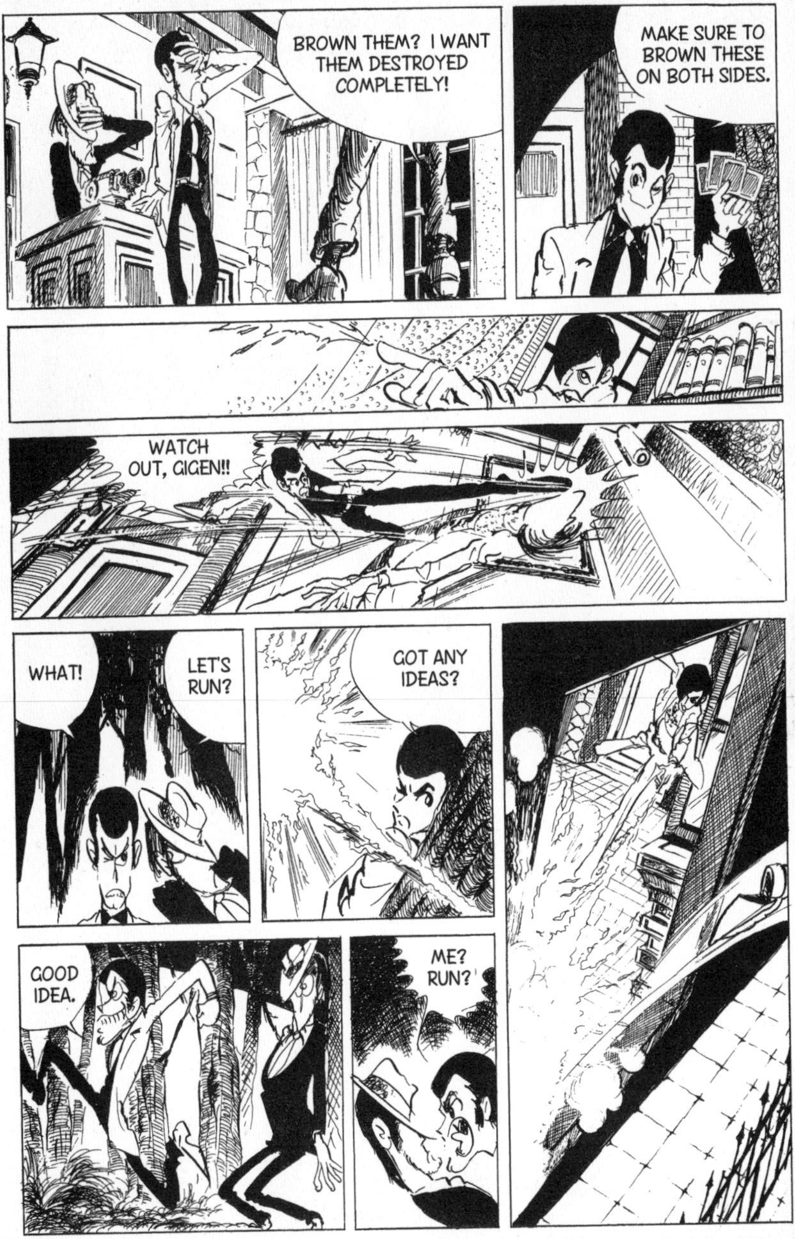
MAKE SURE TO BROWN THESE ON BOTH SIDES.
BROWN THEM? I WANT THEM DESTROYED COMPLETELY!
WATCH OUT, GIGEN!!
GOT ANY IDEAS?
LET'S RUN?
WHAT!
ME? RUN?
GOOD IDEA.

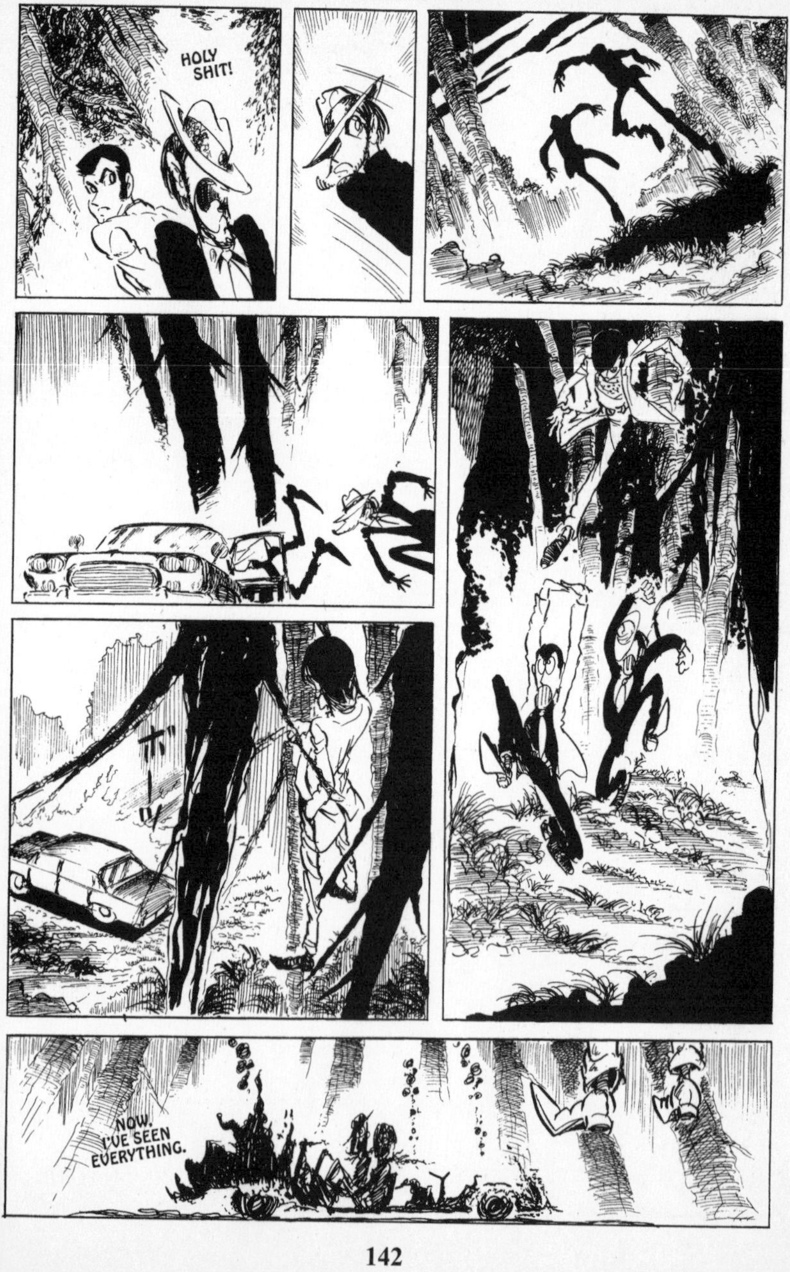
HOLY SHIT!
NOW. I'VE SEEN EVERYTHING.

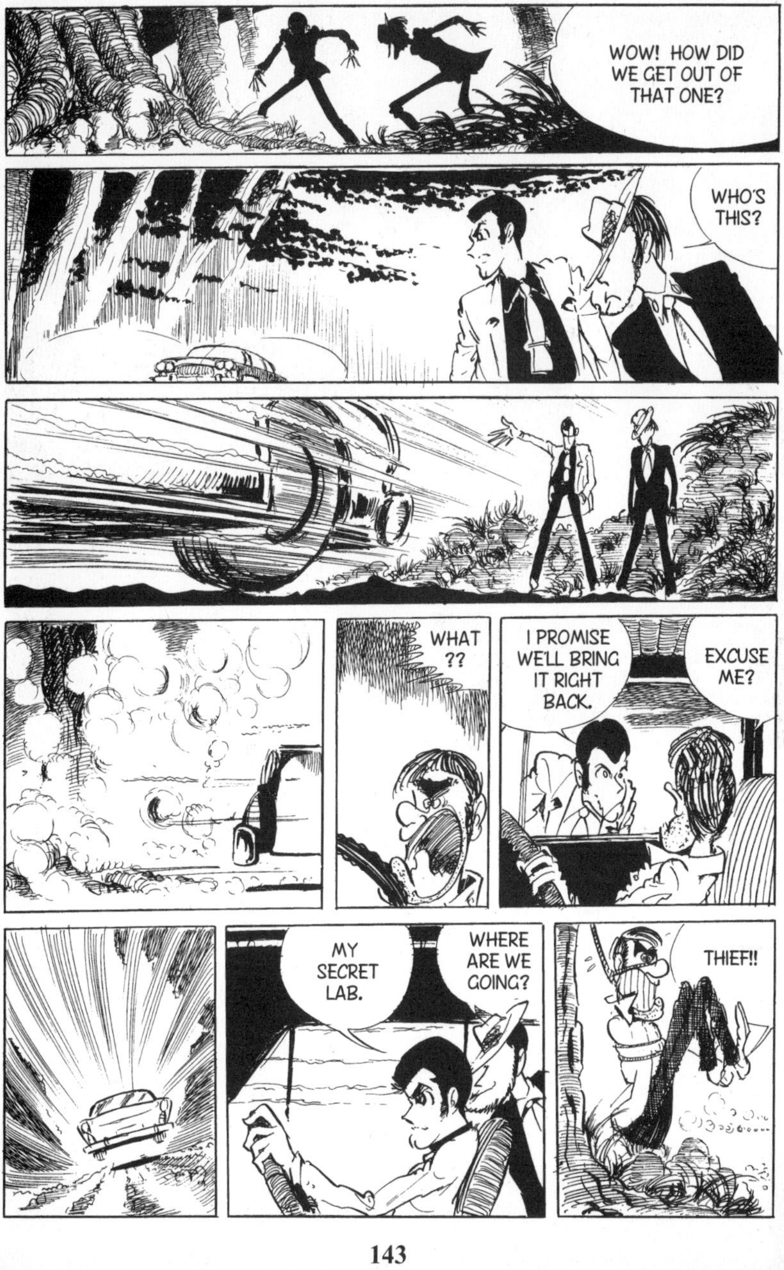
WOW! HOW DID WE GET OUT OF THAT ONE?
WHO'S THIS?
EXCUSE ME?
I PROMISE WE'LL BRING IT RIGHT BACK.
WHAT ??
THIEF!!
WHERE ARE WE GOING?
MY SECRET LAB.

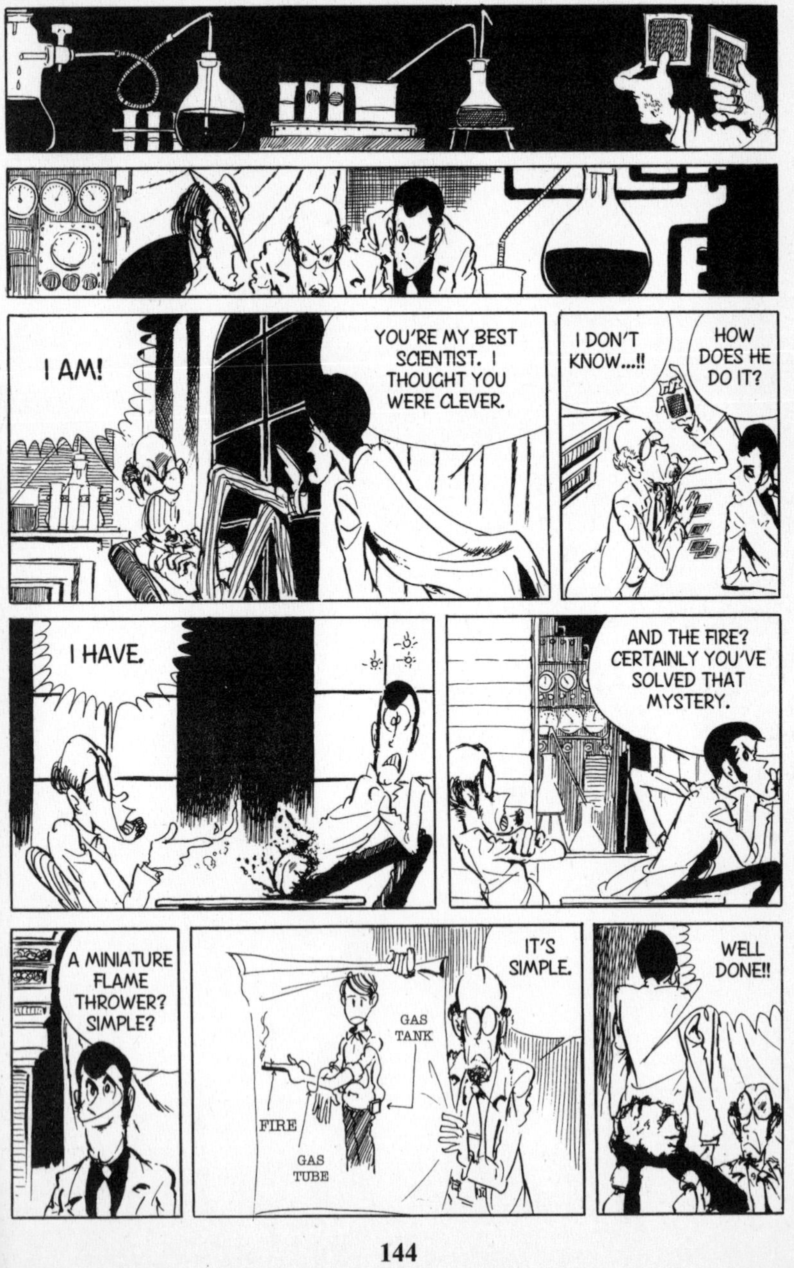
HOW DOES HE DO IT?
I DON'T KNOW...!!
YOU'RE MY BEST SCIENTIST. I THOUGHT YOU WERE CLEVER.
I AM!
AND THE FIRE? CERTAINLY YOU'VE SOLVED THAT MYSTERY.
I HAVE.
WELL DONE!!
IT'S SIMPLE.
GAS TANK
FIRE
GAS TUBE
A MINIATURE FLAME THROWER? SIMPLE?

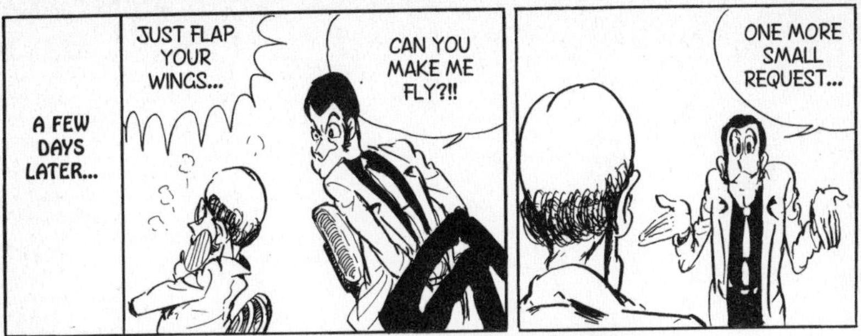
ONE MORE SMALL REQUEST...
CAN YOU MAKE ME FLY?!!
JUST FLAP YOUR WINGS...
A FEW DAYS LATER...

IN THESE FEW PANELS, THE MOST PRIVATE ASPECT OF THE FEMALE FORM HAS BEEN OBSCURED SO AS TO BE SENSITIVE TO DELICATE READERS. HOWEVER, FOR THOSE READERS WHO AREN'T AS SENSITIVE, PLEASE ALLOW YOUR IMAGINATION TO RUN WILD.

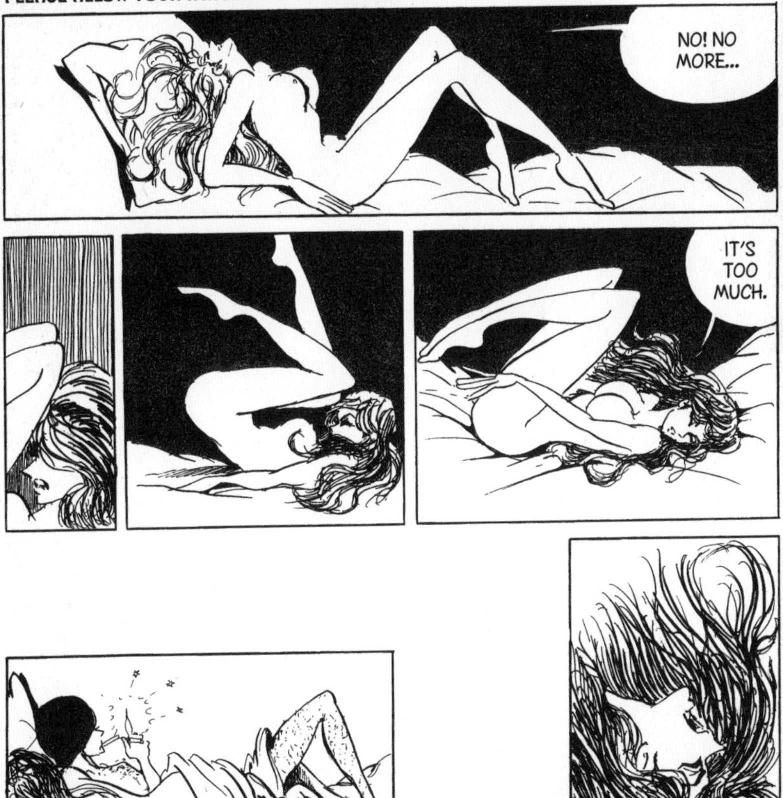
NO! NO MORE...
IT'S TOO MUCH.

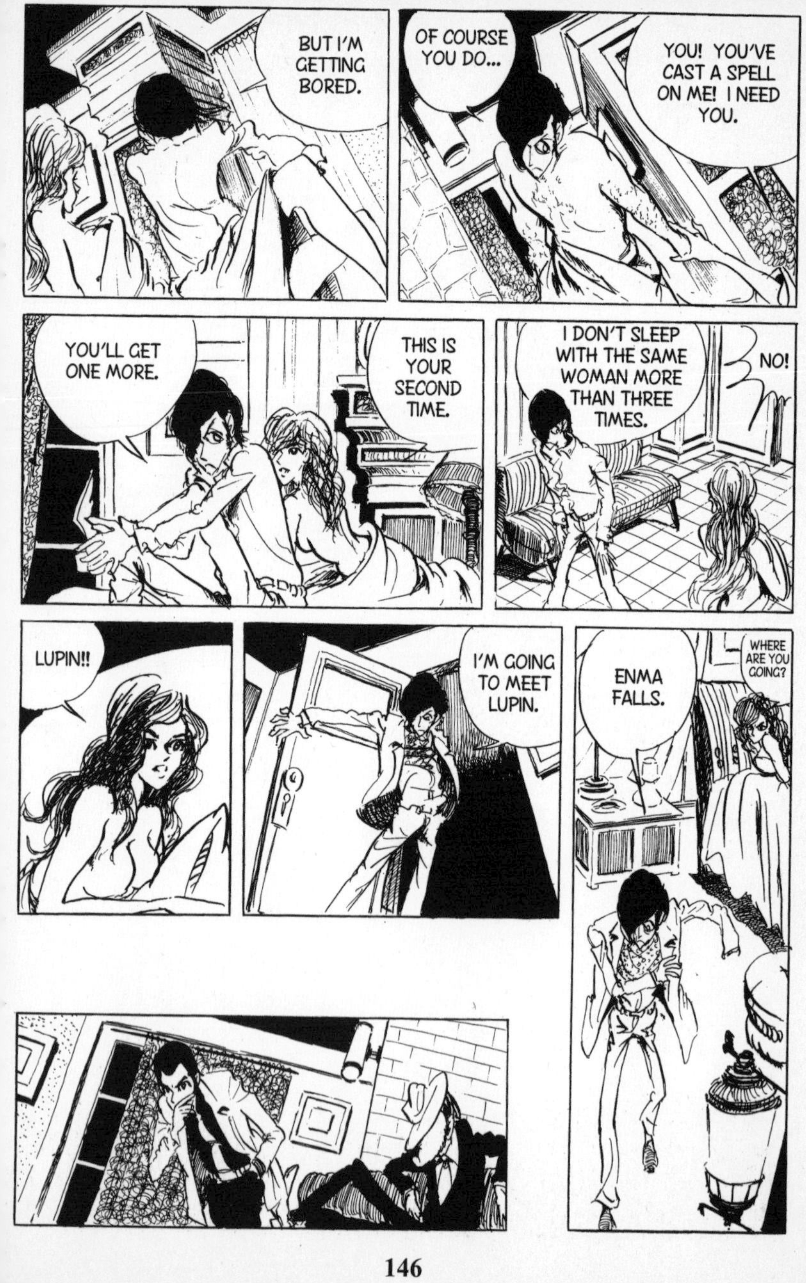
YOU! YOU'VE CAST A SPELL ON ME! I NEED YOU.
OF COURSE YOU DO...
BUT I'M GETTING BORED.
NO!
I DON'T SLEEP WITH THE SAME WOMAN MORE THAN THREE TIMES.
THIS IS YOUR SECOND TIME.
YOU'LL GET ONE MORE.
WHERE ARE YOU GOING?
ENMA FALLS.
I'M GOING TO MEET LUPIN.
LUPIN!!

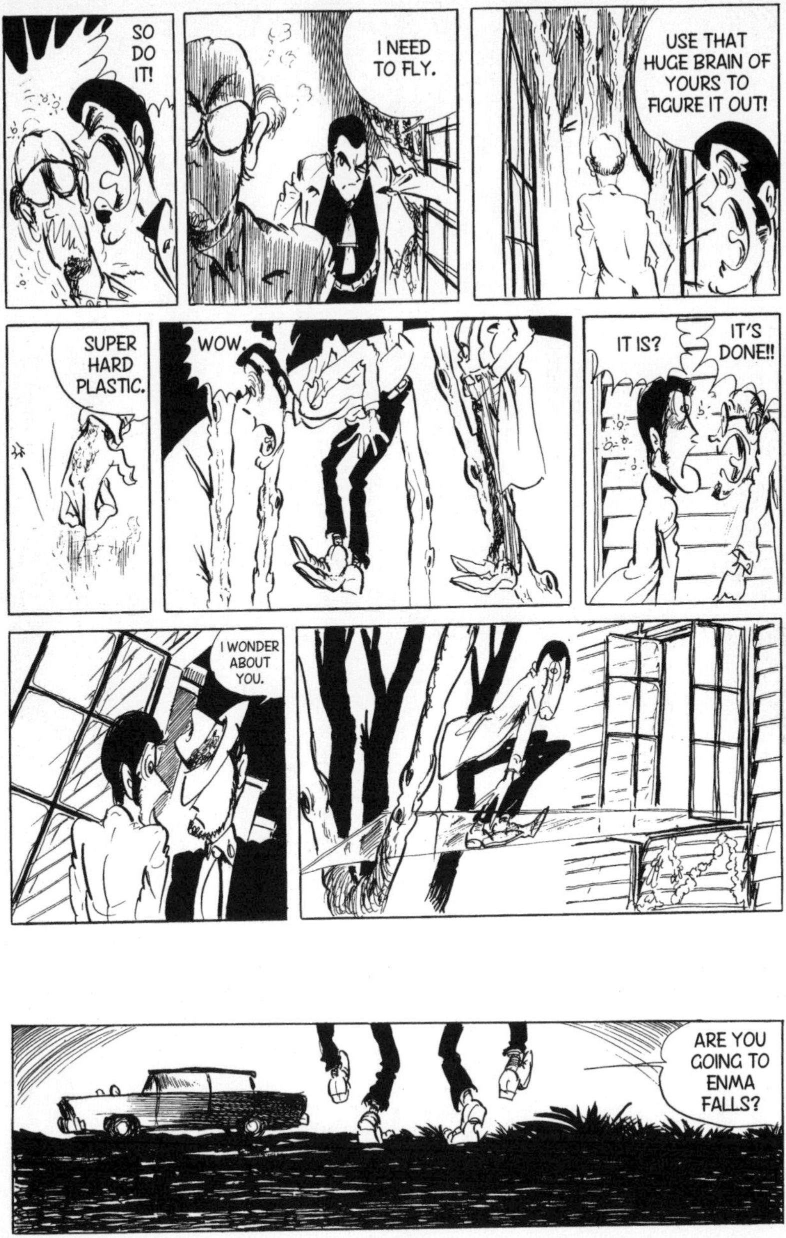
USE THAT HUGE BRAIN OF YOURS TO FIGURE IT OUT!
I NEED TO FLY.
SO DO IT!
IT'S DONE!!
IT IS?
WOW.
SUPER HARD PLASTIC.
I WONDER ABOUT YOU.
ARE YOU GOING TO ENMA FALLS?

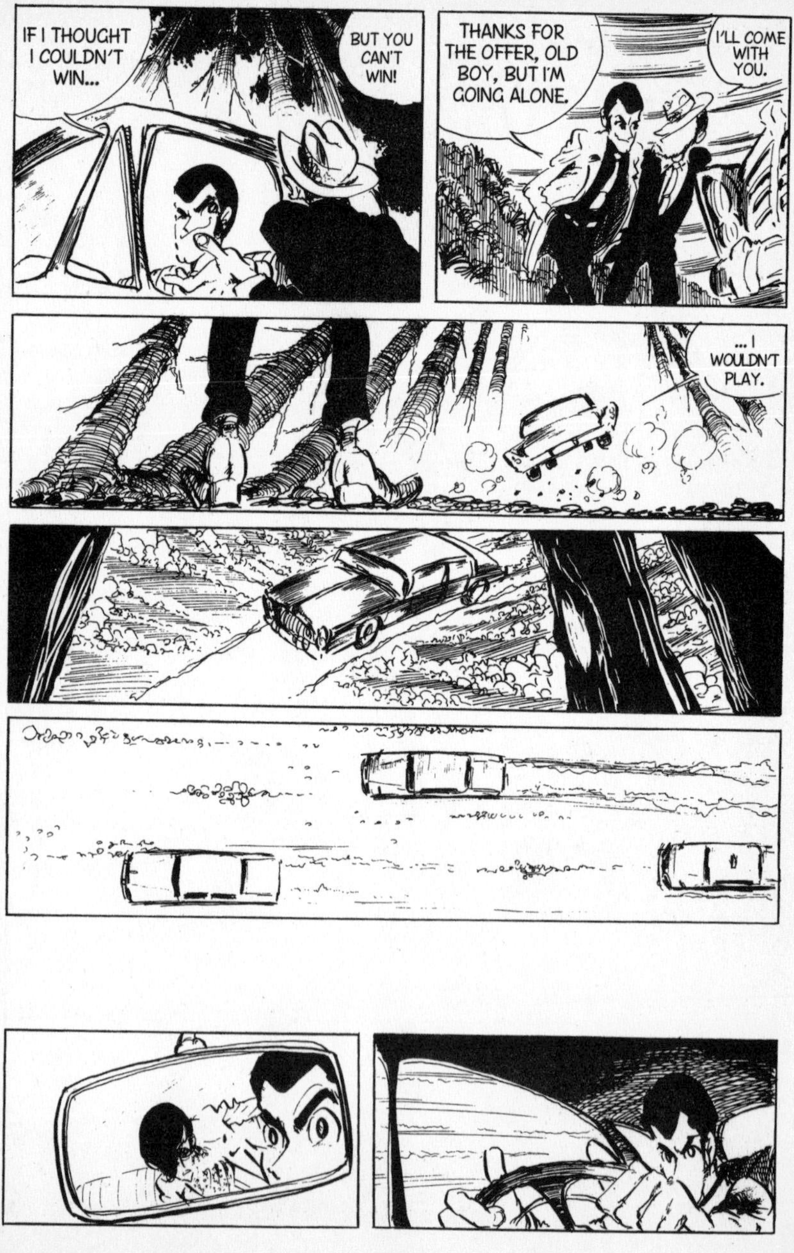
I'LL COME WITH YOU.
THANKS FOR THE OFFER, OLD BOY, BUT I'M GOING ALONE.
BUT YOU CAN'T WIN!
IF I THOUGHT I COULDN'T WIN...
...I WOULDN'T PLAY.

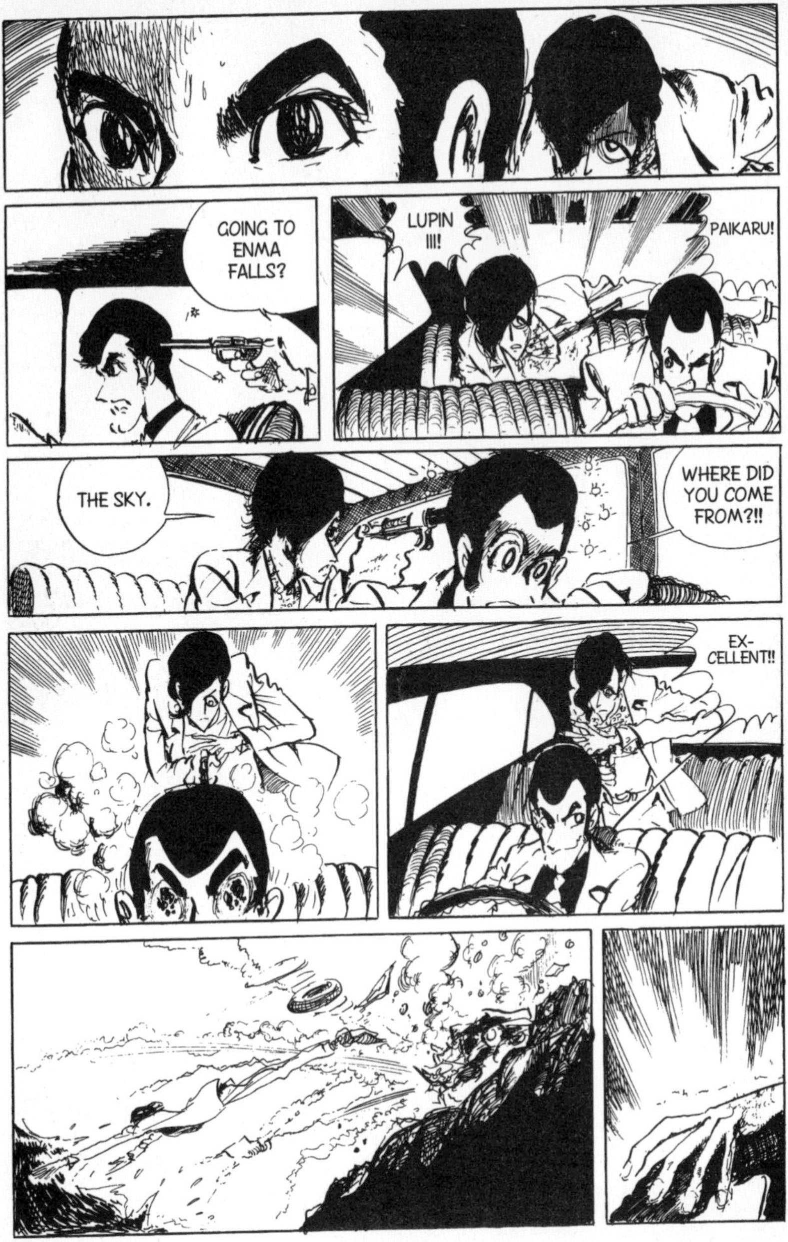
PAIKARU!
LUPIN III!
GOING TO ENMA FALLS?
WHERE DID YOU COME FROM?!!
THE SKY.
EX-CELLENT!!

WAIT!!

DIDN'T I ALREADY KILL YOU ONCE TODAY?

LOOK AT THIS.

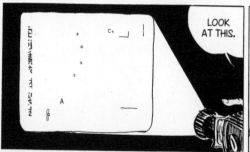

BEFORE YOU KILL ME AGAIN, I WANT TO SHOW YOU SOMETHING.

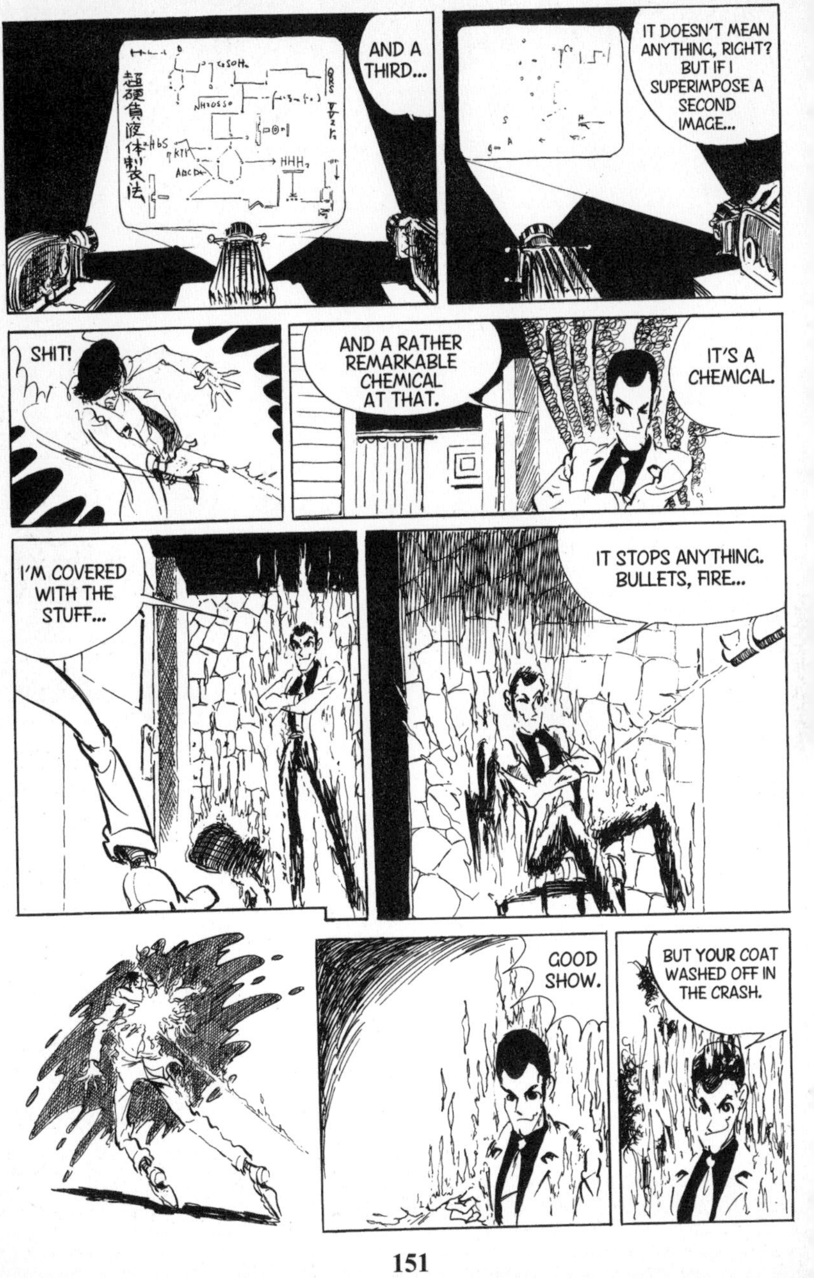
IT DOESN'T MEAN ANYTHING, RIGHT? BUT IF I SUPERIMPOSE A SECOND IMAGE...
AND A THIRD...
IT'S A CHEMICAL.
AND A RATHER REMARKABLE CHEMICAL AT THAT.
SHIT!
IT STOPS ANYTHING. BULLETS, FIRE...
I'M COVERED WITH THE STUFF...
BUT YOUR COAT WASHED OFF IN THE CRASH.
GOOD SHOW.

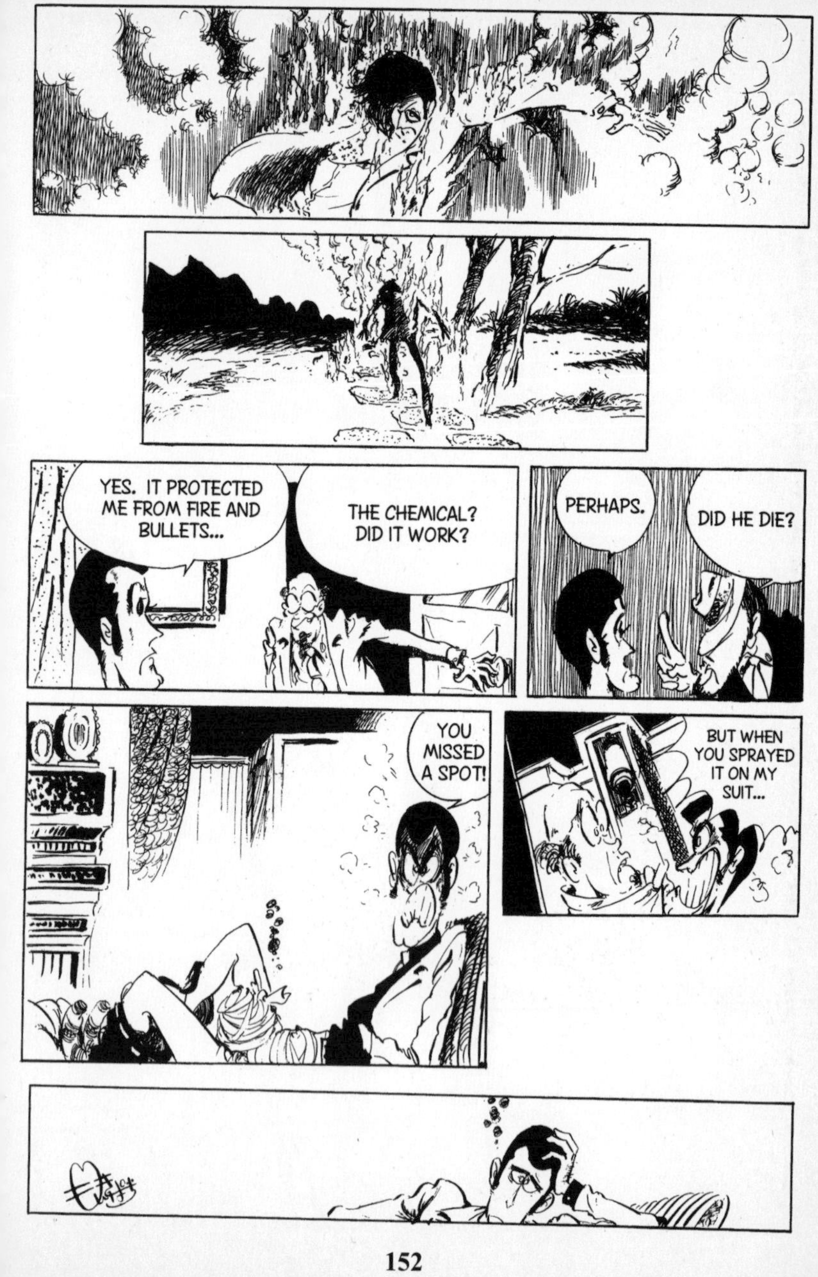
DID HE DIE?
PERHAPS.
THE CHEMICAL? DID IT WORK?
YES. IT PROTECTED ME FROM FIRE AND BULLETS...
BUT WHEN YOU SPRAYED IT ON MY SUIT...
YOU MISSED A SPOT!

CHAPTER 8
"ZENIGATA GETS LUCKY"

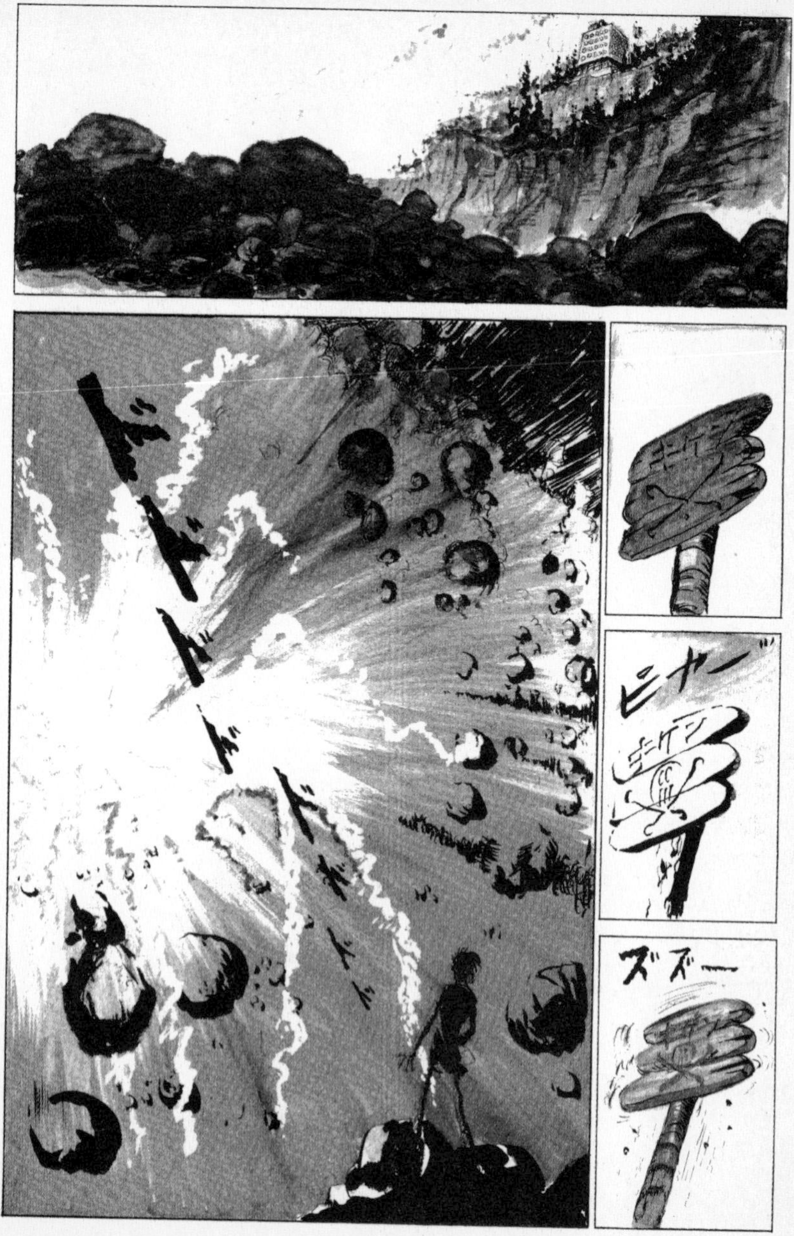
ヒヤー゛
ズズー
ズドドドド

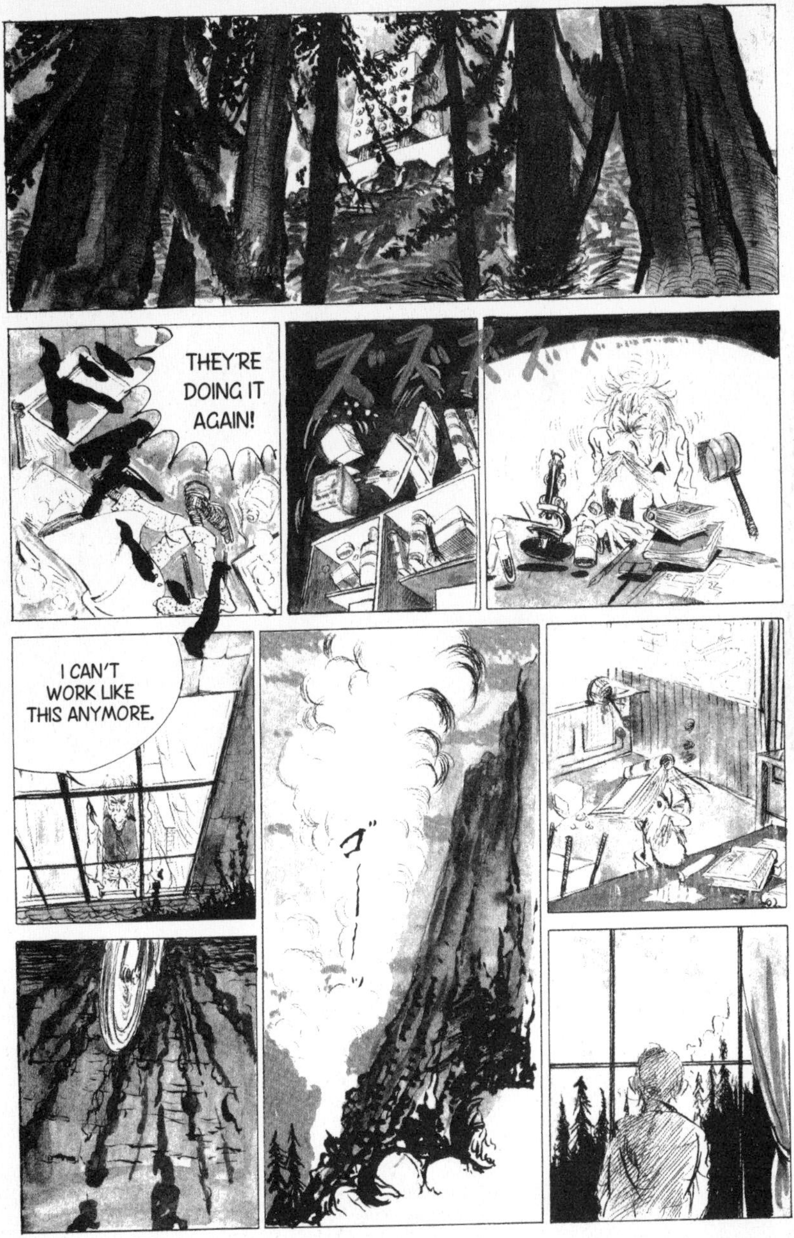
THEY'RE DOING IT AGAIN!
I CAN'T WORK LIKE THIS ANYMORE.

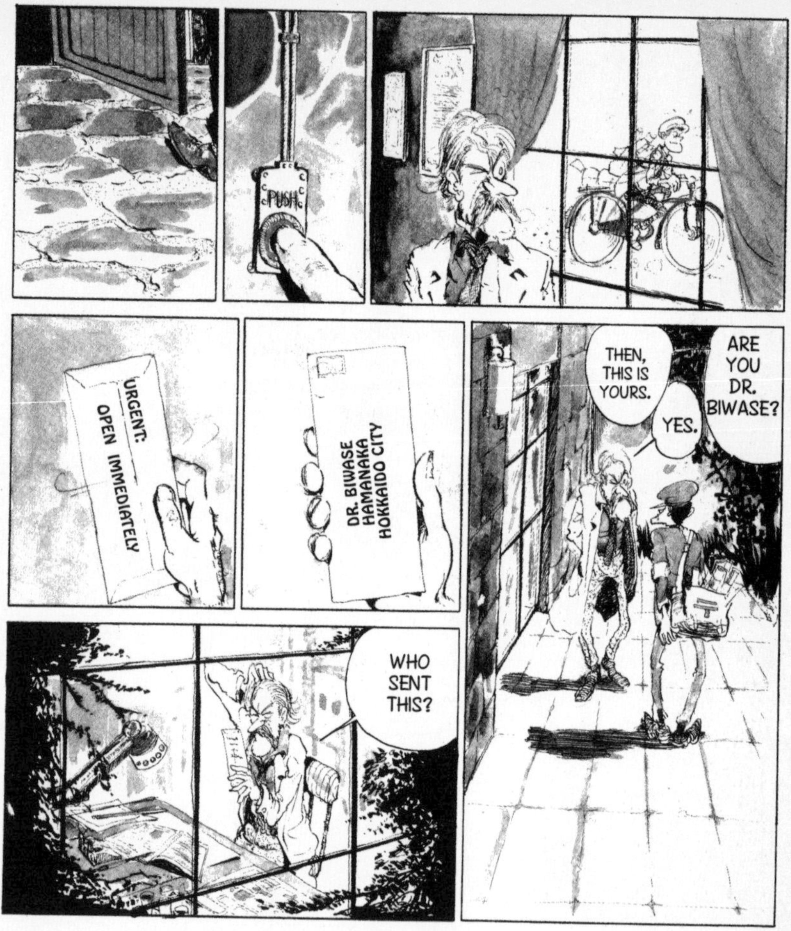
PUSH
ARE YOU DR. BIWASE?
YES.
THEN, THIS IS YOURS.
DR. BIWASE HAMANAKA HOKKAIDO CITY
URGENT: OPEN IMMEDIATELY
WHO SENT THIS?

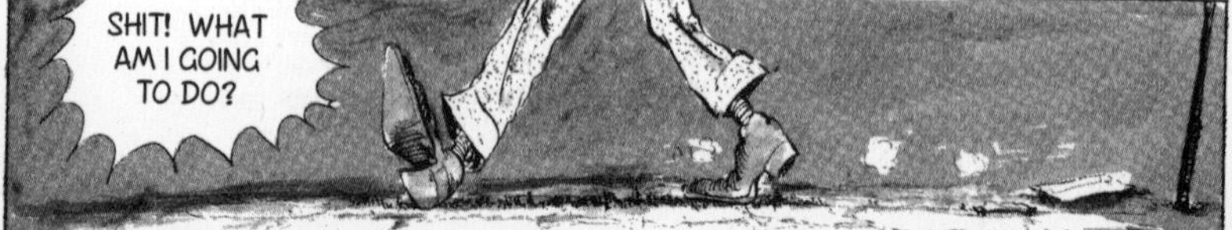
SHIT! WHAT AM I GOING TO DO?

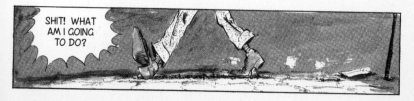

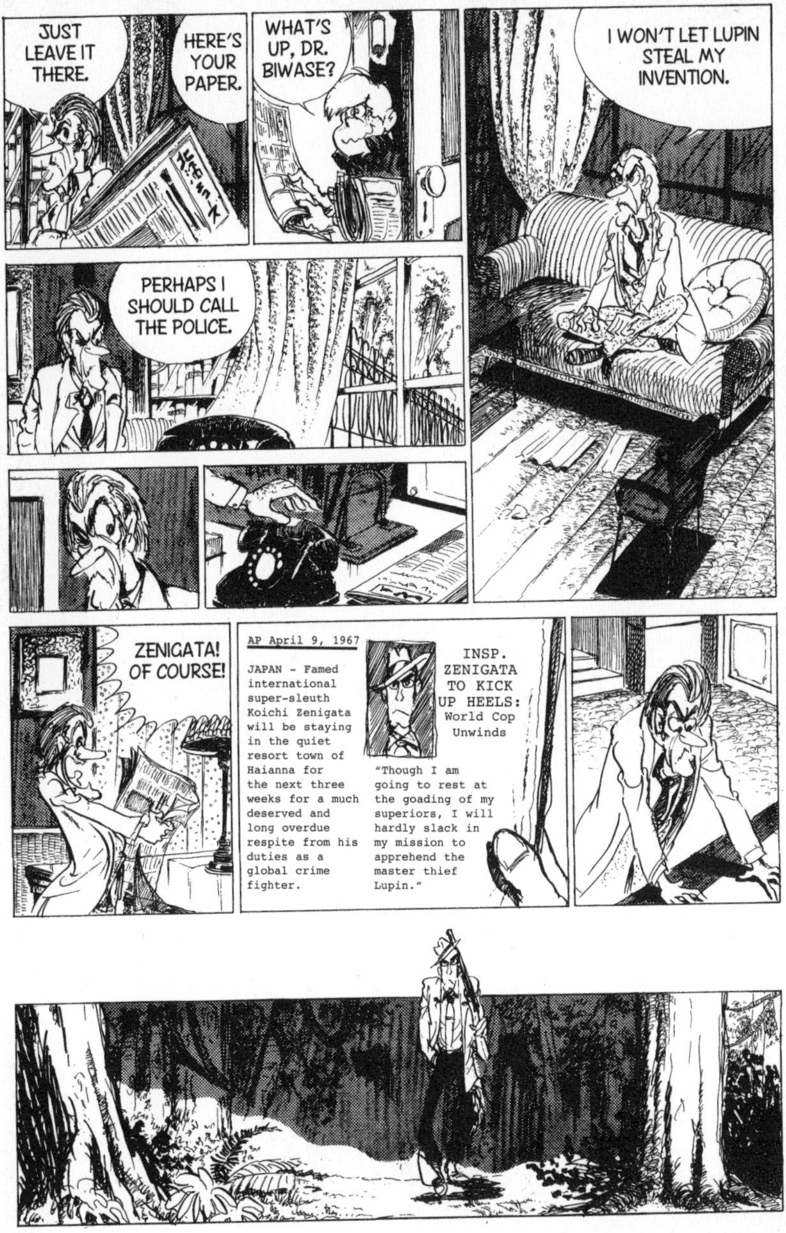
I WON'T LET LUPIN STEAL MY INVENTION.
WHAT'S UP, DR. BIWASE?
HERE'S YOUR PAPER.
JUST LEAVE IT THERE.
PERHAPS I SHOULD CALL THE POLICE.
AP April 9, 1967
INSP. ZENIGATA TO KICK UP HEELS: World Cop Unwinds
JAPAN - Famed international super-sleuth Koichi Zenigata will be staying in the quiet resort town of Haianna for the next three weeks for a much deserved and long overdue respite from his duties as a global crime fighter.
"Though I am going to rest at the goading of my superiors, I will hardly slack in my mission to apprehend the master thief Lupin."
ZENIGATA! OF COURSE!

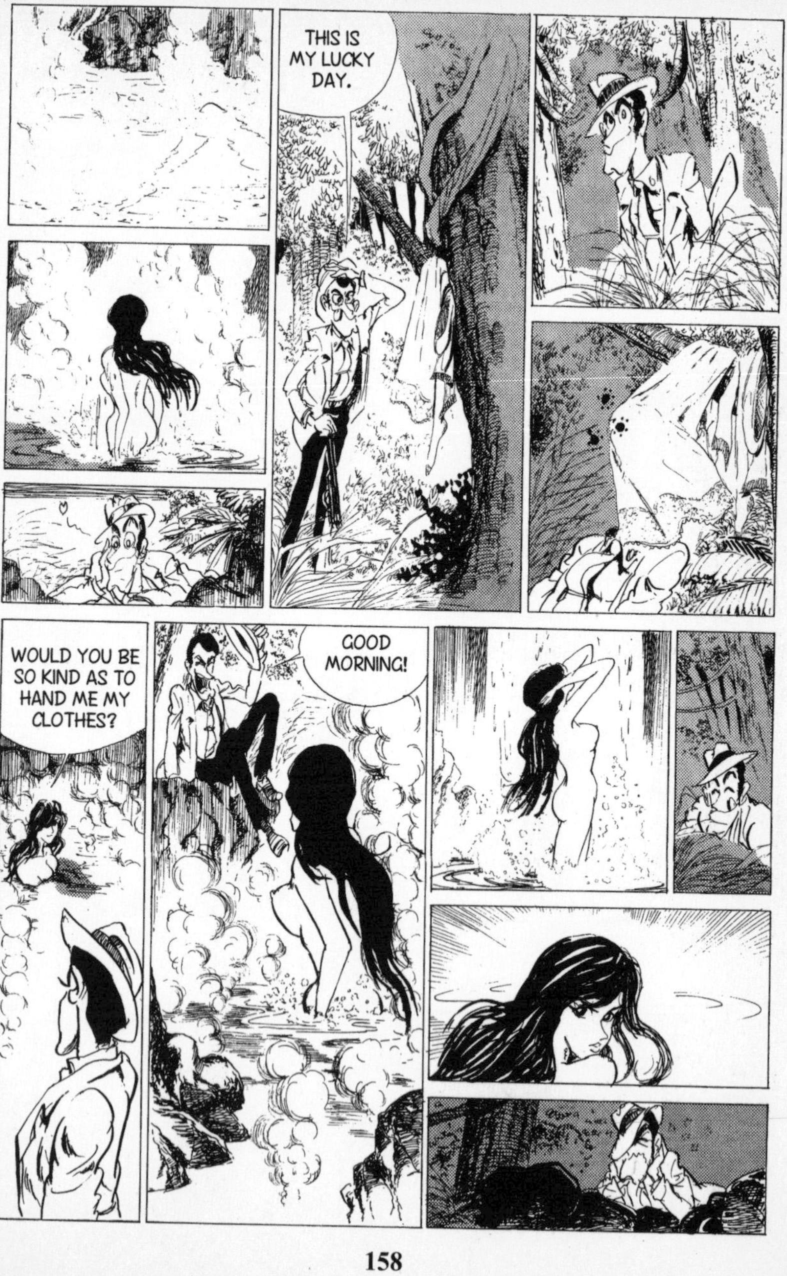
THIS IS MY LUCKY DAY.
GOOD MORNING!
WOULD YOU BE SO KIND AS TO HAND ME MY CLOTHES?

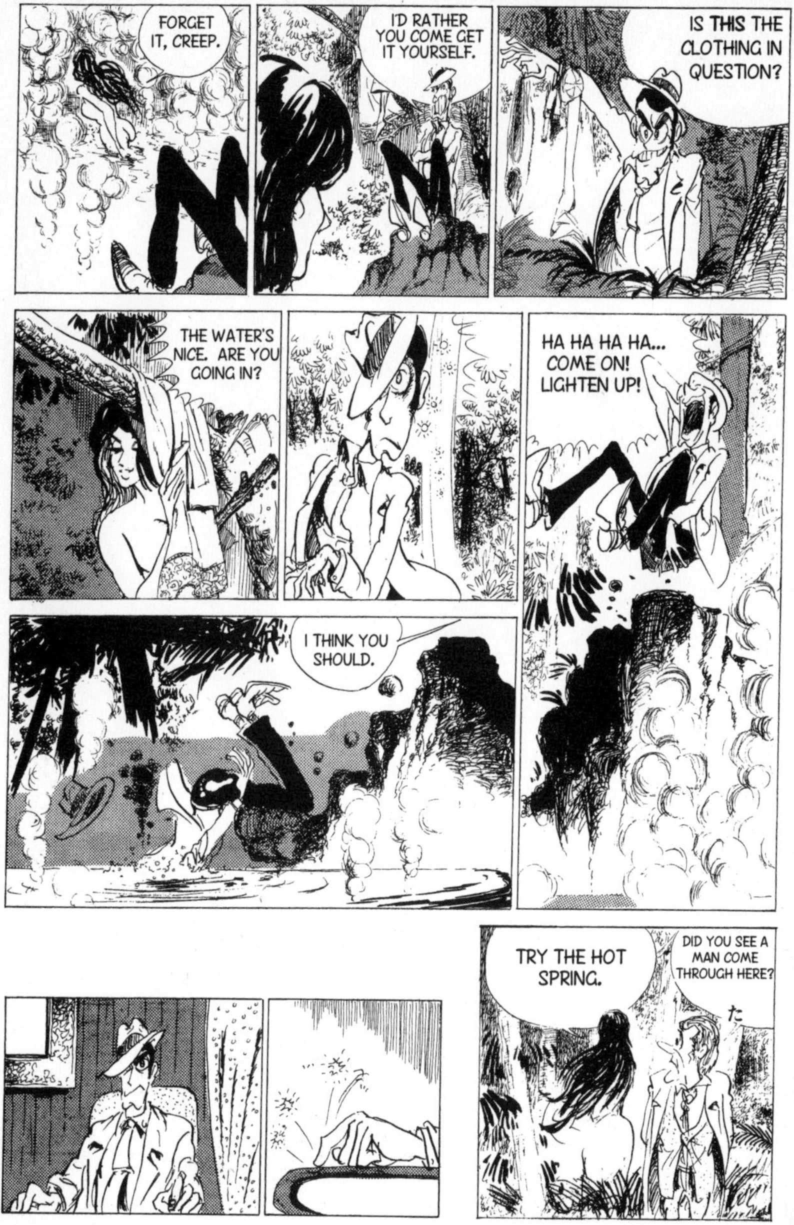
IS THIS THE CLOTHING IN QUESTION?
I'D RATHER YOU COME GET IT YOURSELF.
FORGET IT, CREEP.
HA HA HA HA... COME ON! LIGHTEN UP!
THE WATER'S NICE. ARE YOU GOING IN?
I THINK YOU SHOULD.
DID YOU SEE A MAN COME THROUGH HERE?
た
TRY THE HOT SPRING.

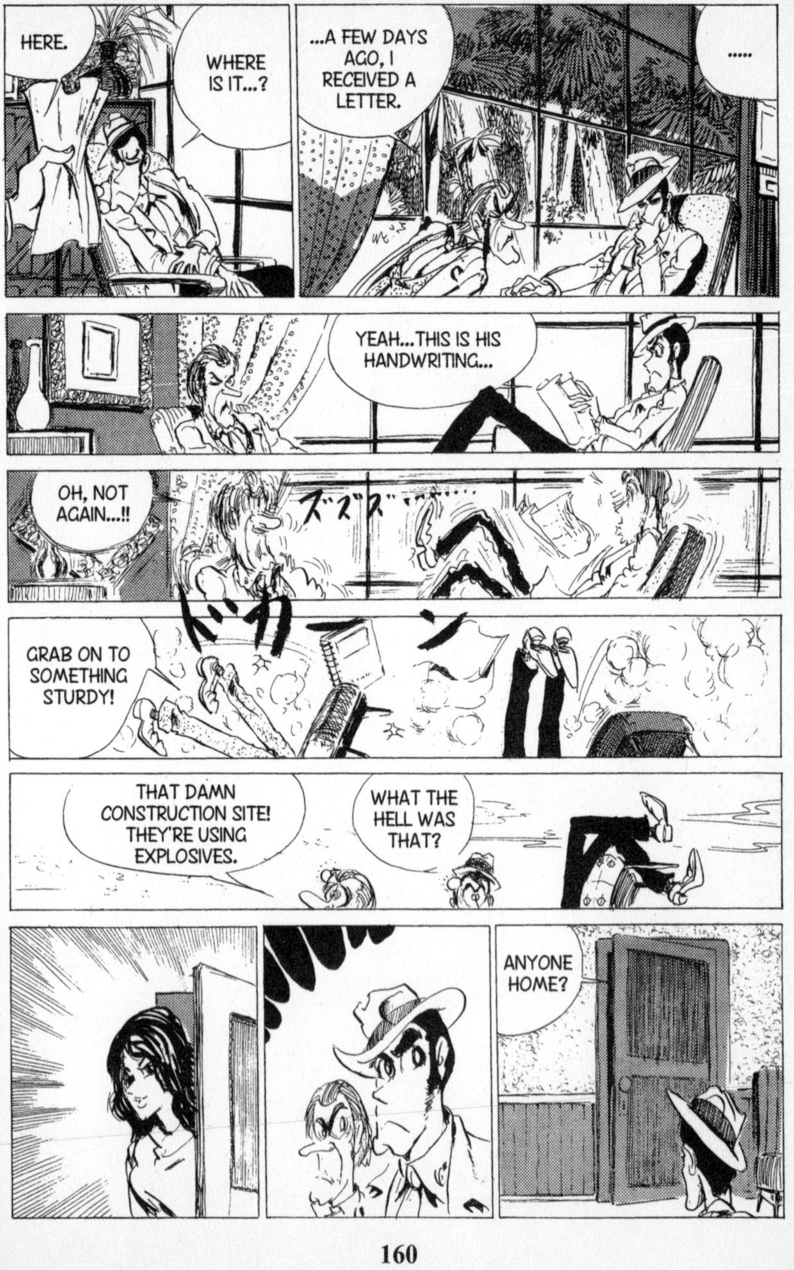
.....
...A FEW DAYS AGO, I RECEIVED A LETTER.
WHERE IS IT...?
HERE.
YEAH...THIS IS HIS HANDWRITING...
ズズズ
OH, NOT AGAIN...!!
ドカーン
GRAB ON TO SOMETHING STURDY!
WHAT THE HELL WAS THAT?
THAT DAMN CONSTRUCTION SITE! THEY'RE USING EXPLOSIVES.
ANYONE HOME?

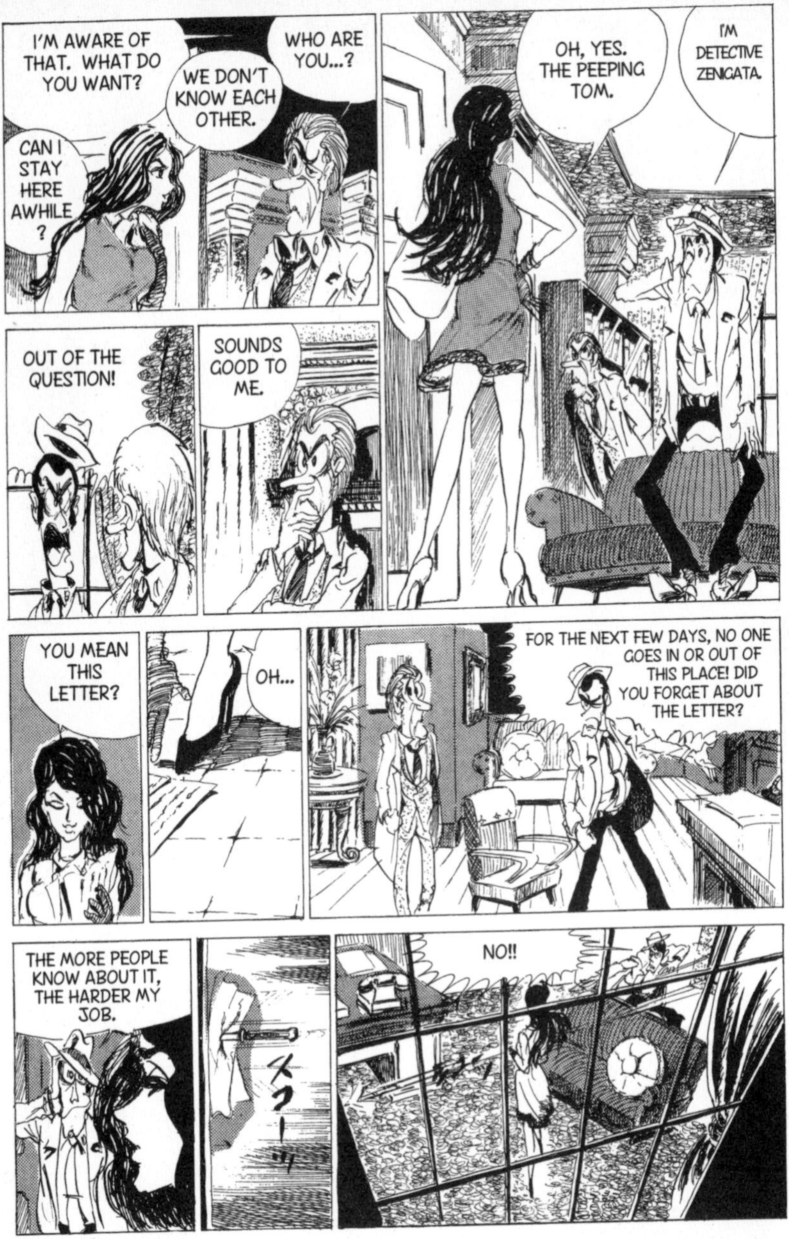
I'M DETECTIVE ZENIGATA.
OH, YES. THE PEEPING TOM.
WHO ARE YOU...?
WE DON'T KNOW EACH OTHER.
I'M AWARE OF THAT. WHAT DO YOU WANT?
CAN I STAY HERE AWHILE?
SOUNDS GOOD TO ME.
OUT OF THE QUESTION!
FOR THE NEXT FEW DAYS, NO ONE GOES IN OR OUT OF THIS PLACE! DID YOU FORGET ABOUT THE LETTER?
OH...
YOU MEAN THIS LETTER?
NO!!
THE MORE PEOPLE KNOW ABOUT IT, THE HARDER MY JOB.

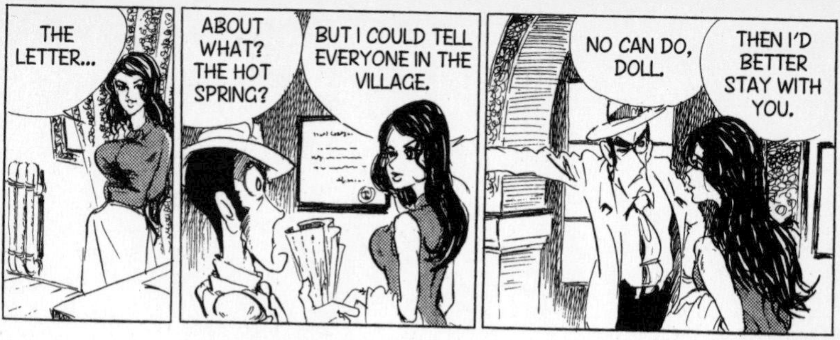
THEN I'D BETTER STAY WITH YOU.
NO CAN DO, DOLL.
BUT I COULD TELL EVERYONE IN THE VILLAGE.
ABOUT WHAT? THE HOT SPRING?
THE LETTER...

CONTENTS OF THE LETTER ...

DEAR DR. BIWASE,
CONGRATS ON THE NEW INVENTION – I HEAR THE "K MACHINE" IS SIMPLY SMASHING. I ALSO HEAR YOU PLAN ON SELLING IT TO A FOREIGN COUNTRY FOR MILITARY PURPOSES. I'M DEEPLY SADDENED BY THIS, AS I FEEL THIS MARVELOUS CREATION SHOULD STAY IN JAPAN. PLEASE, WRAP IT UP AND SEND IT TO ME AT KUSHIRO STATION – OR, IF YOU PREFER, I'LL COME BY TONIGHT AT 12:00 AND PICK IT UP MYSELF.

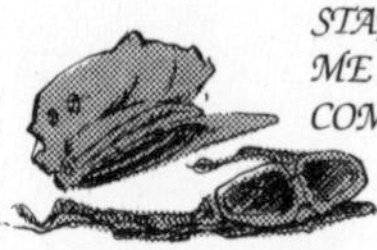

YOURS TRULY, L.

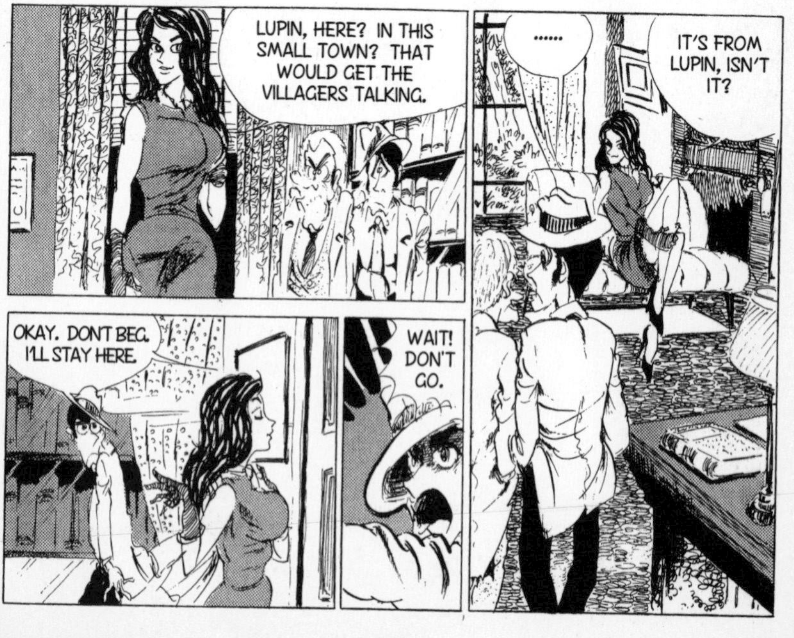
IT'S FROM LUPIN, ISN'T IT?
......
LUPIN, HERE? IN THIS SMALL TOWN? THAT WOULD GET THE VILLAGERS TALKING.
WAIT! DON'T GO.
OKAY. DON'T BEG. I'LL STAY HERE.

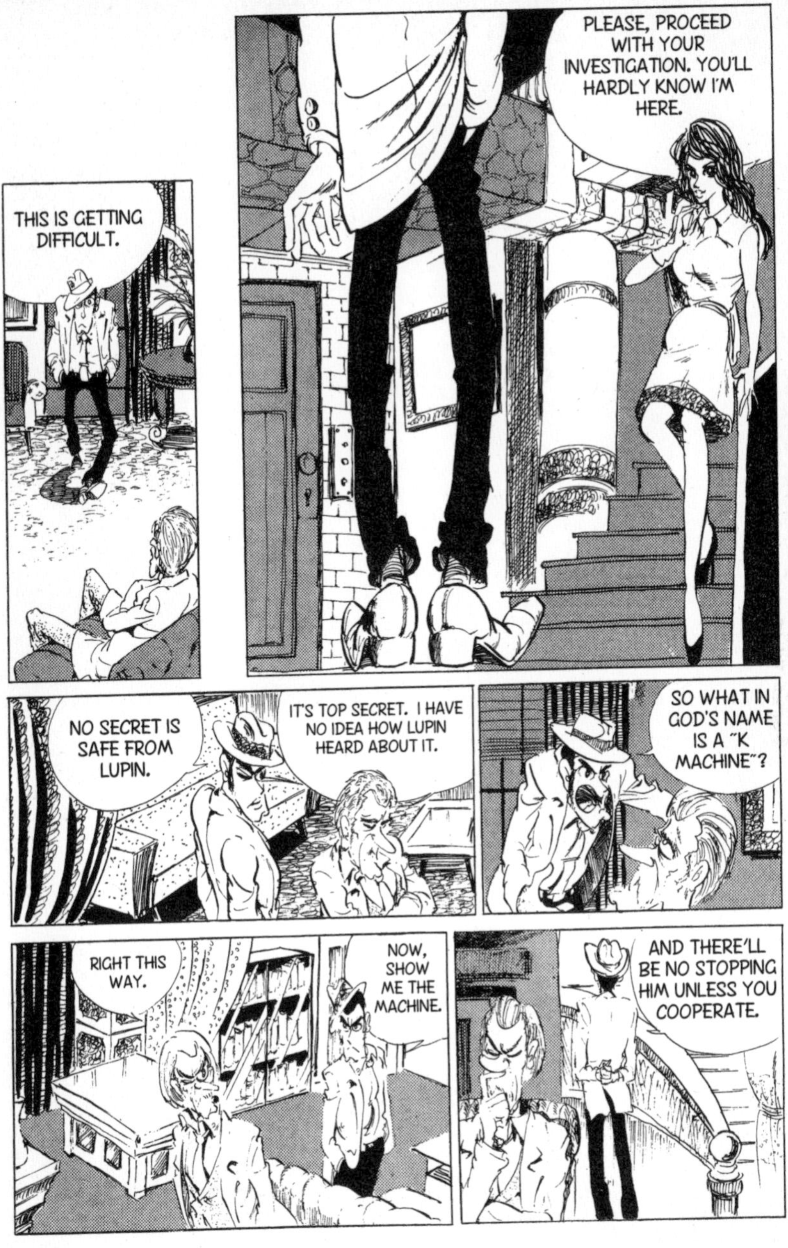
PLEASE, PROCEED WITH YOUR INVESTIGATION. YOU'LL HARDLY KNOW I'M HERE.
THIS IS GETTING DIFFICULT.
SO WHAT IN GOD'S NAME IS A "K MACHINE"?
IT'S TOP SECRET. I HAVE NO IDEA HOW LUPIN HEARD ABOUT IT.
NO SECRET IS SAFE FROM LUPIN.
AND THERE'LL BE NO STOPPING HIM UNLESS YOU COOPERATE.
NOW, SHOW ME THE MACHINE.
RIGHT THIS WAY.

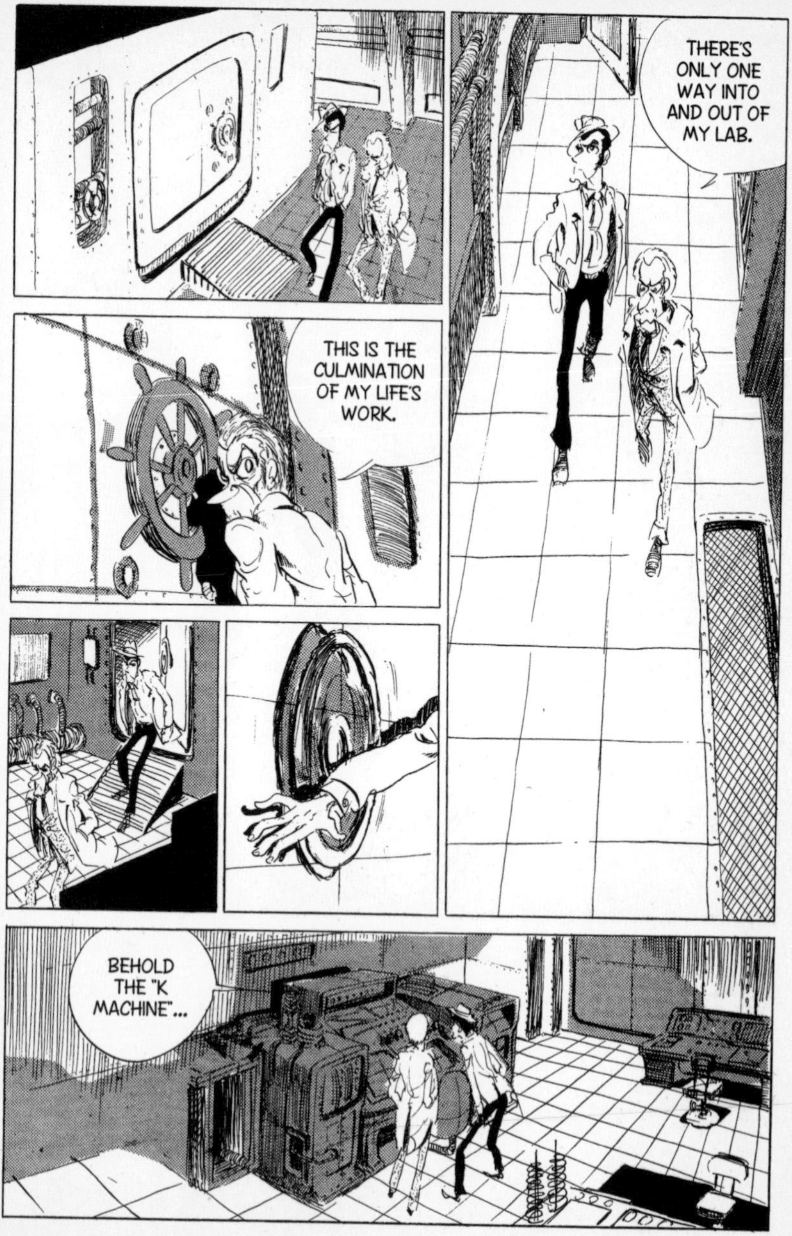
THERE'S ONLY ONE WAY INTO AND OUT OF MY LAB.
THIS IS THE CULMINATION OF MY LIFE'S WORK.
BEHOLD THE "K MACHINE"...

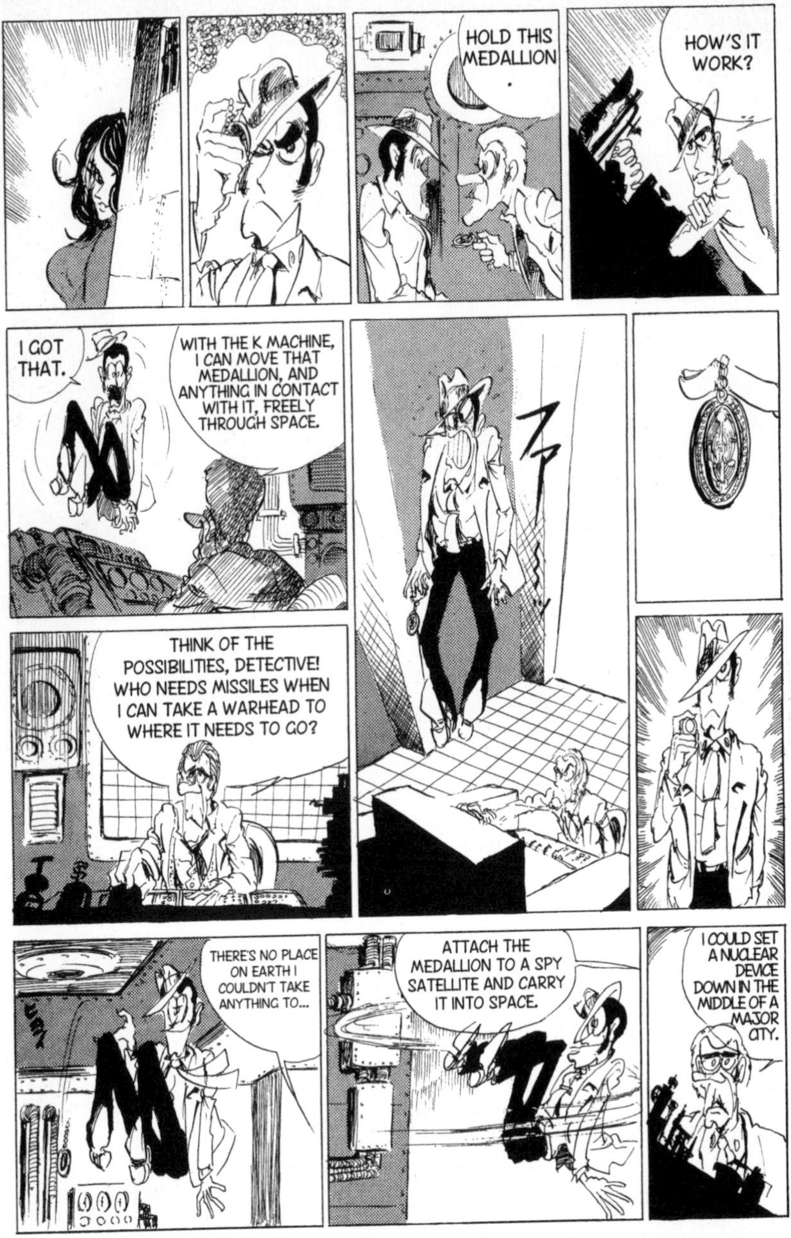
HOW'S IT WORK?
HOLD THIS MEDALLION.
WITH THE K MACHINE, I CAN MOVE THAT MEDALLION, AND ANYTHING IN CONTACT WITH IT, FREELY THROUGH SPACE.
I GOT THAT.
THINK OF THE POSSIBILITIES, DETECTIVE! WHO NEEDS MISSILES WHEN I CAN TAKE A WARHEAD TO WHERE IT NEEDS TO GO?
I COULD SET A NUCLEAR DEVICE DOWN IN THE MIDDLE OF A MAJOR CITY.
ATTACH THE MEDALLION TO A SPY SATELLITE AND CARRY IT INTO SPACE.
THERE'S NO PLACE ON EARTH I COULDN'T TAKE ANYTHING TO...

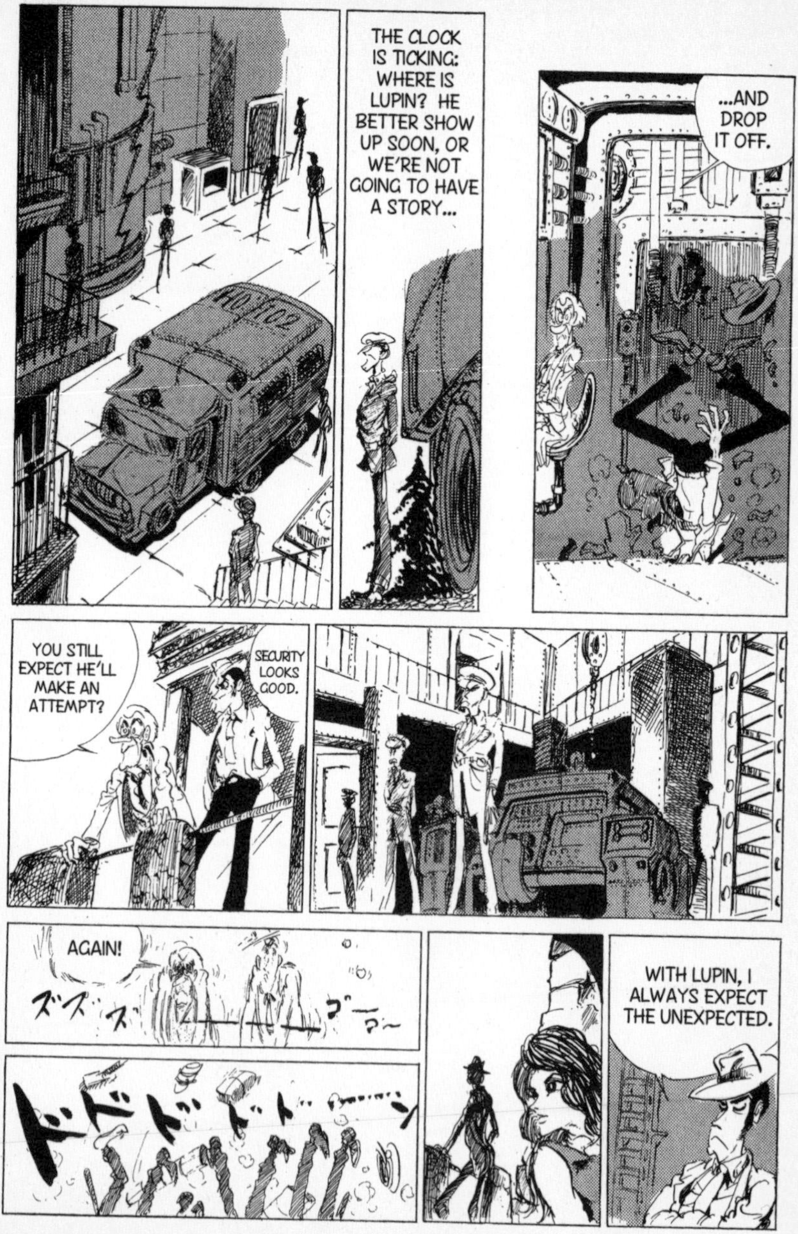
...AND DROP IT OFF.
THE CLOCK IS TICKING: WHERE IS LUPIN? HE BETTER SHOW UP SOON, OR WE'RE NOT GOING TO HAVE A STORY...
SECURITY LOOKS GOOD.
YOU STILL EXPECT HE'LL MAKE AN ATTEMPT?
WITH LUPIN, I ALWAYS EXPECT THE UNEXPECTED.
AGAIN!
ズズ ズ
ゴー
ドドドドト…

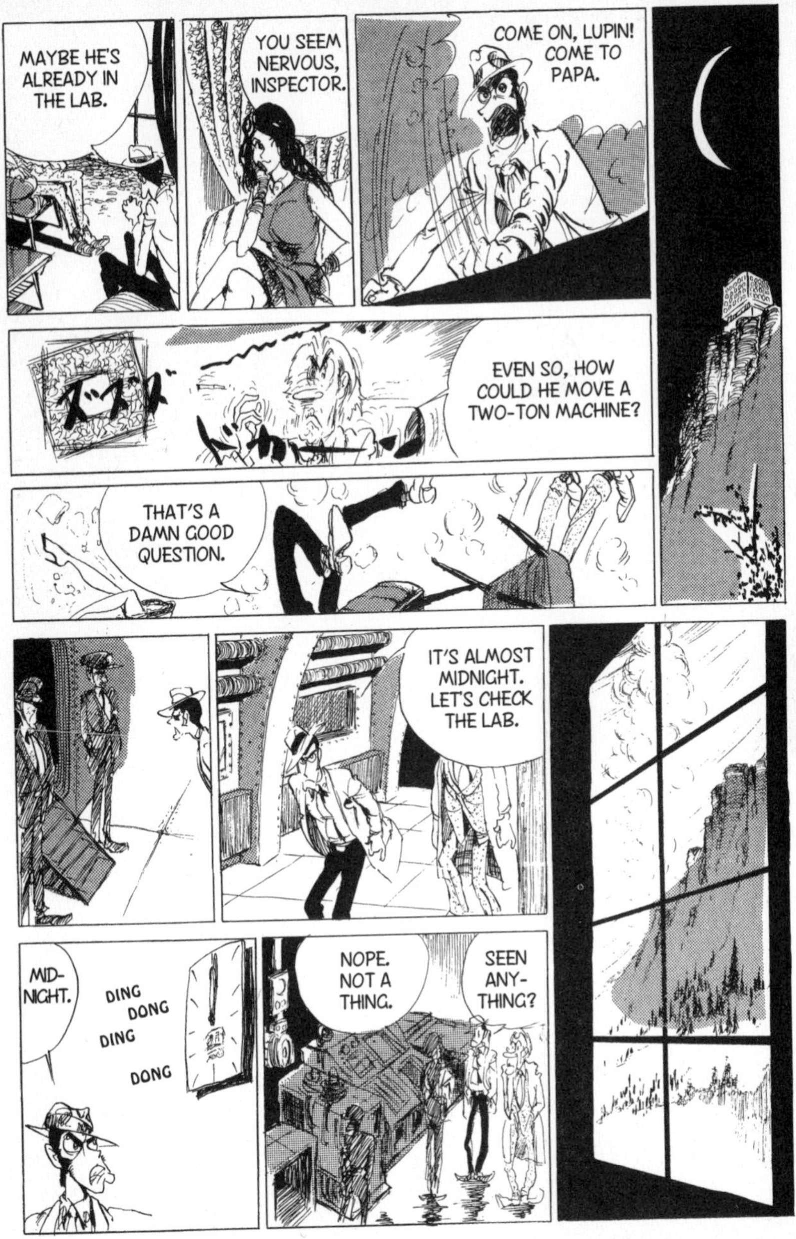
COME ON, LUPIN! COME TO PAPA.
YOU SEEM NERVOUS, INSPECTOR.
MAYBE HE'S ALREADY IN THE LAB.
EVEN SO, HOW COULD HE MOVE A TWO-TON MACHINE?
THAT'S A DAMN GOOD QUESTION.
IT'S ALMOST MIDNIGHT. LET'S CHECK THE LAB.
SEEN ANY-THING?
NOPE. NOT A THING.
MID-NIGHT.
DING DONG DING DONG

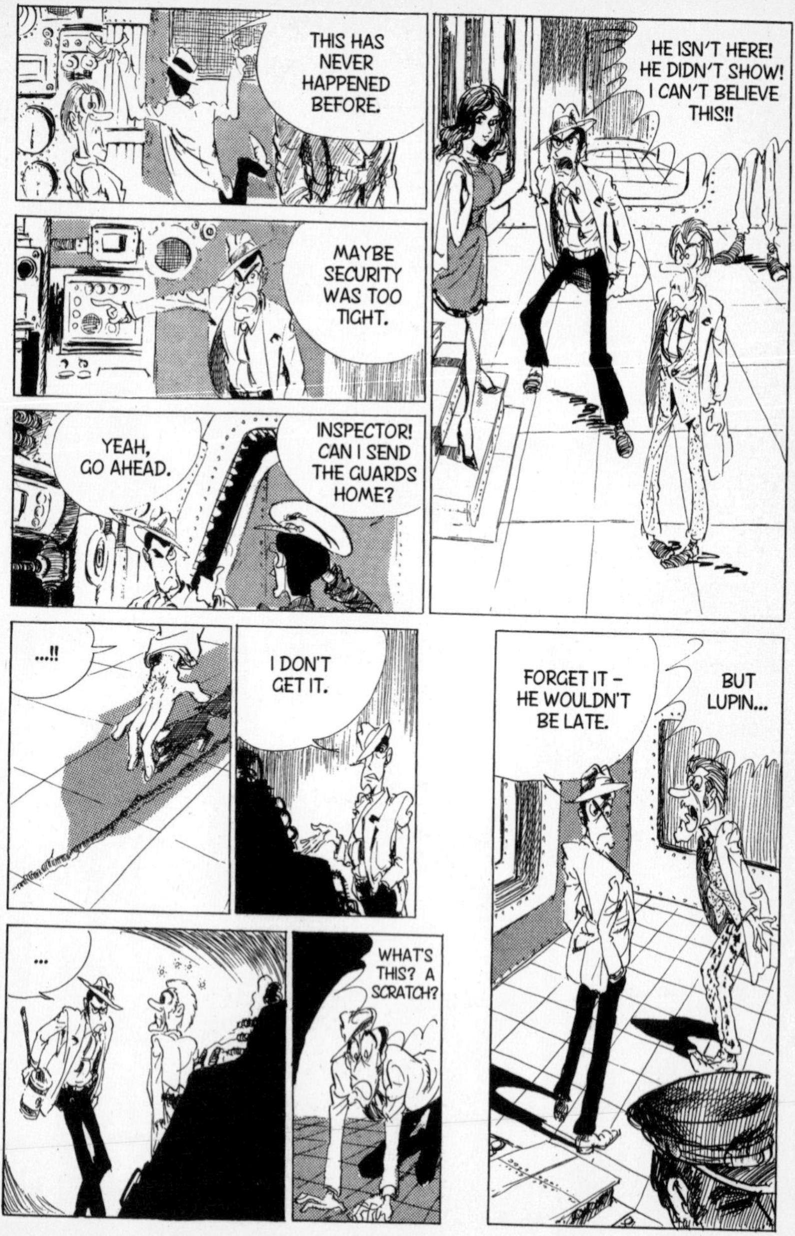
HE ISN'T HERE! HE DIDN'T SHOW! I CAN'T BELIEVE THIS!!
THIS HAS NEVER HAPPENED BEFORE.
MAYBE SECURITY WAS TOO TIGHT.
INSPECTOR! CAN I SEND THE GUARDS HOME?
YEAH, GO AHEAD.
BUT LUPIN...
FORGET IT – HE WOULDN'T BE LATE.
I DON'T GET IT.
...!!
WHAT'S THIS? A SCRATCH?
...

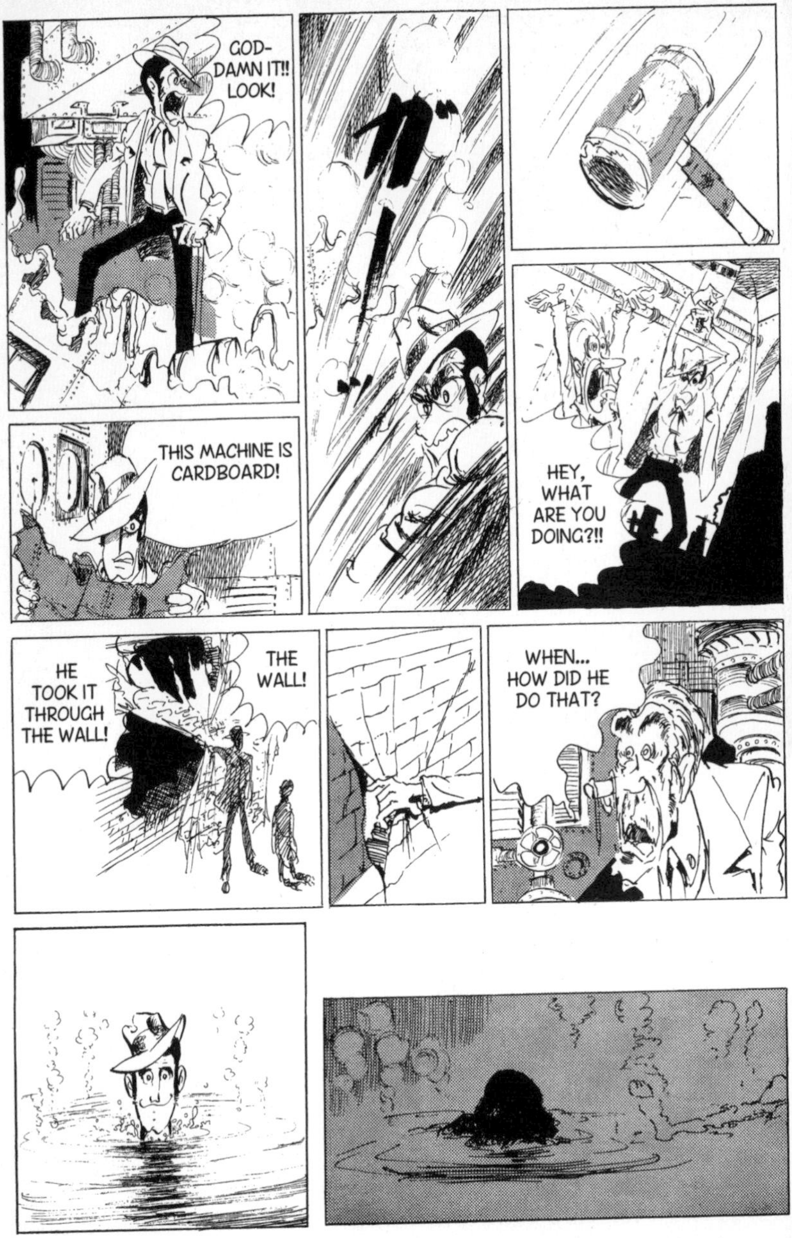
HEY, WHAT ARE YOU DOING?!!
GOD-DAMN IT!! LOOK!
THIS MACHINE IS CARDBOARD!
WHEN... HOW DID HE DO THAT?
THE WALL!
HE TOOK IT THROUGH THE WALL!

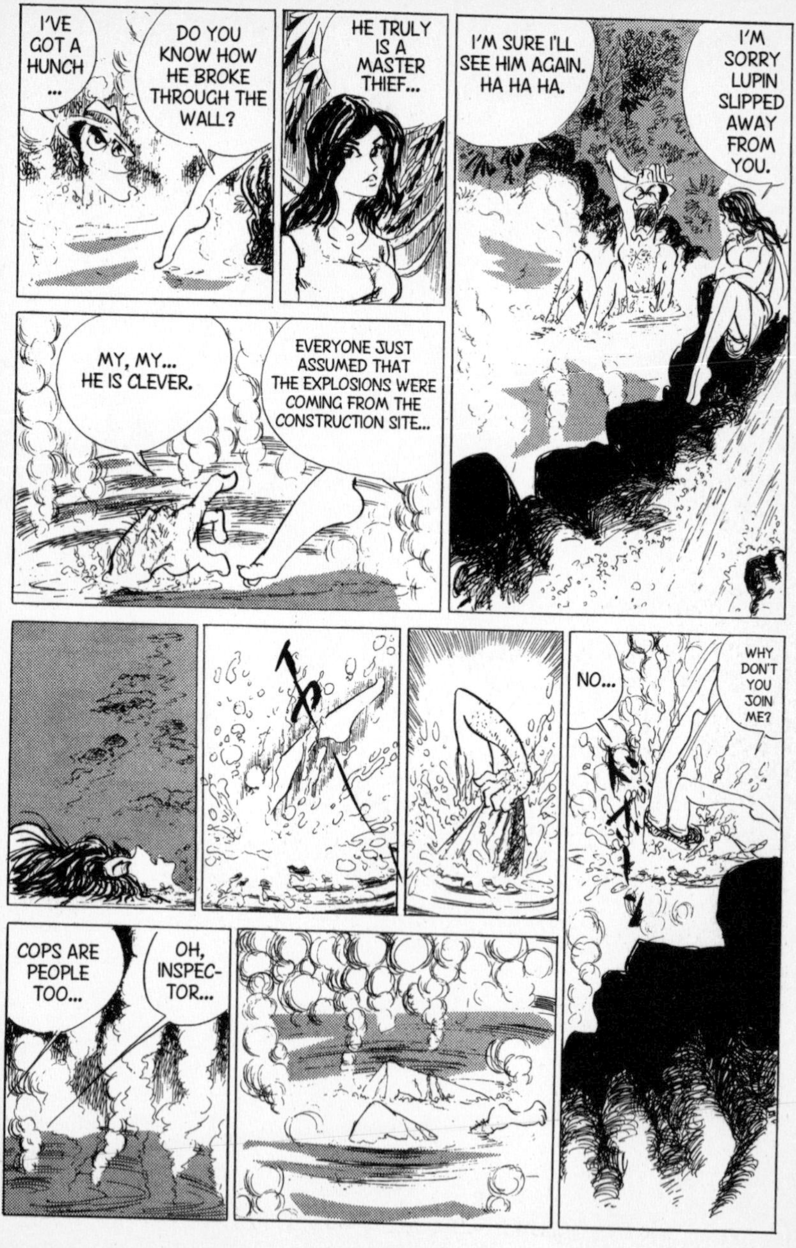
I'M SORRY LUPIN SLIPPED AWAY FROM YOU.
I'M SURE I'LL SEE HIM AGAIN. HA HA HA.
HE TRULY IS A MASTER THIEF...
DO YOU KNOW HOW HE BROKE THROUGH THE WALL?
I'VE GOT A HUNCH ...
EVERYONE JUST ASSUMED THAT THE EXPLOSIONS WERE COMING FROM THE CONSTRUCTION SITE...
MY, MY... HE IS CLEVER.
WHY DON'T YOU JOIN ME?
NO...
OH, INSPECTOR...
COPS ARE PEOPLE TOO...

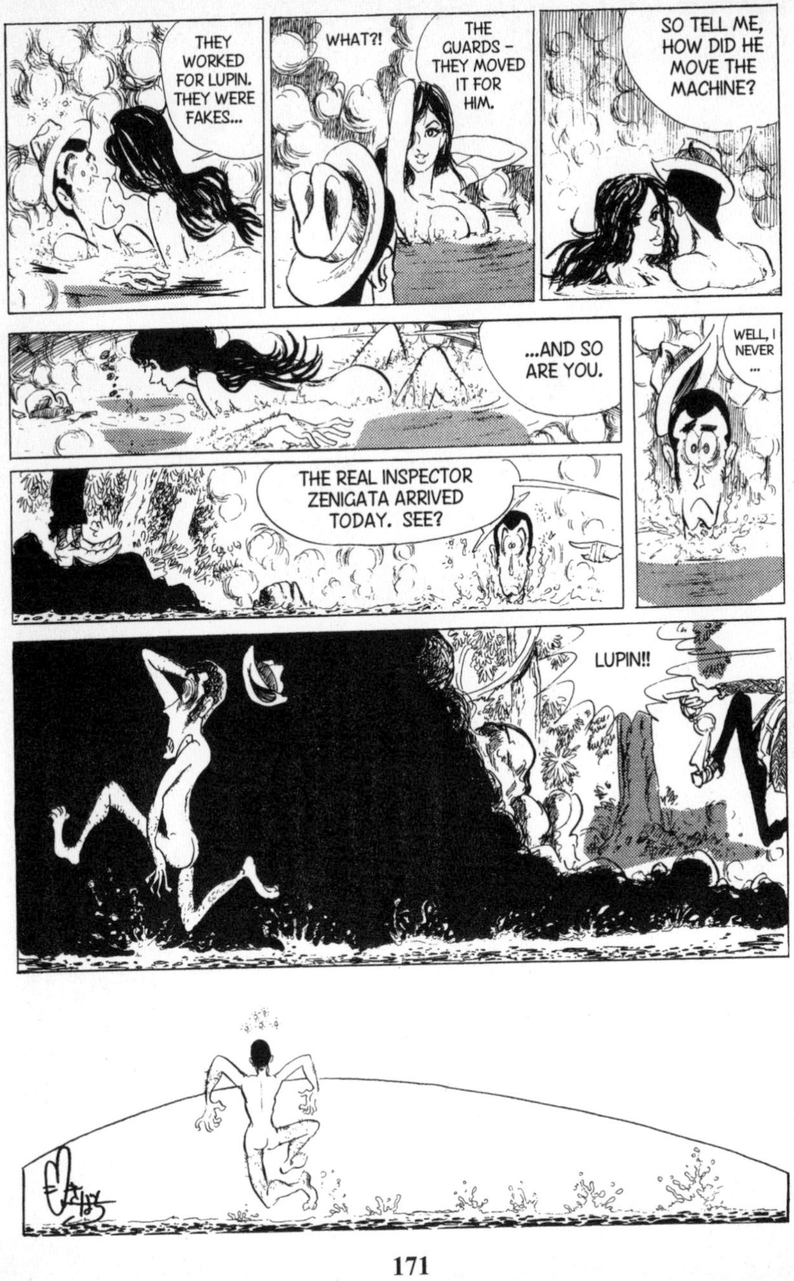
SO TELL ME, HOW DID HE MOVE THE MACHINE?
THE GUARDS - THEY MOVED IT FOR HIM.
WHAT?!
THEY WORKED FOR LUPIN. THEY WERE FAKES...
WELL, I NEVER ...
...AND SO ARE YOU.
THE REAL INSPECTOR ZENIGATA ARRIVED TODAY. SEE?
LUPIN!!

CHAPTER 9
"GATHER YE BAD MEN WHILE YE MAY"

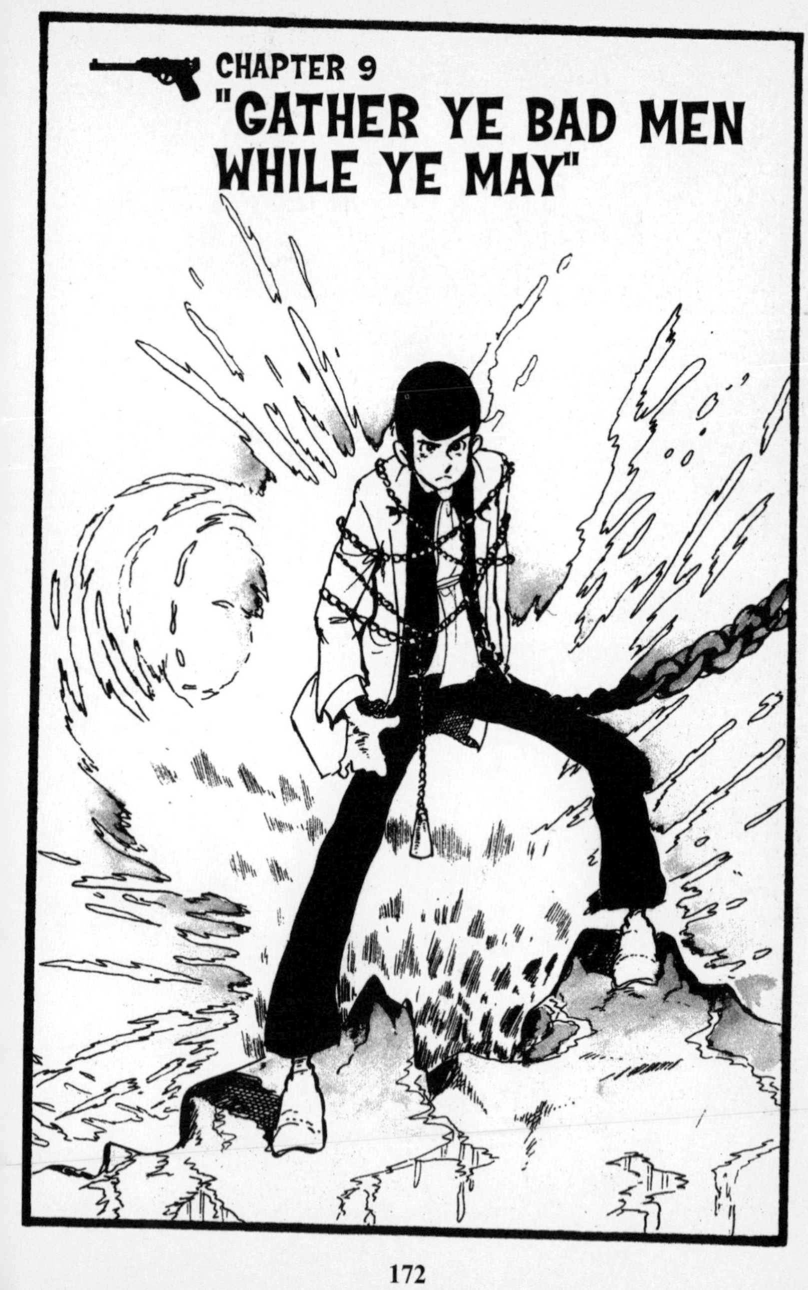

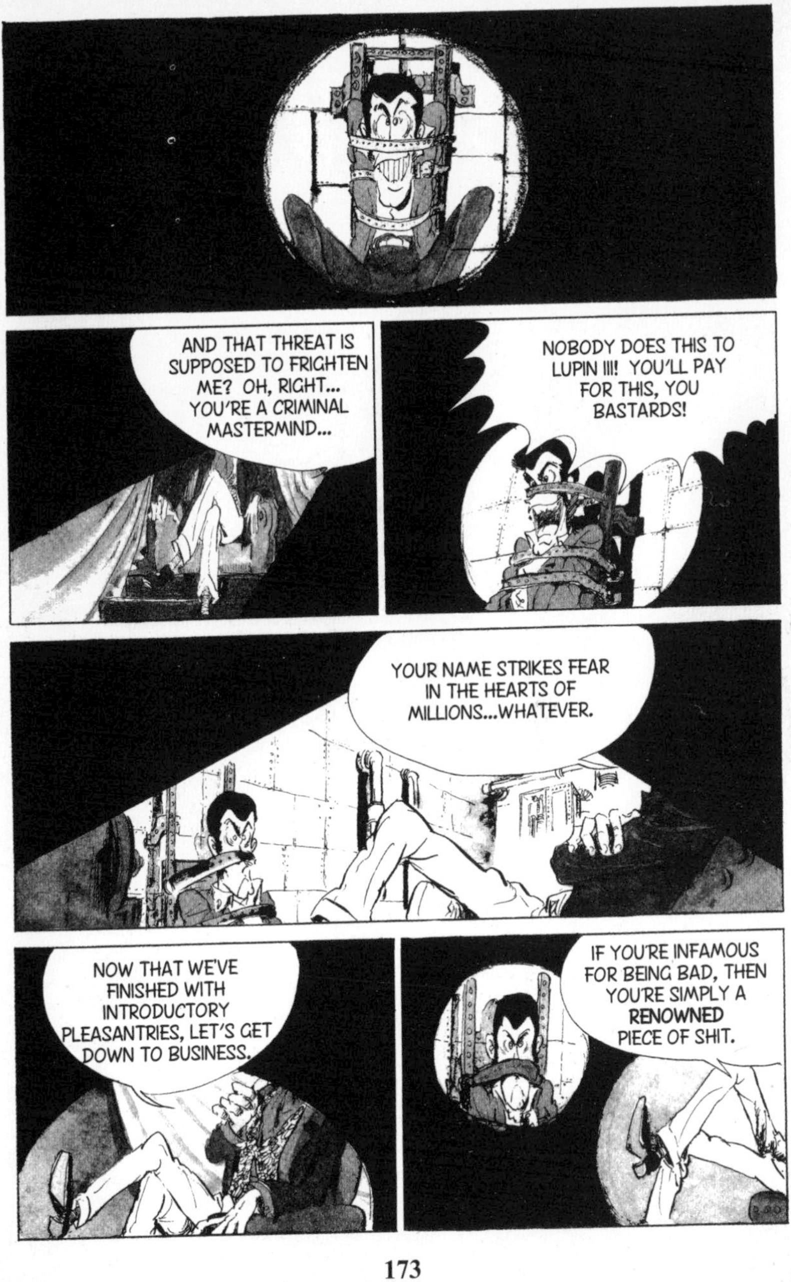
NOBODY DOES THIS TO LUPIN III! YOU'LL PAY FOR THIS, YOU BASTARDS!
AND THAT THREAT IS SUPPOSED TO FRIGHTEN ME? OH, RIGHT... YOU'RE A CRIMINAL MASTERMIND...
YOUR NAME STRIKES FEAR IN THE HEARTS OF MILLIONS...WHATEVER.
IF YOU'RE INFAMOUS FOR BEING BAD, THEN YOU'RE SIMPLY A **RENOWNED** PIECE OF SHIT.
NOW THAT WE'VE FINISHED WITH INTRODUCTORY PLEASANTRIES, LET'S GET DOWN TO BUSINESS.

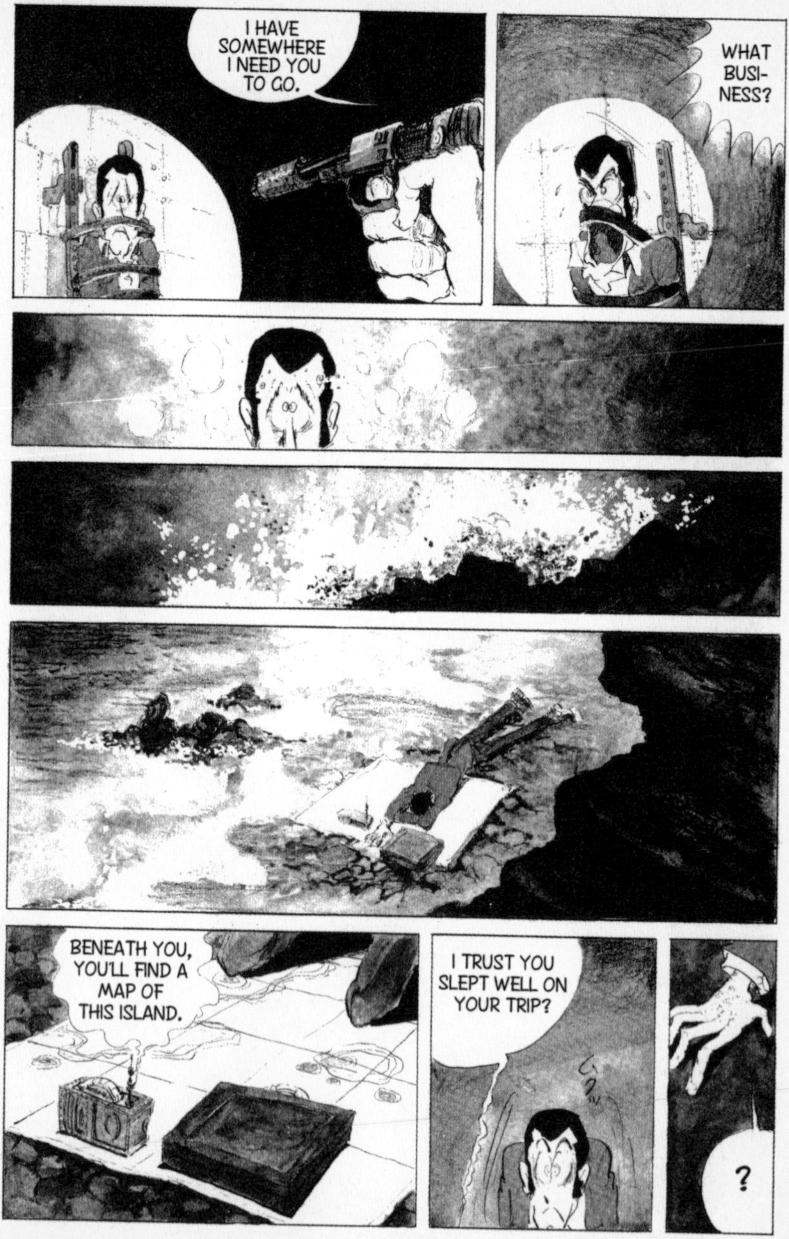
WHAT BUSI-NESS?
I HAVE SOMEWHERE I NEED YOU TO GO.
?
I TRUST YOU SLEPT WELL ON YOUR TRIP?
BENEATH YOU, YOU'LL FIND A MAP OF THIS ISLAND.

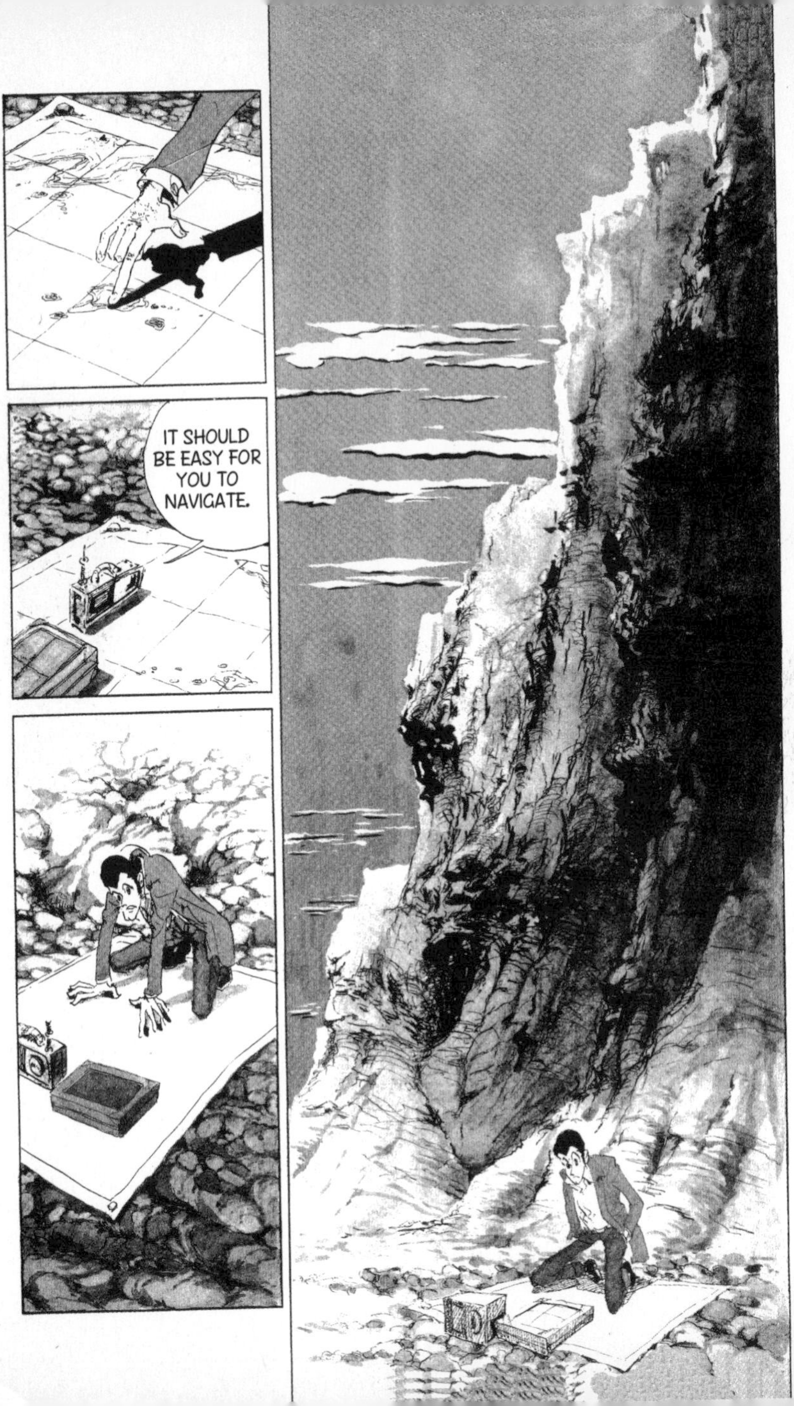
IT SHOULD BE EASY FOR YOU TO NAVIGATE.

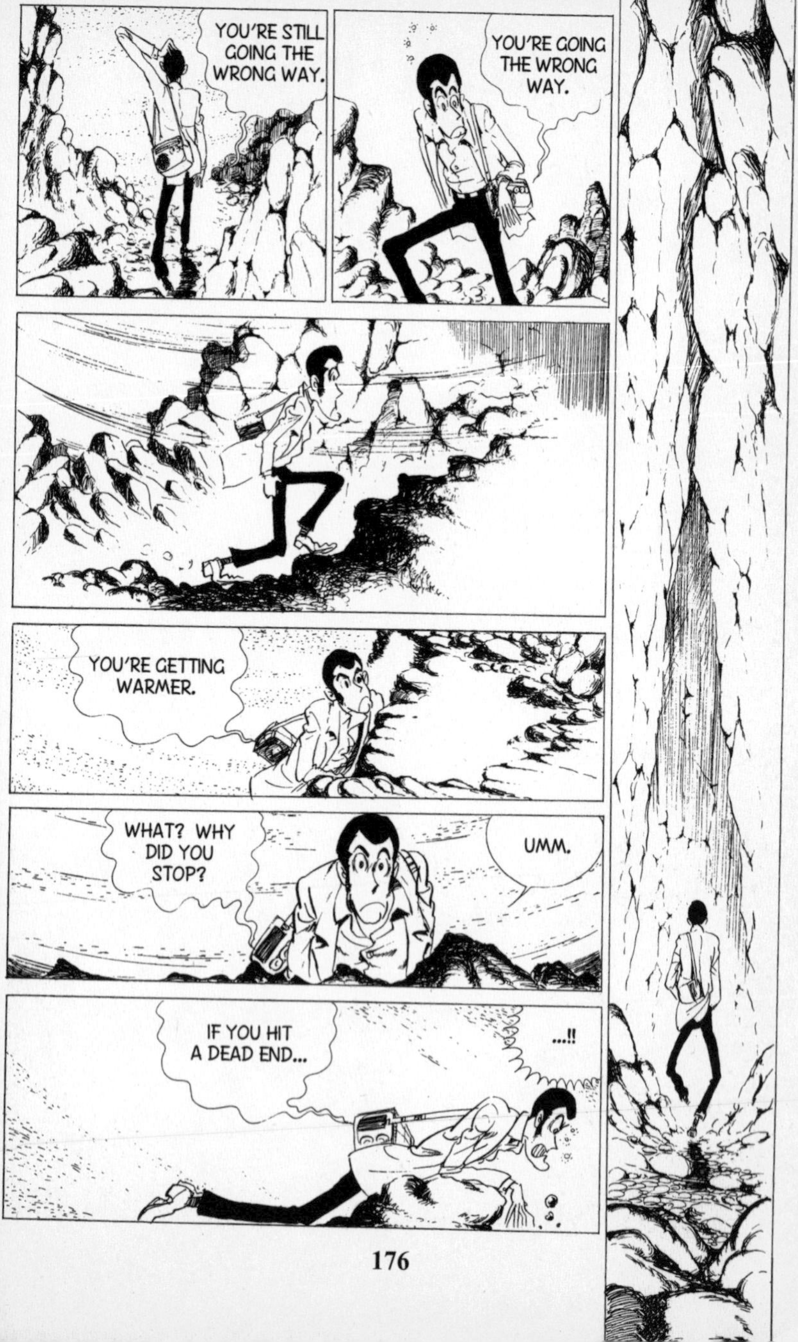

YOU'RE GOING THE WRONG WAY.
YOU'RE STILL GOING THE WRONG WAY.
YOU'RE GETTING WARMER.
UMM.
WHAT? WHY DID YOU STOP?
...!!
IF YOU HIT A DEAD END...

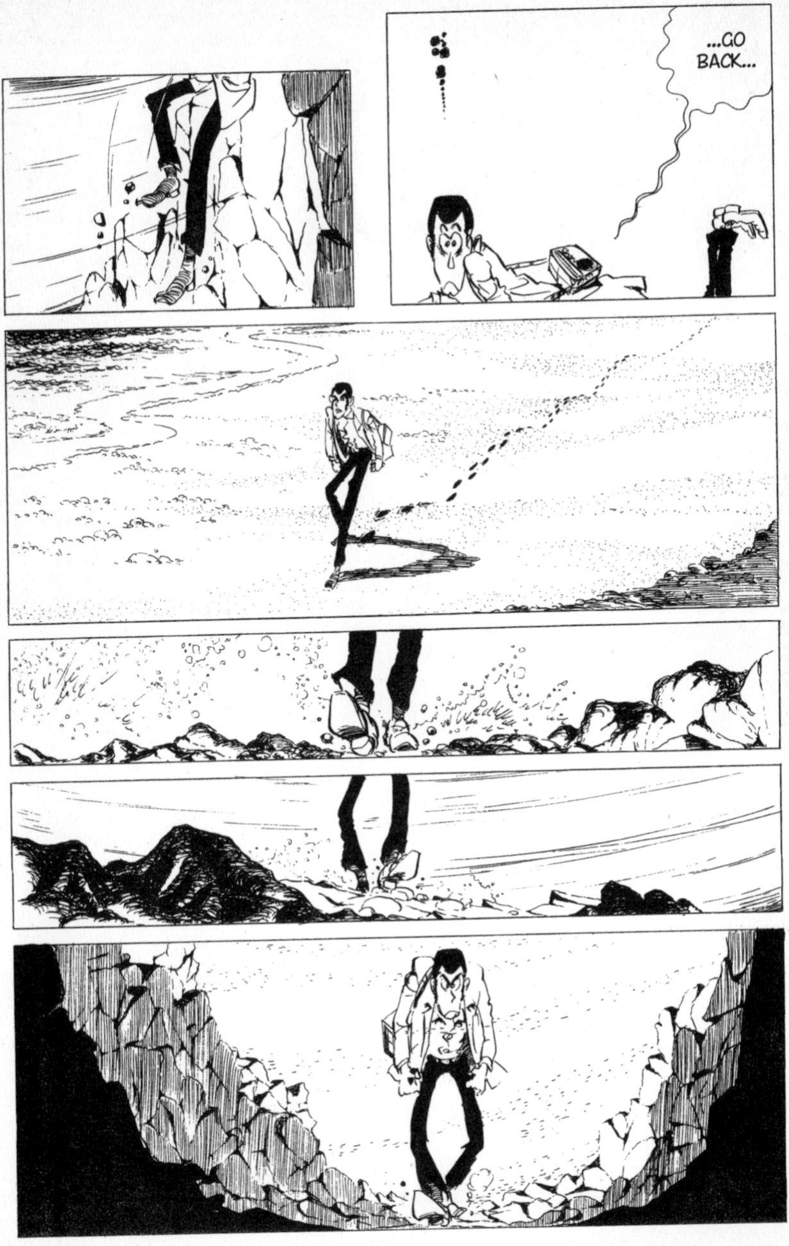
...GO BACK...

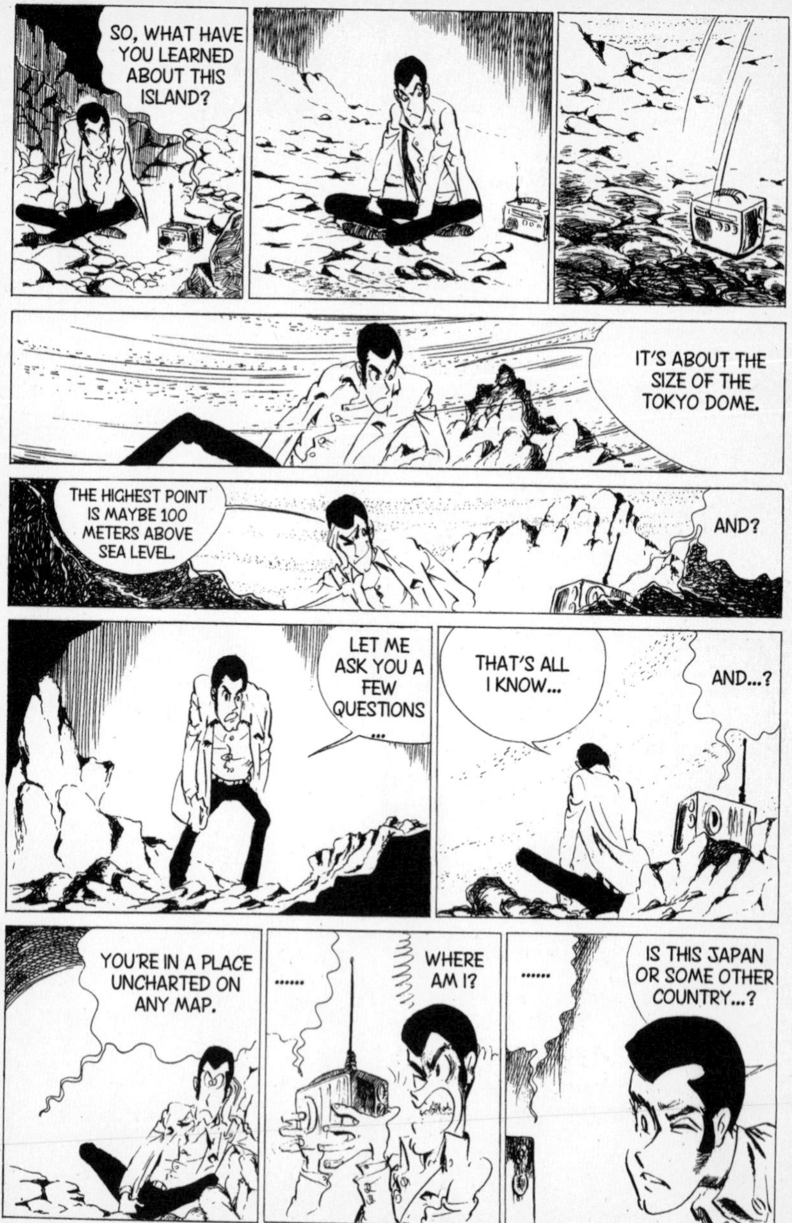
SO, WHAT HAVE YOU LEARNED ABOUT THIS ISLAND?
IT'S ABOUT THE SIZE OF THE TOKYO DOME.
AND?
THE HIGHEST POINT IS MAYBE 100 METERS ABOVE SEA LEVEL.
AND...?
THAT'S ALL I KNOW...
LET ME ASK YOU A FEW QUESTIONS ...
IS THIS JAPAN OR SOME OTHER COUNTRY...?
......
WHERE AM I?
......
YOU'RE IN A PLACE UNCHARTED ON ANY MAP.

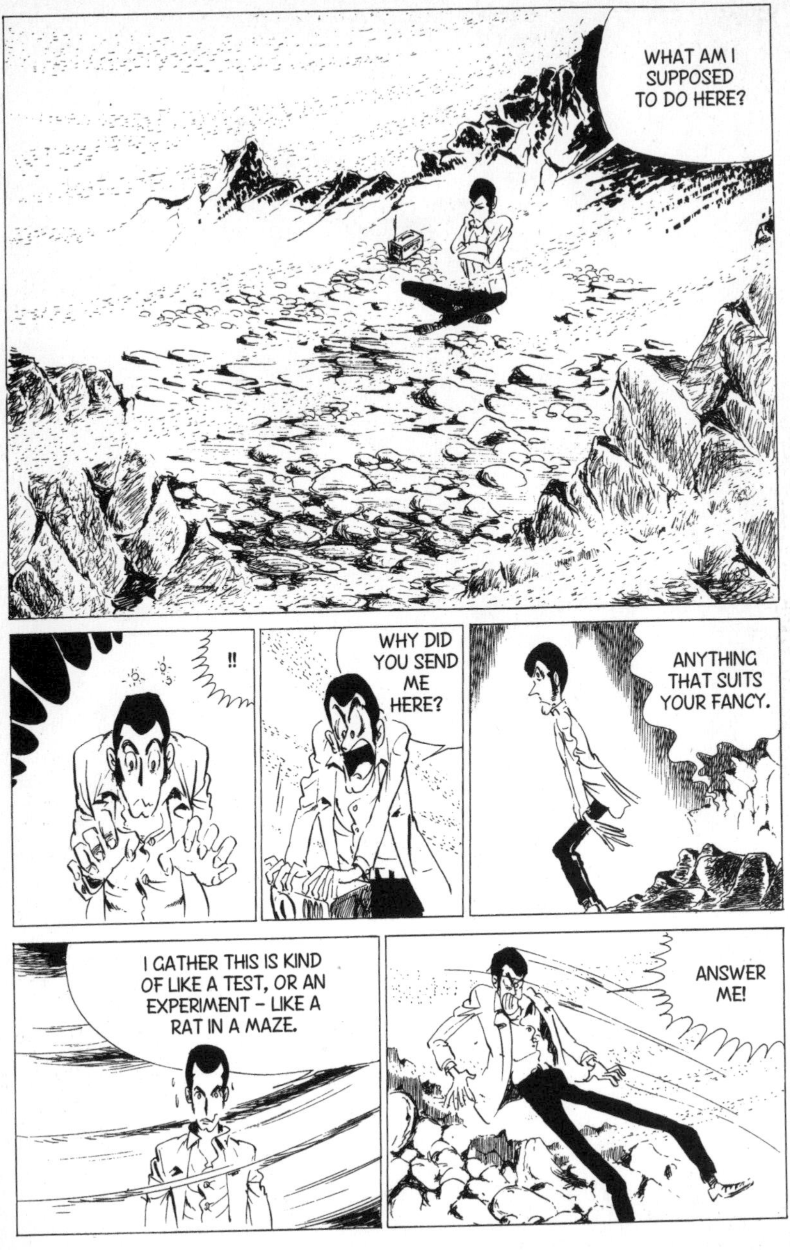
WHAT AM I SUPPOSED TO DO HERE?
ANYTHING THAT SUITS YOUR FANCY.
WHY DID YOU SEND ME HERE?
!!
ANSWER ME!
I GATHER THIS IS KIND OF LIKE A TEST, OR AN EXPERIMENT – LIKE A RAT IN A MAZE.

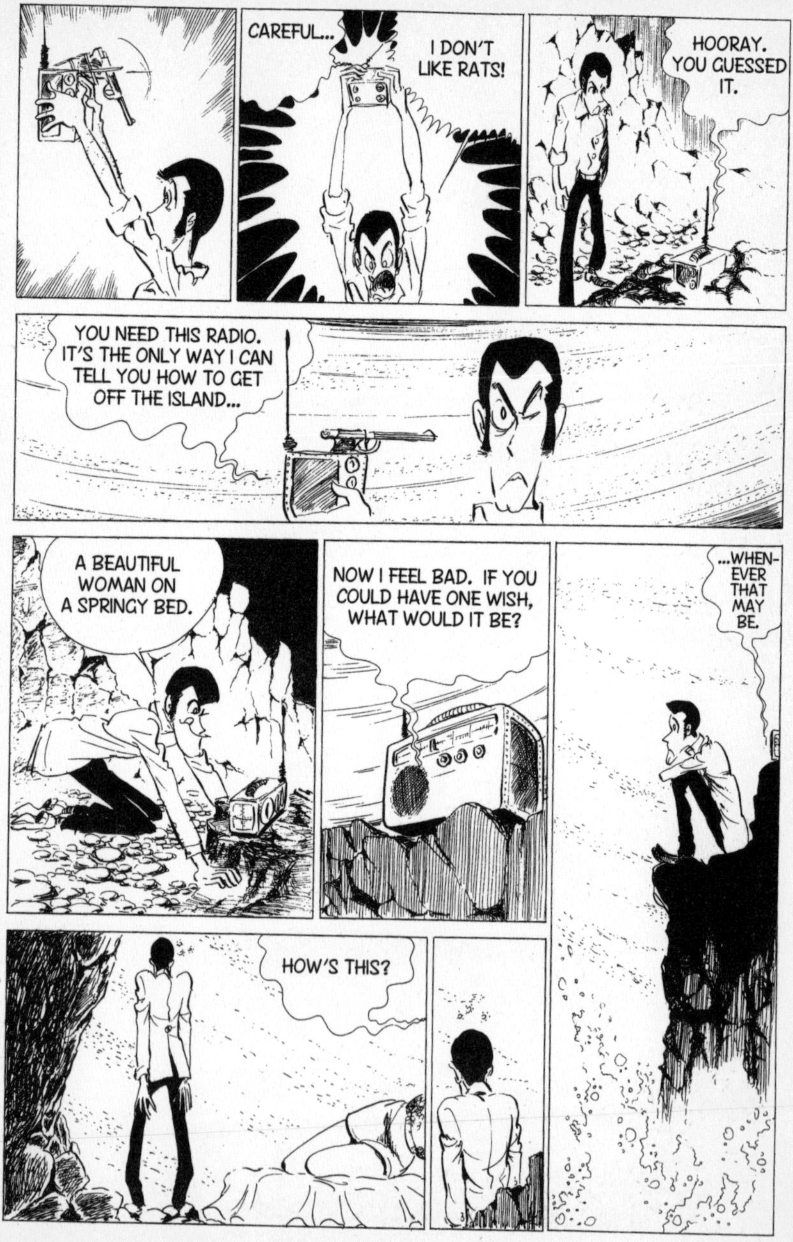
HOORAY. YOU GUESSED IT.
CAREFUL...
I DON'T LIKE RATS!
YOU NEED THIS RADIO. IT'S THE ONLY WAY I CAN TELL YOU HOW TO GET OFF THE ISLAND...
...WHEN-EVER THAT MAY BE.
NOW I FEEL BAD. IF YOU COULD HAVE ONE WISH, WHAT WOULD IT BE?
A BEAUTIFUL WOMAN ON A SPRINGY BED.
HOW'S THIS?

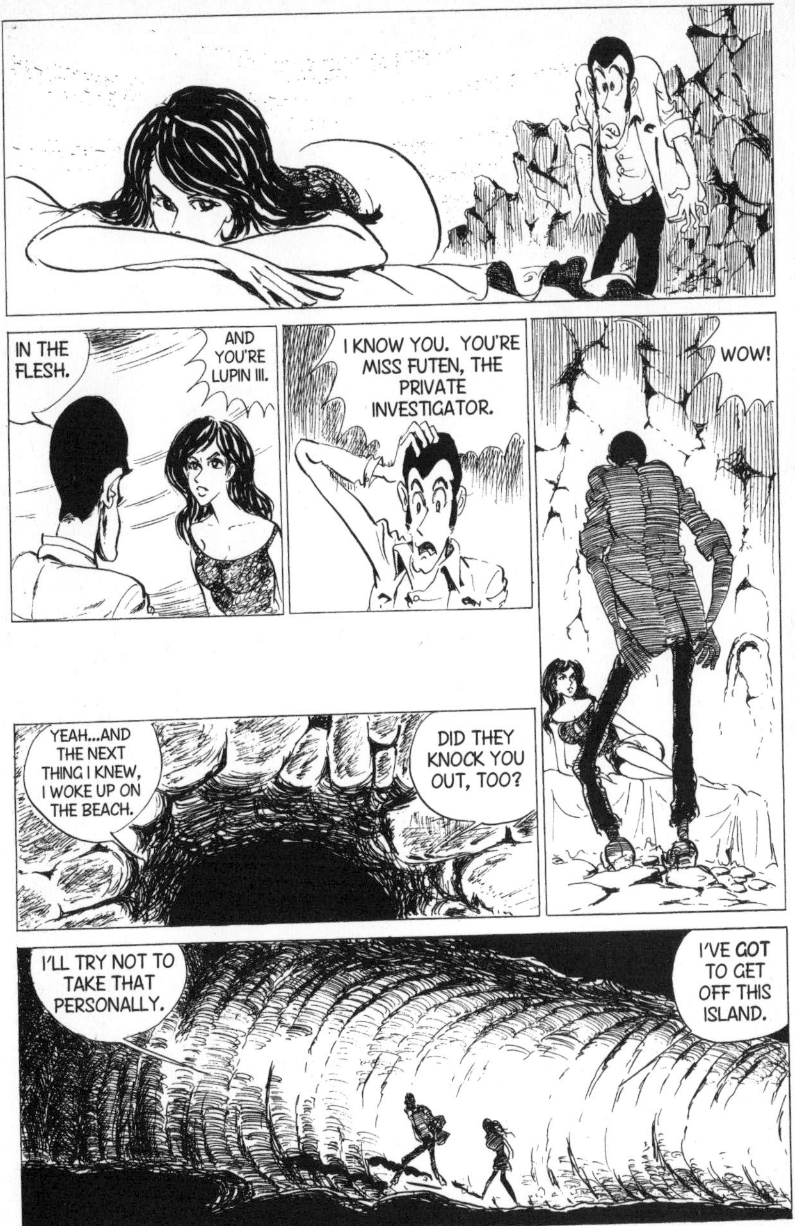
WOW!
I KNOW YOU. YOU'RE MISS FUTEN, THE PRIVATE INVESTIGATOR.
AND YOU'RE LUPIN III.
IN THE FLESH.
DID THEY KNOCK YOU OUT, TOO?
YEAH...AND THE NEXT THING I KNEW, I WOKE UP ON THE BEACH.
I'VE GOT TO GET OFF THIS ISLAND.
I'LL TRY NOT TO TAKE THAT PERSONALLY.

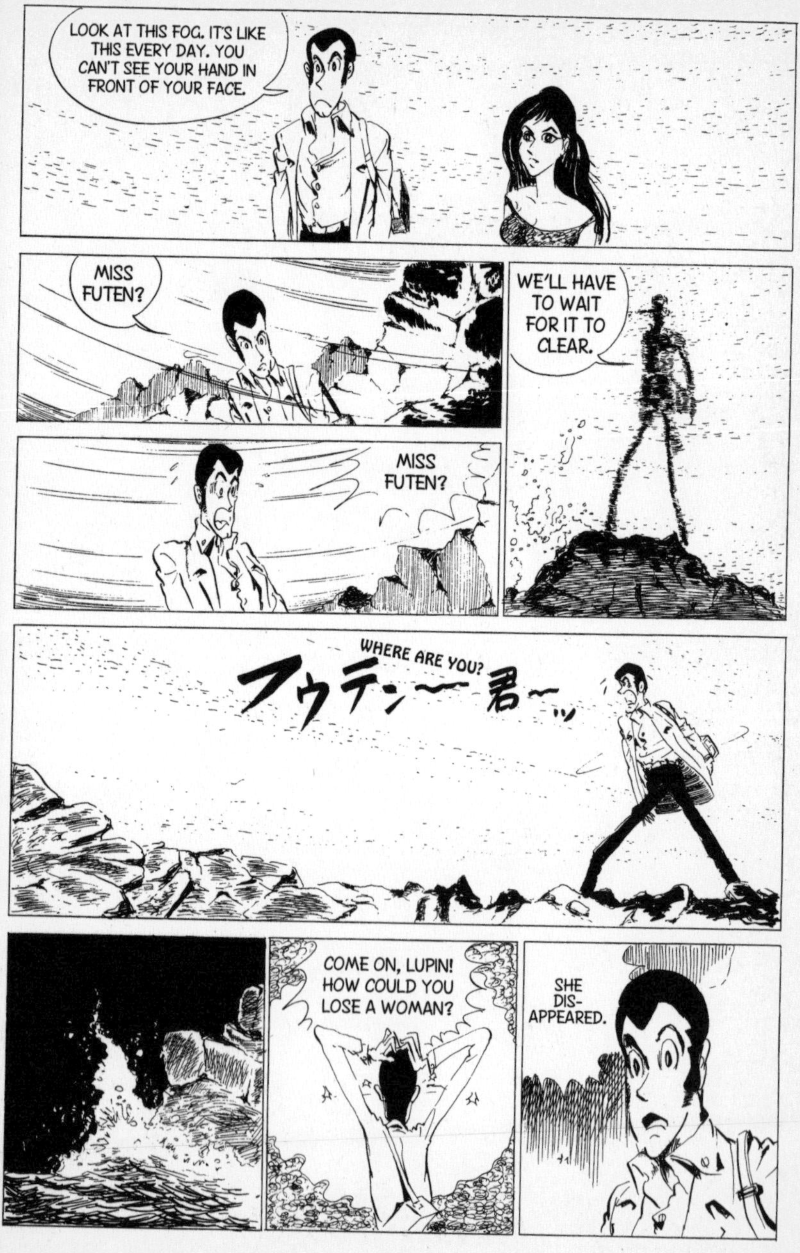
LOOK AT THIS FOG. IT'S LIKE THIS EVERY DAY. YOU CAN'T SEE YOUR HAND IN FRONT OF YOUR FACE.
WE'LL HAVE TO WAIT FOR IT TO CLEAR.
MISS FUTEN?
MISS FUTEN?
WHERE ARE YOU?
フウテン〜〜君〜ッ
SHE DIS-APPEARED.
COME ON, LUPIN! HOW COULD YOU LOSE A WOMAN?

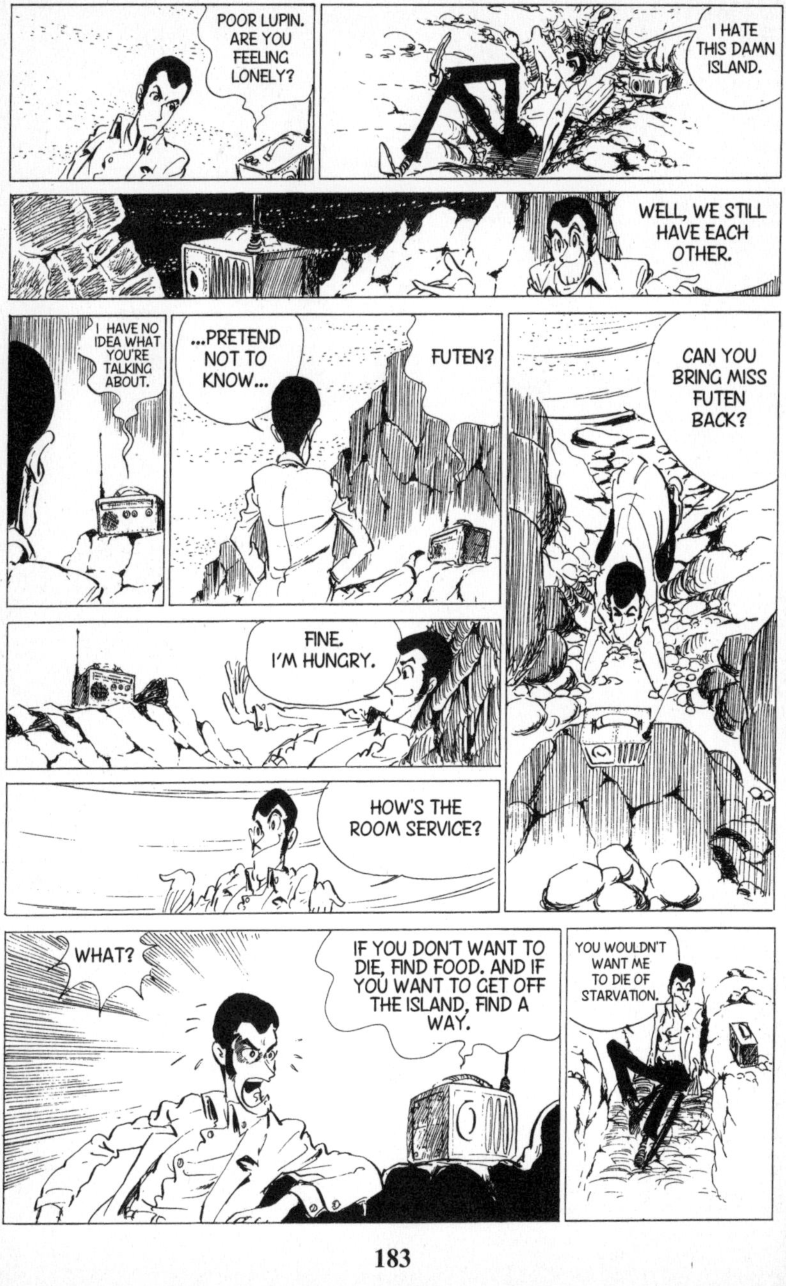
I HATE THIS DAMN ISLAND.
POOR LUPIN. ARE YOU FEELING LONELY?
WELL, WE STILL HAVE EACH OTHER.
CAN YOU BRING MISS FUTEN BACK?
FUTEN?
...PRETEND NOT TO KNOW...
I HAVE NO IDEA WHAT YOU'RE TALKING ABOUT.
FINE. I'M HUNGRY.
HOW'S THE ROOM SERVICE?
YOU WOULDN'T WANT ME TO DIE OF STARVATION.
IF YOU DON'T WANT TO DIE, FIND FOOD. AND IF YOU WANT TO GET OFF THE ISLAND, FIND A WAY.
WHAT?

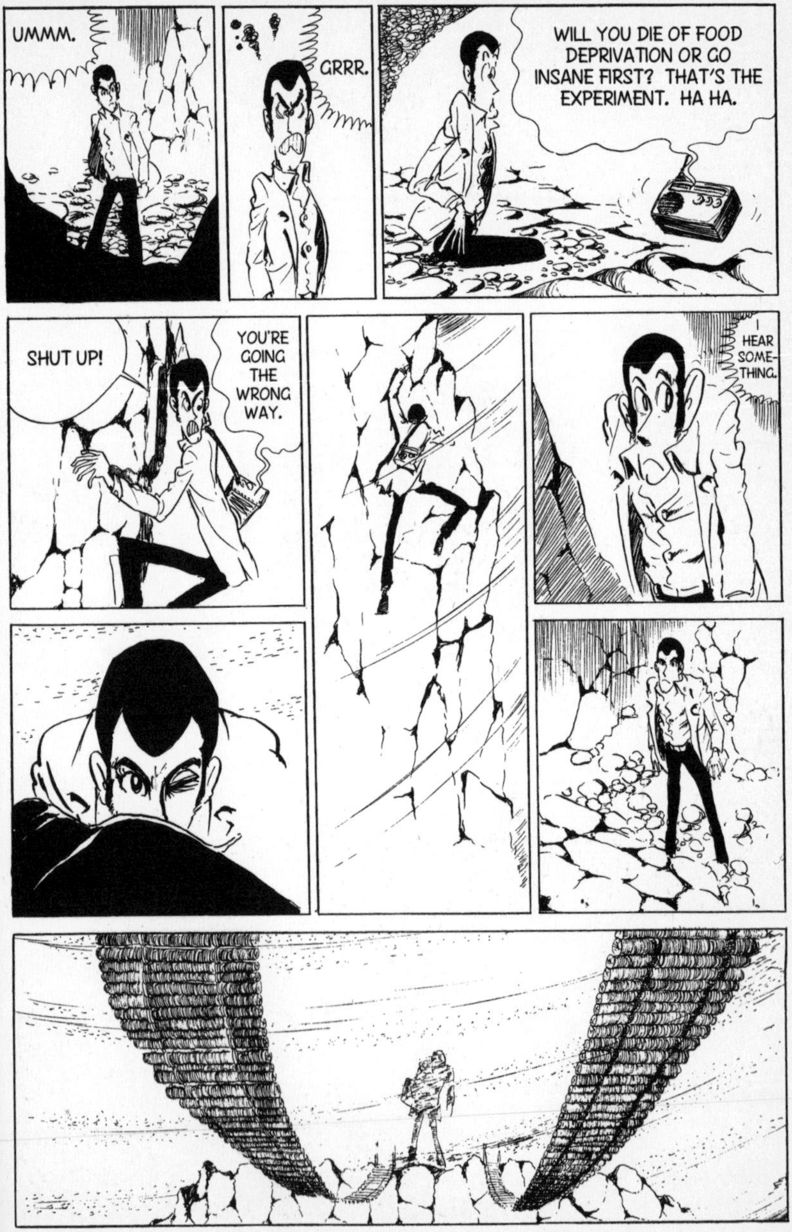
WILL YOU DIE OF FOOD DEPRIVATION OR GO INSANE FIRST? THAT'S THE EXPERIMENT. HA HA.
GRRR.
UMMM.
I HEAR SOME-THING.
YOU'RE GOING THE WRONG WAY.
SHUT UP!

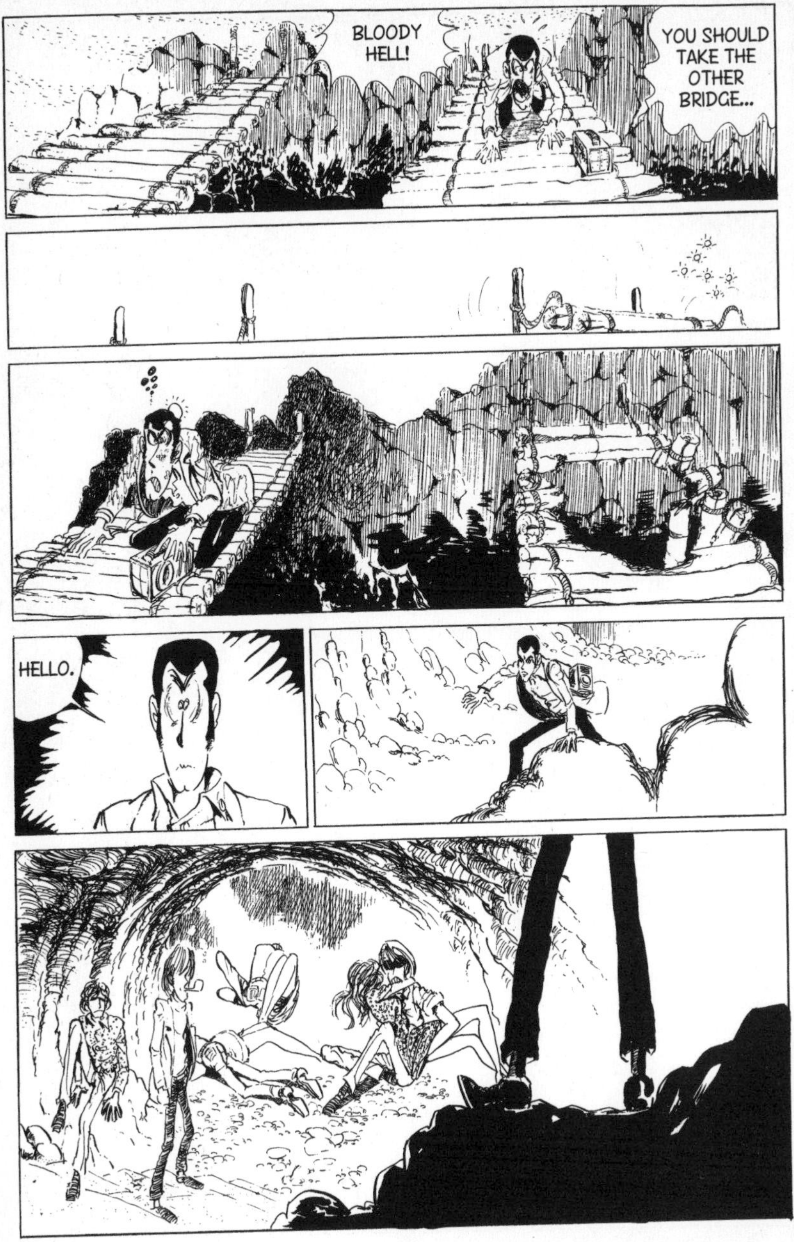
YOU SHOULD TAKE THE OTHER BRIDGE...
BLOODY HELL!
HELLO.

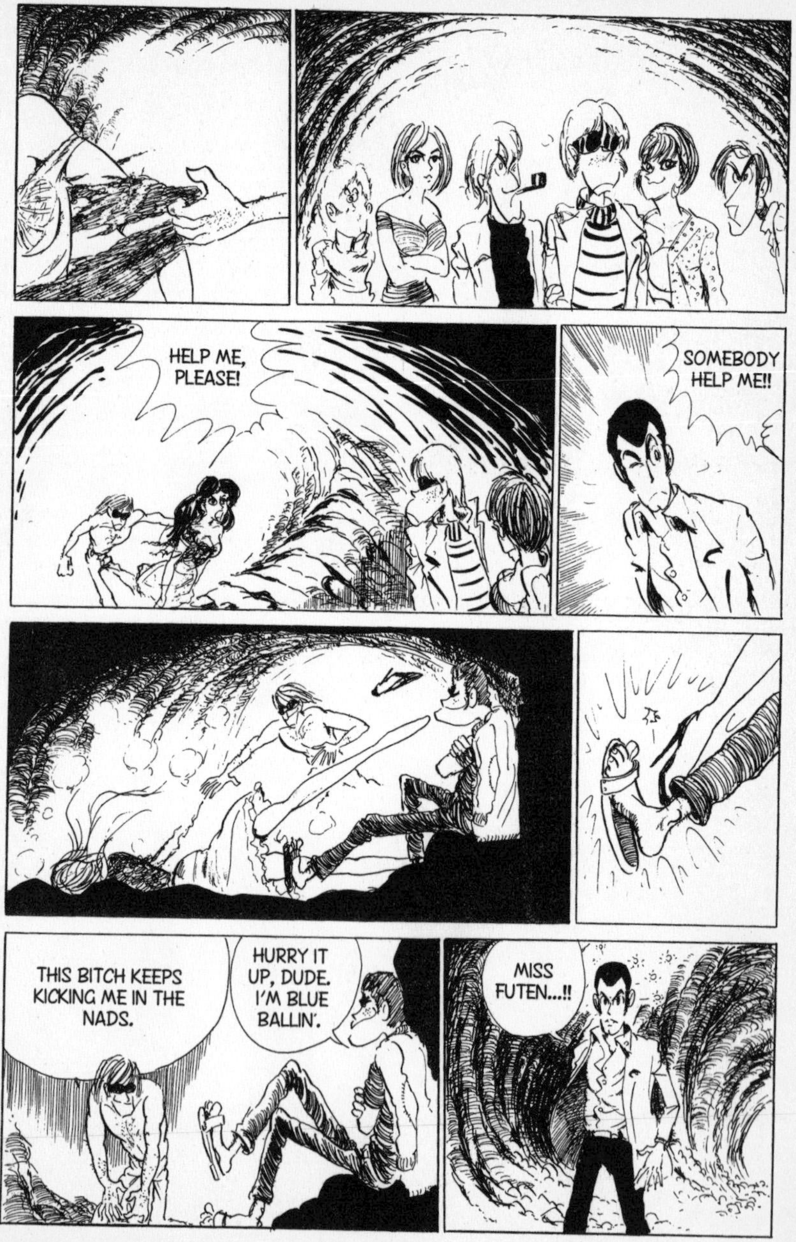
SOMEBODY HELP ME!!
HELP ME, PLEASE!
MISS FUTEN...!!
HURRY IT UP, DUDE. I'M BLUE BALLIN'.
THIS BITCH KEEPS KICKING ME IN THE NADS.

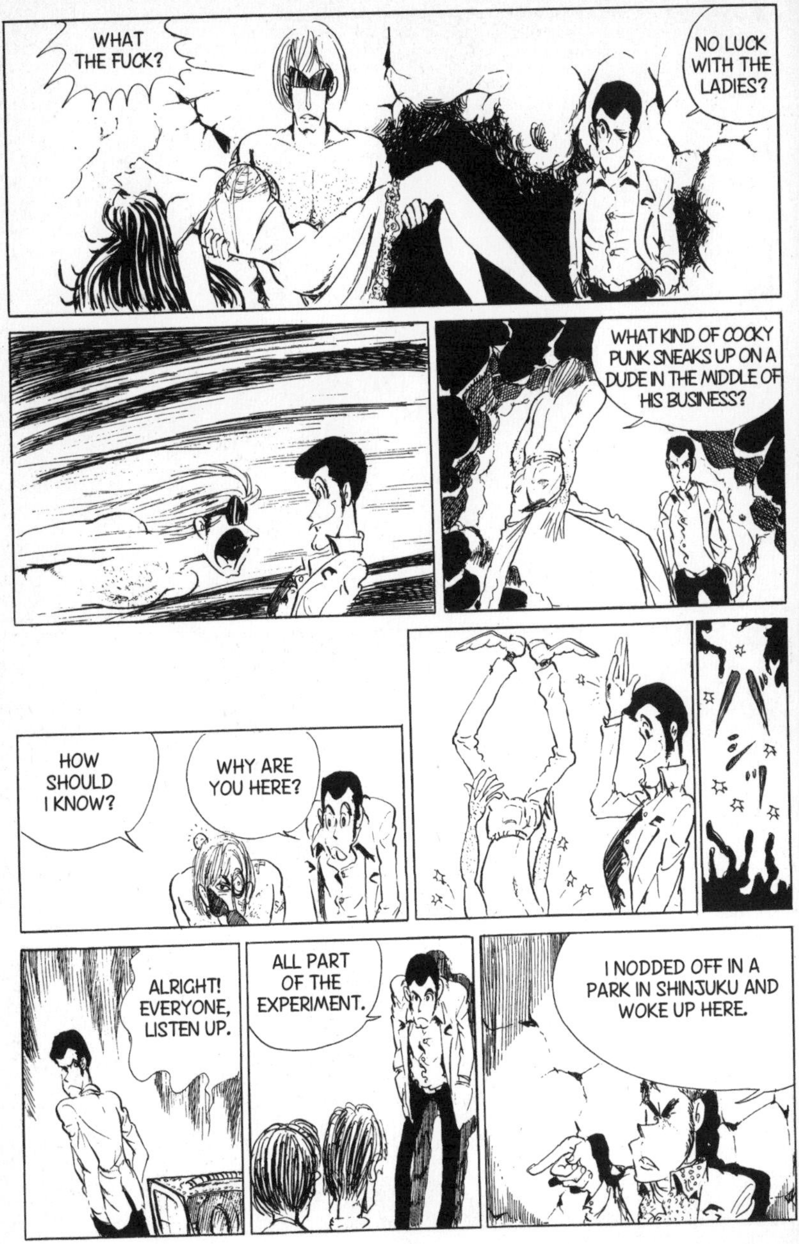
NO LUCK WITH THE LADIES?
WHAT THE FUCK?
WHAT KIND OF COCKY PUNK SNEAKS UP ON A DUDE IN THE MIDDLE OF HIS BUSINESS?
WHY ARE YOU HERE?
HOW SHOULD I KNOW?
I NODDED OFF IN A PARK IN SHINJUKU AND WOKE UP HERE.
ALL PART OF THE EXPERIMENT.
ALRIGHT! EVERYONE, LISTEN UP.

... SO, YES, MR. LUPIN, IT'S ALL PART OF THE EXPERIMENT. I'M CURIOUS TO SEE HOW SHITHEADS RESPOND TO EXTREME CONDITIONS, LIKE BEING TRAPPED ON A BARREN ISLAND...

THIS ISLAND IS GOING TO EXPLODE IN TEN MINUTES...

THIS ISLAND IS FUNNY...

WHAT'S FUNNY?

HA HA HA

...THAT'S GOING TO EXPLODE IN NINE MINUTES.

FIRST OFF, OVER THE LAST SEVERAL DAYS I'VE BEEN HERE, THE TIDE HASN'T CHANGED ONCE...

AND...THE FOG ROLLS IN AT THE EXACT SAME TIME EVERY DAY.

THEN THERE'S THE OCEAN WATER ITSELF, WHICH SHOULD, OF COURSE, BE SALTY.

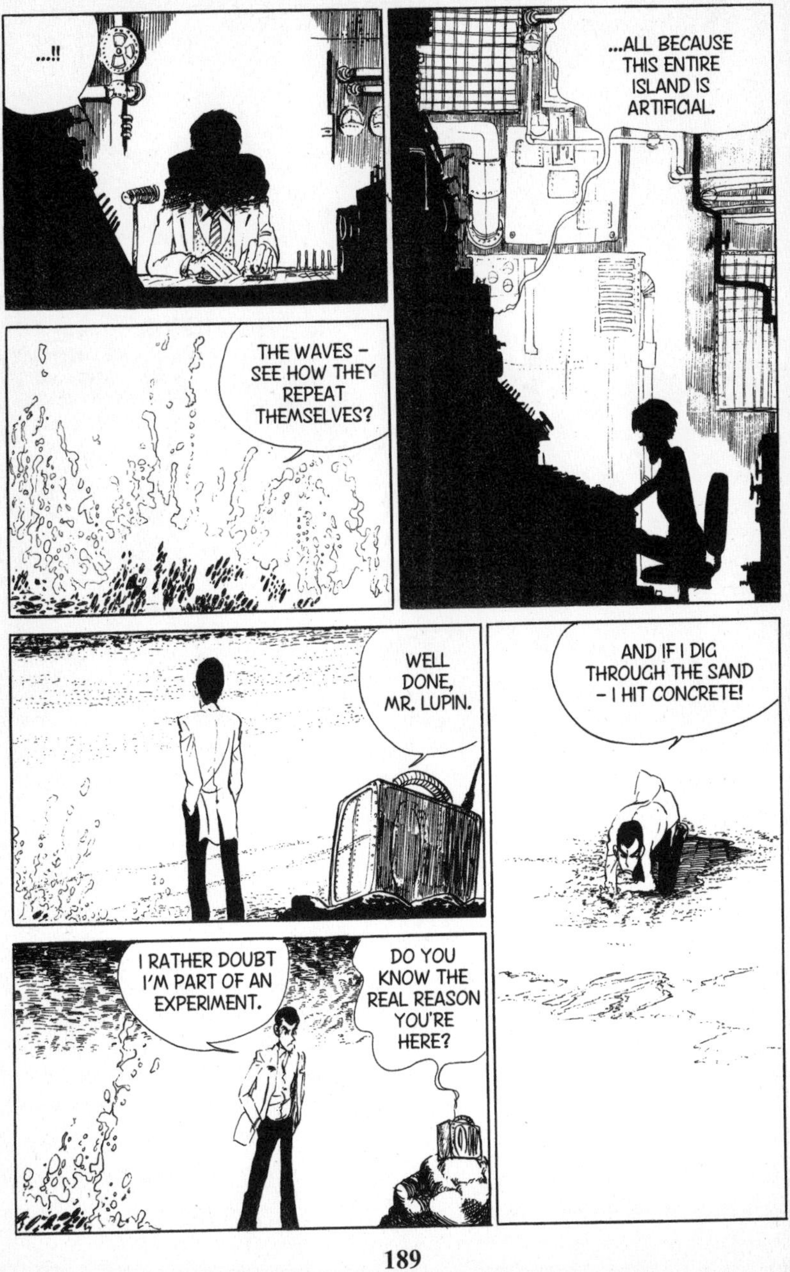
...ALL BECAUSE THIS ENTIRE ISLAND IS ARTIFICIAL.
...!!
THE WAVES - SEE HOW THEY REPEAT THEMSELVES?
AND IF I DIG THROUGH THE SAND - I HIT CONCRETE!
WELL DONE, MR. LUPIN.
DO YOU KNOW THE REAL REASON YOU'RE HERE?
I RATHER DOUBT I'M PART OF AN EXPERIMENT.

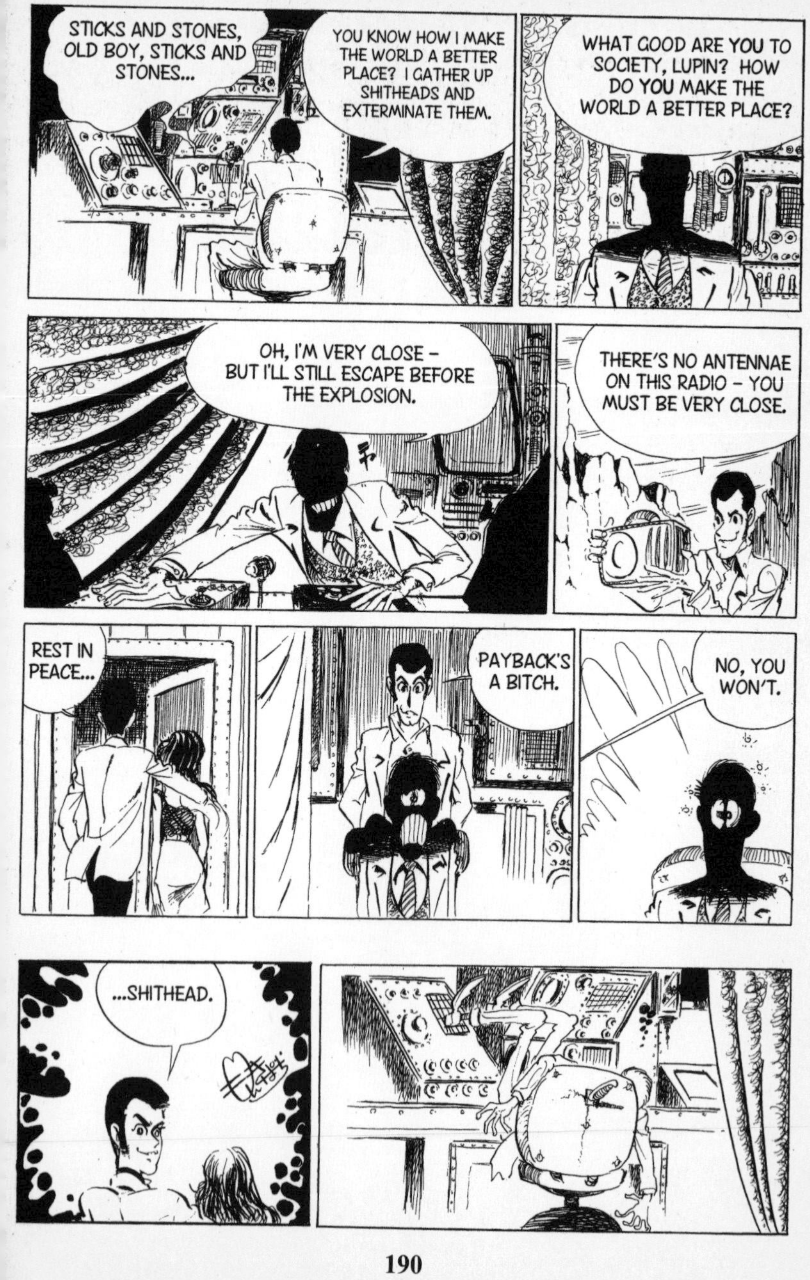
WHAT GOOD ARE YOU TO SOCIETY, LUPIN? HOW DO YOU MAKE THE WORLD A BETTER PLACE?
YOU KNOW HOW I MAKE THE WORLD A BETTER PLACE? I GATHER UP SHITHEADS AND EXTERMINATE THEM.
STICKS AND STONES, OLD BOY, STICKS AND STONES...
THERE'S NO ANTENNAE ON THIS RADIO - YOU MUST BE VERY CLOSE.
OH, I'M VERY CLOSE - BUT I'LL STILL ESCAPE BEFORE THE EXPLOSION.
NO, YOU WON'T.
PAYBACK'S A BITCH.
REST IN PEACE...
...SHITHEAD.